Imperial Projections

Film Europa: German Cinema in an International Context
Series Editors: **Hans-Michael Bock** (CineGraph Hamburg); **Tim Bergfelder** (University of Southampton); **Sabine Hake** (University of Texas at Austin)

German cinema is normally seen as a distinct form, but this series emphasizes connections, influences, and exchanges of German cinema across national borders, as well as its links with other media and art forms. Individual titles present traditional historical research (archival work, industry studies) as well as new critical approaches in film and media studies (theories of the transnational), with a special emphasis on the continuities associated with popular traditions and local perspectives.

For full volume listing, please see page 310.

IMPERIAL PROJECTIONS

Screening the German Colonies

Wolfgang Fuhrmann

berghahn
NEW YORK · OXFORD
www.berghahnbooks.com

First published in 2017 by
Berghahn Books
www.BerghahnBooks.com

© 2015, 2017 Wolfgang Fuhrmann
First paperback edition published in 2017

All rights reserved. Except for the quotation of short passages for the purposes of criticism and review, no part of this book may be reproduced in any form or by any means, electronic or mechanical, including photocopying, recording, or any information storage and retrieval system now known or to be invented, without written permission of Berghahn Books.

Library of Congress Cataloging-in-Publication Data

Fuhrmann, Wolfgang.
  Imperial projections : screening the German colonies / Wolfgang Fuhrmann.
    pages cm. — (Film Europa: German cinema in an international context)
  Includes bibliographical references and index.
  Includes filmography.
  ISBN 978-1-78238-697-1 (hardback : alk. paper) — ISBN 978-1-78533-513-6 paperback— ISBN 978-1-78238-698-8 (ebook)
  1. Documentary films—Germany—History—20th century. 2. Motion pictures—Germany—Colonies. 3. Motion pictures in propaganda—Germany. 4. Germany—Colonies—History—20th century. I. Title.
  PN1995.9.D6F78 2015
  070.1'8—dc23

2014039947

British Library Cataloguing in Publication Data

A catalogue record for this book is available from the British Library.

ISBN 978-1-782328-697-1 hardback
ISBN 978-1-78533-513-6 paperback
ISBN 978-1-78238-698-8 ebook

Contents

List of Illustrations	vii
Acknowledgements	ix
List of Abbreviations	xi
Introduction	1

Part I. The Beginning of Colonial Film Culture in Imperial Germany

1. From the Variety Theatre to the German Colonial Society	27
2. Carl Müller: A Colonial Filmmaker	42
3. The DKG's Film Shows: The Colonies in Motion	64

Part II. Addressing the Masses

4. The 'Hottentot Election' of 1907	83
5. The DKG's Kinematographenkampagne	100
6. Rise and Fall of the Kinematographenkampagne	115

Part III. Ethnographic Filmmaking in the Colonies

7. Karl Weule in German East Africa	133
8. The Expedition in Context: Modern German Ethnography	149
9. Filming in the Colonies: Training and Improvisation	165

Part IV. Tourism, Entertainment and Colonial Ideology

10. Colonial Films in Public Cinema	177
11. The Colonial Travelogue	192
12. Colonial Films in Transition: Robert Schumann's Comeback	224

Part V. Colonial Film Propaganda During the First World War

13. Setting Up Colonial War Propaganda   245

14. The Deutsche Kolonial-Filmgesellschaft (DEUKO)   256

Conclusion. Beyond the Colonial Era   271

Filmography   276

Bibliography   278

Index   302

Illustrations

1.1.	Carl Müller and family	38
2.1.	Jetty in Lomé	47
2.2.	Carl Müller and Herero woman	48
2.3.	Herero children in prison camp	50
3.1.	Trial in Buëa	67
4.1.	Tableau Vivant	88
5.1.	Official Poster of the DKG's Kinematographenkampagne	111
9.1.	Robert Schumann and his operator in German East Africa	171
10.1.	State Secretary Solf arriving in a Riksha. Still from *Staatssekretär Dr. Solf besucht im Oktober 1913 Togo* (1913)	189
11.1.	The marching Togo police troop. Still from *Staatssekretär Dr. Solf besucht im Oktober 1913 Togo* (1913)	205
11.2.	Performing science. Still from *Die Fortschritte der Zivilisation in Deutsch-Ostafrika* (1911)	207
11.3.	Handcraft and imperial kitsch. Still from *Die Fortschritte der Zivilisation in Deutsch-Ostafrika* (1911)	208
11.4.	Geography lesson in a German East African public school. Still from *Deutsch-Ostafrika: Eine große öffentliche Schule in der Provinz Usambara* (1912)	211
11.5.	Listening to the phonograph. Still from *Deutsch-Ostafrika: Eine große öffentliche Schule in der Provinz Usambara* (1912)	212
12.1.	Robert Schumann at the set in German East Africa	231
12.2.	Still from *Löwenjagd in Afrika* (before 1914)	235
12.3.	Still from *Jagd auf den Silberreiher in Afrika* (1911)	236

12.4. Illustration criticizing the slaughter of paradise birds
       for fashion purposes   238
14.1. Still from *Der Gefangene von Dahomey* (1918)   265

Acknowledgements

This book has benefited from many different sources and would not have been possible without the assistance and support of archives, colleagues, friends and family.

I am indebted to the following archives and institutions: Ausstellungs- und Messe-Ausschuss der Deutschen Wirtschaft e.V. (AUMA) in Berlin, British Film Institute (BFI) National Archive (London), Bundesarchiv and Bundesarchiv-Abteilung Filmarchiv, Bundesarchiv-Abteilung Militärarchiv (Freiburg), Deutsche Kinemathek (Berlin), Deutsches Institut für Filmkunde (Frankfurt am Main), EYE Film Institute Netherlands (Amsterdam), Gaumont Pathé Archives (Paris), Historisches Archiv Köln, Historisches Museum Frankfurt am Main, Institut für Ethnologie an der Universität Leipzig, Leibniz-Institut für Länderkunde (Leipzig), Institut für den Wissenschaftlichen Film (IWF) Göttingen (closed in 2010), Landesarchiv Berlin, Museum für Völkerkunde zu Leipzig, Naturschutzbund Deutschland e.V. (NABU), Pro Natura (Basel), Universitätsarchiv der Technischen Universität Dresden, Stadtarchiv Altenburg, Stadtarchiv Leipzig, Thüringisches Staatsarchiv Altenburg and Übersee-Museum Bremen. In addition, I am very grateful for the assistance of the numerous municipal archives that supplied me with copies of advertisements and reviews of colonial film screenings in Germany; too many to mention them all here.

A particularly big thank you goes to Claudia Blaue, librarian of the German Institute for Tropical and Subtropical Agriculture (DITSL) in Witzenhausen, who supported this project from the very first moment and supplied me with relevant literature from the library's vaults. Another major basis for this study has been the retracing of biographies of colonial filmmakers; for information on this I am extremely thankful to Hans-Martin Heinig, Gerhard Groß, Hubert Müller (†), Jutta Niemann (Hans Schomburgk Archive, Paris), Hans-Georg Rogall (†) and Heinz Trebus. Film historian Herbert Birett (†) has always been a great help in finding information on early cinema.

I would like to thank Frank Kessler and William Uricchio for their support and advice. I am grateful to Berghahn Books and the editors of the Film Europa Series, particularly Tim Bergfelder, who encouraged me to publish my work in their series. Philipp Stiasny deserves the credit for coming up with the book's title after a freezing bike ride in Berlin. Special thanks to all my colleagues at the Department of Film Studies at the University of Zurich who have made the last years so enjoyable. Last but not least, I am particularly grateful for Kate Delaney's editing work.

Abbreviations

AMVL	Archiv des Museums für Völkerkunde zu Leipzig
AZSTL	Altenburger Zeitung für Stadt und Land
BArch	Bundesarchiv, Berlin
BArch-MA	Bundesarchiv-Militärarchiv, Freiburg
BUFA	Bild und Filmamt (Photography and Film Office)
DAMUKA	Deutsche Armee-Marine und Kolonialausstellung (German Army, Marine and Colonial Exhibition)
DEUKO	Deutsche Kolonial-Filmgesellschaft (German Colonial Film Company)
DEULIG	Deutsche Lichtbild-Gesellschaft (German Cinematographic Company)
DFV	Deutscher Flottenverein (German Navy League)
DJFG	Deutsche Jagd-Film-Gesellschaft (German Hunting Film Company)
DKG	Deutsche Kolonialgesellschaft (German Colonial Society)
DKZ	Deutsche Kolonialzeitung (German Colonial Newspaper)
DOA	Deutsch-Ostafrika (German East Africa)
DOAL	Deutsche Ost-Afrika Linie (German East Africa Shipping Line)
DOAZ	Deutsch-Ostafrikanische Zeitung
DSWA	Deutsch-Südwestafrika (German South-West Africa)
FDKG	Frauenbund der Deutschen Kolonialgesellschaft (Women's League of the German Colonial Society)
KA	Kolonialabteilung des Auswärtigen Amtes (Colonial Department of the Foreign Office)
RKA	Reichskolonialamt (Imperial Colonial Office)

Introduction

In April 1905 a selected circle of colonial authorities, members of Berlin high society and journalists was invited to a premiere screening of films from the German colonies at the Deutsche Kolonialmuseum (German Colonial Museum). The following day reviews in local and national newspapers reported on the premiere and praised the 'surprisingly vivid image' of the colonies on film, which in this 'simple, faithful form' would considerably contribute to the understanding of the colonial territories.[1] The press coverage of the Berlin screening underlines Benedict Anderson's notion of print media's significance for the formation of a national identity: reading the daily newspaper, the German public was informed about the prosperity of 'their' colonial territories.[2] The coverage, however, also mentions another medium that had its share in the formation of an 'imagined community': cinematography was beginning to communicate the experience of the German colonial empire.[3]

Cinematography started in the era of late imperial colonialism, and its history probably would have taken a different path had the first film operators not had colonial infrastructure to enable them to travel the world and shoot their films. Colonial territories were perfect locations to feed cinema's voracious appetite for ever new topics, actualities, attractions and 'views' from all corners of the world. However, how are we to understand a film that does not offer a clear-cut narrative? What about a film in which shots of African prisoners are followed by a panorama shot of the colonial territory and a scene in which tourists are embarking on an ocean steamer? Such a film suggests a colonial reading, but it cannot exclusively be subsumed under the notion of propaganda, influencing the public's opinion, attitude and behaviour in their support of German colonization.[4] It also stands for a specific film form, aesthetic and viewing experience in early cinema that goes beyond a simplistic interpretation of its images.[5]

Imperial Projections examines the history of German colonial cinematography, roughly between 1904 and the end of the First World War. Written from a filmhistorical perspective, the book is situated at the intersection of both film and colonial history. It investigates the interrelationship between colonialism and early German cinema in terms of production, distribution, exhibition and reception. Colonialism can be described in terms of rational political calculation, economics and scholarly interest, but also in terms of popular entertainment, modernity and adventure.[6] By watching films from the colonies, viewers participated in colonial rule, conquest, racism and salvage ethnography, as well as in virtual travelling, urbanism, moral uplift, visual spectacle and wildlife protection: no contradiction in terms but two sides of the same coin. The study of the history of colonial cinematography, therefore, requires a double focus: firstly, on the history of German colonialism and the way colonialism was represented, shown and understood by the contemporary film audience, with the second focus requiring a sound understanding of the aesthetics of early nonfiction films, as well as of existing film exhibition practices. Hence, the book discusses colonial films in the context of very different exhibition venues and shows how their specific analyses can produce important information about the films and their meaning where traditional film analysis has its limits. *Imperial Projections* shows that the history of German colonial cinematography is more than just putting the colonies on film; it is a cultural and aesthetic experience framed by the conditions of early cinema.

German Colonialism and Visual Culture

German colonialism was greatly influenced by the nation's transformation from an agrarian into an industrial nation in the last third of the nineteenth century and a rising new national self-confidence after the unification of the German Reich in 1871.[7] The risk of playing only a marginal role in future world politics eventually made Germany shift towards active colonial politics and join in the 'Scramble for Africa' at the Berlin Congo conference 1884/85. The purpose of expanding power through colonization was, as the later chancellor Bernhard von Bülow put it simply in 1897, to demand Germany's 'place in the sun'. Colonial advocates supplied German colonialism with the necessary ideology. The need for colonial expansion was mainly explained by Germany's increase in population, in that colonies could be used to channel emigration to national territories rather than to foreign continents such as the United States, a loss that would weaken Germany's 'national energies'.

A second economic argument emphasized Germany's need for new markets and the protection of these markets by the German government. For German industries, colonies were the chance to gain cheap and safe access to resources that, in the long run, could make them independent from world price politics. Plantation, farming or trading were three economic models that characterized colonial economic policy. Finally, colonial advocates were convinced that only overseas possessions could make Germany into a real world power. Within the ambivalence of trying to demonstrate political power on the one hand, and, on the other, the feeling of having played only a secondary role in world politics in the past, German colonial ideology was characterized by variations of social Darwinism. Colonialism was considered a *Kulturmission* (cultural mission) in which the 'superior' race educated and civilized the 'inferior' Other, who was still steps behind on the evolutionary ladder. Being German was never associated with anything other than being white.[8]

Compared to the French or British colonial empires, Germany was a colonial latecomer that acquired most of its colonial territories between 1884 and 1885. In Africa: Deutsch-Südwestafrika (DSWA, German South-West Africa), present-day Namibia; Kamerun (Cameroon), Togo; and Deutsch-Ostafrika (DOA, German East Africa), present-day Tanzania, Rwanda and Burundi. In the Pacific: Deutsch-Neuguinea (German New Guinea), present-day Papua Guinea, Melanesia and Micronesia. Between 1897 and 1899 the empire additionally acquired more islands of Micronesia and the Polynesian Deutsch-Samoa (German Samoa), present-day Samoa, as well as Kiautschou (Kiaochow), today the Jiaozhou Bay area and Qingdao in China. The German colonies measured nearly 900,000 square miles, more than four times the area of the German Reich in Europe. However huge in extent, the German colonial empire was economically unprofitable, militarily insignificant and attracted few Germans to start a new life in the territories: 'The *Kolonialreich* in the end proved the most short-lived of European colonial empires – apparently a venture in futility'.[9]

In contrast to the popular belief that German colonialism was merely a footnote in German history, the 'venture in futility' has left its traces in German public life and designates important historical decades of today's independent nations in Africa, Asia and the Pacific. Two recent centenaries have reminded the German public of its colonial past and its historical responsibility for an era of oppression, enslavement and exploitation: that of the colonial genocide directed at the Herero and Nama peoples during and after the Herero War, 1904–07, in DSWA, which was marked in 2004, and that of the 1905–07 Maji-Maji Rebellion that caused the death of more than a hundred thousand Africans in DOA, which was marked in 2005.

A critical coming to terms with Germany's colonial past would not have been possible without the theoretical and methodological approaches of cultural and postcolonial studies in the German humanities.[10] In addition, the influence of the iconic turn in the humanities has shifted the focus towards colonialism's visuality and medial representation. Images are no longer considered simple illustrations of history but active agents in the making of history due to their specific aesthetics and their social and cultural practices.[11] Following Edward Said's approach in his seminal work *Orientalism*,[12] we see how images and visual media have contributed to the Western imagination of what colonialism and the colonial Other was supposed to be. Research on colonial photography, monuments, architecture, advertisement, *Völkerschauen* (human zoos), trademarks and postcards and trading cards underlines colonialism's presence and meaning, showing its influence on people's everyday life in Imperial Germany.[13]

Colonial cinematography has only marginally been discussed in the context of colonial visual culture. Assenka Oksiloff's *Picturing the Primitive* is one of the very few publications on early German cinema that covers Germany's active colonial period.[14] Oksiloff investigates the relationship between early German cinema and German anthropology's fascination with primitive cultures. The focus on the notion of the primitive as a kind of 'nodal point' that connects ethnographic observation and the earliest discourses on cinema, however, leaves no room for a careful discussion of the emergence of film as an ethnographic research tool during the colonial era, or the history of colonial cinematography in general. *Imperial Projections* touches only to a limited extent on German ethnographic filmmaking, which still is a blind spot in German film history. With a provisional first case study on early ethnographic filmmaking in German East Africa, however, the book focuses on the ethnographers' experience with the new medium and German ethnology's

(*Völkerkunde*) strategies of reaching the public. Racial representation in Weimar cinema has been carefully analysed by Tobias Nagl.[15] Based on the most impressive range of primary sources and a combination of postcolonial criticism and sound filmhistorical understanding, Nagl shows how cinema provided a visual matrix for concepts of race and racism in the cinema that immediately followed Germany's active colonial era. *Imperial Projections* shares with Nagl's book a scholarly interest in studying film in a filmhistorical context that goes beyond aesthetic film analyses. However, it puts a much stronger emphasis on the exhibition context of colonial films and its implications for the conditions of the films' reception. Belgian film historian Guido Convents was likely the first film historian to investigate German colonial filmmaking in a comparative analysis of German, French, British and Belgian filmmaking in sub-Saharan Africa. In his work, which very much inspired the research for this book, Convents points out that it is almost impossible to find any entries in cinema histories on filmmaking in Africa before 1918.[16] The situation has not changed very much since Convents wrote in the late 1980s. The recent anthologies of the British research project 'Colonial Film: Moving Images of the British Empire' give a very detailed overview on the complex relation between British colonialism and the medium film but, unfortunately, provide little information on the practice of early colonial filmmaking in the British colonies.[17] Likewise, studies in colonial Maghreb cinema have attracted more attention than those dealing with French sub-Saharan Africa.[18]

The historiographical marginalization of Africa is all the more surprising since German colonialism shares two thirds of its history with early cinema, usually defined as the period from 1895 to the First World War, a time in which nearly 85 per cent of the earth's surface was controlled by colonial powers.[19] In other words, watching films from unknown regions in early cinema meant watching films from colonial territories. A very pragmatic explanation for the negligence of German colonial films in the discourse of visual colonial culture could be the fact that films from the colonies are archived in different national film archives and are difficult to access. German films have no platform similar to the digitized image collection of the Deutsche Kolonialgesellschaft (DKG, German Colonial Society) or the *Kolonialbibliothek* (colonial library) at the university library in Frankfurt.[20] In addition, surviving colonial films are very often in a precarious condition due to decomposition and decades of unprofessional handling. Carefully restored DVD compilations of colonial films do not exist and are unlikely to be produced because of the costly copyrights to the films.

A more methodological explanation for the neglect of colonial films could be the scope and heterogeneity of the corpus and the lack of film-historical understanding for films that appear so different in style to today's films. Exact figures on the number of films dealing with the German colonies do not exist and can only be provisional.[21] An examination of early film journals suggests that the number of commercial productions was between fifty and sixty films from 1905 to 1918. With the exception of colonial propaganda fiction films produced during the First World War, which will be discussed in length in the final chapters of the book, the majority of colonial films were nonfiction. More films were shot in the African colonies, 'the fantasy topoi of German colonial desire',[22] than in the Pacific colonies. Early cinema was an international cinema mainly dominated by French productions such as those of Pathé Frères or Gaumont, so that films about the German colonies were not shot exclusively by German production companies. Today, the 1911 Pathé Frères film *Die Fortschritte der Zivilisation in Deutsch-Ostafrika* (The Progress of Civilization in German East Africa) is one of very few surviving films that give an idea of the schooling and training practices in the East African colony. While the Pathé film addressed a German audience because of its German colonial context, it is not known to what extent lecturers or intertitles contextualized foreign productions in such a way as to produce a national German colonial patriotic interest. An example for such contextualization is the 1907 Raleigh & Robert film *Die Viktoriafälle* (The Victoria Falls), which was obviously not shot in one of the German colonies but in Rhodesia, today's Zambia and Zimbabwe. What made the film interesting for the German audience was not only the film's aesthetic that showed 'wonderful changing scenes, the cataracts at sunrise, sunset and by moonlight, the beautiful colourings when the enormous mass of water crashes down the abyss', but, as the release advert remarks, that it was an example of how German industry was planning 'very soon to use the enormous power of water for bringing electricity into the interior of Africa'.[23]

Checking film titles for German colonial content and context can be misleading as well. The majority of early films are known only by their title but rarely indicate exactly where a film was shot. One might expect that a film called *Der Kongo* (The Congo) (Messter [Film] Projektion Berlin, 1913) would concern the Belgian Congo. In 1911, however, the territory of the German colony Cameroon was assigned a part of French Equatorial Africa, known as Neukamerun (New Cameroon). It is difficult to say whether all viewers would have been familiar with the new territory that had been acquired two years before, but the film seemed to suggest that the Congo was a new German colony and thus depicts the life of the 'black compatriots of our new colony', as the review put it.²⁴ Studying titles shows that sometimes even film companies were unfamiliar with the geography of the colonial territories. In October 1914 the Deutsche Bioscop GmbH re-released a film called *Sigifälle in Kamerun* (Sigi Falls in Cameroon), though the Sigi Falls was one of the tourist attractions of the East African colony. The error can be explained by the company's hectic efforts to release old material to supply German cinemas with films in the first months of the First World War, but it also might be an indication that film sellers did not pay too much attention to geographic accuracy; who would be able to tell the difference between a giraffe hunt on the British East African or on the German East African plains anyway?

The corpus of German colonial films also includes those films that were not shot in the colonies but had a colonial *sujet*, as well as films that draw the public's attention to their colonial acquisitions in one way or the other. Films like *Der Verräter* (The Traitor) (Georg Alexander, 1917) or *Farmer Borchardt* (Carl Boese, 1917) of the Deutsche Kolonial-Filmgesellschaft (DEUKO, German Colonial Film Company) were successful colonial propaganda films during the First World War, but were entirely shot in and around Berlin. The film *Wie Fritzchen sich die Reichstags-Kämpfe und Neu-Wahlen denkt* (How Fritzchen Imagined the Reichstag's Quarrels and the New Elections) (Internationale Kinematographen- und Licht-Effekt- Gesellschaft mbH, 1907) refers to the election of the German Reichstag in January 1907. Nothing more is known about this film apart from the release advertisement. The cartoon in which different people line up in front of the polling booth suggests that the film was a satirical comment on recent political happenings.²⁵

We should not regard the manageable number of commercial film productions about the colonies as insignificant. The number of productions has to be viewed against the background of countless international productions distributed in Germany depicting other colonial territories. An example of a paneuropean colonial film is *Wie ein Brief von den grossen Seen Zentral-Afrikas zu uns gelangt* (How a Letter Travels from the Great Lakes of Central Africa) (Alfred Machin/Pathé Frères, 1911). The film shows the different stages of the delivery of a letter from Africa to Europe. The film was a French production, shot in one of the British colonial territories, the Sudan, and distributed all over the world. One may doubt whether any viewer was interested in the film's national origin but rather in how a letter from colonial Africa reached the receiver at home – whether in France, England or Germany. German colonial films were part of an international colonial film repertoire, and together these films formed the sediment of the viewer's colonial world view, which made the world available for consumption and appropriation.[26]

Imperial Projections mainly focuses on films that refer to the German colonies in title or in content, and includes paneuropean colonial films that were shown in the German cinemas only to support a specific aspect or argument. A historiography of German colonial cinematography, however, would be incomplete if it concentrated merely on surviving film prints and neglected the so-called 'nonfilmic evidence'.[27] Most colonial films that will be discussed in this book have not survived. In many cases the only proof of the films' existence are references to them in primary sources such as reviews, official and business records and private documents; this applies in particular to amateur footage. There is good reason to believe that a great number of colonial films, perhaps even the majority of colonial films, were shot by amateur filmmakers such as the Altenburg merchant Julius Friedrich Carl Müller (1868–1935) or the forestry assistant Robert Schumann (1878–1914). Both were popular figures in the colonial movement and supplied the German public with some of the very first films from the colonies. The amount of film material supplied by amateurs cannot even be roughly estimated, but their significant contribution to colonial cinematography indicates not only the scope of early cinema but also asks for a reconsideration of nonprofessional filmmaking and informal distribution and exhibition circuits.

Early Cinema's Rediscovery

The study of early cinema would not have been possible without its academic rediscovery at the now legendary FIAF conference, the annual assembly of the national film archives, in Brighton in 1978.[28] At this event archivists and scholars gathered to analyse and discuss early fiction films from the period 1900–06. The conference became a catalyst for a New Film History, which expressed its dissatisfaction with traditional film historiography that told 'the tales of pioneers and adventurers that for too long passed as film histories'.[29] The conference proved that early cinema significantly differs from today's understanding of what cinema is like. Early cinema was a cinema in its own right, and its films often appear incomprehensible to the untrained eye and are considered primitive in form and naïve in content. To understand early cinema means to understand its paradigmatic otherness, as Miriam Hansen put it: 'In contrast to today's films, [e]arly films, although they lacked the mechanisms to create a spectator in the classical sense, did solicit their viewer through a variety of appeals and attractions and through particular strategies of exhibition'.[30] In addition to the aesthetic re-evaluation of early films, filmhistorical research became interested in nonfilmic evidence, such as company papers and the private and public records of filmmakers, organizations and public authorities. The enormous stimulus of the Brighton conference promoted early cinema as 'a complex historical sociological, legal and economic phenomenon' in which films were 'merely one manifestation of the working of the system as a whole'.[31]

Colonial cinematography cannot be discussed without considering the repertoire of visual media and illustrations that already were in practice when the first films from the colonies reached the screens. The colonial experience was not exclusively dealt with in parliamentary committees or other decision-making bodies but was visible through a range of early media. New printing techniques and a fast shutter speed accelerated the availability of photographic images, which turned readers into eyewitnesses and journals into 'visual telegrams'.[32] In the case of the most popular German magazine, *Die Gartenlaube,* Kirsten Belgum has shown that even if the editors 'did not consider colonial involvement a key national cause', the magazine had to increase its coverage on this issue in keeping with Germany's becoming a colonial power.[33] Following the expeditions of German explorers in their discoveries on foreign continents, the illustrated press documented Germany's becoming of one of the last colonial powers and established a visual repertoire that appealed to the public's national patriotic feeling for the Vaterland and supported the image of 'German Glory and German Greatness'.[34] *Kolonialschauen* (colonial expositions) and Völkerschauen represent another media context that familiarized the German public with the colonies. Both were part of the Berliner Gewerbeausstellung (Berlin Trade Fair), a 'local world exposition', operating between May and October 1896.[35] The fair included a colonial exposition that familiarized the visitor with a range of products from the colonies like cacao, coffee and tobacco. Statistics, numbers and data from the colonial economy demonstrated to the public Germany's political, military, economic and scientific achievements. In a colonial reading hall, where the public was offered new colonial literature, visitors could enjoy lectures and lantern slideshows with pictures from the colonies. Visitors who wanted to experience the colonies 'alive' could attend a Völkerschau as part of the colonial exposition.[36] Völkerschauen started to become popular in Germany in 1874 when Hamburg entrepreneur Carl Hagenbeck showed the apparently authentic daily life of the Laplanders in his shop's backyard.[37] Hagenbeck's success inspired many others to imitate this lucrative business idea, and within a decade Völkerschauen became a new form of mass entertainment that regularly toured German and European cities. The shows were often performed in real zoos, a setting that was supposed to underline the shows' exotic appeal. The exhibitions were designed to satisfy the public's curiosity to see previously unheard of 'savage tribes'. Though the organizers of the Berlin trade fair were sceptical at first about displaying colonized people, the exhibition was promoted as an invitation to the public to compare the often propagated cultural and racial differences between Western civilization and the 'primitive' colonized cultures, and to vote for the benevolent act of colonization. The colonial exhibition was visited by more than two million people who had the chance to study the various aspects of colonial life and to walk through its colonies, which were represented by the reconstruction of villages and made alive by more than a hundred 'tribal' people from the African and overseas colonies.[38] Until 1901 colonial advocates favoured the organization of such live exhibitions as being more productive for 'the fanciful lower circles' than museums, lectures or cinematographic recordings, but the prohibition against exhibiting people from the colonies for commercial purposes removed much of a colonial exhibition's attraction.[39] Whatever may have caused the end of the Völkerschau, in the following decades film recordings became a much cheaper and more efficient medium to present 'authentic' images from the German colonies to the public.

Analysing how film communicated the experience of colonialism shifts the focus to the relationship between film and the audience. *Imperial Projections* argues for a consideration of the exhibition context and the specific programming practices in early cinema. Between 1904 and the First World War the exhibition of colonial films was not limited to one particular venue. In his recent publication on early film exhibition in Germany between 1896 and 1914, film historian Joseph Garncarz identifies seven exhibition practices: film screenings in the international variety theatre and the local variety theatre, travelling film shows in the form of fairground cinema (*Jahrmarktkino*) or town hall cinema (*Saalkino*), screenings in a shop cinema (*Ladenkino*), which was similar to a U.S. nickelodeon, in the common cinema theatre (*Kinotheater*), and in the cinema palace (*Kinopalast*).[40] The different exhibition practices did not replace each other but often existed side by side, sometimes in competition, sometimes complementing one another. In his analysis Garncarz shows how the different exhibition venues addressed rather different audiences. In contrast to the international variety theatres with their urbane, worldly programme that targeted an upper-class audience, the local variety theatre or the shop cinema aimed at the petty bourgeois and lower-class audience. While the shop cinema was a major feature of the big city, town hall exhibitors were more successful in small towns and rural regions where a cinema culture was not yet established.

Closely related to the exhibition context is the study of the historical reception of early films. Though it is empirically impossible to explore how films were understood by the historical viewer, one can study the conditions of their reception in a way that allows the drawing of conclusions regarding the intended meaning of the films. Frank Kessler's approach of 'historical pragmatics' links the study of the conditions of the historical reception of early films to the exhibition context.[41] Historical pragmatics is based on French theorician Roger Odin's concept of 'semio-pragmatics', whose goal is to show the 'mechanisms of producing meaning, to understand how a film is understood'.[42] According to Odin, a fiction film is not inherently different from a documentary; a film does not produce 'meaning by itself, but all it can do is to *block* a number of possible investments of meaning'.[43] In other words, for a film to be understood by the spectator as fiction and not as documentary requires external processes like the applying of a specific 'reading mode', in this case a fictionalizing reading mode to the film. Within this perspective, however, it is also possible to read a film in an opposite mode. A film class that analyses a specific stylistic feature in a fiction film does not follow the film as fiction – it resists the film's fictionalization – but applies a documentarizing mode to study the specific aesthetic quality of the film. Kessler is interested in the transhistorical validity of Odin's concept.[44] He considers the variety of exhibition contexts as institutional determinants that conditioned a specific reception. Every exhibition context, therefore, addresses the audience in a particular way and intends a meaning that can be different from the intended meaning on the production side of a film.[45] This also means that the same film can be understood differently depending on the exhibition context: the screening of a colonial film in the context of promoting tourism intends a different meaning than a screening at an event of the colonial lobby.

Garncarz's and Kessler's studies are crucial for the understanding of colonial cinematography's history, as suggested in this book. The exhibition context of the town hall has turned out to be the richest in terms of conceptualizing the exhibition and reception of colonial films.

The most important organizer of colonial film screenings in the very first years of colonial cinematography was a voluntary association, the DKG, which was clearly interested in using film for popularizing colonial issues among the German public. At the time public cinemas became established in Germany, around 1906/07, the branches of the DKG were offering non-theatrical film experiences that document the popularity of film outside the commercial market. Even if screenings at the DKG could not compete with public cinemas in the long run, the record shows that the DKG had its own 'film scene' whose filmmakers did not necessarily enter the public film market in the following years.

Film screenings in associations are still rarely considered in early film studies, but they played an important role in colonial cinematography's nationwide success and contribute to a more refined understanding of early nonfiction cinema.[46] In contrast to the audience structures of public cinemas that are empirically hard to pin down, associations often give detailed information about their membership structure. Especially in places where film screenings in associations were the only venue to watch films, the screenings provide us with valuable demographic information about the early film audience. Sociologically, an association is a group of individuals who voluntarily agree to act as a collective or organization to accomplish a specific purpose. For this an association requires a meeting place, a clubhouse or an assembly room, where members can meet at an agreed time. To inform, entertain and attract new members, associations made use of media of all kinds: speeches, lantern slides, publications, photographs and film. Associations can be considered public spheres in their own right, whose internal structure can be studied with regard to class or gender composition and their common interest. Gender was the category most restrictive to public access and often relegated to the realm of the private.[47] Nancy Fraser notes 'that despite the rhetoric of publicity and accessibility, the official public sphere ... was importantly constituted by ... a number of significant exclusions'.[48] Michael Warner has transformed Jürgen Habermas's concept of the public sphere into a theory of 'counterpublics',[49] and Geoff Eley acknowledges the existence of competing publics 'not just later in the nineteenth century when Habermas sees a fragmentation of the classical liberal model of *Öffentlichkeit*, but at every stage in the history of the public sphere'.[50] According to Eley, it makes more sense to understand the public sphere 'as the structured setting where cultural and ideological contest and negotiation among a variety of publics takes place'.[51] The heterogeneity of the public sphere as an arena of continuous conflict and contest shifts the focus on the role and significance of voluntary associations:

> It [the public sphere] was linked to the growth of urban culture – metropolitan and provincial – as the novel arena of a locally organized public life (meeting houses, concert halls, theatres, opera houses, lecture halls, museums), to a new infrastructure of social communication (the press, publishing companies and other literary media; the rise of a reading public via reading and language societies; subscription publishing and lending libraries, improved transportation; and adapted centres of sociability like coffee houses, taverns and clubs), and to a new universe of voluntary associations.[52]

Associations were considered a 'secondary system of power',[53] and their importance has been emphasized by historians such as Eley, Thomas Nipperdey and Roger Chickering, who see the proliferation of voluntary associations as 'one of the most remarkable cultural phenomena of the Wilhelmine epoch'.[54] Associations represented a network of private and nonprofessional activities and had a significant influence on the formation of the public opinion.

In his study of the Deutscher Flottenverein (DFV, German Navy League) Eley has shown that film screenings constituted an important part of the DFV's propaganda work.[55] The success of the DFV's screenings clearly influenced the introduction of film screenings at the DKG.[56] The Colonial Society, most of whose members were drawn from the upper-middle class, was the most important colonial pressure group in Germany and the 'spokesmen for and the chief agency of the colonial lobby'.[57] Despite statements in the DKG's official histories that suggest the marginal significance of film in the society's propaganda work, the DKG was more than once in its history convinced that film was the most powerful medium to teach the German public about the colonies. From 1905 to 1907 film was a major point of discussion in the DKG's decision-making bodies, and watching films from the German colonies was a leading activity in the DKG's local branches that represented the society throughout Germany.[58] Film screenings at the DKG's branches play a crucial role in the history of colonial cinematography, which underlines not only the significance of voluntary associations as alternative film venues but also the significance of nonfiction films in early cinema.[59] The general importance of voluntary associations with regard to the exhibition of colonial films will return at various stages in the book, either in the form of ethnographic, geographic circles or the wildlife protection movement in the 1910s.

Diversity also characterizes the production context of colonial films. There is no evidence that the German government or the colonial lobby ever produced or ordered the production of colonial films. Rather on the contrary, colonial authorities in the Kolonialabteilung des Auswärtigen Amtes (KA, Colonial Department of the Foreign Office) and, after 1907, the Reichskolonialamt (RKA, Imperial Colonial Office) seemed to be rather cautious about supporting or producing colonial propaganda films on their own. This does not mean that producers of colonial films, professional or amateur, shot their films out of patriotic duty. Filmmakers most likely were colonial enthusiasts and supporters of colonial politics, but they also were entrepreneurs. Significant colonial historical events like the Herero War, 1904–07, the election of the German Reichstag in January 1907, the outbreak of the First World War and the loss of the colonies were events that stimulated amateur filmmakers and production companies to supply the screens with colonial films. However, in contrast to the colonial lobby's clearly patriotic interest in colonial films, the biographies of individual filmmakers show that colonial filmmaking was often closely linked to very personal interests. Carl Müller, Robert Schumann, Paul Graetz (1875–1968) or Hans Schomburgk (1880–1967), filmmakers that will be discussed in the various chapters, were also filming in the colonies for promoting and consolidating their own social status. Carl Müller combined his cinematographic activities with a business trip through the African colonies. While he became a prominent figure in the colonial movement through his film lectures for the DKG, he also used his films for improving the reputation of his business in his hometown, Altenburg – a popular restaurant. Robert Schumann, a passionate hunter, originally planned to film an expedition, and only the outbreak of the war in the German South-West African colony made him change his plans. Later, Schumann became famous for his films on hunting big game in the East African colony, but he never made an appearance as an expert on colonial issues. Like Paul Graetz, who realized that film recordings would promote his large-scale adventure expeditions, Hans Schomburgk was fully aware that shooting fictional films in Africa was still a novelty that would sell at the box office. Last but not least, Leipzig ethnographer Karl Weule (1864–1926) probably was the first to use a film camera in ethnographic fieldwork in the German colonies. Weule must be considered a key figure in early ethnographic filmmaking who knew how to use the new medium to promote his academic career and to consolidate the reputation of the Leipzig museum for ethnography as a modern institution. Operating in a new, fast-growing segment of modern media industry, all five amateur filmmakers aimed at finding and binding their audience in their own particular way.

Nonfiction and Colonial Cinema

Early cinema almost is synonymous with nonfiction films like 'views', actualities, scenics and travelogues, but nonfiction films were excluded from the Brighton conference and have only recently shifted to the top of the Early Film Studies' agenda.[60] The exclusion had partly very pragmatic reasons. As pointed out by film historian Tom Gunning, they 'were difficult to date, trace or identify'.[61] Nonfiction films never reached the same popularity as fiction dramas or early slapsticks. There is no canon of nonfiction masterpieces or famous nonfiction directors. In addition, in contrast to early fiction films with their distinctive narrative style, nonfiction films put narrative in perspective: they are less argumentative but rather descriptive. Curator Nicola Mazzanti has compared looking at early nonfiction films to 'looking at hieroglyphics before the Rosetta stone was deciphered';[62] the films often give little indication of the reason for their production and do not immediately reveal their meaning to the contemporary viewer.[63] Historiographic approaches that focus on a film's intrinsic excellence, influence or typicality in order to constitute a history of film become troubling concepts when applied to a conceptualization of the history of early nonfiction film. The methodological challenge of analysing early nonfiction films' role in film history is therefore to work, as Paolo Cherchi Usai remarks, towards the intelligibility of the visible.[64]

Nonfiction film histories have usually skipped early nonfiction cinema in favour of a safe historical starting point of nonfiction filmmaking, usually somewhere in the 1920s with an established canon of well-known directors and films.[65] Meanwhile several sound studies on early nonfiction have been published in recent years, for example Alison Griffiths's work on the origin of the ethnographic films in the United States, Uli Jung's and Martin Loiperdinger's history of the nonfiction film in Wilhelmine Germany and Jennifer Peterson's study on the film travelogue.[66] They all show the significance and the complex meaning of nonfiction films' form and aesthetic in early cinema. To label colonial films as 'colonialist', however, is 'as redundant as every tautology', as film historian Klaus Kreimeier remarks; he suggests rather that we analyse how the films organized their visual regimes with regard to colonialism.[67] In this sense Peterson's analysis of the most popular nonfiction film form, the travelogue, has a particular significance for the investigation of colonial cinematography. Travelogues are nonfiction films that represent 'place as their primary subject',[68] and they stand for the majority of colonial films that were produced until the First World War. Travelogues, however, depict places in a particular way. They construct their own geography, geographies that exist only on the screen and therefore present, as Peterson states, an 'idealized cinematographic geography'.[69] Following that definition, colonial travelogues then present idealized cinematographic colonial territories that have very little to do with the real colonies. The notion of an 'idealized cinematographic geography' that exists only on the screen recalls Susanne Zantop's study of colonial fantasies in pre-colonial Germany.[70] Zantop shows how different sources such as popular novels, philosophical essays or academic reports produced fantasies of conquest, appropriation and control over territories and men; such fantasies acquired the status of factual 'reality' when Germany became a colonial power. While these fantasies created a 'colonialist imagination and mentality that beg to translate thought into action',[71] colonial cinematography translated these fantasies into a new aesthetic experience: the moving image. Film was considered a substitute for real travelling as well as an extension of the human vision that made it possible to gaze over the earth's surface.[72] The colonial territories were considered national properties of a greater Germany, and film offered the unique chance of sightseeing the colonies without leaving home. The colonial travelogue also added a new visual dimension to the colonial imaginary. Films and film reviews indicate that the depiction of the colonies as 'modern colonies' was one characteristic of colonial films that contrasts with the colonies' representation in colonial literature. The films were more interested in the urban colony rather than in a pastoral untouched territory. The fascination with technology and urban life is not only documented in numerous early nonfiction and fiction films but in the colonies as well. If 'modern life seemed urban by definition',[73] colonial films too were a witness of modern urban life and organized the way of looking at it in a very particular fashion. Almost as a consequence, films from colonial territories are ambivalent by nature – patriotic instruction and virtual adventurous travel, national patriotic navel-gazing of the bourgeoisie and exotic escapism for the masses, the colonies as the extension of the modern metropolis and as the peripheral *Heimat*.

Considering the filmmaker's individual intention in shooting films, the range of venues where the films could be watched and the specific aesthetic of the colonial travelogue, we see how the complex nature of nonfiction films in early cinema suggests that not every viewer became interested in the colonies for the same reason. The travelogue's formulaic composition of combining apparently disparate shots into a single film was a complex visual invitation to the audience to explore colonialism at its intersection with modern culture. The specific case of the colonial travelogue also invites us to think about the film form's wider implication for early cinema. The decrease of film screenings at the DKG around 1908/09 due to the increase of public cinemas and their manifestation in cultural life was not tantamount to a disappearance of colonial propaganda from the screens. The entries in film journals show that early film production had a small but stable output of films from the German colonies, a finding that suggests that public cinemas were taking over important tasks, which informal exhibition circuits, such as associations, could logistically no longer perform. Further research in early nonfiction filmmaking is needed to show to what extent the travelogue provided a visual holding centre for a range of different public interests and preferences.

Sources, Omissions and Book Structure

Imperial Projections draws upon extensive research in various archives and in-depth study of primary sources. However, compared to records on cinematography's role in the DKG's propaganda work and reviews in local newspapers that give information on film screenings in the DKG's local branches, very little is known about how professional film companies organized a shooting in a colony and solved logistical problems of filming in the tropics or about their individual marketing strategies. The analysis of commercial colonial films and their historical reception is based on very disparate sources such as film prints, censorship cards, reviews, release advertisements, articles and discourses in German colonialism. The small body of surviving prints has limited the analysis of differences and variations in the aesthetics of the individual films. This handicap to analysing commercial filmmaking in the colonies could partly be compensated for by bringing in an important field in early nonfiction film practice – amateur filmmaking. Though one can generally agree with Convents that German sources are far more limited than British or French ones, the available sources about Carl Müller or Robert Schumann offer valuable information about the emergence of a national colonial film culture in the Wilhelmine era.

Amateur filmmaking in the colonies also applies to ethnographic filmmaking. The discussion of Karl Weule's films, as well as the existing records on his film expedition and his academic work, give an important first insight into the ambivalent role of the ethnographic filmmaker and his films in colonial Germany. Missing from the group of amateur filmmakers that will be discussed in this book is the African explorer, zoologist and wildlife protectionist Carl Georg Schillings (1865–1921). Schillings was probably the first German who successfully shot films in a German colony. He did this on his last expedition to East Africa in 1903. Though there exists proof of screenings of his films in 1905 and 1906, it is impossible to say why Schillings never mentioned the use of a film camera in any of his publications or surviving private records.[74] Photographic journals reported on Schillings' films, but they were never mentioned in film journals and were entirely ignored by the colonial movement.

The initial attempt to include the role of film in colonial missionary work was stopped at a very early research stage. For many people colonialism still is a loaded word that does not necessarily opens doors for a film scholar. Hence, missionary filmmaking remains to be explored by future film historians. The accessibility of visual sources was also limited due to German colonialism's popularity among collectors of colonial memorabilia. Long before the visual turn entered history studies, private collectors assembled huge archives of colonial postcards and other visual material. Filmmakers often were multi-media entrepreneurs using both the film and the photo camera, or publishing their film adventures afterwards in articles and books. For example, Carl Müller's passion for not only filming but taking photographs as well on his journeys gives us today the chance to have samples from his film travels. In contrast to his films that could not be located in an official film archive, his photographs have become collectibles at specialized picture-postcard fairs. Some of them are reprinted in this book; the majority remain behind closed doors. Last but not least, *Imperial Projections* covers a broad range of aspects in colonial cinematography, but it excludes cinema culture in the individual colonies. A study of colonial records in Tanzania, Namibia, Cameroon, Togo or the Pacific remains a project for the future.

The book is divided into five chronological parts that focus on different exhibition contexts. Part One and Part Two discuss colonial cinematography in the context of the German variety theatre and the DKG as a voluntary association. German cinema's rooting in the variety business suggests that the first films from the colonies initially appeared in the programmes of high-class, international variety theatres around 1904, the year of the Herero Uprising. While colonial topicals quickly disappeared from the variety programmes, the DKG's lecture halls offered a more stable venue for colonial films in the following years. For the colonial lobby films from the colonies were the major attraction at every screening at the DKG's branches, where they were considered as an important complement of the association's propaganda activities. The films were supposed to demonstrate the colonies' political stability and economic power. The phasing out of DKG film screenings around 1908/09 was due not to a decreasing interest in colonial films. As local cinemas became more established and cinema-going became a common cultural practice, demand for new films grew. Voluntary associations such as the DKG could not compete with an emerging new media industry that was quickly establishing a professional network of production and distribution. If people wanted to watch films from the colonies, they could easily attend a local cinema at almost any time or day.

German Völkerkunde, as will be discussed with the case study on Karl Weule in Part Three, aimed at exploring the colonies in the most systematic way and at making ethnological knowledge available to colonial administrators. Sharing the DKG's conviction that film's mechanical reproduction was the most objective and authentic way of representing the filmed object and subject, filming became part of colonial ethnographic field work. However, while ethnographers primarily wanted to understand cinematographic recordings of indigenous people from Africa or New Guinea as scientific records, shots of barebreasted African women could trigger rather unscientific 'viewing pleasures' if screened in a local cinema.

Part Four discusses colonial films in public cinema. Unlike the DKG, cinema owners had to address a broad audience. Film programming in the public cinemas required a certain skill from the exhibitor, and programming a film from the colonies was not necessarily aimed at offering a specific colonial viewing experience. The focus on the colonial travelogue shows the ambivalence of the films. The overtly racist degradation of individual African workers into a depersonalized mass of 'Arbeitsmaterial' (material for labour), as cited in a review of the film *Die Wilden beim Eisenbahnbau* (The Savages Constructing Railway) (Raleigh & Robert, 1907), needs no elaborate deconstructive analysis to show German colonialism's racist orientation.[75] However, colonial films could also offer an aesthetic experience, such as virtual time travel, or provide an association with a new Heimat or the thrilling entertainment of big game hunting. Films on hunting are a particular case in point. Were the films made for the enthusiastic hunter and adventurer or were they propaganda for the emerging wildlife protection movement?

The last two chapters, Part Five, shift the focus from nonfiction to fiction and discuss feature-film-length colonial propaganda dramas, which were shown in prestigious cinema palaces during the First World War. The films of the DEUKO aimed at addressing the broad cinema public. Unlike nonfiction films that gave viewers the chance to explore the colonies from the perspective of the colonizer, the colonial tourist, the ethnographic scholar or the intrepid German hunter killing African 'beasts', the DEUKO's melodramatic colonial potboilers offered an identification with the white hero or the suffering but ultimately passionate heroine. Through their nationwide distribution the films joined the official discourse of war propaganda by creating an ideological bond between the colonies and the German Heimat.

Notes

1. *Vossische Zeitung*, 12 April 1905; *Berliner Börsenzeitung*, 11 April 1905.
2. B. Anderson, *Imagined Communities: Reflections on the Origin and Spread of Nationalism*, rev. edn, London: Verso, 1991.
3. Cf. I. Christie, '"The Captains and the Kings" Depart: Imperial Departure and Arrival in Early Cinema', in L. Grieveson and C. MacCabe (eds), *Empire and Film*, London: Palgrave Macmillan, 2011, 22.
4. Cf. G. Maletzke, 'Propaganda: Eine begriffskritischen Analyse', *Publizistik*, 1972, 17(2), 156.
5. The 2000 annual FIAF conference in Rabat was dedicated to the colonial film heritage and challenged the 'mechanical link' between colonial cinema and colonial ideology. A. Benali, 'Le cinéma colonial: patrimoine emprunté', *Journal of Film Preservation*, 2001, 63(10): 4.
6. See H. Gründer, *Geschichte der deutschen Kolonien*, 5th edn, Paderborn: Schöningh, 2004, 25.
7. Ibid., 25–33.
8. K. Roller, '"Wir sind Deutsche, wir sind Weiße und wollen Weiße bleiben" – Reichstagsdebatten über koloniale Rassenmischung', in U. Van der Heyden and J. Zeller (eds), *Kolonialmetropole Berlin. Eine Spurensuche*, Berlin: Berlin Edition, 2002, 73–79.
9. A. J. Knoll and L. H. Gann (eds), *Germans in the Tropics. Essays in German Colonial History*, New York, Westport, CT, London: Greenwood Press, 1987, xiii.
10. For an overview see S. Lennox, 'From Postcolonial to Transnational Approachers in German Studies', in U. Lindner, M. Möhring, M. Stein and S. Stroh (eds), *Hybrid Cultures – Nervous States. Germany and Britain in a (Post)Colonial World*, Amsterdam and New York: Rodopi, 2010, xlvii–lxxiii.
11. See G. Paul, *Visual History. Ein Studienbuch*, Göttingen: Vandenhoeck & Ruprecht, 2006.
12. E. Said, *Orientalism*, New York: Pantheon Books, 1978.
13. An overview of recent publications is given in the bibliography.

14. A. Oksiloff, *Picturing the Primitive. Visual Culture, Ethnography, and Early German Cinema*, New York: Palgrave, 2001.
15. T. Nagl, *Die unheimliche Maschine: Rasse und Repräsentation im Weimarer Kino*, Munich: Edition Text und Kritik, 2009.
16. G. Convents, *A la recherche des images oubliées: Préhistoire du cinéma en Afrique: 1897–1918*, Brussels: Organisation Catholique Internationale du Cinéma et de l'Audiovisuel (OCIC), 1986, 13.
17. Grieveson and MacCabe (eds), *Empire and Film*. On the Boer War see: J. Barnes, *The Beginnings of the Cinema in England, 1894–1901*, Exeter: University of Exeter Press, 1997.
18. A. Benali, *Le Cinéma colonial au Maghreb*, Paris: Éditions du Cerf, 1998; F. Ramirez and C. Rolot, *Histoire du cinéma colonial au Zaïre, au Rwanda et au Burundi*, Brussels: Musée royal de l'Afrique central, 1985.
19. E. Shohat and R. Stam (eds), *Unthinking Eurocentrism. Multiculturalism and the Media*, New York: Routledge, 1994, 16.
20. Retrieved 28 March 2014 from http://www.ub.bildarchiv-dkg.uni-frankfurt.de/Default.htm. Exemplary for the preservation and accessibility of a colonial film heritage is the database of the above-mentioned project 'Colonial Film: Moving Images of the British Empire', retrieved 28 March 2014 from http://www.colonialfilm.org.uk/home.
21. It is impossible to say how much film material actually has survived. A screening of all the film material from the German colonies that was located during the research for this book probably would not last longer than an evening screening. A list of all available films can be found in the filmography at the end of this book.
22. J. Blankenship, '"Leuchte der Kultur": Imperialism, Imaginary Travel, and the Skladanowsky Welt-Theater', *KINtop: Jahrbuch zur Erforschung des frühen Films*, 2006, 14/15: 41.
23. *Der Kinematograph*, 10 July 1907.
24. Ibid., 19 February 1913.
25. Ibid, 13 January 1907.
26. See also: T. Gunning, 'The Whole World within Reach: Travel Images without Borders', in R. Cosandey and F. Albera (eds), *Cinéma sans frontières 1896–1918. Images Across Borders*, Lausanne: Nuit Blanche Editeurs/Edition Payot, 1995, 24.
27. R. Allen and D. Gomery, *Film History: Theory and Practice*, New York: McGraw-Hill Inc., 1985, 38.
28. E. Bowser, 'The Brighton Project: An Introduction', *Quarterly Review of Film Studies*, 1979, 4(4): 509–38. The conference is documented in R. Holman (ed.), *Cinema 1900–1906: An Analytical Study. Proceedings of the FIAF Symposium Held at Brighton*, FIAF, 1978, vols 1 and 2.
29. T. Elsaesser, 'The New Film History', *Sight and Sound*, 1986, 35(4): 246.
30. M. Hansen, *Babel and Babylon*, Cambridge, MA: Harvard University Press, 1991, 24.
31. Elsaesser, 'The New Film History', 247.
32. F. Heidtmann, *Wie das Photo ins Buch kam*, Berlin: Verlag Arno Spitz, 1984, 512.
33. K. Belgum, *Popularizing the Nation: Audience, Representation, and the Production of Identity in 'Die Gartenlaube', 1853–1900*, Lincoln: University of Nebraska Press, 1998, 151.
34. D. Barth, *Zeitschrift für alle. Das Familienblatt im 19. Jahrhundert. Ein sozialhistorischer Beitrag zur Massenpresse in Deutschland*, Ph.D. dissertation, Universität Münster, 1974, 203.
35. Bezirksamt Treptow von Berlin (ed.), *Die verhinderte Weltausstellung. Beiträge zur Berliner Gewerbeausstellung 1896*, Berlin: Berliner Debatte, 1996. For the success of the Cinématographe Lumière at the fair: M. Loiperdinger, *Film & Schokolade. Stollwercks Geschäfte mit lebenden Bildern*, Basel, Frankfurt: Stroemfeld/Roter Stern, 1999.

36. On the German Völkerschau see: H. Thode-Arora, *Für fünzig Pfennig um die Welt: Die Hagenbeckschen Völkerschauen*, Frankfurt: Campus Verlag, 1989; B. Staehelin, *Völkerschauen im Zoologischen Garten Basel 1879–1939*, Basel: Basler Afrika Bibliographien, 1993; A. Dreesbach, *Gezähmte Wilde. Die Zurschaustellung 'exotischer' Menschen in Deutschland 1870–1940*, Frankfurt: Campus Verlag, 2005.
37. E. Ames, *Carl Hagenbeck's Empire of Entertainments*, Seattle and London: University of Washington Press, 2008.
38. R. Richter, 'Die erste deutsche Kolonial-Ausstellung 1896. Der "Amtliche Bericht" in historischer Perspektive', in R. Debusmann and J. Riesz (eds), *Kolonialausstellungen-Begegnungen mit Afrika?*, Frankfurt: IKO-Verlag für interkulturelle Kommunikation, 1995, 25–41.
39. Anon., 'Die Ausführung von Eingeborenen aus den Kolonien zu Schaustellungszwecken', *Koloniale Zeitschrift*, 1901, 2(13), 183. The remark on cinematographic recordings is interesting as it points out the possibility of film screenings for colonial propaganda. While there exists no evidence that this was the case in 1901, topicals already covered events such as an African exhibition. *Bilder aus Leipzig* (1897) (Distributor: Bartling, Leipzig). H. Birett, *Das Filmangebot in Deutschland 1895–1911*, Munich: Filmbuchverlag Winterberg, 1991, 78.
40. J. Garncarz, *Masslose Unterhaltung. Zur Etablierung des Films in Deutschland 1896–1914*, Frankfurt, Basel: Stroemfeld, 2010. For an English introduction to the different exhibition venues in Germany: J. Garncarz, 'The Origins of Film Exhibition in Germany', in T. Bergfelder, E. Carter and D. Göktürk (eds), *The German Cinema Book*, London: BFI, 2002, 112–28.
41. F. Kessler, 'Historische Pragmatik', *montage AV*, 2002, 11(2), 104–12.
42. Cf. R. Stam, 'Semiotics Revisited', in *Film Theory: An Introduction*, Malden, Oxford: Blackwell Publishing, 2002, 254.
43. R. Odin, 'For a Semio-Pragmatics of Film', in R. Stam and T. Miller (eds), *Film and Theory: An Anthology*, Malden, MA and Oxford: Blackwell, 2000, 55.
44. Kessler, 'Historische Pragmatik', 106.
45. Ibid., 109.
46. Cf. W. Fuhrmann, 'Trans-Inter-National Public Spheres', in M. Braun et al. (eds), *Beyond the Screen: Institutions, Networks and Publics of Early Cinema*, London: John Libbey, 2012, 307–14.
47. M.P. Ryan, 'Gender and Public Access: Women's Politics in Nineteenth Century', in C. Calhoun (ed.), *Habermas and the Public Sphere*, Cambridge, MA: MIT Press, 1992, 259–88.
48. N. Fraser, 'Rethinking the Public Sphere: A Contribution to the Critique of Actually Existing Democracy', in C. Calhoun (ed.), *Habermas and the Public Sphere*, Cambridge, MA: MIT Press, 1992, 109–42.
49. M. Warner, *Publics and Counterpublics*, New York: Zone, 2002; J. Habermas, *The Structural Transformation of the Public Sphere: An Inquiry Into a Category of Bourgeois Society*, Cambridge, MA: MIT Press, 1991.
50. G. Eley, 'Nations, Publics and Political Cultures: Placing Habermas in the Nineteenth Century', in C. Calhoun (ed.), *Habermas and the Public Sphere*, Cambridge, MA: MIT Press, 1992, 306.
51. Ibid.
52. Ibid., 291.
53. T. Nipperdey quoted in R. Chickering, *We Men Who Feel Most German. A Cultural Study of the Pan German League, 1886–1914*, Boston: George Allen & Unwin, 1984, 25.

54. Chickering, *We Men Who Feel Most German*, 183. See also T. Nipperdey, 'Verein als soziale Struktur in Deutschland im späten 18. und frühen 19. Jahrhundert', in *Gesellschaft, Kultur, Theorie. Gesammelte Aufsätze zur neueren Geschichte*, Göttingen, 1976, 174–205.
55. G. Eley, *Reshaping the German Right. Radical Nationalism and Political Change After Bismarck*, New Haven, CT, London, 1980, 220–22. The Navy League's role as a film exhibitor is discussed by M. Loiperdinger in 'The beginnings of German Film Propaganda: The Navy League as Travelling Exhibitor 1901–1907', *Historical Journal of Film, Radio and Television*, 2002, 22(3), 305–13.
56. There exists no comprehensive study on the history of the DKG from the society's beginning until its end in 1933. The major reference for this book is R.V. Pierard's 'The German Colonial Society, 1882-1914', Ph.D. dissertation, Iowa State University, 1964. The period until the end of the Bismarck era is covered by K. Kauß in 'Die Deutsche Kolonialgesellschaft und die Deutsche Kolonialpolitik von den Anfängen bis 1895', Ph.D. dissertation, Berlin (Ost): Humboldt-Universität Berlin, 1966. The colonial activities of the DKG in Bavaria are covered by M. Seemann in *Kolonialismus in der Heimat. Kolonialbewegung, Kolonialpolitik und Kolonialkultur in Bayern 1882–1943*, Berlin: Ch. Links Verlag, 2011. Official histories, and therefore rather apologetic in their description of the society's activities, can be found in E. Prager, *Die deutsche Kolonialgesellschaft 1882-1907*, Berlin: Dietrich Reimer, 1908; W. von Stuemer and E. Duems, *Fünfzig Jahre Deutsche Kolonialgesellschaft 1882–1932*, Berlin: Deutsche Kolonialgesellschaft, 1932.
57. Pierard, 'The German Colonial Society', 2.
58. See also W. Fuhrmann, 'Locating Early Film Audience: Voluntary Associations and Colonial Film', *Historical Journal of Film, Radio and Television*, 2002, 22 (3), 291–304.
59. The DKG was not the only colonial association. The Deutscher Kolonialbund (German Colonial Association) was founded in 1900; four years later the Deutsch-Nationaler Kolonialverein (German-National Colonial Association) came into being. Both associations seemed to have had considerably less influence than the DKG, and there is no evidence that these two associations were involved in film projects.
60. For studies on early nonfiction cinema please consult the bibliography. In 1995 the two Italian film festivals Il Cinema Ritrovato in Bologna and the Giornato del Cinema Muto in Pordenone focused on early nonfiction films. Today, discoveries and restorations of early nonfiction films are integral parts of the festival programmes.
61. T. Gunning, 'Before Documentary: Early Nonfiction Films and the "View" Aesthetic', in D. Hertogs and N. de Klerk (eds), *Uncharted Territory. Essays on Early Nonfiction Film*, Amsterdam: Stichting Nederlands Filmmuseum, 1997, 12.
62. Hertogs and de Klerk, *Nonfiction From the Teens*, 12.
63. Ibid.
64. Ibid., 14.
65. See for example R.M. Barsam, *Nonfiction Film: A Critical History*, Bloomington: Indiana University Press, 1992; E. Barnouw, *Documentary. A History of the Nonfiction Film*, 2nd edn, New York: Oxford University Press, 1993.
66. Griffiths, *Wondrous Difference*; U. Jung and M. Loiperdinger (eds), *Geschichte des dokumentarischen Films in Deutschland, Bd. I: Kaiserreich 1895–1918*, Stuttgart: Reclam, 2005; J.L. Peterson, 'World Pictures: Travelogue Films and the Lure of the Exotic 1890–192, Ph.D. dissertation, University of Chicago, 1999.
67. K. Kreimeier, 'Mechanische Waffen und Haudegen überall. Expeditionsfilme: das Bewaffnete Auge des Ethnografen', in J. Schöning (ed.), *Triviale Tropen: Exotische Reise- und Abenteuerfilme aus Deutschland 1919–1939*, Munich: edition text + kritik, 1997, 47.

68. Peterson, 'World Pictures', 12.
69. Ibid., 1.
70. S. Zantop, *Colonial Fantasies, Conquest: Family, and Nation in Precolonial Germany, 1707-1870*, Durham, NC, London: Duke University Press, 1997.
71. Ibid., 3.
72. G. Melcher, 'Von der Lebenden Photographie und dem Kino-Drama,' *Der Kinematograph*, 17 February 1909.
73. L. Charney and V. Schwartz (eds), *Cinema and the Invention of Modern Life*, Berkeley: University of California Press, 1995, 3.
74. A recent biography gives no information on this. M. Becker, *Bwana Simba. Der Herr der Löwen. Carl Georg Schillings. Forscher und Naturschützer in Deutsch-Ostafrika*, Düren: Hahne & Schloemer, 2008.
75. *Der Kinematograph*, 10 February 1907.

PART I

THE BEGINNING OF COLONIAL FILM CULTURE IN IMPERIAL GERMANY

Chapter 1

FROM THE VARIETY THEATRE TO THE GERMAN COLONIAL SOCIETY

The first appearance of films from the colonies in Germany coincided with the moment when the colonial movement had almost come to a complete standstill. The enthusiasm of the first years of German colonialism had dissipated into a broad disinterest in colonial matters. In the German Reichstag the social democrat Wilhelm Liebknecht soberly summed up the results of colonialism: 'Murder, robbery, homicide, syphilis and Schnaps'.[1] Despotic rule and conflicts with the natives' traditional sociocultural values and beliefs were the main reasons for the revolts in the African colonies. To counteract the revelations of colonial scandals, the colonies' economic unproductiveness and the outbreak of the Herero War in January 1904, a positive image of the colonies' national value for Germany was badly needed.[2]

Togo, the smallest of the four African colonies and considered the 'model colony' of the German Empire, was the only African colonial territory that did not experience revolt or war, though maltreatment of the Togolese population was part of the daily colonial practice. Between 1904 and 1907 the colony Cameroon experienced revolts caused by the despotic rule of Cameroon's governor, Jesko von Puttkammer (1895–1907). The governor was one of the biggest stockholders of German plantation societies and supported overtly the colony's division among the plantation societies at the expense of the population's total expropriation and proletarization. The most violent and disastrous conflicts for the African population happened in the South-West African and the East African colonies.

The outbreak of the Herero War on 12 January 1904 in German South-West Africa hit the German Empire quite unexpectedly. The cause of the outbreak could be found in Germany's ignorance of pre-colonial African economics and the effort of trying to apply European economic concepts in Africa. The colonial government considered the Herero's accumulation of livestock as pure economic abundance and not as a traditional signifier of political and social power and prestige. After the loss of their cattle in the devastating cattle plague in 1897, many Herero were forced to work for the new white settlers. Settlers used this chance and exploited the new workers by paying minimum wages, and since the Herero no longer had a monopoly on cattle, the settlers took the leading position on the cattle market. The Herero War lasted for more than half a year until October 1904, and killed between 75 and 80 per cent of the Herero population. After the Herero's defeat another ethnic group, the Nama (who also were scornfully called the 'Nama-Hottentotten'), rose up against the German colonizers. Massacred like the Herero, more than 50 per cent of the Nama died during the war, which lasted until March 1907 when the state of war was officially declared to be over in German South-West. On the German side, 1,500 Germans died in the battles or from the extreme climate conditions that drove many soldiers into madness and suicide.

In a situation similar to that in the South-West African colony at the beginning of the Herero War, a head-and-hut tax (*Kopf- und Hüttensteuer*) drove the native population in the German East African colony into poverty and wage labour. Compulsory work was introduced either on public projects or on the private plantations of German farmers and corporations. The inhumane conditions and hard work on the plantations killed – sometimes within a short time – 10 per cent of the recruited workers. In July 1905 the Maji-Maji Rebellion broke out in the colony;[3] for more than two years German troops, supported by African soldiers, the Askari, fought against several tribes in East Africa. Although the official figures estimated that seventy-five thousand Africans were killed between 1905 and 1907, the economic consequences of Germany's military strategy of 'scorched earth' caused starvation among the population and probably killed between two-hundred-and-fifty thousand and three-hundred thousand East Africans.

Word of uprisings, war, atrocities, favouritism and other colonial scandals reached the German public and presented German colonialism less as an act of patriotic idealism than as a regime of oppression. General Trotha's proclamation that not only 'every Herero, with or without a gun, with or without cattle, will be shot'[4] and even women and children were no longer accepted in the South-West colony provoked social democrat August Bebel in the Reichstag to compare Trotha's military strategy with 'slaughter methods' that did not require a general or a higher officer, but was a strategy that could be executed by 'every butcher's boy'.[5]

In addition to German colonial policy's devastating result, the colonial economy was not doing any better and offered little that could deflect the public's attention from the violent situation in the colonies. People preferred to emigrate to the United States rather than to Africa, a continent that never lost its reputation as a place for failures. In 1907 fewer than eight thousand Germans were living in the African colonies. The colonies' productivity was equally low; in 1904 the colonial economy contributed only 0.5 per cent to Germany's balance of trade. The political and economic situation in the colonies made the German public doubt whether all the efforts and sacrifices that had been made would finally pay off in the end. A positive public image of the colonies was badly needed. While public media exploited the Herero War as an entertaining spectacle, it became the colonial lobby's major task to transform the public's critical attitude into a new colonial enthusiasm.

The Herero War and Popular Media

The geographic distance between Germany and the African colony made it difficult for the media to immediately respond to the outbreak of the Herero War. The *Deutsche Kolonialzeitung* (*DKZ*, German Colonial Newspaper) could not offer photographs with images from the battles in the South-West African colony before May 1904.

Faster than illustrated reports was the popular panorama. In February the first painted panoramas were offered to the travelling fair business,[6] and in April exhibitioners could order panoramas with the 'Blutiger Kampf gegen Hereros bei Owikokorea' [sic] (Bloody Battle Against Hereros at Owikokorea).[7] The battle details needed for the production of panoramas at this early stage of the war probably did not come from photographs but from reports in the daily newspapers. Though panoramas were technically limited in illustrating the live character of a battle, the disadvantage was compensated for through the precise attention to details of the depicted moment.[8] The purpose of colonial panoramas was to illustrate the so-called *Befriedungsfeldzüge* (pacification campaigns) against the colonized enemy and to glorify German soldiers and the superiority of the troops.[9] The fair, however, offered more than panoramas of the ongoing colonial war. Motivated by newspaper reports and illustrations of brave German soldiers, male visitors could arm themselves and virtually join the colonial troops. In June 1905 a glass manufacturer offered a new business idea to owners of shooting galleries: for the price of two marks, owners could purchase for their shooting clients a hundred 'deceptively real-looking' reconstructions of Herero heads made of glass.[10]

Another form of entertaining spectacle of the Herero War was offered by the Circus Busch in Berlin, where the monumental pantomime 'South-West Africa' premiered in September 1904.[11] The show enjoyed great popularity among all classes and ages. With more than a hundred actors and an exact staging, the spectacle was a choreographed music show about the military campaign against the Herero. The show illustrated the decisive battle against the Herero at the Waterberg Plateau that had taken place a few weeks before. The show's purpose was not to present the reality of war and its atrocities, which caused the agonizing death of more than six thousand Herero warriors and their families in the Omaheke desert, but, as Sylke Kirschnick points out, it aimed at practicing and confirming current racist prejudices that justified military action against the Herero.[12] The punishment of the colonized enemy also seemed to dominate other theatrical presentations, like the performance of a touring Herero group in a variety theatre in Breslau (Wroclaw) in January 1905.[13] The group, which according to their manager was 'well-disposed to the German audience and did not show any solidarity with their people in Africa', performed artistic versions of prayers, dances, songs and club and sword plays. The main attraction, however, was the 'out-of-the-everyday' scene of the capturing and conviction of a thief caught red-handed, whose decapitation was 'authentically done by our black compatriots'.[14]

It is impossible to exactly date the very first film screening of a colonial film in Germany, but cinema's rooting in the variety theatre business suggests that it was in the context of popular entertainment.[15] Film quickly entered the variety business around 1900 for two reasons: firstly, following a structure of contrasts and climaxes, the variety tried to combine artistic performances with the presentation of new technical sensations such as film projection. Secondly, film was a perfect closing number for a programme that was usually difficult to finish with a human artist.[16] Joseph Garncarz distinguishes between two kinds of varieties: the international variety theatre for the wealthy upper class and the local variety theatre for the petty bourgeoisie. Though both variety forms offered film shows to their audience, only the international variety theatre showed an early form of cinema newsreels, the *Optische Berichterstattung* (visual report).[17] The visual report offered a panorama of topicals, for example images of the German emperor, the German navy, major political events or militant conflicts like the Boxer Uprising of 1900/01 or the Russian-Japanese War of 1904/05. Addressing the upper class, the visual report conveyed a specific world view so that screenings of topics of national interest made the report into a kind of 'national naval gazing'.[18] The visual report, therefore, was the perfect setting for images from a war that addressed the audience's imperial patriotism.

In April 1904 the Internationale Kinematographen-Gesellschaft GmbH from Berlin announced in the variety trade journal *Der Artist* that material would be soon available, 'Natur-Aufnahmen aus Deutsch-Südwestafrika (Herero Aufstände)' (Scenics from German South-West Africa [Herero Uprisings]). Meanwhile it was already offering two interesting 20 m shots that were not re-enactments.[19] According to the title the film could be used as a visual report to comment on the latest events in the colony. Though new films seemed to have reached the company in May, the lack of any additional adverts in the following weeks suggests that the films must have been of low quality and were probably economically unviable.

Visual reports at the international variety theatres could not compete in timeliness with the daily newspaper, as the moving images from the Herero War illustrated an event that had been known to the audience for months. The emphasis in the advert that the films were not re-enactments, however, indicates that film companies were trying to comment on the political events in more than one way. Staging the Herero War in film was another way to join the existing media coverage and will be discussed in more detail below. Analyses of re-enactments in early cinema show that the films were not necessarily considered as frauds but as the staging and visualization of an actual event.[20] The cinematographic vision (*kinematographische Traumbild*) *Die Schwarze Hölle* (The Black Hell), which premiered in July 1904 at the Belle-Alliance-Theater in Berlin, is an example of how the Herero War was re-enacted as a combination of cinematographic representation and theatrical performance, embedding the idea of a visual report within a dramatic stage play:

> A young German joins the battle against the Herero. Of course, his bride cannot join the battle and she is dreaming at home about her lover. In one of the dreams (the 'Bioscope' depicts the fantasy image [*Phantasiegebilde*] in living pictures) the young hero has a serious fight with a particularly bloodthirsty Herero – the dreamer loudly cries out, her uncle shouts:

'What is going on?' – the doorbell rings – and the brave Herero fighter enters safe and sound in his uniform! General emotion, embraces – and the 'cinematographic vision' [*Traumbild*] is over.[21]

According to reviews in the local newspapers, the film projection added a new quality to the traditional stage play. The re-enacted fight between the German soldier and the Herero was presented in form of a dream shot of the bride's vivid nightmare. It did not depict any moment of the battle beyond the most spectacular one, the fight between the young German hero and the African enemy. The emphasis on a 'particularly bloodthirsty Herero' suggests that the film tried to show the Herero in the most negative way through costume, makeup, mime and gesture. It obviously aimed at creating empathy with the German soldier and arousing colonial-racist prejudices against the colonial enemy. The combination play did very well with the audience, but the trade press considered it inappropriate for a variety's closing number.[22]

The lack of further adverts for films from the colonies in the variety's trade press, and the sparse information on similar stage plays like the *Die schwarze Hölle,* suggest that the Herero War as a film sujet sold only for the time that it was breaking news. The decisive battle against the Herero people at the Waterberg Plateau in August 1904, the warfare against the Nama people or the Maji-Maji Rebellion in German East Africa did not result in broad film coverage as visual reports at the international variety theatres. However, another exhibition context started to become a much more reliable venue for watching films from the colonies: the town hall and the network of a voluntary association that addressed itself to the promotion of the colonial idea in the German public – the German Colonial Society (DKG). In contrast to the fair or the variety theatres, colonial film screenings at the DKG were planned to be more than an amusing intermezzo but a long-term project to win over the public to the colonial idea.

The Deutsche Kolonialgesellschaft (DKG)

The DKG was founded in 1887 in Berlin as an amalgamation of the Deutscher Kolonialverein (German Colonial Association) (1882) and the Gesellschaft für deutsche Kolonisation (Society for German Colonization) (1884). Compared to the German Navy League, another important patriotic society in Wilhelmine Germany, the DKG was small in membership and reached its peak shortly after the outbreak of the First World War in October 1914 with 43,244 members.[23] The society's official organ was the illustrated *DKZ*, which provided its readers with articles about all topics related to colonialism and the work of the local branches.

The DKG was concerned about the preservation of a German national identity abroad and represented the colonial variant among a group of patriotic societies such as the Allgemeiner Deutscher Sprachverein (General German Language Association) and the Allgemeiner Deutscher Schulverein (General German School Association), which considered the German *Volk* as a unified ethnic entity defined by language and culture.[24] The DKG considered itself a centre for all colonial matters and saw its mission in the national work of German colonization and carrying an appreciation of the importance of this endeavour into ever larger circles. This work included fostering practical solutions to colonial questions and the support of national German colonial enterprises, to find solutions for questions concerning German emigration and to maintain and enforce the commercial and spiritual cohesion between Germans abroad and the fatherland.

With hundreds of local branches, the DKG was a decentralized organization, but policy was laid down by central organs in Berlin, which from 1911 operated from the so-called Afrikahaus (Africa House) near Potsdamer Platz. The society was composed of a presidium, Duke Johann Albrecht zu Mecklenburg, a *Vorstand* (board of directors) and the *Ausschuss* (executive committee), which handled the society's administration.[25] The committee dealt with and discussed almost every issue that was passed to the society and ran the publicity commissions that played an important role in the institutionalization of colonial cinematography in the DKG. Leadership positions, such as presidium and board, were usually filled by prominent public figures. That was not only a question of prestige for the society but also provided the DKG with a means of making its influence felt in high places.[26] Maintaining a close working relationship with the government, the director of the KA (Colonial Department of the Foreign Office) considered the DKG a great ally in the work of colonial development of the German empire, and the DKG and the colonial administration together formed a close community.[27] The society's significance was even recognized by the German emperor Wilhelm II, who declared that he could always count on the support of the DKG in his endeavours for Germany's greatness beyond the seas.[28]

A member of the society usually belonged either to an *Abteilung* (local branch) or a smaller *Ortsgruppe* (local group), which was organized within a larger *Gauverband* (district association). The high number of local branches, 333 branches and eight regional associations in 1900, ensured the society's presence in almost every German city and town. The branches were semi-autonomous and could be highly organized or could exist as only a small social gathering. Bigger branches, such as the Berlin branch with over a thousand members, ran their own clubhouse with a colonial library and a meeting room. The DKG was open to all, but a high annual membership fee of six marks and an additional one or two marks fee for the local branch made the society rather unattractive for people with low incomes. The DKG was an organization represented by a 'small top group with professional overseas interests and a broad base in the upper-middle class'.[29] The few existing statistics on the different professions represented by the DKG's members show that government officials, military and naval officers, merchants, manufacturers and businessmen made up more than half of the society's members.[30] Branches in industrial cities like Essen had among their members big industrialists like Krupp von Bohlen und Halbach, who generously supported the colonial movement; branches in university towns usually had more academics and those that hosted a garrison more army members.[31] The society's membership in proportion to the total population was strongest in smaller cities, less in commercial centres such as Hamburg, Bremen or Frankfurt am Main, and weakest in the large industrial strongholds such as Berlin, Munich, Cologne, Dortmund or Breslau. The geographical aspect, as will be shown later, was not unimportant for the development of colonial film screenings.

Geoff Eley has described the internal relations of the DKG as 'particularly lifeless'; the main activities were located in the Berlin headquarter rather than in the local branches.[32] A more detailed look at the branches' activities, however, shows that it was largely through the branches' efforts that the DKG articulated its voices in the public sphere. It was particularly due to the response and pressure of the local branches that the DKG was forced to improve its propaganda activities. The most important medium used by the branches to address the public was the organization of public lectures.

From Lantern Slides to Moving Images

Before the turn of the twentieth century, the DKG grew continuously in numbers and took many initiatives to popularize colonialism among the German public. Besides the production of an inexpensive colonial atlas in paperback form for mass consumption, the DKG started to supply German newspapers with weekly press releases about colonial matters. Even though the DKG was able increase its influence on many people and double its membership between 1896 and 1900 to thirty-six thousand, the society's propaganda activities before 1900 were not too successful in converting the masses to colonial policy.[33]

Starting in the second half of 1900 and continuing for the following four years, the DKG noticed a growing public disinterest in colonialism, which was mainly caused by the revelation of colonial scandals and the virtual non-productiveness of the colonies. The decrease in membership led the DKG to be concerned not only about how to win and re-win members, but also about how to bind existing members to their branches. To manage the increasing work of coordinating the propaganda efforts of the DKG, the society appointed in January 1898 a *Werbekommission* (publicity committee).[34] The committee's task was complex: it scheduled lectures in the branches, tried to organize new branches, prepared the DKG's own lantern slide collections on the colonies and disseminated to the public informative literature about the society.[35]

Chickering has emphasized the importance of the social activities and gatherings in local branches; even though they had no particular historical importance, they translated ideology into political action.[36] The most powerful medium in the DKG's colonial propaganda work was the organization of public lectures on colonial issues. In order to reach the largest possible audience lectures were usually for free and held during the society's publicity campaigns from October to April. To offer the audience the freshest impressions from the colonies, the DKG put much effort into recruiting lecturers, colonial civil servants or farmers as officers, who either were on vacation in Germany or had spent at least some time in the colonies and could give therefore first-hand information. Some speakers occasionally used lantern slides to illustrate their lectures, and this new lecture mode became extremely popular among the DKG's members, stimulating the society to establish its own picture archive in 1891. Confident that illustrated lectures would become a 'crowd-pulling' medium able to 'create a vivid idea' of the colonies, the DKG planned to expand its activities in this field in the future.

In subsequent years the DKG worked on the standardization of illustrated lectures by editing small introductory booklets with background information on every image in the individual series. In 1895 the DKG offered a one-hundred-slide series about the East African colony that was edited together with a small booklet recommending that images be organized in an order that suited the branches' own interests and that lectures be limited to fifty images.[37] The confidence in a successful future with lantern slide lectures for propaganda purposes is illustrated by an event in which the DKG had the chance to introduce a very new visual medium for colonial propaganda. In May 1898 the society's executive committee discussed a proposal requesting financial support for the production of films in the colonies;[38] the committee sympathized with the project but turned down the motion for financial reasons and because illustrated lectures were considered sufficient for the society's propaganda work in the branches. Consequently, the DKG's picture archive increased year by year through the purchase of new slides and through donations of originals or duplicates from official, commercial or private collections. The lantern slides were usually compiled into larger series and covered all aspects of colonial life: sciences including geology and mining; schools and missions; traditional trade and traffic; vegetation and native agriculture; introduction of modern infrastructure such as harbour docks, railways and streets; studies of landscapes and animals; the work of natives and of white settlers; economic development through European efforts; and the very popular and often requested series on the German colonial army and the Herero War.

Attending an illustrated lecture on the colonies was an 'edutainment' in which history joined geography, and ethnographic images were followed by spectacular shots or romantic views. The 1901 introductory series, 'Eine Wanderung durch unsere Kolonien' (A Walking Tour Through Our Colonies), of sixty-eight images created a sense of 'being there' by imitating a steamship journey through the colonies, starting from Hamburg and anchoring in different colonial harbours. The lecture was aimed at satisfying 'the audience's thirst for knowledge'.[39]

With the publicity campaign of 1902/03 more lantern slide series were ordered than non-illustrated lectures. The popularity of individual series changed from year to year; while the Boxer Rebellion made Kiaochow the most interesting topic in 1900, in the following years attractions varied from the South-West African colony to the exotic appeal of Samoa and Togo in 1902/03. The outbreak of the Herero War created an increase in lantern slide series on this topic; in 1904 almost 55 per cent of the total demand was for slide series on this war. In contrast to this demand, the Maji-Maji Rebellion in the East African colony in 1905 seemed to inspire only limited interest from the local audiences.[40]

By 1905 the DKG had a well-organized network of local branches all over the country and had institutionalized the illustrated lecture as the most important medium in the society's propaganda work. Yet, in the same year, the society had to face new challenges in this area; the DKG's annual report for 1905 mentions the growing dissatisfaction within the local branches. Though public lectures were still considered the most powerful medium for colonial propaganda, the society came to recognize that non-illustrated lectures were poorly attended and even illustrated lectures did not 'develop the full attraction any more'.[41] Impressed by the German Navy League's successful film shows in their branches, the DKG's members were also asking for colonial film screenings. The society was urged to adapt the propaganda work to the 'signs of the time'.

The chance for the DKG's leadership to study film as a new medium for colonial propaganda came in April 1905, made possible through the films from the African colonies of the Altenburg citizen, merchant and brewery owner Carl Müller. Müller officially addressed the DKG's executive committee in March, proposing the exhibition of his lantern slides and the cinematographic films from the East African and the South-West African colonies that he had shot during a trip through Africa in the winter of 1904/05:

> The merchant and brewery owner Mister Karl (sic) Müller from Altenburg, who made a series of cinematographic and lantern slide pictures in German East- and German South-West Africa, wishes to exhibit them in a fortnight to the members of the presidium and executive committee of the German Colonial Society, the boards of both Berlin branches and some invited guests. He asks the German Colonial Society to arrange a date and issue the invitations. The executive committee gives its agreement and proposes, if the two Berlin branches' boards consent, to exhibit the images on Monday April the 10th.[42]

The committee's positive response to Müller's request and the invitation to Berlin was a something of a formality, because his plan to produce films in the colonies did not come as a surprise. In September of the previous year Müller had already presented his project to colonial officials, including the DKG's presidium.

In September 1904 Carl Müller contacted the DKG and the KA in Berlin and presented his plan of travelling to the colonies in the winter of 1904/05. He planned to stay two months in the African colonies: one month in the East African colony, then a half-month stay in South-West Africa and finally eight days each in Cameroon and Togo. In his letter to the KA Müller explained in detail his project, which had two major goals:

Figure 1.1. Carl Müller and family (ca. 1910). Reproduced courtesy of Gerhard Gross.

> With one of the best cinematographic apparatus, that I have already been using for months I intend to make a trip to Africa, especially to our colonies, in order to show in film screenings Germany's land and sea power as well as her greatness. I will especially screen manoeuvers and films of the sea fleet, as well images of our biggest cities to show our compatriots what Germany looks like now but also to give the natives an idea of Germany's power.[43]

The quote reveals that the purpose of Müller's first trip was not only to shoot films in the colonies but also to exhibit in the colonies films from Germany and spread propaganda for Germany among the African population. Films of military manoeuvres, the German sea fleet and German cities would inform the German audience abroad and impress the colonized Africans with Germany's power. The second part of his journey was dedicated to cinematographic recordings in the colonies, which were to be used for propaganda screenings back home in Germany. Müller's reference to the new quality of moving images from the colonies compared to common photographic images shows that he was quite aware that he would be exploring a new visual field in colonial representation:

Furthermore I have an excellent camera to shoot in return all interesting occurrences, life of the natives, scientific recordings, harbour scenes and everything that is of interest and to show them in Germany. I am convinced that not just for high officials but for all colonial friends it will be of utmost interest to see facilities, institutions, life not just in photographs as it has been the case until now but in living images.[44]

Müller did not expect any direct financial support from the KA but asked for a military escort, free rides on the colonial railways and bed and breakfast in the quarters of the Schutztruppen. The KA viewed Müller's project with sympathy and wished Müller success in overcoming the well-known difficulties of using film in the tropics. However, because of official regulations and to avoid setting a precedent for other petitioners, the KA did not grant most of Müller's requests but promised to send a letter of introduction to the individual colonial administrations with the recommendation to 'support the productions of living pictures of the populations of the protectorates (*Schutzgebiete*) as long as this did not require special expenditures of particular means'.[45] Although in the official letter Müller emphasized the patriotic spirit of his intended journey, in addition to patriotic considerations he was influenced by his sense for business. Müller successfully combined his own commercial interest with the political situation in 1904 that affected the Altenburg local public in a particular way, as will be shown later in this study.

Very little is known about Müller's stays in the individual German colonies, meaning that summaries of his two journeys must be based on the sparse reports that were given in the local colonial newspapers and the information about places that are mentioned in his lectures. At least his stay in the East African colony on his first trip can be almost completely reconstructed. Although no official tourist guidebook existed at the time Müller was travelling in the colonies, he seemed to visit those tourist sights that later formed the official tourist route recommended by the first tourist guide to the East African colony in 1914.[46] Though he was also a tourist on his second journey, it seems that his second route was much more dictated by the interest of his various sponsors.

Notes

1. Wilhelm Liebknecht quoted in G. Noske, *Kolonialpolitik und Sozialdemokratie*, Stuttgart: Verlag von I.H.W. Dietz Nachf. GmbH, 1914, 78.

2. The following overview is based on Gründer, *Geschichte der deutschen Kolonien*.
3. The name Maji-Maij derives from a sacred water-medicine that was supposed to make African warriors invulnerable against German bullets.
4. Trotha's proclamation has become known as the *Vernichtungsbefehl* (extermination order), which is quoted in full length in J.B. Gewald, 'Colonization, Genocide and Resurgence: The Herero of Namibia 1890–1913', in M. Bollig and J.B. Gewald (eds), *People, Cattle and Land: Transformations of a Pastoral Society in Southwestern Africa*, Cologne: Rüdiger Köppe Verlag, 2000, 187–226.
5. Noske, *Kolonialpolitik und Sozialdemokratie*, 113.
6. *Der Komet*, 13 February 1904, 32.
7. *DerKomet*, 23 April 1904, 25.
8. E. Roters, *Jenseits von Arkadien- die romantische Landschaft*, Cologne: Du Mont, 1995, 127.
9. Cf. J. Zeller, 'Berliner Maler und Bildhauer im Dienste der Kolonialidee', in *Kolonialmetropole Berlin*, 2002, 160.
10. *Der Komet*, 03 June 1905, 19.
11. S. Kirschnick, '"Hereinspaziert"! Kolonialpolitik als Vergnügungskultur', in A. Honold and O. Simons (eds), *Kolonialismus als Kultur*, Tübingen and Basel: Francke, 2002, 221–41.
12. Ibid., 225.
13. *Der Artist*, 29 January 1905.
14. Ibid.
15. See C. Müller, *Frühe deutsche Kinematographie. Formale, wirtschaftliche und kulturelle Entwicklung 1907–1912*, Stuttgart, Weimar: Metzler, 1994; J. Garncarz, *Masslose Unterhaltung*, Frankfurt and Basel: Stroemfeld, 2010.
16. Garncarz, *Masslose Unterhaltung*, 21.
17. Ibid., 30–51.
18. Ibid., 39.
19. *Der Artist*, 24 April 1904. 20 metres corresponds to a projection time of one minute.
20. Garncarz, 'The Origins of Film Exhibition in Germany', 114; see also S. Bottomore, 'Filming, Faking and Propaganda: The Origins of the War Film, 1897–1902', Ph.D. dissertation, Utrecht: Utrecht University, retrieved 20 February 2014 from http://dspace.library.uu.nl/handle/1874/22650.
21. *Der Artist*, 10 July 1904.
22. Ibid.
23. Pierard, 'The German Colonial Society', 106. A third influential patriotic society was the Alldeutscher Verband (Pan-German League), with seventeen thousand members (calculated for 1912). The DFV had 331,493 members in 1914. Eley estimates that, together with members in corporately affiliated organizations, the DFV had more than a million members (Eley, *Reshaping the German Right*, 366).
24. Chickering, *We Men who Feel Most German*, 38.
25. Pierard, 'The German Colonial Society', 99.
26. Ibid., 98.
27. Ibid., 248.
28. Ibid., 210.
29. Gründer, *Geschichte der deutschen Kolonien*, 42.
30. Pierard, 'The German Colonial Society', 109; see also U. Soénius, *Koloniale Begeisterung im Rheinland während des Kaiserreiches*, Cologne: Rheinisch- Westfälisches Wirtschaftsarchiv zu Köln e.V, 1992, 40-44.
31. Pierard, 'The German Colonial Society', 111.

32. Eley, *Reshaping the German Right*, 119–20.
33. Pierard, 'The German Colonial Society', 284.
34. The work of the Werbekommission is documented in the records of the DKG at the Bundesarchiv-Berlin only from 1911 onwards. The names of members of the publicity committee that appear in the executive committee's discussion about film screenings indicate that the publicity committee was the driving force in the institutionalization of film in the Colonial Society.
35. Pierard, 'The German Colonial Society', 209.
36. Chickering, *We Man who Feel Most German*, 152.
37. Deutsche Kolonialgesellschaft, *Material zur Ausarbeitung von erklärenden Vorträgen zu den Lichtbildern der Deutschen Kolonialgesellschaft über Deutsch-Ostafrika*, Berlin: Julius Sittenfeld, 1895, 1.
38. Deutsche Kolonialgesellschaft, *Berichte über die Sitzungen des Ausschusses der Deutschen Kolonialgesellschaft*, Berlin: Deutsche Kolonialgesellschaft, 10 May 1898, 6 (henceforth cited as DKG, *Ausschuss*).
39. Deutsche Kolonialgesellschaft, *Wanderung durch unsere Kolonien*, Berlin: Deutsche Kolonialgesellschaft, 1901, 5.
40. For detailed numbers see W. Fuhrmann, 'Propaganda, Sciences, and Entertainment. German Colonial Cinematography: A Case Study in the History of Early Nonfiction Cinema', Ph.D dissertation, Utrecht: Utrecht University, 2003, 29.
41. Deutsche Kolonialgesellschaft, *Jahresbericht der Deutschen Kolonialgesellschaft: bearb in d. Geschäfsstelle*, Berlin: Deutsche Kolonialgesellschaft, 1905, 11 (henceforth cited as DKG, *Jahresbericht*).
42. DKG, *Ausschuss*, 24 March 1905, 19.
43. Bundesarchiv (henceforth cited as BArch), R 1001/662,86.
44. Ibid.
45. BArch, R 1001/6620, 88.
46. O. Karstedt, *Deutsch-Ostafrika und seine Nachbargebiete. Ein Handbuch für Reisende*, Berlin: Dietrich Reimer (Ernst Vohsen), 1914.

Chapter 2

CARL MÜLLER

A Colonial Filmmaker

Müller's First Journey: October 1904 to February 1905

Carl Müller started his first journey in the middle of October and stopped initially in Italy, where he shot his first films of Naples and Rome. From Naples Müller continued his journey to East Africa and carefully documented his stops in Suez, Aden and British East Africa with his photo camera. Müller arrived in Tanga, German East Africa, mid-November and spent the rest of the month taking pictures and filming in and around Tanga, from which he made several short trips into the northern highlands.

In the colony Müller filmed a market scene and a plantation of the Sisal Agave Society in Amboni, and he documented the strict segregation of the compartments for white, Indian and black passengers of the Usambara railway. By train he travelled to the Biological-Agricultural Institute in Amani in the Usambara mountains and to Kwamkoro, where he shot scenes of coffee processing at the Prince Albrecht coffee plantation. Most likely inspired by the forest's beauty in the region of Kwamkoro, Müller shot a film scene of this idyll in which 'just the singing of the birds echoed through the sublime silence', as he described it afterwards in one of his lectures. With a small colonial steamer he continued his travel through the colony. On his way to Dar es Salaam he stopped for shooting in Pangani and Bagamoyo. Müller reached Dar es Salaam in the first days of December and spent most of his time filming scenes around the harbour: the panorama of the harbour, the little ships' loading and unloading at the custom office, the transport of the government-owned ivory to the office, exercises of the local colonial troops, streets scenes and the transport of slaves. Reviews underlined the beauty of Dar es Salaam's European architecture: churches and public buildings and a 'wonderful palm avenue'.[1]

Letters from the DKG and the KA to colonial authorities in the colony and an article in the *Deutsch-Ostafrikanische Zeitung* (DOAZ) at the end of October 1904 about Müller's arrival informed the local colonial public about his plan to stay between four and six weeks in the colony.[2] More important than Müller's intention to shoot films in the colony was the news that he wanted to show films from the Germany. For that purpose Müller spent the first weekend in Tanga giving two film shows, Friday and Sunday, at the local clubhouse;[3] his film shows had rather different purposes depending on whether they were addressed to the German or the African public. There exists no evidence of Müller's contact with Christian missionaries, but screening the 'Oberammergau passion play' to a native audience clearly played into the hands of missionaries' goal to Christianize African people. On the other hand, films of the German army or the German sea fleet were shown to impress the African population with Germany's greatness and power. In this sense, films about the army or navy functioned as a preventive measure to nip in the bud any resistance against German colonizers. In its letter of recommendation that introduced Müller's project to the KA, the DKG emphasized that the success of Müller's work largely depended upon its influence on the coloured population that was going to see his films.[4] The handwritten note that was 'compulsory' on this recommendation, which could have been made by a colonial official, indicates that the KA, at least considered compelling the native population to watch Müller's films from Germany. If this was in fact the case cannot be said, but an extra screening for the African people at the Tanga market became a success and was heavily applauded by the African audience.[5]

The applause was probably not exclusively due to the instructional and educational character of his films but additionally because the audience found the films entertaining. This was also surely the case for the German audience. In contrast to stories that depicted life in the colonies as either romantic, adventurous or both, actual daily life offered very few cultural distractions for the European colonists. For this reason the local German audience welcomed Müller's film shows primarily as an interesting change in the daily rhythm of colonial life that often was described as a 'palm-desert tropical treadmill'.[6] The success of the Tanga screenings raised the expectations of the Dar es Salaam public, but problems with the projection lamp spoiled the screenings. In contrast to the success of his film show for the African population in Tanga, a similar screening in Dar es Salaam led the reviewer of the *DOAZ* to remark that the films were ill-suited and largely incomprehensible for the African public.[7]

It is not known when Müller left the East African colony. According to his own plans, he intended to visit Zanzibar, Mozambique, Johannesburg, Pretoria and Cape Town. Reviews of his lectures indicate that Müller surely stayed in Durban, where he filmed 'Street life in Durban' and carried out some shooting in the Natal region.[8] The most interesting aspect of Müller's stay in Durban is his contact with one of the key figures in early South African cinema, Wilhelm Wolfram.[9] Little is known about Wolfram himself. Of German origin, Wolfram probably came to South Africa to find employment in the mining industry but soon became interested in moving pictures.[10] Wolfram's cinemas were especially remembered for the quality of their film programmes. The contact with Wolfram was not limited to Müller's stay in Africa but also influenced his work as a film exhibitor in Altenburg, as will be discussed later.

Details about Müller's stay in the South-West African colony are not known. The local newspaper did not report about him as had the papers in East Africa, probably because all attention was concentrated on the Herero War. Due to the political situation, it seemed that Müller stayed in South-West Africa not the half month he had planned originally but for only a few days on his way back to Germany. Such a turn of events seems likely based on reviews of his 1905 film lecture tour, which mentions only lantern slides and films shot around the coastline and not in the interior of South-West. However, though the depiction of DSWA in Müller's film programme was limited to scenes from the Swakopmund harbour and Lüderitzbucht, reviews show that the meagre quantity of local films was compensated for by the novelty of watching the first moving images from the South-West colony. By 3 February 1905, Müller was back in Germany.

Müller's Second Journey: January to May 1906

At the first screening in Berlin, Müller already indicated the possibility of travelling once again to Africa. In retrospect, Müller's first journey was only partly successful; he spent little time in the South-West African colony and failed to visit Cameroon and Togo. Moreover, Müller was critical of his own work and considered his first films far from *'mustergültig'* (exemplary) and merely a first attempt to shoot films in the tropics.[11] Critical remarks in some reviews pointed out that the films were not entirely perfect, but these flaws were excused because of the exceptional nature of the content.[12]

On his second journey Müller therefore travelled together with a technical assistant, Max Burghard, from a local photo shop in Altenburg. The result of this collaboration seemed to be successful; the *Vossische Zeitung* remarked later that one could not fail to see the helping hand of an experienced director.[13] Given the experience of his first trip and the success of his film screenings in the DKG's local branches, Müller was more self-confident when he made his second request to the KA in December 1905 than he had been a year earlier, documenting the success of his film shows all over Germany and enclosing reviews and the programme of a Hamburg screening. In his request he emphasized the advantage of his films being the best form of instruction on colonial matters and remarked that 'more will be believed of what the eye sees than the strongest spoken assurances'.[14] In contrast to his previous request in 1904, Müller asked this time for a grant, a translator and military escort for his travels inside DSWA. Even though Müller could be sure that this second trip would again bring him recognition in colonial circles, Müller asked the KA to promote his project up to the highest ranking colonial officials and to recommend his films for colonial education. The department reacted in the same way as they had one year earlier and recommended his project to the colonial administrations. Since grants for this kind of projects did not exist, Müller received no financial support and no military escort, and was even warned against travelling to the interior of the DSWA as peace had not yet been re-established.

Equipped with 3,000 m of unexposed film, Müller started his second colonial journey in Hamburg in January 1906. In the following weeks he reported regularly to the DKG about his travels.[15] Müller's arrival and stay in DSWA, where he planned to spend between three and four weeks, was again not covered by the local press. Despite the warning of the KA, Müller left Swakopmund, where he shot several scenes, and travelled 400 km into the interior of the colony. He rode to the end of the Otavi railway and travelled beyond Windhuk (later Windhoek). On his train trip he shot a phantom ride.[16] Müller stayed in Windhuk until the first days of March, from where he left for a short stay in Swakopmund. Müller went further south to Lüderitz before continuing his travels to

Cameroon, where he was expected in the last week of March. Detailed information about Müller's stays in Togo and Cameroon do not exist because the two colonies did not have their own colonial newspaper. Reviews and the surviving picture postcards suggest that Müller did not travel to the interior of either Cameroon or Togo but rather stayed along the colonies' coastlines. In Cameroon he travelled to Kribi, Duala (later Douala) and Victoria. In Buëa, the administrative centre of the colony, he filmed an open air trial that became one of the attractions in his later film shows. The review in the *Vossische Zeitung* gives an impression of the content of his material from Cameroon, including shots of the German education system in the colony and its 'achievements':

> The work of the blacks in the big government workshops in Duala, in a Woermann trading post when a steamer from Europe arrives or departs, and in the governments' botanical garden in Viktoria, the proceedings at a trial in Buëa, the vivid bustle in the market in Duala, the funny, joyful bath of the Negroes in the current of the Cameroon river, the artistic structure of the hairstyles of the Duala Negresses, the diligent labour of bricklayers, carpenters, and cabinet makers at their work were rewarding designs for more cinematographic recordings.[17]

In Togo Müller spent his time filming the market in Lomé, as well as the harbour and the city's train station. By the colonial railway he travelled eastwards to the cotton plantation Kpeme, where he filmed production processes such as planting, harvesting and transport, and made recordings of the African population: 'You saw the landing station, the unloading of goods from a steamer into the wagons of the Togo railway, the children of the Togo Negroes in school and on the athletic grounds, Negroes picking cotton and harvesting copra, the impressive Lomé train station, a vivid scene from market life in Lomé, and natives transported in a dance of joy'.[18]

In contrast to the sparse information on Müller's travels in the individual colonies and the loss of his films that could tell us more about Müller's cinematographic impressions and 'views', surviving picture postcards from his second journey give some additional information about Müller, his attitude towards the African population and the circulation of his images in colonial Germany. As a passionate amateur photographer Müller used to take hundreds of pictures on his travels. Most of them he distributed as picture postcards or projected them as lantern slides in combination with his films.[19] One private postcard that Müller sent to his wife in March 1906, from Windhuek in DSWA, documents his everyday life as a colonial tourist in which the ex-

Figure 2.1. Jetty in Lomé. Photographer: Carl Müller. Reproduced courtesy of Übersee-Museum, Bremen, Historisches Bildarchiv, P. 03335.

ploitation of an African woman for his own needs seemed to be rather normal:

> Windhouk 5/3. 06
> Dear Clara and children, in this picture you can see how a fresh and actually warm drink tastes. Only hot water comes from the earth. I am always doing fine and I hope you do as well. Today 250 witboois have arrived, I have shot nice pictures of them. Tomorrow morning I will leave for Swakopmund where I will arrive on evening the 6th + on the 8th to Lüderitzbucht with Hans Wörmann and with this steamer also to Cameroon [unidentifiable word, W.F.] Duala where I will arrive the 23rd. I am longing for you all the time and looking forward to seeing you again. I found the best family-like reception at Mr. Fierler's. The woman lying next to me by the water is a prisoner who carries my luggage but is indispensable. Thousand greetings and kisses, your Daddyman.[20]

The photograph shows him lying next to the African woman. Both are drinking water from a small beaker. In contrast to Müller, who is properly dressed, the African woman is barefoot, and her clothes appear shabby and scattered. Müller's personal words to his family and the photography on the front are not congruent and provide a basis for speculation about Müller's relationship to the woman that he simply calls 'a prisoner'.

Figure 2.2. Carl Müller and Herero woman in DSWA, February/March 1906. Reproduced courtesy of Hans-Martin Heinig.

His passionate, warm longing for his wife and his family stands in sharp contrast to the sober description of his female African bearer, whose family life did not seem to exist for him. It was quite common for African male and female prisoners to be forced to perform hard labour in the colonial economy on farms or construction sites, and Müller's mentioning of the woman as being a prisoner suggests that he benefited from this kind of 'travel service' that probably corresponded to regulations of the local colonial administration.[21] However, in the photograph one does not see any luggage that would provide evidence of the woman's job as his servant. It is quite possible that Müller tried to calm down the fears of his wife who may have heard about the interracial relationships in the colonies that existed and were endlessly debated in German politics and among the public.[22]

The aspect of social distance that Müller's words try to establish but which is absent in the image also characterizes a picture postcard from Cameroon. The photograph shows a street leading to a small village in the background. The person on the left side of the picture can be identified as Müller, while in the picture's centre and at some distance from Müller stands a group of Africans lining up for the camera. Müller's Western tropical suit contrasts with the clothing of the Cameroonians. From today's perspective the shot composition appears awkward; a similar tourist snapshot would place the tourist in a kind of 'going native' manner among the Africans. This is not the case in this picture. Müller is separated from the group of Africans, indicating that he does not belong to them. This kind of '"entertaining" narrative of evolution' that juxtaposes the white tourist with native people was quite common in early popular representations of the Other, as pointed out by Tobing Rony.[23] The 'desire to transfix a dynamic cultural confrontation into a still life',[24] as Sara Suleri puts it, reveals what Tobing Rony calls the 'shielding gesture' of the picturesque.[25] The juxtaposing of Müller with the native Africans established a safe subject-positioning that allowed the viewer to identify with the modern Western traveller. Müller's position in this picture is quite similar to that of a lecturer, who presents the 'exotic, strange Africa' for the viewer at home.

Reviews of Müller's film shows mention images of African prisoners but mainly in the context of lantern slides. One can assume that Müller did not make any film recordings in the African concentration camps, a term commonly used for the colonial prisoner-of-war-camps that were especially erected for the Herero people during wartime and offered disastrous living conditions, on his first trip but did so during his second journey in 1906.[26] The fact that reviewers do not expand on this aspect of colonial reality in detail might be an indication that images of prisoners were only one visual attraction among many others. This is confirmed by Mülller's own impression; the arrival of 250 Nama prisoners, the so-called 'witboois', with whom the Germans had been at war since October 1904, seemed to be just one more 'nice' visual attraction, as he comments in his postcard.

One of Müller's picture postcards that were taken in one of the concentration camps started a rather popular distribution history. The picture shows sixteen underfed children, some wearing an identity tag, two of them holding a newspaper. In April 1906 Müller sent the photograph to editors of the hometown newspaper *Altenburger Zeitung für Stadt und Land*, who exhibited it in a local shop window in Altenburg. The few lines in an article that comment on the picture say that to document the 'circulation' of the local Altenburg newspaper Müller took a picture of sixteen 'Negerbabys' (NegroBabys), two of them holding an issue of the Altenburg paper. With a comic undertone the article speaks of a 'perfect picture' of the 'little black compatriots'.[27] There is little doubt that the children's parents had either been killed in war or were doing hard labour for the colonizer's economy. Shocked by the situation in one of those camps, the German missionary Heinrich Vedder remarked that 'such a ruthless brutality [*Roheit*], lecherous sensuality, brutal mastership [*Herrentum*] spread out among troops and civilians' made it almost impossible to exaggerate the description of the living conditions there'.[28] No such comments were included in any of Müller's lectures. One may wonder what he – himself a father – thought about children living in a prison camp and what made him take pictures of them.

One important function of such pictures was, as Joachim Zeller points out, the visual humiliation of the enemy.[29] Following the circulation history of this particular image we can see how the photographs entered and racialized domestic space.[30] From its display in a show window the photograph circulated in Germany as a picture postcard and turned into a consumer item that could be purchased, sent, sold or exchanged. In 1908 the photograph was reprinted in a popular reading book as 'Herero Children in a Prison Camp', and it became the front cover of the January 1909 issue of the popular colonial journal *Kolonie und Heimat* (Colony and Home).[31] It is the same picture that was shown in the Altenburg shop window three years before but obviously retouched and reframed in order to fit as an entertaining cover. In the context of a concentration camp, the new title of the photograph appears as the most cynical comment: 'Happy New Year, Kolonie und Heimat'. The subtitle below the photograph 'Idyll in a Herero Werft' pretends that the picture was taken in a typical Herero location around a white co-

Figure 2.3. Herero children in prison camp. Photographer: Carl Müller. Archive: Wolfgang Fuhrmann

lonial city. The new context and editing of the photograph in a popular journal that addressed the whole family raises important questions about the reception of the image: is it possible that readers knew the real origin of the photograph but were amused by the 'faking'? Did they believe in the subtitle or did they want to believe in the subtitle in order to transform the memory of a war that killed thousands of Herero and Nama people into a happy idyll? The examples of Müller's picture postcards show how images were part of a media practice that produced a colonial reality that downplayed the real social context of the African population during and after wartime by transforming the images into objects of visual entertainment.

On 1 May 1906 Müller returned to Germany from his second African journey with 2,000 m of exposed film and various African animals, including four ostriches. The premiere of Müller's new film material was again hosted by the Colonial Museum in Berlin on 29 June, and the DKG's vice president welcomed a group of invited guests drawn from an exclusive circle of colonial personalities. For two hours the audience watched the work of the colonizers. The films were 'remarkable for their great freshness and vitality and afforded an insight into the life and activity of Africa'.[32] As he had done the previous year, Müller toured again with his new films through the DKG's branches. Since he returned at the beginning of the summer season, he did not set up special premieres in his hometown of Altenburg, but integrated the screenings of his new films into the weekly changing film programme of his restaurant-beer garden, the Insel.

Carl Müller was never mentioned as a member of the DKG or any other patriotic society that would make his patriotic commitment and travels more obviously justifiable. Nevertheless, he became a well-known person in the colonial movement and his films were seen by colonial officials, politicians and members of the royal family. Being a nonprofessional film exhibitor makes him particularly interesting for the study of film exhibition in early cinema. Studying his work in the years between 1905 and 1907 one can identify several different exhibition contexts: in his hometown Müller used his national reputation to consolidate his position in the Altenburg region and to promote his cinema as a quality venue; as a travelling film exhibitor for the DKG and his major sponsor, the Woermann shipping line, his pictures and films demonstrated the progress and growing efficiency in the colonies. While Müller's films were an invaluable source to demonstrate the shipping company's patriotism and to promote its business all over Germany, the DKG had a powerful medium at their disposal that was much easier to handle and seemed to be more effective than any other colonial medium. Müller's films were a chance to demonstrate that German colonialism was no futile endeavour and that the colonies were economically productive territories. Like a colonial exposition, Müller's films illustrated a range of different colonial topics, but in contrast to statistics or diagrams that tried to convince the visitors to such exhibitions of the colonies' efficiency, film actually placed the viewers right into the colonies and let them see what economic and technical achievements had been attained. Who would doubt that the diligent work of Africans on German plantations did not disprove the notorious critics of German colonialism who emphasized the colonies' unprofitability?

Colonial Films: The Altenburg Quality Film Programme

Born in Altenburg, near Leipzig, Carl Müller was a local legend in his hometown.[33] He was an extremely clever and innovative businessman and epitomizes the image of the modern entrepreneur who understood how to make money from the growing appetite for leisure and entertainment. In 1897 Müller started his own business with a company specializing in a coffee substitute, which quickly expanded in the following years. In 1901 he purchased a brewery in Wuitz near Altenburg, and in 1902 signed a lease for the Insel (*Insel,* meaning island), a popular tourist restaurant located on a little island in the lake of the city of Altenburg, which became one of the most popular attractions in the local region. Probably also due to the fact that the Insel could be visited only by using small ferry boats, Müller's restaurant soon became known as the 'prettiest place on earth' and a major attraction for all kinds of entertainment.[34] Though the Insel was primarily a summer-season business, Müller tried to turn it into a year-round attraction: 'Parties on Ice' with ice skating, fireworks and illumination in winter, a beer garden with concerts of local and regional marching bands, popular singers, beauty contests and a rowboat rental concession in summer. The establishing of a little zoo on the island indicates Müller's preference for the exotic as well as his commercial spirit. He regularly presented new exotic animals, including monkeys, seals, ostriches, flamingos, bears, crocodiles and coatimundis, which he had ordered in Hamburg, and began to refer to the island as the 'Zoological Garden of Altenburg'. In summer the Insel attracted three thousand people daily, and the press cited the Insel's 'jungle life'-like atmosphere.[35]

At the beginning of 1904 Müller realized that cinema was becoming a major new attraction for public entertainment. Likely inspired by film shows he had seen in Altenburg and other cities, Müller purchased a projector and started running his own open-air cinema on the island in April 1904.[36] During the summer season Müller regularly showed films on various topics: special screenings for children in the afternoon, while for adults he offered entire sea fleet programmes or films on local events, such as a mining disaster in a nearby town for which Müller personally sent an operator to shoot the scenes. Müller's film shows represented the only permanent cinema in Altenburg prior to 1907. After having sold his films to the DKG in December 1906 Müller disappeared from the colonial scene. In late 1909 he offered his technical equipment for sale in the *DKZ*, reminding the prospective buyer that with this apparatus he had once shot his successful moving pictures from Africa.[37] With the presence of a recruiting depot and the construction of a provisional bridge at the outbreak of the First World War, the island lost its idyllic atmosphere. In January 1919, Müller asked for early termination of the lease. Private reasons, including banking business on the Berlin stock market, made continuation impossible. Müller died 27 February 1935, remembered by the Altenburg public as the 'Insel-Müller'.

Müller's motivation for travelling to the colonies came from different sources. Private family records report that Müller responded to a company's advertisement in a Hamburg newspaper that was looking for an experienced merchant who could travel independently to the South-West African colony and explore it for trading possibilities. Müller applied for the job and was accepted.[38] Müller's business interest coincided with the political situation around 1904, as there probably existed no German newspaper that did not report on colonial issues, and the Altenburg newspapers were no exception. Especially after the outbreak of the Herero War in January 1904, the local public had a particular interest in the situation in DSWA. Some Altenburg citizens had started a new life in the colony, and young men from Altenburg families were fighting in the colonial army.[39] A letter to his mother from a young Altenburg citizen who was fighting in the colony was reprinted in one of the daily newspapers and made his private fate a public matter in a small town like Altenburg.[40]

For patriotic or commercial reasons, Müller shared the local public's concern and organized a charity event for the support and reward of returning *Altenburger Landeskinder* (Altenburg natives) in June 1904.[41] The charity event was a multi-media happening of speeches, music performances (live and from a phonograph), a lantern slideshow with pictures from DSWA and films with slapstick shorts. Only a few days before this event Müller showed the film *Ein Herero auf der Insel* (A Herero on the Island), which leads to speculation about the production of this film. Was Müller filming with a black-face actor mimicking a Herero on Müller's island? The review of the charity event reports that some of the films shown were 'ridiculously funny', which suggests that Müller tried to exploit the patriotic topic for comic and commercial purposes.

To let the local audience participate in his first African journey and to thus create a demand for his film souvenirs, he organized a farewell evening the day before he left Altenburg in autumn 1904.[42] During this evening the audience had the chance to learn about his itinerary as well as the purpose of his long journey, and Müller also used the chance to rehearse the film show that he was going to present to the African public in the following months. The programme included the 'Oberammergau passion play', newsreels, scenics, slapstick shorts, lantern slides of German princes and well-known local and national business companies, which most likely were sponsors of his journey. The local press acclaimed Müller's colonial project and his patriotic commitment, but just as important was the fact that Müller was travelling as an experienced operator and film exhibitor. It was the superb technical equipment such as his projector, which allowed him to show films without any flickering, that was remembered by the local press. Based on the experience of the farewell evening, the Altenburg public could expect to see perfect filmic souvenirs of African sights after Müller's return. Müller left Altenburg the following day and started his travels 'with God, to Germany's honor and for the benefit of his family'.[43]

After his return from his first journey Müller became extremely busy. In the middle of March 1905 he travelled to Berlin, where he oversaw the further processing of his films that were arriving from Paris. Together with the DKG he arranged the colonial film premiere in April at the Colonial Museum in Berlin; parallel to this he was taking care of his business in Altenburg. He prepared the first screening in his hometown for 19 March, along with the opening of the summer season with new film screenings on the island. Müller bridged the time until the first screening in Altenburg with an exhibition of a small selection of his African souvenirs in a local shop window in Altenburg. People could see antlers, teeth and furs of African big game, as well as handicrafts and Müller's topee. The souvenirs became part of Müller's own colonial museum, which he opened on the island in May 1905 and constantly updated with new colonial products and ethnographic objects that he received from Hamburg or from friends in the colonies. School classes from the region came to see the museum, which gave Müller's island the veneer of being a place for patriotic education.

The Altenburg film premiere was not a single event but spread over two days, each divided into two parts and more expensive than normal film screenings. The day of the first premiere started with a visit to Müller's African exhibition with all kinds of souvenirs and ethnographic objects before attending in the afternoon his screenings that were titled 'My journey from Naples to Cape Town'.[44] Four hundred people attended Müller's two-hour show of 180 lantern slides, films from Rome, Naples, the East African colony and South Africa, along with additional entertaining and educational films. A specific local aspect of the show featured pictures of former Altenburg citizens who were now living in the East African colony and had been visited by Müller. The programme indicates that not all of his material was shown that day. Images and films from the South-West African colony were not shown at this first premiere but only two weeks later at the opening day for the summer season at the island.

Like the first premiere, the second premiere on 2 April 1905 was again divided into two separate programmes. In the afternoon Müller organized a children's session in which he combined his screenings from Africa with the fairy tale film *Ritter Blaubart* (Bluebeard) and his own accounts about Christmas in Africa. In the evening Müller finally presented the second part of his African journey with films from DSWA. As he had done two weeks before, Müller combined the Africa films with other films such as *Krönung des Königs Edward* (King Edward's Coronation) and *Begräbnis der Königin Viktoria* (Funeral of Queen Victoria), which, according to Müller, give a very precise picture of celebration and funeral processions in England.[45]

The inclusion of British films on the premiere programmes is significant, and might have been influenced by Müller's contact with Mr Wolfram in South Africa. It appears that Müller followed Wolfram's style of film programming, which he had had the chance to study while he was staying in Durban. South African film historian Thelma Gutsche describes Wolfram as a cinema owner who 'exercised scrupulous care in the choice of his programmes', which were especially remembered for their exceptional quality and made people think they were watching superior and interesting, as well as entertaining, films.[46] Wolfram achieved this quality through the balance of British productions that represented to him the educational aspect in film, while French productions stood for the fantastic side of cinema.

A sample of Wolfram's quality programme could also be seen in Altenburg at the end of July 1905, when Wolfram made a short stop in Altenburg during a trip through Europe and showed French and British productions to the Altenburg public. The screening evening was promoted in a big advertisement as a programme worth ten thousand marks, which had never been shown in Germany before, and reviews underlined the quality of this screening evening.[47] Wolfram left his films in Altenburg, and they were used by Müller for different programmes in the DKG's branches. Programming British films with his own films from DSWA offered Müller a chance to give his own films the same quality image for which British films were known. They were integrated into an educational programme whose quality was generally not questioned. Like Wolfram in Durban, Müller was not interested in exploiting the cinema on get-rich-quick principles but to establish his island cinema as a superior venue. His concern about the right balance in his film programmes and his intention to be entertaining as well as educational indicate that Müller's colonial films were not exclusively shown to strengthen the public's patriotism but also to attract the Altenburg public with a quality programme. His lecture activity for the DKG was extremely useful in this regard, as the following quote from an advertisement for a film show illustrates; emphasizing his success in the German metropolis he underlined the exclusivity of his films and gave the local Altenburg public the feeling it was participating in a big city event: 'Presentation of my films taken in Africa with a lecture that I have shown with the greatest success in Hamburg and Berlin. Given the interest raised by the films from all sides outside Altenburg, I hope that also here I will find understanding for my work'.[48]

The year 1905 became an extremely successful one for Müller. His travel was exploited in every possible way to promote the island cinema and to make Müller, and his family, prominent in Altenburg. His success certainly had a positive influence on the city's decision to award Müller the concession for the main marquee of the Thüringische Kreisturnfest (Thuringian Gymnastics Festival) in Altenburg at the end of July, where he organized a film show every night. Müller received more official recognition for his work and his outstanding achievements in late summer and in November 1905. In November he was asked to present a private screening at the residence of the Duke Ernst I of Saxonia-Altenburg and was honoured after the screening with the title of a *Hoftraiteur* (purveyor to the court).[49]

In contrast to the film's local and regional meaning, which helped to consolidate Müller's reputation in Altenburg, the films had a different significance for members of the colonial lobby, such as the Woermann shipping line.

The Woermann Shipping Line

Letters of recommendation from the Colonial Department, the DKG, and from the DFV were important for Carl Müller as they gave his journeys the imprimatur of a national endeavour. In this respect his second trip differed from his first. Although Müller's first trip had no direct support from commercial interests, names and motifs in the reviews of his second set of colonial films suggest that his second journey had much more the character of a contract job for certain companies, and the itinerary was directed by the recommendations of the different sponsors.

The list of companies that supported his travel through the West African colonies, either by covering some of the travel expenses or by recommendations that gave Müller and his assistant free housing and lodging in the colonies, reads like a 'Who's Who' of German colonial industry. Scenes of the colonial railway and locomotives, the Essersche Kakaoplantage, the cotton and copra plantations, the mission school in Togo or properties of the Woermann company in Cameroon were not accidental recordings but represented Müller's contract shooting of the companies' colonial properties.[50] His work, however, was not limited to the visual documentation of colonial industries. He also had a commission to conduct 'scientific research' on his travels. The Geographische Institut (Geographic Institute) of the Friedrich-Wilhelms-Universität (later Humboldt Universität) in Berlin asked Müller to make photographs of ocean waves,[51] and after his return these images became part of the Allgemeine Photographen-Ausstellung (General Photograph Exposition) at the Prussian House of Representatives in Berlin, where Müller showed the pictures in the section for scientific photography. Müller was neither a colonial expert nor an academic, but the list of his sponsors and the institute's request show his important role as a travelling film and photography amateur for the colonial lobby. The wide reception of his first films led companies to approach him at the beginning of his second trip and ask him to conduct specific tasks during his travels, with one of the most important patrons of Müller's trips being the Woermann shipping company.

Founded by Carl Woermann in 1837, the Woermann-Linie (Woermann-Line) was one of the biggest shipping lines in the world, largely thanks to the efforts of Carl's son Adolph Woermann.[52] Even before Germany became a colonial power, the company had several trading stations along the West African coastline, and the colonization of Cameroon would not have been possible without Woermann's support. No one better illustrates the multiple interrelations between colonial policy and commercial interests than Adolph Woermann himself. In addition to being the chairman of the board of the Woermann AG he sat on the boards of the Deutsche Ost-Afrika Linie (DOAL, German East Africa Shipping Line), the shipyard company Blohm und Voss, the Norddeutsche Bank and the DKG, and was a member of the *Kolonialrat* (colonial council). It is unclear whether Müller, through his Hamburg business connection, already knew Woermann before his first trip, but the correspondence between Müller and Woermann concerning Müller's plan to shoot films in the colonies seems to have started in October 1904. Though information on the cooperation between Woermann and Müller is extremely limited, there are good reasons to consider the business connection as rather successful. Woermann was very interested in Müller's project and promised to reimburse all his travel expenses under the condition that he shoot films of the colonial harbours.[53] To guarantee the success of this film travel, Woermann informed the captains of the Woermann-Linie and the DOAL that Müller and his assistant were allowed to interrupt their trip according to their itinerary and to switch to the smaller coastal liners in the colonies.[54] The financial support that Müller was promised explains his preference for shots of the colonial harbours. In Tanga, for instance, he filmed the arrival of the Woermann steamer Feldmarshall.

After his return to Germany from his first African journey, the results of Müller's filming were immediately examined by Woermann. Two days after the Berlin screening Müller presented his films to the directors of the Woermann-Linie and the DOAL at the Woermann Afrikahaus (Africa House) in Hamburg.[55] The film evening proved a success, and Müller's travel expenses were reimbursed. The evening was most likely also the beginning of the preparations for Müller's second trip, for which Woermann took care of the travel expenses in advance. Woermann and the DOAL offered Müller a first-class ticket, with a second-class ticket for his assistant, on their way to Africa.

Müller's films and his work as a film exhibitor were interesting for Woermann in many ways. During his first voyage Müller planned to show his films on board the ships, which gave Woermann the chance to experiment with a new form of shipboard entertainment. Müller was not allowed to charge admission for the screenings and not every passenger was allowed to attend them. The luxury of watching films as part of shipboard entertainment was reserved exclusively for first-class passengers:

> Furthermore, Mr. Müller is allowed, as long it does not disturb the order and work on board, to exhibit living photographs and lantern slides for the passengers' entertainment on board our steamers. However, they are not allowed to charge admission but only to take voluntary donations. Where and when screenings may take place is up to you. If you permit a screening, then you have to make sure that the necessary electricity and the connection, as far as it is possible, are available on the ship. Furthermore, Mr. Müller and his assistant are allowed to join the first class on days of screening.[56]

Film screenings on board ocean liners were an absolute novelty at this time, and became regular shipboard entertainment only around 1914.[57] There exists no account of the reception of the film screenings, but it is easy to imagine that passengers enjoyed this new form of shipboard entertainment during the voyage, which lasted almost three weeks. Another marketing strategy that combined the improvement of the onboard travel experience with the public promotion of the company was the decision to have Woermann's own publishing company issue Müller's picture postcards. It was a synergetic relationship: while Müller had a sure customer in Woermann, Müller's travel expenses could at least partly be covered by selling Müller's postcards as souvenirs on board the ships.

More important than postcards of African sights were films that showed the company's ships on their way to the colonies. The mentioning of ships of the Woermann Line and trading posts in Müller's film lectures suggests that Müller wanted to present the company in the best possible light, which was probably also part of the agreement between Müller and Woermann. Since Müller had already started to document his trip by filming on board, scenes of the 'extremely entertaining life on board' could be used to interest the public in booking a cruise with Woermann.[58] On the other hand, film images that showed the company's economic efficiency in the colonial harbours had a particular importance during the Herero War. The German Navy was too small to solve the logistical problems of military transport to the South-West colony so the Woermann Line became the 'unofficial carrier' for troops, horses and military equipment.

Filming the unloading of ships in the heavy South-West African surf was therefore not only a spectacular scene to watch: the shots of the transfer of mules, cattle and vehicles onto rafts, as described in the reviews, indicate that these sequences were linked to the Woermann company's logistical achievements during the war. Images like these showed the film-viewing audience the company's importance and underlined Woermann's patriotic service during wartime. To increase this positive patriotic image, Woermann asked Müller to make additional film recordings. These were made in May 1905 by filming the embarkation of the colonial troops on the steamer Eduard Woermann. The reception of these patriotic scenes became rather successful and effective as colonial propaganda and as promotion of the company. A very similar boarding scene was filmed again on 1 September. The film of 280 m was mentioned in many reviews afterwards and was considered one of the highlights in Müller's film programme.[59] In addition to the nationwide propaganda for the Woermann Line, film screenings with images of the company could also be used to underline their economic position in the region, as screenings by the northern branches on the North and Baltic sea coasts document.

Shots of the Woermann Line did more than just present the company's supporting efforts during the war. Francesca Schinzinger has pointed out that neither the size of the German ocean-going fleet nor the size of the merchant fleet was sufficient to conduct a colonial policy 'in grand style', and Woermann was a leader among those who urged the expansion of the German merchant and sea fleet.[60] Screenings at which his concept found the strongest support were film screenings for the DFV, and screenings that were organized by the DKG together with the DFV.[61] It was most likely Woermann himself who put Müller in contact with the DFV. Woermann sponsored DFV-organized trips for students and teachers to the German harbours during the summer break; to host the groups he offered free board and lodging on his ships that anchored in the harbours. In 1905 and 1906 Müller's colonial film shows were part of the daily programmes of these visits. At such screenings Müller's films served to demonstrate the need for a strong merchant fleet for colonial trading, and a powerful ocean-going fleet to protect trading and the colonies. The recent events in the South-West colony were an additional argument to emphasize Germany's military presence in the colonies, and it does not come as a surprise that many naval officers attended his screenings in the harbour cities. In his lectures Müller often emphasized the necessity for a better colonial infrastructure, which made him almost a spokesman for Woermann's interests. The emphasis on colonial trading and the sea fleet remained two significant aspects in Müller's lectures: 'The lecturer, who gave short relevant comments to the individual pictures, pointed out in his closing remarks the need for conserving and well-planned cultivation of our colonies and the necessity for a new strengthening of the fleet. To serve both was the purpose of his cinematographic screening'.[62] Müller's closing remarks made him the perfect spokesman for the DKG's colonial propaganda.

Notes

1. *Vossische Zeitung*, 12 April 1905.
2. *DOAZ*, 29 October 1904.
3. *Usambara-Post*, 26 November 1904. The *Berliner Börsenzeitung*, 11 April 1905, reports that Müller developed his photographs and films immediately after shooting and showed them to the African people.
4. BArch, R 1001/6620, 90.
5. *Usambara-Post*, 26 November 1904.
6. *DOAZ*, 8 July 1905. The quote is taken from an article describing a visit to a variety theatre in Dar es Salaam in July 1905.
7. *DOAZ*, 10 December 1904.
8. *Afrika-Post*, 29 April 1905, 119.
9. See T. Gutsche, *The History and Social Significance of Motion Pictures in South Africa 1895–1940*, Cape Town: Howard Timmins, 1972, 60 (footnote 1).
10. Ibid.
11. DKG, *Jahresbericht*, 1905, 11.
12. *Weser-Zeitung*, 6 December 1905.
13. *Vossische Zeitung*, 30 June 1906.
14. BArch, R 1001/6621, 36.
15. BArch, R 8023/683, 83. Unfortunately Müller's correspondence with the DKG has not survived.
16. *General Anzeiger für Elberfeld-Barmen*, 19 September 1906; *AZStL*, 16 January 1906; *DKZ*, 30 June 1906, 259.
17. *Vossische Zeitung*, 27 November 1906.
18. *Vossische Zeitung*, 30 June 1906.
19. Müller's picture postcards from his second trip can be easily identified since his name is printed on the backside.
20. I would like to thank Heinz Trebus (Altenburg) for the reproduction and transcription of the postcard.
21. Joachim Zeller points out that it was quite common for African men and women prisoners to be forced to perform hard labour for white economy on farms or construction sites. J. Zeller, 'Orlog in Deutsch-Südwestafrika. Fotografien aus dem Kolonialkrieg 1904–1907', *Fotogeschichte. Beiträge zur Geschichte und Ästhetik der Fotografie*, 2002, 22(85/86): 36.
22. Cf. Roller, 'Wir sind Deutsche, wir sind Weiße und wollen Weiße bleiben', 73–79. That the colonies were always good for an excuse to leave one's wife was also mentioned by Müller at his first film premiere in Berlin. He remarked that many men from Altenburg had abandoned their wives while pretending to take a journey to Africa (*Vossische Zeitung*, 12 April 1905).
23. F. Tobing Rony, *The Third Eye: Race, Cinema, and Ethnographic Spectacle*, Durham, NC and London: Duke University Press, 1996, 83.

24. S. Suleri, *The Rhetoric of English India*, Chicago: University of Chicago Press, 1992, 76 (quoted in Tobing Rony, *The Third Eye*, 80).
25. Ibid., 80.
26. For a discussion of photographs from African prison camps during the Herero War see J. Zeller, '"Wie Vieh wurden hunderte zu Tode getrieben und wie Vieh begraben." Fotodokumente aus dem deutschen Konzentrationslager in Swakopmund/Namibia 1904–1908,' *Zeitschrift für Geschichtswissenschaft*, 2001, 49(3): 226–43.
27. *Altenburger Zeitung für Stadt und Land* (henceforth cited as *AZStL*), 10 April 1906.
28. Quoted in Zeller, 'Wie Vieh wurden hunderte zu Tode getrieben und wie Vieh begraben"', 227.
29. Zeller, 'Orlog in Deutsch-Südwestfrika', 35.
30. Cf. A. McClintock, *Imperial Leather: Race, Gender and Sexuality in the Colonial Contest*, London: Routledge, 1995.
31. O. Beta, *Das Buch von unseren Kolonien*, Leipzig: Hirt & Sohn, 1908, 60; *Kolonie und Heimat* 2(8), 3 January 1909.
32. *DKZ*, 7 July 1906, 268.
33. H. Trebus, 'Carl Julius Friedrich Müller, genannt der "Insel Müller". Eine legendäre Persönlichkeit von Altenburg', *Familienforschung in Mitteldeutschland*, 2001, 14(4), 160–64.
34. M.L. Noirot, Landmann Chronik, typescript, 1966/67, 14.
35. *AZStL*, 2 August 1904.
36. *AZStL*, 23 April 1904.
37. *DKZ*, 2 October 1909, 661. I would like to thank Joachim Zeller (Berlin) for this information.
38. Noirot, Landmann Chronik, 5–11, 13–14.
39. In December 1905 the Altenburg newspaper could name eighty-four people either from the duchy of Sachsen-Altenburg or in some way related to it who were fighting in DSWA (*AZStL*, 3 December 1905).
40. 'Brief eines Altenburgers aus Südwestafrika', *AZStL*, 7 August 1904.
41. *AZStL*, 8 June 1904.
42. *AZStL*, 14 October 1904.
43. Ibid.
44. *Altenburger Landes-Zeitung*, 18 March 1905.
45. *AZStL*, 2 April 1905.
46. Gutsche, *Motion Pictures in South Africa*, 61.
47. *AZStL*, 28 and 29 July 1905.
48. *AZStL*, 4 June 1905.
49. *AZStl*, 22 November 1905.
50. Müller's idea for travelling once again to Africa did not meet unmixed enthusiasm at the KA. According to an official who commented on Müller's request, with a small handwritten remark on the letter, Müller's journey was just a commercial enterprise (BArch, R 1001/6621, 26). The colonial official's reservation against this kind of popular colonial propaganda was not a unique reaction. With the growing popularity of film as a new form of entertainment, colonial authorities became even more sceptical about the commercial exploitation of a serious matter such as colonial policy.
51. *AZStL*, 16 January 1906.
52. The DOAL was founded in 1890. Although the Woermann group had only a share in the DOAL, the company was part of Woermann's responsibilities. F. Schinzinger, *Die Kolonien und das Deutsche Reich. Die wirtschaftliche Bedeutung der deutschen Besitzungen in Übersee*, Wiesbaden: Franz Steiner Verlag, 1984, 147.

53. BArch, R 1001/6620, 86.
54. Letter from Woermann and the Deutsche Ost-Afrika Linie to Müller, October 1904. I would like to thank Hubert Müller for a copy of this correspondence.
55. *Altenburger Landes-Zeitung*, 16 April 1905.
56. Letter from Woermann to captains, October 1904. I would like to thank Hubert Müller for a copy of this correspondence.
57. I would like to thank the shipping historian Arnold Kludas for this information. Correspondence, 3 May 2001; see also M. Töteberg. 'Exotik und Tourismus. Die Reisefilme der Hapag', *Hamburger Flimmern*, 1999, (5): 2–6.
58. *Vossische Zeitung*, 12 April 1905.
59. *Hamburger Fremdenblatt*, 18 October 1905.
60. Schinzinger, *Die Kolonien und das Deutsche Reich*, 142–47.
61. The local newspaper *Kieler Zeitung*, 15 October 1905, reports that Müller's screenings in Breslau, Lübeck, Frankfurt, Stuttgart and Nuremberg were organized jointly by the DKG and the DFV.
62. *Weser-Zeitung*, Bremen, 6 December 1905.

Chapter 3

THE DKG'S FILM SHOWS

The Colonies in Motion

Film stood for a rather new visual experience at the turn of the twentieth century and was different from the lantern slideshows that had shaped the audience's visual knowledge about foreign territories until then. The possibility to show the colonies in *moving* images became an extremely important motivation for the DKG to support the introduction of film screenings. It was through motion that the colonies could be presented as prosperous and technologically advanced territories.

In contrast to still photography's achievement of freezing a moment on the photographic plate, the moving image was regarded as a medium that made it finally possible to overcome the photographic moment and to follow people's activities by contextualizing them in time and space. The moving image did not present a cut slice of reality but was associated with wholeness. In film single moments were joined together and therefore allowed a more complex understanding of the filmed reality, thus surpassing the spoken word and the photographic image that had to remain incomplete and insufficient.[1] From Müller's films viewers obviously expected more than watching just a photographic moment. The new quality was also acknowledged by reviews that emphasized that in contrast to the Sciopticon (a kind of magic lantern) the cinematographic apparatus 'produces apparently living, moving images'.[2] The phrase of watching 'the hustle and bustle in the colonies', which was often used in reviews of colonial film screenings, illustrates that film was associated with watching life flowing and passing by in front of the viewers' eyes. It was not the observation of a particular moment but a continuous change of different activities that people expected to see in the films. Müller himself was convinced that, in contrast to the present standard of the photographic image, film's new visual quality could also be of interest for colonial concerns. In his first letter to the Colonial Department in 1904, Müller emphasized that he was convinced 'that not just for high officials but for all colonial friends it will be of utmost interest to see industrial-plants, installations, life not just on photographs as it has been the case until now but in living images'.[3]

The projection of lantern slides, however, did not become obsolete with the beginning of film screenings in the branches. Until the exhibition of colonial film in the branches was taken over by a professional exhibitor in October 1907, Müller's film lectures included lantern slideshows and film projection. The combination of lantern slide projection and film screening illustrated the transition from still photography to the moving image and also became a kind of exhibitional dramaturgy, which was quite similar to the first public screenings of the Lumière brothers in Paris in December 1895. The technical setting in motion of a film image was first of all a fantastic experience of reality for the audience.[4] The study of details like steam or the wind in the leaves became a sensuous experience that was not comparable to a photographic image. Viewers who first watched slides and then later moving images from the colonies must have undergone a similar experience. While slides were able to illustrate the exotic beauty of nature in the colonies, film could go beyond this first impression and make the pictures come alive. Though people were quite familiar with images from the colonies, it was only through the moving image that audiences seemed to get a real impression of what life in the colonies must be like:

> Much has been heard and read from our protected territories and also seen in lantern slides, at least from the blood-soaked Hereroland, so that the most adults have an accurate idea of this field of knowledge. But one thing was still missing, the literal reviving of the West African world in moving photography. How different fixed images are from the slowly dragging Kafferoxen..., the sea spray that is whirling up in the surf's waves.[5]

Müller seemed to be quite aware of the representational differences of the two media, as the reviews and picture postcards from his second journey show. Motifs such as *Kamerun. Gruss aus Victoria* (Cameroon. Greeting from Victoria) or *Deutsch Südwest-Afrika. Partie in Klein Windhuk* (German South-West Africa. Trip in Klein Windhoek) could establish their aesthetic quality without focusing on motion or requiring necessarily the pan of the camera. The photographs' aesthetic was rather rooted in the late eighteenth-century aesthetics of the picturesque, which focused on the sublime and on the beauty of nature, framing the perception of the exotic unknown in early tourism.[6] Though reviews of Müller's film lectures show that panorama shots were also part of his film repertoire; they followed another visual regime as they unfolded a sight in time and space. Filming a panorama adhered to imperial ideology in which the newly colonized regions of the world were made 'accessible and visible, glorifying the imperial state, and imposing the illusion of order onto the fabric of the rapidly urbanizing cities of Europe and America'.[7] In contrast to Müller's photographs, the film set the colonies literally in motion and created a sense of realism that the society's lantern slide series could not achieve. The audience could follow for the first time 'the enormously difficult landing situation'[8] of the boats in the heavy surf on the South African coastline – a problem that was familiar to everybody who was interested in the colonies – and got a *Gesamtbild* (general picture) of the East African timber forest.[9] Instead of just looking at photographs of the work on the jetty in Lomé, the audience now could see how the economic productivity in the colonies was achieved. Likewise, while photographs of the *Regierungswerkstätten* (government's workshops) or *Faktoreien* (trading posts) in the colonies gave an impression of the architecture and size of the buildings, films showed their actual use and how the colonized Africans were trained and educated and 'more and more brought up to well-ordered activities'.[10] Finally, moving images of, for instance, an African open-air trial gave the viewer an impression of the physical and emotional character of such an event: 'A gripping representation was a trial held outdoors. In a lively way you could see the blacks defending their affairs'.[11]

Not all pictures from the German colonies were considered useful for colonial propaganda. Film's ability to show life in motion could help get the public interested in the colonies, but not every moving image from the colonies represented the DKG's idea of what the colonies stood for. At the executive committee's discussion of the purchase of Müller's films in November 1906, one member did not want to focus exclusively on Müller's films but also wanted to contact the Austrian anthropologist Rudolf Pöch, who was staying at that time in Berlin, where he had given a film lecture at the Gesellschaft für Erdkunde zu Berlin (Geographical Society of Berlin). The DKG suggested asking Pöch for duplicates of his ethnographic films from his last ethnographic expedition to the New Guineas. The idea initiated a short but significant

Figure 3.1. Trial in Buëa. Photographer: Carl Müller. Reproduced courtesy of Übersee-Museum, Bremen, Historisches Bildarchiv, P. 03704.

discussion that reveals a little bit of the society's particular interest in Müller's films. The first objection that was raised against the idea was that Pöch was not a *Reichsdeutscher* (citizen of imperial Germany), but Austrian. Secondly, it was argued, if Pöch's films were to be purchased, one should carefully make a selection of his films because most of the material depicted exclusively natives and that would finally tire the viewer.[12]

The discussion at the committee's meeting shows that the DKG put much emphasis on the patriotic character of the films. Müller's films therefore were not just showing scenes from the German colonies, they were also a demonstration of a German citizen's patriotic spirit. Although films from the colonies included images of the life of the colonized Africans, the DKG was not interested in screening exclusively ethnographic films. Though ethnographic shots were a perfect substitute for the face-to-face encounters with colonized people that had been prohibited at colonial exhibitions since 1901, Müller, as a colonial tourist, produced films that were characterized by the range of different topics in which economic aspects, such as *Kaffeeernte auf der Prinz Albrecht Plantage in Kwam Koro* (Coffee Harvesting on the Prince Albrecht Plantation in Kwam Koro), were combined with ethnographic shots like *Negermarkt in Amboni* (Negromarket in Amboni) and touristic sights, such as *Rundblick in Amani* (Panorama in Amani) or *Fahrt mit R.-P.-D. Prinzregent von Swakopmund nach Lüderitzbucht* (Trip with the R.P.D. Prinzregent from Swakopmund to Lüderitz Bay). This variety of colonial sights seemed to be much better suited for giving new momentum to the promotion of the colonial idea among the public than would a programme made up exclusively of 'tiring' ethnographic shots.

Creating a positive colonial image through the depiction of progress and civilization in the colonies was also important because of the recent uprisings in DOA and DSWA. Although Müller could not travel extensively in the interior of DSWA and his screenings were not regularly promoted with regard to the situation in the colonies, it was reported that his films gave an idea of 'the traces of the long lasting war' and illustrated the extreme difficulties the colonizers and the government were facing in the colonies.[13] According to the speaker of one branch, Müller's films were therefore the most effective way to build up a bulwark to respond to the common mistrust against the colonies. The purpose of Müller's films was not to show the damage caused by the war. The DKG expected the film's objectivity to disprove the supposedly devastating results of German colonialism and to spark new public interest in German colonialism. In the DKG's strategy to establish a positive image of the colonies among the public, the significance of the moving image cannot be underestimated. Müller's films, often promoted – as the *Berliner Börsenzeitung* titled his first premiere – as 'The life in Germany's African colonies and their economic significance',[14] showed that the uprisings in the colonies did not result in a complete standstill of colonial life but rather, on the contrary, that economy and social life in the colonies were literally in motion:

> This way the apparatus showed, among other things, the work of the Negroes on a coconut plantation, as well the Negro-market in Amboni to which on Sundays hundreds of natives bring their products. Another picture shows the traffic in Dar es Salaam. It showed the difficult handing over of goods from the steamer 'Sassari' to the Imperial mail steamer 'Kanzler', and also the unloading of barges. Another shot gave us an impression of the difficult transport to the customs office.[15]

Images of trains, ships and the loading and unloading of goods in the colonial harbours represented technical development and colonial mobility, and illustrated the unstoppable progress of German colonization. Images like these also corresponded to the new approach in colonial policy that emphasized technology's role as the colonizer's most important complementary science, as Colonial Secretary Bernhard Dernburg pointed out: 'Whereas colonization was once carried out by means of destruction, today we are able to colonize by means of preservation. This includes the missionary and the doctor, the railway and the machine, that is to say, the advanced theoretical and applied sciences in all fields'.[16]

While Müller's film screenings inside the colonies established the cinematographic apparatus itself as a kind of a colonizing machine, his screenings in Germany became an important tool for documenting technology's efficiency in colonization – an aspect that was exploited by commercial film companies in the following years. The focus on railway construction, cotton production or the 'cultivation of the virgin soil' showed the 'blessings' of German colonization, as the Berlin *Vossische Zeitung* put it.[17] To demonstrate that the colonies were in 'good administration and diligent workers are available' it was as important to show the working and learning colonized population in scenes that depicted the colonized as they 'eagerly work as bricklayers, carpenters and cabinet-makers, or workers on the plantation'.[18] Images like these and their reception had a double purpose. Besides demonstrating the colonies' productivity, supported by the Africans' work, they also illustrated the success of colonial education according to the Eurocentric ideology, which held that civilization could be understood only in terms of disciplined labour: vivid scenes such as market life in Lomé, Africans joyfully dancing or scenes from a botanical garden, 'with its cultivation done by Negroes',[19] represented a peaceful harmony of colonizer and colonized in the colonies.

Film: A New Propaganda Medium

Müller's first film screening at the Colonial Museum in Berlin in April 1905 was a social event, hosted by the society's executive vice president. The guest list included the boards of the two Berlin branches, a range of prominent figures from the Berlin colonial movement with their wives, high-ranking members of the society and the Berlin press. Major local Berlin newspapers and national papers reviewed the premiere, all emphasizing the screening's positive influence on the colonial idea and recommending that their readers view the films.[20] The fact that Müller's programme included scenes of the DKG's president's own coffee plantation in the East African colony was not only emphasized by the reviews as particularly interesting, but was also a clever move to arouse the DKG leaders' interest.

The DKG internally and cautiously announced the premiere as a *Probevorführung* (test screening), but the society was obviously speculating on the success of the film premiere for which the Colonial Museum's director offered Müller all possible support.[21] To 'test' a new medium for its propaganda use also seemed to be an accurate characterization of the first public screening of Müller's film at the meeting of the board of the Saxonian-Thuringia district association at the prestigious Kristallpalast on 7 June in Leipzig, and this 'testing' underlined the careful nature of the society's introduction of the new medium. The Saxonian-Thuringia district association was the DKG's biggest regional association, so a positive response from its representatives made successful film screenings in other branches more likely.

The society's caution with the new medium might explain the limited information that the *DKZ* gave its readers about the screening. There was no official announcement of the screening and only a small article on the premiere appeared at the end of April in the paper's weekly column on the branches' activities.[22] Even though it is hard to understand why the DKG did not prominently market the premiere as an outstanding propaganda event, at a time when colonialism was hard pressed to come up with positive news, the article did acknowledge Müller's achievement as being the first to return from the tropics with films of a reasonable quality, and recommended the screening to the society's branches. One week later, the *DKZ* informed its readers that Müller had agreed to give film lectures in the branches. Not until May, three weeks after the first article, did the readers of the *DKZ* finally learn more about the films and receive a more detailed description of them. The source for this article was not, as one might expect, a first-hand review of the premiere, but a quote from a review in the Hamburg *Afrika-Post*, the public organ of the Woermann Line.[23] This second-hand coverage of Müller's films reveals the screening's wider recognition in the colonial movement, as well as Woermann's influence as one of the major colonial advocates.

According to the *Afrika-Post*, films from the German colonies had not yet been shown before in Europe; coffee processing in the East African colony could be seen most clearly, and for the first time one could see the extremely difficult landing conditions on the South African colony's coastline.

In the following months Carl Müller toured through many of the DKG's local branches, including Hamburg, Kiel, Frankfurt, Stuttgart and Berlin. In almost every city where he lectured as accompaniment to his films his screenings became successes and were highly acclaimed by the local press. Müller's lecture days often included various screenings on a single day. While film lectures in the afternoon were organized for local schools, evening screenings were reserved for the adult public. Advertisements and announcements for his film lectures emphasized that his shows would be a 'delightful' evening that nobody should miss. Because of the high fee charged, two hundred marks per screening plus the travel expenses of a second-class train ticket and a third-class ticket for his assistant, film lectures took place primarily in bigger cities and rarely in smaller cities like Neumünster, Homburg (near Frankfurt) or Pirna. In the case of the Pirna screening, the advert shows that the novelty character of films from the German colonies was promoted by emphasizing the films' screenings in the biggest German cities: attending a colonial film screening in a small town was linked to the idea of participating in a big-city-event.[24] As early as November 1905 the *DKZ* reported that Müller's films received applause 'as usual'.

The introduction of colonial film screenings into the DKG's propaganda work was not the result of a top-down order from the Berlin office. The elite of the German colonial movement had had the chance to be the first to watch films from the colonies, but it was the rank and file of the DKG in the local branches that urged the leadership to search for new methods to improve the society's lecture activities. The DFV's film shows with images of the imperial sea fleet provided the opportunity to observe this new mode of lecturing with film screenings. Since double or triple membership in associations was not unusual, and contacts between the DKG and other patriotic societies were much more common than official statements suggest, one can suppose that many of the DKG's members had attended at least once a sea fleet film programme at one of the DFV's branches.

The DFV used film propaganda for the first time in Kattowitz, Silesia, in March 1901. Supported by the Deutsche Mutoskop- und Biograph-Gesellschaft and their 68 mm film shows, the DFV organized nineteen screenings that were attended by of twenty-four thousand viewers, including many parties of schoolchildren.[25] Encouraged by this instant success, the DFV continued with film screenings and could report annually on the success of film screenings in the local branches: sea fleet film shows became enormously popular, and the DFV realized that naval exhibitions did not attract audiences that had already been to a film show once.[26] In 1902 the Navy League therefore extended their film propaganda by buying 35 mm projectors that made it possible to organize film shows for the countryside and smaller halls, and to work independently from the Deutsche Mutoskop.

By 1904, film shows with sea fleet images had become a standard in the league's propaganda work. At the time when Müller presented his films to the DKG in Berlin, the DFV's public organ *Die Flotte* lists four naval film shows for the Berlin area alone.[27] From October 1906 sea fleet film shows were arranged by the Deutsche Bioscop, under a contract signed in May of the same year by the league. Reports of the DFV's branches that thousands of new members enlisted in the branch after film screenings could not have passed unnoticed by the DKG's leaders. Since a competitive atmosphere existed among patriotic societies, the societies had to work constantly on improving associational life. Low dues and motion pictures made the DFV a formidable competitor, and the DKG admitted frankly the influence of the Navy League's film shows on the decision to introduce film shows into the society's propaganda work as well.[28] With the introduction of film screenings the DKG could finally present itself as a modern organization that was up to date with new technologies, from which it obviously expected a decisive jump in popularity that would attract new members as well as bind current members to their branches.

The DKG's decision spoke for itself. The overall response to film screenings was positive; newspapers noted that Müller's films gave the audience a much better idea of the colonies than lectures and still photographs. The boasts in the local advertisements that Müller's films were the only existing authentic original shootings, that the estimated production costs of the films were about eleven thousand marks or that his films were most likely the first ever to be shown in Europe were chances to promote the extraordinary event of a colonial film screening in town and to draw public attention to the branch's activity.[29] For many branches the film screening presented a special highlight in their local campaign. While in Duisburg the screening became the opening lecture for the branch's winter campaign and a 'worthy' introductory evening for this purpose;[30] the reviewer of the screening in Homburg auf der Höhe concluded: 'This way the local branch of the Kolonialverein [sic] fulfils the endeavour to arouse the interest and understanding for our colonies, in a pleasant and successful way, so that we can join the request of all that were present yesterday: vivat sequens, in German: *Bald wieder*! [soon again]'.[31] Despite the competition, close cooperation on the local level with branches of other associations was not impossible; indeed, from an economic perspective, it was advisable.

The DKG's most important partner for the organization of common film screenings became the DFV. Film programmes about the colonies could easily establish the connection between colonial trade and the protection of the colonies through a strong ocean-going fleet. Cooperation with other associations such as Bürgergarde (Burgher Guard), the voluntary fire brigade, the War Association of the Red Cross, Vaterländische Frauenverein (Patriotic Women's Association) and the Volksverein (People's Association) existed as well. Another example of close cooperation between the local branches of patriotic societies was reported by the DKG Esslingen branch. Branches of the Alldeutscher Verband (Pan-German League), the Schulverein (School Association), the DFV and the DKG were pooling their resources by jointly founding the Nationale Vereinigung (National Association). One of their common activities was the organization of three film screenings with moving images of the imperial sea fleet by the Deutsche Bioscop in October 1906. The two afternoon school screenings and the evening screening attracted approximately three thousand viewers.[32] In pooling their resources the associations not only reached a larger audience than with a singular lecture at an individual branch but also minimized expenses and administrative burdens and averted the 'psychological as well as financial catastrophe of a half-empty meeting hall'.[33] In addition to the advantageous financial aspect, collaborations also provided a chance to promote the colonial idea in a double sense.

While film screenings gave the DKG the opportunity to emphasize the political aspect of Germany's role in world politics, the collaboration with merchant associations emphasized the exploration of the colonies for German trading and business. Müller's films were often identified with the colonies' economic significance and power. Though film programmes were much more varied, the economic character of the films was often supported by Müller's own interest and knowledge as a businessman. In Lübeck Müller mentioned that on his next trip to Africa he was planning to invest his money in South-West Africa; on another occasion he suggested that 'practical businessmen' should be hired for the colonial administration and recommended the South-West colony to young adventurous businessmen. To promote the colonies as a new market and as an option for starting new business, several screenings were organized in cooperation with local merchant associations in communities such as Posen or Zeitz. Screenings in Chemnitz and Bremen were not just organized together with the local mercantile associations but even exhibited in the rooms of the associations. The close contact of the Magdeburg branch with local industry and trade made possible two free film screenings during the branch's publicity campaign in the winter of 1907/08; both screenings resulted in overcrowded lecture halls and became huge successes for the branch.

Strict guidelines on how to organize the propaganda work in the branches did not seem to have existed so that branches most likely decided individually about their programme for the coming publicity campaign. However, some advice concerning the organization of public lectures existed. The DKG recommended organizing lectures in large, popular restaurants rather than in expensive hotels in order to avoid the image of exclusivity.[34] That this advice was not always followed is evidenced by screenings at exclusive events, such as the meeting of the board of the Saxony-Thuringia district association in Leipzig in June 1906.

The DKG considered lectures informal social gatherings at which the presence of the lecturer should be used for discussions afterwards, with the hopes of convincing people who had become interested in colonial topics to join the DKG. The organization of special afternoon screenings, sometimes two on the same day, for local schools or military personnel, shows that almost every branch used the lecturer's presence for promotional activities. Some branches used the advertisements for film screenings in the newspapers to give information on how to join DKG or laid out sign-up sheets at the entrance of the lecture hall where new members could enrol. Events at film lectures usually followed the same order as other lectures, whether illustrated by lantern slides or not. The evening started with an introductory speech by the branch's director or secretary, who explained the purpose of the gathering and outlined briefly the DKG's purpose and aims. The speech finished with a cheer for the German emperor, and then the actual film lecture started. To make a film lecture evening a pleasant social event the cultural setting for a film lecture changed from branch to branch, with some preferring musical performances by the local marching band and others combined the screening with performances of local singers.[35] Other branches decided to emphasize the film lecture's colonial character. With reference to the current fighting of the colonial troops in DOA and DSWA, the Lübeck branch decided to give its October 1905 screening a particular charity character. The financial surplus of the screening was to be donated to the soldiers to 'brighten up the Christmas for the brave troops in the field'.[36]

The colonial character of a film evening could be emphasized by creating a special 'colonial atmosphere' via the decoration of the lecture hall with colonial paintings or ethnographic objects. In Magdeburg the colonial spirit of the screening was additionally illustrated by different ethnographic objects that were positioned on a table below the screen: a war mask from the Massai, a huge antler from a kudu, East-African spears, a peculiar Hottentot rifle, throwing clubs from the Ovamboland and dance axes from Togo.[37]

Müller's Lecturing for the DKG

The DKG's cautious introduction of the new medium into its propaganda work also might have had another reason. With the beginning of colonial film screenings the society was outsourcing the propaganda work to a private film exhibitor – a risky step. There exists no indication that Carl Müller was a paying member of the DKG, only offering his service to the association. Müller's role as a town hall film exhibitor characterizes an exhibition practice that was, as Garncarz notes, 'even more crucial in shaping film's development into a new mass medium'.[38] Fairground film exhibitors and town hall film exhibitors belonged to the travelling film business, which can be traced back to the beginning of cinematography. The town hall exhibition context was the most heterogeneous of all exhibitions forms in imperial Germany, mainly addressing associations, congregations or schools. The purpose of such screenings was either entertainment, propaganda, education or the viewer's religious uplift. In contrast to the variety theatres located in larger and middle-sized cities, a town hall exhibitor could play even the smallest places without a financial risk.[39]

Müller's evening film shows usually lasted between one and a half and two hours, and were longer than the afternoon screenings for schools that ran approximately an hour. He began his film lecture with a short introductory speech in which he outlined the purpose of his travels. As mentioned above, Müller did not start at once with screening the films, but created a certain atmosphere by projecting first his lantern slides and later the moving images. From his collection of around 450 slides from his 1905 trip, he chose roughly one hundred slides, divided into fifty from DOA and fifty from DSWA, which were selected to show the characteristics of the individual territories. The film programme of Müller's lecture in Hamburg in September 1905 shows that Müller presented his films in the form of a travelogue in which the different 'views' showed the most interesting places of the journey. The programme was divided into two parts and followed the geographical route of a journey from East to West Africa. Part one, *Lebende Photographien aus Deutsch Ost-Afrika* (Living Pictures from German East-Africa) included films from Tanga-Amboni-Amani-Dar es Salaam. After a ten-minute break, the second part, *Lebende Photographien aus Durban, Hamburg und Deutsch Südwest-Afrika* (Living Pictures from Durban, Hamburg and German South-West Africa) showed Durban, Swakopmund and Lüderitzbucht, and the troops boarding ships in the Hamburg harbour.

Studying Müller's programme in more detail one can see that he did not present a simple permutation of 'views' of colonial places, but varied them by combining views of places with views of production processes.[40] Müller achieved with this combination a rhythmic change from spatial to temporal views in the colonies, which also created a tension between rapid and slow movements: the panorama of the Tanga harbour is followed by scenes on a coconut plantation; the panorama in Amani by the traffic in Dar es Salaam. The comparatively small quantity of films from DSWA in the second half of the programme was not felt as a lack. The novelty of watching the South-West colony in film for the first time at all, and the recent uprisings of the Herero and the Nama in DSWA, made the available film material a sensation regardless and seemed to outweigh the limited number of 'views'. However, to compensate for this lack, Müller supplemented his films from DSWA with statistics that informed the viewer either about square-metre prices of property in Swakopmund, 'that were almost as high as in better suburbs of Berlin',[41] or prices for cattle and cart material. The information was not considered superfluous or boring, but, as the Stuttgart newspaper put it: 'what the eye could not convey that was said more clearly by numbers'.[42]

The programming of military scenes at the end of each part recalls the aesthetic of the apotheosis, which was quite common in the early *féerie* genre.[43] Similar to the visualization of a story's heavenly happy ending, the military scenes in Müller's programme functioned as short glorifications of Germany's power. The films from Durban that often concluded Müller's film programme had a similar purpose. Even though they might appear unnecessary or misplaced in a German colonial film programme, the images had a significant function in the context of promoting German colonialism to the national public. They simply had to convince the audience of colonialism's positive results. With reference to the colonial British neighbour, who was often used as an example of a positive colonial policy and economy, images from 'Street life in Durban' were supposed to show what colonialism in general was able to achieve.[44]

Müller's second film lecture tour through the DKG's branches in the second half of 1906 did not change significantly in style but improved in quality and quantity. The projection of slides was extended to approximately 150, partly coloured slides, and as indicated in some reviews, some of his new material was also presented – this time in colour. The most important change in the film programme was, however, that the quantity of films available in 1906 allowed Müller to present a comprehensive programme, including all the African colonies, as he did, for example, in Pirna in December 1906. Reviews show that Müller's film lecture programmes were not exclusively compiled from colonial films, which made his lectures also interesting for a non-colonial audience. Running his own seasonal cinema on the island in Altenburg he was sufficiently experienced as a film exhibitor to vary the individual programmes with short films from other genres.[45] The first screening that included a second part with slapstick shorts and other films is reported from Chemnitz, which seem to have been one of the first screenings in the publicity campaign of 1905/06. The films that were shown were Goerge Meliès's fairy tale *Le Royaume des Feés* (1903) and *Eine Fahrt in den Schweizer Alpen* (A Trip in the Swiss Alps). Since not every review mentions the screening of non-colonial films, it is difficult to say whether this part was shown only at an individual branch's special request or as part of the regular programme. The fact that the popular part was not taken out of the programme during the campaign – they are occasionally mentioned in later screenings as well – indicates that the Berlin headquarters at least tolerated the blending of the serious colonial topic with pure entertainment. Not every viewer seems to have been satisfied with the popular part in the colonial programme, as a review in a local newspaper shows; the paper complained about the screening of films from other genres, which, in the paper's view, should have been omitted.[46] Even though the criticism of the Chemnitz screening was understandable from the point of view of arousing the audience's interest in colonialism rather than in entertaining fantastic films, it was exactly the exclusively patriotic character of colonial film programmes that ran the danger of boring the audience rather than winning them for the colonial idea.

The fact that Müller toured through the DKG's local branches for almost two years, and the positive reputation he gained inside the colonial movement during that time, suggest that the DKG must have been satisfied with the general concept of his lectures. By the end of his second film tour for the DKG, reviews called Müller an *Afrikareisender* (Africa traveller), which made him an expert on the colonial situation in Africa in the eyes of his audience and even led one reviewer to mistake Müller for somebody who had lived for years on the African continent. His film lectures became a confirmation of the DKG's confidence in the new medium: 'One could really feel what an excellent tool for illustration living pictures have become and how they are much better suited for conducting propaganda in an efficient way than usual lectures and explanations'.[47] However, while printed texts were sent to the branches together with the DKG's lantern slide series, no written guidelines existed for a film lecture. Müller was a travelling town hall exhibitor, whose lectures were in the first instance personal accounts of someone who had travelled in the African colonies, and his comments did not provide unmixed support for German colonial policy. In Essen, in December 1905, he remarked critically that the colonies would be in a much better state if they were not treated as a reformatory for unpopular state servants and officers, and he complained in Stuttgart in March 1907 about the problem of *Assessorismus* (excessive bureaucracy) in the colonies. The picture of Governor Puttkammer's palace in Buëa in Cameroon was accompanied by Müller's comment that the amount of money that had been spent on the construction of this building would have been better invested in the local railway.[48] Remarks like these do not necessarily turn Müller into a critic of German colonialism, but upcoming changes in the exhibition practice suggest that in the future the DKG aimed at more control over the films, the programme and the politically correct reception of the films.

The transition to cinematographic screenings at the branches became a major element in the DKG's propaganda work. The publicity committee of the DKG carefully studied Müller's colonial film lectures during the propaganda campaign of 1905/06 and came to the conclusion that it should support, if possible, the purchase of cinematographic films and projectors for 1906.[49] In addition to getting control over the exhibition of the films, the DKG realized that cinematographic screenings had become the new standard and were already being employed by other organizations such as the DFV. Film shows did not cost more than normal lantern slide lectures and required only a larger initial investment; the investment would pay off in time since film shows were expected to become a new source of income for the society.[50] In November 1906 the publicity committee finally informed the DKG about ongoing negotiations for the purchase of Müller's films and lantern slides. In December the DKG bought Müller's films, including all rights, for the price of 3,200 marks.[158] With that, the DKG made the first step towards its own colonial film archive.

Notes

1. G. Strahl, 'Kinematographen', *Der Kinematograph*, 26 June 1907.
2. *Holsteinischer Courier*, 13 October 1905.
3. BArch, R 1001/6620, 86.

4. See M. Loiperdinger, 'Lumières Ankunft des Zugs – Gründungsmythos eines neuen Mediums', *KINtop: Jahrbuch zur Erforschung des frühen Films*, 1996, 5: 44–50.
5. *Der Altmärker*, 8 December 1910.
6. P. Märker and M. Wagner, 'Bildungsreise und Reisebild: Einführende Bemerkungen zum Verhältnis von Reisen und Sehen', in P. Bopp, P. Märker and M. Wagner (eds), *Mit dem Auge des Touristen. Zur Geschichte des Reisebildes*, Tübingen: Eberhard-Karls-Universität, 1981, 7–18.
7. A. Miller, 'The Panorama, the Cinema and the Emergence of the Spectacular', *Wide Angle*, 1996, 18(2): 34–69.
8. *Afrika-Post*, 29 April 1905, 119.
9. *DKZ*, 22 April 1905, 159.
10. *Berliner Tageblatt*, 29 November 1906.
11. *Afrika-Post*, 9 August 1906.
12. DKG, *Ausschuss*, 9 November 1906, 8–9.
13. *Stuttgarter Neues Tageblatt*, 4 November 1905.
14. *Berliner Börsenzeitung*, 11 April 1905.
15. *Hamburger Fremdenblatt*, 20 October 1905.
16. Bernhard Dernburg quoted in J. Noyes, *Colonial Space. Spatiality in the Discourse of German South West Africa 1884–1915*, Chur: Harwood Academic Publishers, 1992, 130.
17. *Vossische Zeitung*, 27 November 1906.
18. *AZStL*, 6 July 1906.
19. *Afrika-Post*, 9 August 1906.
20. *Vossische Zeitung*, 12 April 1905.
21. BArch, R 8023/646, 384.
22. *DKZ*, 22 April 1905, 159.
23. *DKZ*, 13 May 1905, 188.
24. *Pirnaer Anzeiger*, 12 December 1905.
25. Eley, *Reshaping the German Right*, 220.
26. Deutscher Flottenverein, *Jahres-Bericht des Deutschen Flotten-Vereins e.V. für das Jahr 1903*, 4 (henceforth cited as DFV, *Jahres-Bericht*).
27. *Die Flotte*, May 1905, 76–77.
28. DKG, *Jahresbericht*, 1905, 11.
29. *Pirnaer Anzeiger*, 12 December 1906.
30. *Rhein- und Ruhrzeitung*, 16 December 1905.
31. *Taunusbote*, 13 December 1905.
32. *DKZ*, 3 November 1906, 440.
33. Chickering, *We Men Who Feel Most German*, 195.
34. DKG, *Jahresbericht*, 1906, 42.
35. *Stadt- und Landbote*, 5 October 1907.
36. *Lübecker Generalanzeiger*, 21 October 1905.
37. *Magdeburgische Zeitung*, 16 October 1907.
38. Garncarz, 'The Origins of Film Exhibition in Germany', 115.
39. Garncarz, *Maßlose Unterhaltung*, 134.
40. Tom Gunning differentiates between 'views' of places and 'views' of processes whose individual aesthetic lies in their spatial or temporal emphasis. The 'view' aesthetic and the travelogue genre will be discussed in more detail in Part IV.
41. *Vossische Zeitung*, 12 April 1905.
42. *Stuttgarter Neues Tagblatt*, 4 November 1905.
43. The genre emerged as a popular form of stage entertainment in the late eighteenth century and is described as a play 'presenting a fantastic subject where the spec-

tacular elements of the mise en scène, the sets and the costumes are foregrounded whereas the narrative serves largely as a pretext to introduce all sorts of marvellous effects'. The féerie was immediately adopted by film and established as a popular filmic genre in the first decade of cinematography, before it disappeared around 1910. F. Kessler, 'On Fairies and Technologies', in J. Fullerton and A. Soderbergh-Widding (eds), *Moving Images: From Edison to Webcam,* Sydney: John Libbey & Company Pty Ltd, 2000, 39. See also the seminal essay on this subject: K. Singer Kovács, 'George Méliès and the Féerie', in J.L. Fell (ed.), *Film Before Griffith,* Berkeley, Los Angeles and London: University of California Press, 1983, 244–57.
44. *Berliner Tageblatt,* 29 November 1906.
45. Reviews of the first screenings in Berlin and Leipzig do not mention additional films from other genres, so that these 'serious' screenings can be seen as different from later film lectures.
46. *Chemnitzer Tageblatt und Anzeiger,* 27 September 1905.
47. *Pirnaer Anzeiger,* 9 December 1906.
48. *Der Grenzbote. Heidenheimer Tages-Zeitung,* 4 March 1907.
49. DKG, *Jahresbericht,* 1905, 11.
50. Deutsche Kolonialgesellschaft, *Berichte über die Sitzung des Vorstandes der Deutschen Kolonialgesellschaft,* Deutsche Kolonialgesellschaft, 7 June 1906, 42 (henceforth cited as DKG, *Vorstand*).
51. DKG, *Ausschuss,* 14 December 1906, 9.

PART II

ADDRESSING THE MASSES

Chapter 4

THE 'HOTTENTOT ELECTION' OF 1907

The purchase of Carl Müller's films was a first step towards the institutionalization of colonial film screenings in the DKG's propaganda work, although the society's decision-making bodies had yet to develop concrete plans to implement the new media policy. The political events in December 1906, which unexpectedly interrupted the DKG's publicity campaign, showed the necessity for a solid policy regarding the use of film screenings in the branches. On 13 December 1906, Chancellor Bernhard von Bülow declared that the Reichstag was to be dissolved. The dissolution was preceded by a heated debate over the government's request for an emergency supplement to the colonial budget, which was refused by the Reichstag.[1] The new election, in which 'colonialism and the entire question of imperialism and *Weltpolitik* became the principal issue', was scheduled for 25 January 1907.[2] The Herero War and the Nama uprising in German South-West Africa became the campaign's central issue, which led the election to be known as the '*Hottentot*-election'.[3]

The DKG did not want to become involved in party politics, but Chancellor Bülow had a very clear idea about the society's role in this campaign. A government working paper about how the election campaign should be conducted emphasized that the society had first of all to run a popular and aggressive propaganda strategy for the campaign.[4] The society's task was less the rational than the emotional persuasion of the public. This could be achieved either through interesting first-hand information from the colonies, even if it came from 'African ne'er-do-wells', or from apolitical lantern slide shows:

> The German Colonial Society could do much here. It must (perhaps as a cover address [*deckadresse*]) mobilize, including with money, all the old Africans to enter the campaign. If nothing else is possible, then it should at least act 'apolitically' and [provide] projection images to accompany the candidates. Also hire with money African ne'er-do wells for lectures before the opposition does it. Not loyal but interesting speakers achieve the most. Farmers, merchants, they all must get on.[5]

The new political constellation in December led the DKG to set up rapidly a propaganda programme for the election campaign. Two days after the Reichstag was dissolved, the DKG's president delineated the society's position on the colonial issue in an appeal to the branches in which he emphasized the election's national importance. The colonial question, according to the DKG's president, was neither a question of political parties nor of national economy or politics, but affected all the nation's circles, parties and classes.[6] In another confidential letter to the branches, the DKG's president Duke Mecklenburg called the dissolution of the Reichstag a 'favour of fate' (*Gunst des Schicksals*), which created the 'extraordinary positive chance' to work towards the nomination of many pro-colonial representatives in the new Reichstag.[7] Even if it was not the society's task to publicly support any particular party, the DKG could strengthen the colonial consciousness of the voting masses by organizing numerous public lectures free of charge.

In order to open every German's eyes to the fatherland's 'vocation' to a strong overseas policy and to explain what the Reichstag's refusal meant in terms of the disloyalty to the 'heroic soldiers in South-West',[8] the society organized free public lectures and made additional money available in order to pay the lecturers and their travel expenses. Following Mecklenburg's reminder that the 'brave warriors' in the colony were now unprotected and abandoned, almost every topic touching on the situation in the South-West African colony was used for propaganda. A broad literature campaign supplied the branches with more than a million copies of the leaflet *Deutschland halte fest an deinen Kolonien* (Germany, Hold on to Your Colonies), eighty-five thousand copies of the brochure *Deutsche Kolonialpolitik* (German Colonial Policy) and one-hundred-and-fifty thousand copies of *Soldatenbriefe aus Deutsch-Südwestafrika* (Letters from Soldiers in German South-West Africa). The society distributed in total more than four million leaflets and brochures during the campaign in which the DKG also strengthened its cooperation with other patriotic societies. All publications and information were exchanged with the Navy League and vice versa.

A large share of the propaganda workload fell upon the shoulders of the local branches, which had to organize additional lectures. During the campaign the DKG could report on almost five hundred lectures,[9] and by January 1907 the DKG had forty lantern slide series available so the society could now support even smaller branches that could not afford outside speakers and non-associated societies that wanted to use the slide series for their lectures.[10] Corresponding to the campaign's focus on the colonial war, the most requested lantern slide series in 1907 were those dealing with the South-West African colony and the Herero War. With 229 requests out of 527, the series represented nearly the half of the yearly output. The most popular series proved to be the first part of *Kriegsbilder aus Deutsch-Südwestafrika*, (War Scenes from German South-West Africa) with fifty-two images, whose success led the society to quickly produce four extra copies of this series especially for the campaign.[11]

The election was won by the colonial alliance, and the Herero War was officially declared to be over at the end of March 1907. The uprisings and the public discussion that were caused by the colonial scandals resulted in a new direction in German colonial policy. In May 1907 Bernhard Dernburg, who had become the director ad interim of the KA in September 1906, became the first state secretary of the independent RKA, and launched a reform of the colonial administration. The Dernburg era became synonymous with a more rational colonial policy, marked by new political and economic reforms and the recognition of the colonized African people as the colonies' 'most important activum' – though not for humanitarian but rather for economic reasons.[12] However, approaches that suggested the erasure of the African people's identity in order to create one coloured working class, as articulated by colonial lobbyist Paul Rohrbach, show that racist ideology was still part of colonial political debates.[13]

Colonial Living Pictures

Lectures and publications belonged to the DKG's traditional propaganda media, but given the government's expectation that the society conduct an aggressive campaign, the DKG decided to experiment with a new medium, which, according to Pierard, was 'the most unusual scheme of all for agitation'.[14] In a telegram from 11 January 1907, the

DKG's president suggested the performance of living pictures (*lebende Bilder*) from the war in South-West:

> I have been made aware from different sides that it would be advisable for the influence of the public mood [*Stimmung*] to perform living pictures from army life in South-West Africa in theatres, circuses and similar institutions. If possible with a stirring text, perhaps with the support from authorities. Images like: Farewell, Battle, Death seem to be appropriate. Uniforms are available at the office. Performance, if possible, before the 22.[15]

The recommendation of 'living pictures' in this context did not mean moving images. Mecklenburg was rather thinking of the traditional performance of tableaux vivants, in which members of the local branches performed for a set period of time images of the Herero War, showing the suffering and privation of German soldiers.[16] The president's emphasis on the importance of influencing public mood, however, was also significant with regard to colonial film screenings. Parallel to the performance of the colonial tableaux vivants in the branches, Carl Müller started working again as a film lecturer for the DKG.

The day after Mecklenburg's telegram the branches were sent a letter in which specific colonial stage plays and subjects for tableaux vivants were recommended for performance. The most prominent author on this list was Adda Freifrau von Liliencron, whose tableaux *Unsre Braven* (Our Brave Ones) became one of the most performed tableaux vivants in the campaign.[17] The branches had rather mixed feelings about the idea of performing tableaux vivants; the majority simply ignored it.[18] While one branch declared that theatrical performances would not have any influence on the final result of the election, another complained about the lack of time for the organization of a performance that in the end would do more damage than good for the promotion of the colonial idea. Other branches reported practical problems: one had neither a theatre nor a circus in which to perform tableaux vivants; another reported that because of the forthcoming carnival season every large hall in town was booked. Other branches followed Mecklenburg's idea and reported successful performances in theatres and school halls using amateurs, students and real army members. In Brzeg (Brieg) the performance of *Unsre Braven* was part of a larger 'Patriotic Festive Presentation', which at the behest of the president of the DKG included the demonstration of uniforms and costumes. The political significance of this event only three days before the election made every other theatrical performance secondary, so that even the announcement of William

Shakespeare's *Othello* was relegated to the bottom of the event's advertising poster.

Unsre Braven consists of five tableaux, each of which illustrates an important moment in the life of the fighting troops in the South-West. The following description of the play comes from a performance at a charity event for the soldiers in DSWA – which was quite common during the Herero War – in Schwerin in 1904[19]:

1. *Sergeant Dietrich bringt Meldung vom Aufstande* (Sergeant Dietrich Reports on the Uprising): it is the story of the brave Sergeant Dietrich who has fought his way through the hostile lines and reports the revolt to the headquarters. Music: 'Auf der Wacht' (On the Watch).
2. *Freiwillige nehmen Abschied von den Ihren* (Volunteers Bid Farewell to Their Families): the message arrives in Germany and causes the mobilization of the troops in the barracks. Volunteers bid farewell to their families. Music: 'Morgen muss ich fort von hier' (Tomorrow I Have to Leave).
3. *Das Patrouillengefecht* (The Patrol's Battle): the German troops arrive in South-West and confront the enemy in a first battle. Music: 'Morgenrot, Morgenrot, leuchtest mir zum frühen Tod?' (Dawn, Dawn, Do you Light my Young Death?).
4. *Lagerruhe* (Camplife): the troops are resting. Far away from their families in an unknown but somehow fascinating country. Music: 'Steh ich in finstrer Mitternacht' (I Stand in Darkest Midnight).
5. *Die Feldpost kommt an in Afrika* (The Military Postal Service Arrives in Africa): it is already Christmas time and the soldiers wish to be at home together with their families. The military postal service arrives with messages and presents from home. Music: 'Stille Nacht, heilige Nacht' (Silent Night, Holy Night).

The idea and purpose of performing *Unsre Braven* at the branches was clearly not to teach the viewers about difficult colonial policy. This lack of complexity was in keeping with the government's idea of how to address the masses. In a secret memorandum to Bülow, state secretary Posadowsky remarked that 'only clear simple questions' would impress the voting masses,[20] and *Unsre Braven* seemed to be an appropriate medium for this 'simple' way. It addressed the German public emotionally rather than rationally; in a very direct way, the audience had to decide between being a patriot or not. However, to reach the

Figure 4.1. Tableau Vivant. 'Sergeant Dietrich reports on the uprising.' First tableau of *Unsre Braven*. Source: *DKZ*, no. 51, 22.12.1904, p. 505.

desired result the correct performance of the play and a high degree of authenticity were important.

The author, Adda Freifrau von Liliencron, had very precise ideas about how to stage the tableaux. After the main curtain has risen the audience sees first a lecturer – dressed in civilian clothes – standing on the stage. A second, elevated stage is located behind another curtain in the background. After the introduction of the tableau, the background curtain rises and offers a view of the tableau for thirty to forty-five seconds. Each tableau will be shown several times with a fifteen-second break. All scenes are illuminated by one single spot light on the floor of the stage. Only for the battle scenes did Liliencron recommend coloured illumination.[21] The dramaturgy of Liliencron's play was supported by the historical authenticity of the tableaux. In their study on the representation of history in early fiction films of the U.S. *American Vitagraph* company, which can also be applied to the characterization of Liliencron's colonial tableaux vivants, William Uricchio and Roberta Pearson describe four different strategies for the conveyance of historical authenticity.[22]

'Key event' and 'key image' refer to the public's familiarity with a historical event's chronology or a historical person's biography, so that specific images could be immediately identified as being authentic and historically significant for this period or person. The Herero War was *the* key event in German colonial history and became widely discussed by the German public. The daily coverage in all local newspapers on battles, victories and defeats of the German troops produced a broad range of popular texts and images. The government's decision to make the Herero War the election campaign's central theme in 1907 was therefore not accidental. It could count on the public's familiarity with the event and an intertextual knowledge that made Liliencron's *Unsre Braven* a perfect ideological vehicle for promoting national patriotism. 'Correct period detail' relies on a widely accepted sense of correctness. The correspondence between the office and the branches shows that painstaking accuracy was paid to the creation of historical authenticity by using authentic uniforms and props. The fourth and last strategy, 'iconographic consistency', is based on an agreed notion of the historical figure's appearance. Though *Unsre Braven* does not focus on a famous and widely known historical figure, Liliencron manages to address the sentiments of a broad public by presenting images of the fate of the 'unknown' average German soldiers that every viewer could easily relate to.

Tableaux vivants are much older in tradition than lantern slide shows or film screenings, but there exist interesting parallels between *Unsre Braven* and the two projection media, which suggest the possibility of a blending of different media experiences at the performance of the tableaux: firstly, the single spot in the tableaux directs the viewers' gaze to the action on the stage in a fashion similar to the way the projector lamp illuminates the screen. Secondly, the explanatory role of the lecturer and his mid-position between the second stage and the audience is similar to that of the slide/film lecturer between the audience and the screen. Thirdly, the loose narrative in *Unsre Braven*, divided into five individual pictures, is similar to a slide show and the 'view' aesthetic in single shot films, which will be discussed later in more detail. Fourthly, though the static character of each tableau suggests a comparison with the projection of lantern slides, *Unsre Braven* also indicates the possibility that in this very specific case the tableaux were also used as a kind of surrogate for the limited availability of topical visual information. *Unsre Braven* then was not the representation of a historical event in the distant past but of a contemporary event. Even though *Unsre Braven* was not a new play, as the performance in Schwerin in 1904 shows, the specific exhibition context in 1907 gave the tableaux a new topicality. The topical character was even more emphasized by the final tableau, 'Christmas in Africa', which, at the time of performance, was only a month past and still present in the viewers' mind.

Entries in the *DKZ* show that some branches followed the DKG's advice to perform 'living pictures'. The organization of tableaux vivants, however, also created logistical problems. The performances required the participation of a number of people and time for rehearsing, and very small branches could not provide enough actors for the entire cast. Performing a tableau did not require professional acting skills but probably not everybody was willing to perform on a stage. Moreover, the task of each branch was not just to offer instruction to its members and the public, but also to bind the members to the branch with new entertaining activities. This could not be achieved through theatrical performances in which the members themselves were required to act. Last but not least, the tableau was very limited in what it could represent. *Unsre Braven* was hardly suited to furthering the DKG's interest in promoting progress and 'civilizing' efforts in the colonies.

It is hard to say to what extent the DKG was already aware of these disadvantages when recommending the performance of tableaux vivants to the branches, but the mention of a film lecture on 14 January in Zeitz suggests that the president's message to the branches also resulted in the re-activation of Müller as a film lecturer. Though only two entries on film screenings during the election campaign are mentioned in the *DKZ* – both of them local successes – it is most likely that more were organized. The screening in Zeitz attracted more people than the lecture hall could take and made many viewers into new 'friend[s] of the colonies'.[23] Four days later a screening in Quedlinburg was organized in cooperation with the local branch of the DFV.

In contrast to the colonial tableaux vivants, Müller's films presented a broad range of aspects. Though he could not offer scenes of the colonial troops in action, his films covered the loading of troops and horses, their departure from Hamburg, captured Herero, a fortress in Windhuk and the Swakopmund harbour.[24] Reviews during and after the election show that the lack of films of the colonial troops was not necessarily a disadvantage or nor did it make his film lectures less popular. Rather to the contrary, having still a kind of monopoly on films from DSWA gave his films a new topical interest. Recontextualized through his lectures and the individual introduction of the branches' speakers, his films were now viewed as visual background information to the fighting in the South-West African colony.

Müller continued to exhibit his films for the DKG until the end of the publicity campaign in March 1907, which became one of the most successful campaigns ever in the society's history. Reports on film screenings in March 1907 demonstrate the new colonial euphoria among the German public: a screening in Stuttgart was attended by twelve hundred school children, eleven hundred soldiers and seven hundred adult, civilian viewers. Three days later the Heidenheim branch had about a thousand school children for the afternoon and six hundred adult viewers for the evening screening. The following two days the Ulm branch counted five thousand members at a screening for the local army troops, three thousand school children in the afternoon and eight hundred adult viewers in the evening.[25] The Ulm film shows were probably the last time that Müller presented his films in one of the DKG's local branches, but a second colonial film exhibitor had already started to show his films from the colonies in the branches. At the end of January 1907 Robert Schumann joined the DKG's publicity campaign with moving images from the Herero War and thus satisfied the public's need for melodramatic action.

Robert Schumann's Journey to South-West

There exists little biographical information on Robert Schumann. Born in April 1878 in Damen, a small town near Belgard/Pomerania, Schumann did his military service in Potsdam and attended the school of forestry in Tharandt/Dresden in October 1899, where he also took his exams as a forestry assistant in August 1900. In August/September 1903 Schumann travelled as a tourist to DSWA, where he planned to go on an expedition in the East of DSWA and South Africa. His plans were changed when the Herero War broke out, however, and he joined the colonial army. Schumann spent one year in the army and returned to Germany after being wounded and decorated for his service as a vice sergeant of the reserve in 1906.

Schumann started to work as a film exhibitor for the DKG at the end of January 1907, when he showed films about 'War- and peace time in South-West Africa' in the society's Kolonialheim (colonial club house) in Berlin.[26] The screening was not mentioned in the local press and only briefly commented on by the *DKZ*, which does not report again on Schumann before April. One reason for this could be that Schumann had another contract at this time with the prestigious Berlin variety theatre the Wintergarten, the leading international variety theatre, where his films became part of a charity event for the African soldiers under the patronage of the German crown prince.[27] In April Schumann showed his films at least six times in the DKG's branches (Hagen, Coblenz, Morhange, Neustadt-Haardt and Tuttlingen). His last reported screening at the Sigmaringen branch was a 'worthy closing' for the winter's publicity campaign in the branch.[28]

Carl Müller and Robert Schumann were never compared with each other and not considered competitors in their exhibition work for the DKG. Their films were clearly distinguished by their content and the reception context. Müller's possibilities to visit the South-West African colony during the war were rather limited. Though his films from DSWA were viewed with a 'vivid interest', they nevertheless were only 'related' to the battles in the colony.[29] Schumann's films presented a novelty. He had unique film material with scenes from the army life in DSWA. Though his films were about war *and* peacetime, and also included scenes of German settlers and natives, it was primarily the military aspect and only secondarily the economic aspect for which Schumann's films were remembered by the viewer:

> In the beginning the lecturer portrayed his experiences as a participant fighter in the hard, full of privation but nevertheless happily welcomed combats in South-West Africa and made the listener familiar with warfare through a long series of living pictures including the marching out of the first troops of Major von Estorff, the reconnaissance ride of Count Brockdorff to the rocks etc. Further quite nice pictures from peacetime existence were shown and the lecturer explained in a gripping and humorous way the hustle and the bustle of farmers and natives. At the end the lecturer reported briefly about the heavy combat with the Hottentots where he had to be sent back to Windhoek after being wounded. At the end of his extremely interesting performance the lecturer received vivid applause. Tonight the performance will be repeated, attendance at which can be highly recommended.[30]

While the few entries in the *DKZ* on Schumann's film lectures make it difficult to draw conclusions on the films' influence on the election's aftermath, it is possible to situate Schumann's films and his role as a film exhibitor within the context of the popular representation of the Herero War. Like Müller, Schumann was working as a town hall exhibitor for the DKG too, but his performance was very different in kind to that of Müller. Schumann was not a businessman who travelled the colonies but presented himself as experienced soldier. According to the reviews, the success of his film shows came from Schumann's ability to present a kind of 'cinematographic equivalent' to the literary figure of the brave German colonial soldier that had already been established by colonial literature.

The colonies had been quickly discovered as a new source for literary inspiration and hundreds of so-called colonial novels were published in Germany before the First World War.[31] The colonial novel mainly dealt with three major motifs: travelling and the encounter with the exotic Other, emigration and settling, and military actions. Binary oppositions such as the memories of the good and clean Heimat in contrast with dirty places that are inhabited by uncivilized Africans or the brave German soldiers and the noble civilizing efforts of the colonizer in contrast to the savage African warriors and their blind destruction were essential features of colonial narratives. The purpose of the binary oppositions was not only to support the establishing of ideological differences between the colonizer and the colonized Other; the transportation of 'familiar forms and themes into a milieu where the "usual and customary" predominate' was a chance to create a collective national feeling in the reader.[32]

Colonial literature targeted a broad readership, but young readers, both male and female, were particularly attracted by stories that triggered the imagination, such as thrilling adventures or a passionate love story in an exotic setting.[33] The novels were repeatedly criticized by reform educationalists as being 'trashy literature' (*Schundliteratur*) that harmed the mind of the German youth;[34] however, with the outbreak of the Herero War, the colonial war novel became the most successful sub-genre in colonial literature. It was especially favoured for the detailed descriptions of battles and close combat. The message of a colonial war novel was rather simple: 'Overseas military service instead of professional training, colonial war as fitness training for the fight for survival'.[35]

The most prominent war novel was Gustav Frenssen's *Peter Moors Fahrt nach Südwest*.[36] The book became immediately a bestseller, a colonial classic from the moment of its publication in 1906 and even was published in English, *Peter Moor's Journey to Southwest Africa*, in 1908. *Peter Moor* was recommended for reading in school, and by 1910 it was present in almost every school library. The book tells the story of young Peter, who volunteers for military service in order to fight for his German fatherland in the South-West African colony. On his passage to South-West Peter meets for the first time in his life African people and realizes the fundamental differences between him and Africans. The steamer arrives in the colony and a march full of privation takes him and the troops to the interior of the colony. Heat, diseases, thirst and hunger cause frustration among the soldiers. During the first battle Peter gets wounded. The battle is lost and frustration grows among the soldiers. Peter suffers from typhus but recovers. In the final battle the German troops achieve victory over the Herero. Peter returns to Germany, having become a man and learned about the meaning of the colonial war: war and killing are part of a higher order. In an infamous dialogue, which reveals the novel's racist colonial ideological body of thought, a lieutenant explains to Peter:

> These blacks have deserved death before God and man, not because they have murdered two hundred farmers and have revolted against us, but because they have built no houses and dug no wells. ... God has let us conquer here because we are the nobler and more advanced people. That is not saying much in comparison with this black nation, but we must see to it that we become better and braver before all nations of the earth. To the nobler and more vigorous belongs the world. That is the justice of God.[37]

Written in a first-person narration, *Peter Moor* was no biographical account of a single individual soldier, nor was it a fictional adventure story. Frenssen tried to create an authentic report of the war and a young man's reflection by combining information drawn from official records of the Great General Staff (Großer Generalstab), pictures, literature, letters from soldiers and interviews with army members returning from South-West with his own creative imagination of life during wartime.[38] The impact of *Peter Moor* on the German reader illustrates a reviewer's first contact with the book: 'In state of fever' he had read the book the very night of the day the Reichstag was dissolved and imagined a thirsty, tired troop of German soldiers learning about the shameful actions in the German Reichstag.[39]

As the government's working paper on the election campaign shows, the government clearly counted on the popularity of stories from the Herero War and their melodramatic effect on the public. Voters should not be influenced through statistics or economic forecasts but through striking written and visual accounts:

> No figures and colonial pipe dreams [*Zukunftsmusik*], but concrete, graphic stories, the more violent the better, because the melodramatic needs of the mass always demands sensational literature [*Kolportageliteratur*]. If some images from African soldiers can be found – so much the better. People in the backwaters [*Heckendörfer*] cut out this kind of thing, put it on the wall, and the suggestion starts to work.[40]

It is not difficult to situate Müller and Schumann's different roles in this simple concept, which also seemed characteristic for the DKG's publicity campaign in the election's aftermath. In contrast to Müller's film shows, which were much closer to the 'colonial pipe dreams' and represented the economic discourse of progress, Schumann obviously stood for the melodramatic part, which attracted the 'people in the backwaters' to his film lectures. It is not hard to imagine that at the special school screening in Neustadt in April for many young viewers Peter Moor must have come alive in Schumann's performance as a film lecturer. He represented the type of lecturer Chancellor Bülow had in mind. As a volunteer in the colonial army he was not just a perfect and interesting lecturer, but someone who conformed to the popular image of the 'simple soldier'. Comparing the different reviews of Schumann's screenings one notes that his simple appearance and clear and modest explanations were not equated with an insufficient understanding of political or military issues but rather as the reason for the popularity of his screenings: 'Assistant Schumann understood to speak in a simple and clear and therefore popular way. That is why he also received keen attention'.[41] The lack of any 'compulsive posing or pompousness' characteristic of a real 'warhorse', as one review emphasized, made him a prototype of the average German soldier, quite similar to a Peter Moor. Like Moor, who immediately joined the colonial army when he heard about the outbreak of the war – 'We have to go' – Schumann presented himself in the same way. In contrast to Moor, who was in Germany when he heard about the war, Schumann had been on an expedition in South Africa when the war broke out, and he boarded a ship in Cape Town immediately to return to DSWA and join the army.[42]

Readers of *Peter Moor* must have been quite familiar with the images and stories of Schumann's lecture, which included many of the novel's motifs. Schumann's film lecture started with images of the soldiers' arrival in Swakopmund, still in their proper uniforms.[43] He showed and described the extremely slow treks of ox-drawn wagons, driven by young 'speedy Kafferboys'. The audience learned about baking bread in the African desert, the extreme climate conditions of cold nights and hot days, and the funny incidents that let the soldiers forget about the war for a few minutes. Quite similar to the lieutenant's exculpation for the killing of Africans in *Peter Moor*, 'they have built no houses and dug no wells', one reviewer of Schumann's film show came to the conclusion: 'with our advanced technology we will manage to subdue the country and make its treasures available to the German Fatherland'.[44] From the reviews it remains unclear to what extent Schumann could illustrate every anecdote and story in his lecture with film material, but he was not to be taken as somebody who was making up a fictional character. The films he was showing were set in sharp contrast to any kind of faked films or staged 'composed pictures' from the Herero War, as the announcement of his screening in Tuttlingen underlines:

A whole year he was standing in the field, during this time he took a number of living pictures, as it happened by chance or on occasion. That he had to overcome extraordinary difficulties does not need particular emphasis; however, it must be said that these pictures are the first, only and will remain the only pictures from the war area, that means just original recordings and no re-enactments [*gestellte Bilder*] taken at the coast or in a peaceful region, that are screened under fantasy titles.[45]

The review indicates that the author was familiar with re-enactments that either could have been shot on the beaches in the South-West African colony or in peaceful Germany. Fakes or re-enactments of war scenes already were on the wane around 1907, but had a short-lived tradition in cinema dating back to the Greco-Turkish War in 1897.[46] According to David Levy, the phenomenon of re-enactments in early cinema was too widespread to have been accidental and too strong to be explained away as the work of international plagiarists.[47] With reference to L.W. Dickinson's experience in the Boer War, which became a popular topic for re-enactments, Levy argues that such films mostly dramatized the 'medium's bogus promise to capture, simply and mechanically actual life on celluloid'.[48] Even being present at a key event was no guarantee that sufficiently thrilling footage would be obtained. In her study of early ethnographic filmmaking, Alison Griffiths points out that the artifice of the re-enactment was defended in pragmatic and ideological terms against the occasional charges of trickery. If the public had an interest in viewing a representation of a noteworthy event, this representation was under no obligation to render reality with complete exactitude.[49] Griffiths's suggestion that re-enactments should be understood in the context of different viewing interests is illustrated by Maurice Normand's short story *Vor dem Kinematographen* (In Front of the Cinematograph) from 1900.[50]

In the story a young Irish lady, Delia Flaherty, who faints in a local cinema in Paris after having seen a newsreel from the Boer War in which she believed she saw her lover, Jerry, being seriously wounded. When Delia awakens several people are gathered around her. Trying to calm her down, a man explains that the films were just re-enactments of the war and actually shot in a Parisian park. Delia does not believe the man and explains that she knows from a letter that was sent by her lover that a camera operator was present when the troops were arriving. Thus she is quite sure that what she just saw was a true depiction of the events in South Africa. For the owner of the cinema and the newspaper that reported on this incident the following day, this incident was just one more piece of proof regarding the authenticity of the cinematographic apparatus and its realist effect. A day later Delia receives another letter from Jerry in which he reports that after his arrival he got sick and therefore could not fight, so would soon be home again.

The short story illustrates the different aspects surrounding re-enactments that were obviously exploiting nonfiction's realism for commercial gain. Historical authenticity could be created through different strategies, and the different interpretations of the story show that it also could have been rather difficult for some viewers to distinguish real footage from re-enacted war scenes. While Delia considers the films to be the depiction of real events, the sceptical man enjoys the films exactly for the display of a faked spectacle that was especially set up for the film viewer. For the cinema's manager, the question of whether there is fakery or not does not seem to matter at all. His concern is mainly the commercial exploitation of such films. The coverage of Schumann's screenings in the local papers and the *DKZ* suggests that screenings of Schumann's films had to deal with a similar problem. In their announcements of Schumann's screenings, branches emphasized that his films were taken on the spot during a military campaign and that they were the only existing shots that were taken from reality.[51] The *DKZ* underlined that members of an African expedition corps confirmed the films' true-to-life images, and reported that even a member of the Schutztruppe recognized himself in one of Schumann's film shows.[52] The DKG obviously seemed to care about the authenticity of Schumann's films, whose credibility was threatened by existing re-enactments. If some of the colonial literature was already considered to be of poor quality and classified as trashy literature, faked or re-enacted war films could shift a national and patriotic issue into the same dubious light of cheap entertainment.[53]

The election campaign of 1906/07 marked only a very short period in the DKG's history, but the society benefited from the new colonial euphoria by increasing its membership by almost 13 per cent. With regard to their propaganda work, the election campaign showed the DKG that if the masses were to be reached, new propaganda strategies were needed. Though the DKG never gave up emphasizing the serious character of their colonial work, it nevertheless realized that 'popular' strategies such as tableaux vivants or film lectures of an *Afrikakämpfer* (Africa combatant), like those of Robert Schumann, could become successful propaganda events. Even though film screenings could support the election campaign only in a limited way, reports about the size of the film audiences at Carl Müller's film lectures and the success of Robert Schumann's films in the election's aftermath show that colonial film screenings could attract the masses. It was now time for the DKG to institutionalize film screenings as an integral part of their propaganda work in order to bind the masses to the society.

Notes

1. On the 1907 election, see G.D. Crothers, *The German Elections of 1907*, New York: Columbia University Press, 1941.
2. Pierard, 'The German Colonial Society', 300.
3. The dissolution of parliament that led to the election was caused by its failure to approve a supplementary budget for the German troops that were fighting the Nama people in South-West Africa, derogatorily called the 'Hottentotten' in DSWA.
4. The working paper *Vorschläge zur Führung des Wahlkampfes durch die Regierung*, 14 December 1906, is reprinted in D. Fricke, 'Der Deutsche Imperialismus und die Reichstagswahlen von 1907', *Zeitschrift für Geschichtswissenschaft*, 1961, 9(3): 538–76.
5. Ibid., 553.
6. J.A. Herzog zu Mecklenburg, 'Die Auflösung des Reichstages und die Deutsche Kolonialgesellschaft', *DKZ*, 22 December 1906.
7. DKG, *Jahresbericht*, 1907, 47.
8. Ibid., 48.
9. 247 additional lectures as well as the 245 regular ones. DKG, *Jahresbericht*, 1907, 46.
10. Pierard, 'The German Colonial Society', 306.
11. DKG, *Jahresbericht*, 1907, 45 (footnote 2).
12. Gründer, *Geschichte der deutschen Kolonien*, 242.
13. Ibid., 124.
14. Pierard, 'The German Colonial Society', 309.
15. BArch, R 8023/510, 2.
16. On tableaux vivants, see also L. Nead, *The Haunted Gallery*, New Haven, CT and London: Yale University Press, 2007, 69–82.
17. A. von Liliencron, *Unsre Braven. Fünf Bilder aus dem Leben unsrer braven Truppen in Südwestafrika*, Mühlhausen in Thüringen: Verlag von G. Danner, 1905.
18. Pierard, 'The German Colonial Society', 310.
19. *DKZ*, 22 December 1904, 505–06.
20. Quoted in Fricke, 'Der deutsche Imperialismus', 547.
21. Liliencron, *Unsere Braven*, 1.
22. W. Uricchio and R.E. Pearson, *Reframing Culture: The Case of the Vitagraph Quality Films*, Princeton, NJ: Princeton University Press, 1993, 115–21.
23. *Zeitzer Neuesten Nachrichten*, 15 January 1907.
24. *Der Grenzbote. Heidenheimer Tageszeitung*, 6 March 1907.
25. *DKZ*, 16 March 1907, 112.
26. *DKZ*, 2 February 1907, 52.
27. Schumann mentions that he met the crown prince on 10 March 1906. BArch, R 1001/6621, 120–21. It seems more likely that Schumann mixed up the years and showed his films in March 1907 at the colonial charity event. A short article in the local newspaper mentions that the biograph showed some scenes from 'hot Africa'. *Berliner Lokal Anzeiger*, 11 March 1907.
28. *Hohenzollerische Volkszeitung*, 5 May 1907.

29. *Der Grenzbote. Heidenheimer Tages-Zeitung,* 6 March 1907.
30. *Hagener Zeitung,* 18 April 1907.
31. For her study on German colonial literature, Sibylle Bennighoff-Lühl located more than five hundred colonial novels that were published between 1884 and 1914. S. Benninghoff-Lühl, *Deutsche Kolonialromane 1884–1914,* Bremen: Im Selbstverlag des Museums, 7.
32. J. Warmbold, *Germania in Africa. Germany's Colonial Literature,* New York, Bern, Frankfurt and Paris: Peter Lang, 1989, 146.
33. The most prominent novelist of exotic adventure stories was Karl May, though he never published stories set in one of the German colonial territories and never supported the colonial discourse.
34. Benninghoff-Lühl, *Deutsche Kolonialromane 1884–1914,* 183.
35. M. Christadler, 'Zwischen Gartenlaube und Genozid', *Politik und Zeitgeschichte,* 1977, 27(21): 18–36.
36. G. Frenssen, *Peter Moors Fahrt nach Südwest. Ein Feldzugbericht,* Berlin: G. Grotesche Verlagsbuchhandlung, 1906. In English: *Peter Moor's Journey to Southwest Africa. A Narrative of the German Campaign,* trans. M.M. Ward, London: Archibald Constable/Boston and New York: Houghton Mifflin, 1908.
37. Frenssen. *Peter Moor's Journey to Southwest Africa,* 233–34.
38. Warmbold, *Germania in Africa,* 70.
39. Leo Berg quoted in Benninghoff-Lühl, *Deutsche Kolonialromane 1884–1914,* 136.
40. Quoted in Fricke, 'Der deutsche Imperialismus', 553.
41. *DKZ,* 4 May 1907, 184.
42. *Gränzbote,* 26 April 1907.
43. *Gränzbote,* 6 May 1907.
44. Ibid.
45. *Gränzbote,* 26 April 1907.
46. See S. Bottomore, 'Filming, Faking and Propaganda', Chapter III.
47. D. Levy, 'Re-constituted Newsreels, Re-enactments and the American Narrative Film,' in R. Holmann (ed.), *Cinema 1900/1906: An Analytical Study,* Brussels: Fédération Internationale des Archives du Film, 1982, 243–60.
48. Ibid.
49. A. Griffiths, 'Wondrous Difference', 216.
50. Maurice Normand's 'Vor dem Kinematographen' was originally published in 1900 in the French weekly magazine *L'Illustration.* The German translation was published in the same year in *Frankfurter Zeitung* und *Handelsblatt.* The discussion is based on the annotated reprint of Normand's short story under the title 'Delia im Kinematographen und der Burenkrieg', in *KINtop: Jahrbuch zur Erforschung des frühen Films,* 1997, 6: 11–29.
51. *Hagener Zeitung,* 17 May 1907; *Gränzbote,* 25 April 1907.
52. *DKZ,* 4 May 1907, 184. Recognizing people in film was a popular topos in early cinema. S. Bottomore, 'Le théme du témoignage dans le cinéma primitif', in P. Guibbert (ed.), *Les premiers ans du cinéma français,* Perpignan: Institut Jean Vigo, 1985, 155–61.
53. In a similar vein Stephen Bottomore points out for the film business: 'As far as the early film industry went, it seems that leading figures saw that a betrayal of trust between film industry and public was taking place. Charles Urban ... warned his customers about fakes or "representations". He saw that such deception ultimately would have a detrimental effect on the reputation and future of the business'. Bottomore, 'Filming, Faking and Propaganda', 16.

Chapter 5

THE DKG'S *KINEMATOGRAPHENKAMPAGNE*

The outcome of the colonial election strengthened the DKG's position within the colonial movement but also made it clear that if the society wanted to keep its hegemonic position in the movement it would have to adopt new directions in its propaganda efforts. At the executive committee's first meeting after the election in February 1907, the society's secretary reported that the publicity committee was already working on a new project that, although still 'up in the air', depended only on the committee's general support for its financing.[1] As the executive committee welcomed any new plans that tried to instruct the general public with word and image on colonial matters, they recommended that society's board be contacted regarding the financial aspects of the plan. The most important project the publicity committee was working on in the first half of 1907 was the preparation of the contract with an official film exhibitor for the upcoming publicity campaign of 1907/08, which became known as the *Kinematographenkampagne* (cinematograph campaign).[2] The motivation for the DKG to institutionalize film shows was based in the society's hope of exploring new sources of income and a new way of promoting the 'colonial idea' among the broad public.

Film screenings in the branches had usually been organized by the branches, which decided individually about admission prices and admission conditions. While some branches offered free admission for members (Neumünster, Lübeck, Posen, Weimar, Homburg), others had price reductions for members and their relatives (Bremen, Kiel). In contrast to the privileges extended to members in these branches, members of other branches had to pay the same full price as non-members, which was usually between 0.5 and one marks. Afternoon film lectures were the cheapest way to watch colonial films. Though advertised as 'school screenings', with an average price of about 0.2 marks, many afternoon sessions could be attended by adults as well. Screenings in the major cities were usually more expensive than those in smaller cities and towns, meaning that viewers in Leipzig or Stuttgart (two marks for a front seat) were charged double what viewers in Chemnitz or Kiel had to pay.[3] The reason for this price difference seemed to be the same as the one that Corinna Müller pointed out in her study on early German cinema. Ticket prices were usually not targeted at specific classes but depended rather on the cultural setting.[4] Since cultural competition was much stronger in the big cities one can conclude that some branches considered their screenings cultural events that stood in direct competition with other entertainment events in town. The presence of the king at the Stuttgart screening in November 1905 definitely made Carl Müller's film lecture an outstanding event for which many citizens were willing to pay a higher price.[5] Müller's remark, however, needs to be qualified in respect of the DKG's aim to reach a broad public.

As the DKG was primarily interested in addressing people with financial and political influence, expensive ticket prices were barriers for people with low income. Studying the reviews on colonial film screenings in the local branches, one discovers that advertisements and reviews about the screenings were not published in local left-wing newspapers but preferably in conservative ones. Nevertheless, comparing the number of viewers with the population of the individual town in which a film lecture was organized illustrates the cultural and social significance of such an event. A screening in Weilburg in 1905 attracted two thousand viewers, representing half of the population. With about twelve thousand citizens in 1905, almost 5 per cent of the Heidenheim population saw Müller's films from the colonies, and evening screenings in small cities like Homburg, Höxter, Pirna or Velbert must have been at least the talk of the day. The *DKZ* only occasionally mentioned the size of film audiences for individual screenings, but the comparison of existing numbers with the average admission charge gives at least some information on the financial aspect of film screenings. Considering Müller's fee, travel expenses, hall rental and advertising costs, film screenings could open the door to new money. Even when a screening only covered expenses it could still pay off in the long run: the Neumünster branch reported it had won ten new members after a screening in October 1905.⁶

Screenings in the election's aftermath must have been safe financial propositions. A screening in Stuttgart in March 1907 reported seven hundred viewers at an evening show,⁷ and the Leipzig branch's cashbook mentions a net profit of 343.9 marks for film screenings in 1908.⁸ For smaller branches film screenings could also be an attractive source of income. The Ulm branch, with seventy-eight members in 1903, attracted eight hundred viewers for two screenings,⁹ and the Höxter branch, with only nine members in 1903, made 260 marks with three afternoon and one evening screening.¹⁰ The novelty of films from the German colonies, however, was not always a guarantee for a sold-out lecture hall, as some of the reviews show. High ticket prices were most likely the reason for the weak attendance at Müller's second film lecture in Leipzig in June 1905, and the branch decided to reduce the prices for the following screening by more than 60 per cent. The explanation offered for the reduction, however, was not the poor attendance at the previous screening but, as one of the local Leipzig papers remarked, Müller's 'generosity' in making the screenings even more popular in the Leipzig public.¹¹

That film lectures also had to compete with more 'attractive' events can be seen from the case of a poorly attended film lecture in Duisburg in December 1905. Müller's film lecture was far less popular than the erotic performance of the famous Broadway dancer Saharet, who had performed some weeks before. While Saharet's show attracted a huge audience, the speaker of the Duisburg branch complained that Müller's films that had never been shown in Europe before aroused little interest in the local public.¹² Four screenings in Pirna in December 1906 were also poorly attended. Probably encouraged by the success of Müller's film screening the year before, the branch seems to have been rather optimistic about the prospects for the new films, and booked Müller for three evening shows at the weekend and an additional family screening on Sunday afternoon. Even though the local newspaper gives no indication about other cultural events occurring on those dates that could have competed with the colonial screenings, Müller's film shows, according to the *Pirnaer Anzeiger*, were a financial flop.¹³ Though the last examples show that not every screening became a success, the majority of reviews suggest that, from an economic point of view, film lectures were rather attractive for the branches and thus the DKG. The society primarily lived from its members' annual dues and interest from capital investments, which in turn determined the DKG's budget for the following year, including the propaganda budget. Any new financial sources were therefore quite helpful in expanding the society's colonial activities. Financial success, however, was not possible without addressing a larger audience.

The Working-Class Audience

In his analysis of the DKG, Pierard points out a dilemma concerning the society's class composition. On one hand, the society could influence the government because of its good relation with the Reichstag, but was it isolated 'from the labouring and peasant classes', which made it extremely difficult to 'convert these groups to colonialism and thus instil the colonial idea in the masses'.[14] For years the society had been struggling with the idea of integrating the working class into the colonial movement. Although the working class was never explicitly excluded from membership it – in contrast to engineers, businessmen, medical doctors or teachers – it was never particularly addressed by the society's propaganda.[15] Even in industrial regions like the Ruhr Metropolitan, members from the working class usually did not join the local branches.[16] The reason was less an antipathy for associative life – there existed several working-class associations in the Ruhr region – than the barrier of the high annual dues of eight marks. Though branches addressed non-members in particular, and were encouraged by the DKG to do so, one may have some doubts as to whether the society was really interested in a socially mixed audience. Although reaching the working class was discussed as an important issue by the society's decision-making organs, it is fair to say that attempts in this direction remained rather half-hearted.

It was noted above that advertisements for film screenings were preferably published in 'conservative' newspapers. In this way the DKG could exclude undesired viewers from the outset. The pricing policy for the tickets was another way to make attendance at a colonial screening rather unattractive for the working class. Expensive tickets for screenings, as in Leipzig or Stuttgart, were affordable only to a wealthy audience. This tactic also corresponded to the DKG's interest in primarily targeting an audience of people able to support the colonial movement financially and politically. In other words, the society tried to reach the educated and prosperous circles first. However, in a letter from December 1907 addressed to the colonial secretary, Dernburg, a man from Hannover complained about the society's practice of recruiting members 'only from cultivated and well-to-do levels of society'.[17] He proposed that the DKG and the branches be put on more popular ground. The ordinary citizen, as the writer put it, had no sympathies for exclusive gatherings and would lose interest in an association's work as soon as he realized that only 'the upper ten thousand of the city' belonged to the association. As the experiences of the election campaign of 1906/07 showed, the DKG could indeed no longer target only the financially strong or politically influential parts of the German public if encouraging a broad interest in colonial matters in the German public was desired. A major task for the future had to be therefore the intensification of popular lectures that also addressed a working-class audience.[18] In addition to showing the significant link between the colonies' natural resources and the worker's own job in the processing of these resources, colonial lectures had to show that the colonies presented an alternative for the 'ordinary' worker for starting a new life as an independent craftsman, farmer or settler.[19] In this regard the role of the Berlin-Charlottenburg branch was especially acknowledged during the election campaign. The branch organized several illustrated lectures in Berlin's suburbs with an entrance fee geared towards the income of the working class. The positive response to the lectures, one of them having been 'enthusiastically received' by about eight hundred listeners, led the branch to plan to hold film screenings for craftsmen and the working public.[20] In May 1907 the DKG's board considered film screenings as an important tool to reach circles not yet part of the colonial movement.[21]

Reports in the *DKZ* on local activities after the election show that branches were indeed trying to address the working class with their lectures. In Rheydt, which was also called the German 'Manchester' due to the strong presence of textile industries, the film lecture was aimed at 'reviving' interest in the colonies among the youth and the local industrial population. The reduced admission price for associations at this screening indicates the possibility that members of workers' associations may have been among the fifteen hundred viewers that made the two screenings crowded events. However, one may doubt whether a ticket price of one mark could really motivate a large proportion of the industrial population to attend the screenings.[22] The best way of reaching a large audience was to offer free screenings, as was done by the Magdeburg branch, which attracted an audience from all social classes. Trying to address the working class with film lectures, the Weilburg branch asked all its members to recommend the screening to relatives and friends and in particular to employees and servants. As was emphasized in the advertisement, the film lecture was meant to correct the 'wrong impression' of the colonies, which conveyed a 'certain side', especially to the 'strata our workers and service personnel come from'.[23] Insinuations like this one were clearly directed against the social democrats, who continued to attack the government for the failings in colonial policy.

Even if the DKG's attitude seemed to have changed after the outcome of the colonial election in January 1907, the society did not succeed in converting the masses to colonial politics, as a new discussion on this topic in 1913 in the society shows. In April of that year the Harburg branch passed a motion for the general assembly, which demanded recognition of the fact that the instruction of German workers on colonial matters was now more necessary than ever.[24] Trying to improve this situation, the branch made its first successful experiment in January 1914. A film screening on the production of rubber was attended by almost one thousand workers, three-quarters of them from a nearby rubber factory.[25] Commenting on this new discussion, the *DKZ* saw a major difficulty in the fact that most lectures exceeded the comprehension of workers, and did not emphasize the significant link between resources in the colonies and the labour of the workers.[26]

The outbreak of the First World War in August 1914 made it impossible to continue the work of the Harburg branch in experimenting with specialized lectures for the working class, and it is hard to say whether this time the DKG was on its way to becoming a popular organization. In 1913 the society still emphasized that 'once industrialists, directors and employers are convinced of the colonial idea, there will also be the time and opportunity to teach employees and workers about the colonies'.[27] The explanation that colonial film lectures were considered unintelligible to the working class points to a growing problem that the DKG had faced from the beginning of their film activities. Sober instruction in colonial economics was not necessarily what people wanted to listen to after a long, hard, working day. Regardless of the social strata, people probably preferred to watch colonial films within an entertaining programme, and the DKG had to realize that exclusively colonial film programmes started to bore even the 'educated' members.

The Female Colonial Viewer

In her study on German women's participation in German colonialism Lora Wildenthal has shown that 'the colonies were a fantasyland for both German men and German women.'[28] The German Colonial Society was a primarily male organization, but women could join it with the same rights and duties as the male members. Though the society's president considered the presence of women at official parties merely to be a 'brightening up',[29] women made up a substantial percentage of the association's lecture audiences as they paid admission charges and 'filled seats in halls that otherwise would have remained half-empty'.[30]

Little information exists on the gender composition of the colonial film audience, but several reviews of colonial film screenings at the DKG branches show that women made up part of the film-viewing audience. Especially where films from the colonies were shown for the first time or screened in a particular social context, screenings were not gender-specific events.[31] The remark on the invitation card for one of Müller's screenings in Leipzig in February 1907, that women are requested to take off their hats during the exhibition of projected images, indicates that the presence of women during illustrated and film lectures was not only rather common but their attendance expected. Sometimes the screenings were combined with a social event, such as a banquet, where female guests were expected.[32]

A particular female interest in German colonialism was articulated by the Deutsche Frauenverein für Krankenpflege in den Kolonien (DFKK, German Women's Association for Nursing in the German Colonies) and the Frauenbund der Deutschen Kolonialgesellschaft (FDKG, Women's League of the German Colonial Society), which, in spite of its name, was formally independent of the DKG.[33] The FDKG was more successful than the DKG in recruiting female members for a colonial association, and the success in attracting even men irritated the DKG. The DFKK's work of training nurses for medical support in the colonies and the FDKG's project to supply the colony with 'simple, unpretentious German girls'[34] in order to fight the cohabitation of German settlers with African woman offered a public arena for active female involvement in colonial politics. The very scarce information on film screenings for an exclusively female audience make it impossible to analyse the exhibition of colonial films in the individual associations, but a correspondence between the president of the FDKG's branch in Berlin and the DKG in October 1910 about available colonial films shows that the FDKG was aware of the possibility of using film for the association's propaganda work in the branches.[35] Even though the purpose of this particular enquiry is not known, one can speculate on the screenings' meaning and on how films from the colonies were used for schooling the members of the female colonial associations for their work in the colonies.

In her sociological study on the early film audience, *Zur Soziologie des Kino* (On the Sociology of the Cinema), Emilie Altenloh suggested that female viewers often preferred to watch nature spectacles because of their aesthetic appeal.[36] Though this could also apply to colonial films in this particular context, films often included shots of the colonial flora and fauna, it is more likely that the female interest was much more pragmatic. For women interested in working in the colonies or getting married to a German farmer, film could give the first authentic impression of what life in the colonies was like. The very few remarks on German farmers and settling in reviews of screenings in the DKG's branches, however, make it difficult to assess to what extent film could depict the everyday life of a *Farmersfrau* in the colony, which, according to Wildenthal, created its own mystique in female colonial discourse.[37]

A practical interest in films from the colonies or related topics framed the reception of a screening in November 1913 in Wiesbaden. In collaboration with the Verein der Ärzte Wiesbadens (Society of Medical Doctors in Wiesbaden) and the Deutsche Frauenverein vom Roten Kreuz für die Kolonien (German Women's Association of the Red Cross for the Colonies), as the DFKK was called after 1909, the DKG branch organized a film screening lecture on tropical hygiene. The director of the German Institute for Medical Missions, Dr Olpp, showed films on the topic of 'The fight against tropical pathogens'.[38] Screenings of this kind that were repeatedly mentioned in the *DKZ* show the significance of film as a teaching instrument in this discipline. While they documented the efforts and achievements of German tropical medicine on one hand, the films took away fears of possible infections and prepared future nurses for their work in the colonies on the other. As important as an instrument for medical training was the addressing of young viewers.

A Crusade for Colonial Education

A major target group for the DKG was the German youth, which, according to the society, represented the future of German colonialism. The DKG therefore supported using all available means in the colonial education of German youth. Since 1896 the DKG had been trying to influence the schools' curriculums concerning the introduction of colonial topics.[39] The promotion of colonial education in schools became part of a school reform that worked towards the transformation of the traditional school system into a system adapted to the needs of a modern industrial nation.⁴⁰ *Staatsbürgerliche Erziehung* (civic education became the reform's buzzword and primarily meant educating school children to become patriotic German citizens and strengthening their interest in colonialism, the naval fleet and the monarchy.⁴¹ To reach this goal reformers emphasized the use in history and geography classes of 'characteristic illustration material,' such as wall paintings, maps and slides, which gave an 'immediate impression'.⁴²

In November 1904 the German Colonial Society set up a special text book committee (*Lesebuchkommittee*), whose task was to assemble readings on the German colonies and the navy into small publications that could be used for colonial education in school. After the DKG's president personally approached the Prussian minister of education, asking him to accept the society's collection of readings, colonial atlas and wall maps of the colonies for use in the public schools, the minister, in a circular, urged all schools to order the society's colonial teaching materials.⁴³ Pedagogues welcomed good illustrations, coloured if possible, from the colonies as a 'vitalization' of school lessons.⁴⁴ Likewise sourcebooks with texts about the colonies were supposed to be read out loud to the children to makes lessons more exciting and emphasize the emotional moments.⁴⁵

Hosting the premiere of the first colonial film screening at the Berlin Colonial Museum in 1905, the DKG could once more underline its pedagogical commitment to colonial education. Founded in October 1899 and transferred into the hands of the DKG in 1900, the museum exhibited ethnographic objects and collectibles of Berlin's colonial exposition of 1896, and was considered a place for exhibition and instruction for the propaganda of colonial and naval issues.⁴⁶ In contrast to the academic interest and purpose of the Berlin Museum for Ethnology, the colonial museum abstained from a profound scientific contextualization of its collection, as that could never produce a 'really vivid image' of the colonies.⁴⁷ Being a popular institution for colonial education, the museum focused instead on aspects of daily colonial life that were presented in *in situ* dioramas. The construction of a lecture hall in 1901 was another contribution to the museum's 'permanent attractional appeal'.⁴⁸ Regularly organized lantern slideshows became part of the museum's exhibition concept and were particularly addressed to schoolchildren. In 1904 the society urged that the *DKZ* and all other newspapers 'standing under the society's influence should refer now more than ever to the colonial museum and the events that are organized in it'.⁴⁹ Carl Müller's film premiere in April 1905 corresponded to the museum's didactic concept of 'giving a vivid image of the natural and economic characteristic as well as the hustle and bustle of the natives in our protectorates'.[50]

The DKG's branches started to address the German youth with special afternoon screenings immediately after the introduction of Müller's films. Film lectures were considered more appropriate for education than any academic lecture, as one review put it, recommending the DKG's colonial film lectures especially for young people.[51] Regarding the DFV's film propaganda work, Martin Loiperdinger pointed out the double function of such special school screenings, an observation that can also be applied to the DKG. The school screenings contributed to the patriotic education of the children, and the children in turn 'functioned as little sales agents telling to their parents what they had seen on the Navy League's screen'.[52] Their curiosity aroused by the children's enthusiasm, parents purchased tickets for the evening screening. Complaints of travelling film exhibitors about film screenings in local branches of patriotic societies suggest that wherever an associational film screening was offered, the attendance seemed to become part of the local schools' curriculum.[53]

It was again after the election in January 1907 that the question of colonial education received new attention. Colonial secretary Dernburg's appeal to German teachers to join the crusade for colonial education initiated a new discussion about the best method for teaching children about the colonies' importance.[54] Though many colonial products could already be shown to the children '*in Natura*', pictures and illustrations were recommended to show the colonies' ethnographic, geographic and economic significance.[55] Men who had been living in the colonies started to tour through the schools and lectured about their personal experiences and showed lantern slides. Entries in the *DKZ* show that film screenings were also used as an important teaching aid in colonial education: twelve hundred school children in Stuttgart, one thousand in Heidenheim and three thousand in Ulm were counted at such screenings.[56] The Ulm screening was attended by local and regional school children, and the screening served as an occasion to distribute the colonial atlas and colonial reading books to the teachers for use in school. The largest number of young viewers was reported from the Barmen branch where Müller's films were said to have been seen by eight thousand children.[57]

Film screenings were 'extreme fun' for school children, as remarked by one reviewer after a screening in September 1906, saying that it was a special pleasure to observe the youth at such an event.[58] But the popularity of colonial film screenings among German youth often mentioned in the reviews may well have been due to something that initially was not in the DKG's mind. The popularity of colonial literature discussed above also seemed to have made film a kind of visual blueprint for colonial adventure fantasies, which may explain the fascination among young viewers for Müller's, and even more for Schumann's, films *and* their performances.

The position of colonial propaganda at the intersection of sober colonial instruction and thrilling entertainment is also illustrated by the DKG's official film poster for colonial film screenings for the DKG's Kinematographenkampagne of 1907/08. The colourful poster, lit by a bright yellow sun, shows an African warrior standing on top of a small mountain; in the background a native village can be seen. The poster does not reveal much of the DKG's interest in using film for serious colonial instruction, which aimed to represent the colonies as a safe place for living and to emphasize their economic and political significance. The illustrated scene created a popular image of the colonies as was recommended by different teachers' journals: 'That's why no long treatises on the necessity and purpose of the colonies but on the wings of fantasy freshly placed into the magic of the jungle and the mysterious silence of the steppe'.[59] As if following this didactic advice, the poster foregrounds the exotic and the adventurous flair of the colonial film lecture, an attraction further emphasized by the warrior's spear and shield. In contrast to a scene that shows Africans working on plantations and being integrated within the different production processes of colonial goods, the poster shows Africans still untouched by civilization. After colonial film screenings came to an end at the society's branches, the DKG's plan to continue colonial education using the society's lantern slides was doomed to failure. A test by the publicity committee in 1912 to attract young people with a lantern slideshow was poorly received by the children, all of whom, according to the publicity committee, preferred to watch moving images.[60] Though the DKG could not continue acting as *the* colonial educator for German youth, colonial films did not vanish from the teaching agenda in schools.

The overview of the different audiences shows that, at the beginning of the DKG's first official Kinematographenkampagne, the society had good reason to believe in the success of film screenings in the branches. While the election campaign had initiated a new interest in German colonialism, the great crowds at colonial film lectures in the first half of 1907 indicated that film lectures could become a new source of income for the society. Watching colonial films was neither a class-, gender- nor age-specific cultural activity. In other words, with film lectures the

Figure 5.1. Official poster of the DKG's Kinematographenkampagne for a screening in Frankfurt, 12 February 1908. Reproduced courtesy of Historisches Museum Frankfurt.

DKG could count on the interest of wide strata of the society, and it was now up to the DKG to sustain the public's interest in colonialism. What was missing was a reliable partner that could take over the exhibition of the films.

Notes

1. DKG, *Ausschuss*, 1 February 1907, 4–5.
2. The term '*Kinematographenkampagne*' was mentioned for the first time during the board's meeting in June 1908. DKG, *Vorstand*, 11 June 1908, 22.
3. To give a sort of benchmark for ticket prices in 1907, the average food prices in Prussia in 1907 were: 1 kg butter: 2.47 marks; 1 kg pork: 1.57 marks; 1 kg potatoes: 0.06 marks. Königlich Preußisches Statistisches Landesamt, *Statistisches Jahrbuch für den Preußischen Staat 1907*, Berlin: Verlag des Königlich Statistischen Landesamtes, 1908, 65. In the same year a coal miner from an industrial town like Dortmund earned 1402 marks a year (or 26.96 marks a week) and an ore miner from Clausthal earned 752 marks (14.46 marks a week.) Königlich Preußisches, *Statistisches Jahrbuch*, 83. Even though the typical colonial film viewer did not belong to the working class, the figures suggest that ticket prices between 0.5 and 2 marks excluded all but a wealthy audience.
4. Müller, *Frühe deutsche Kinematographie*, 23–27.
5. *Stuttgarter Neues Tagblatt*, 4 November 1905.
6. *DKZ*, 21 October 1905, 452.
7. *DKZ*, 16 March 1907, 112
8. Archiv für Geographie im Institut für Länderkunde e.V., Leipzig, Deutsche Kolonial Gesellschaft (box 434).
9. *DKZ*, 16 March 1907, 112.
10. *DKZ*, 9 November 1907, 456.
11. *Leipziger Neueste Nachrichten*, 29 June 1905.
12. *Duisburger Generalanzeiger*, 18 December 1905.
13. *Pirnaer Anzeiger*, 11 December 1906.
14. Pierard, 'The German Colonial Society', 113.
15. Soénius, *Koloniale Begeisterung*, 46.
16. Ibid., 41.
17. BArch, R 1001/6688, 88.
18. DKG, *Ausschuss*, 1 February 1907, 4–5.
19. Benninghoff-Lühl, *Deutsche Kolonialromane 1884–1914*, 40.
20. BArch, R 1001/6688, 92.
21. DKG, *Vorstand*, 22 May 1907, 32.
22. *Rheydter Zeitung*, 22 October 1907.
23. *Kreis-Blatt für den Ober-Lahn-Kreis*, 19 October 1907.
24. DKG, *Ausschuss*, 25 April 1913.
25. *DKZ*, 7 March 1914, 169. The Harburg screening was not a film from the colonies but a selection of images from Brazil. The purpose of this screening was, however, to instruct the working-class audience about the importance of colonial resources with regard to the worker's labour.
26. 'Koloniale Werbung und Aufklärung,' *DKZ*, 10 July 1913, 482–83.

27. Soénius, *Koloniale Begeisterung*, 46.
28. L. Wildenthal, *German Women for Empire, 1884–1945*, Durham, NC: Duke University Press, 2002.
29. Soénius, *Koloniale Begeisterung*, 85.
30. Chickering, *We Men Who Feel Most German*, 171.
31. A special 'female' colonial contribution was reported from the Heidenheim branch, where a generous Heidenheim female citizen supported the local screening with a donation of one hundred free tickets for the top classes of the local *Knabenvolksschule* (boys' grade school), *Der Grenzbote. Heidenheimer Tages-Zeitung*, 6 March 1907.
32. Deutsche Kolonial- Gesellschaft, invitation card (box 434), Archiv für Geographie, Leibnitz-Institut für Länderkunde, Leipzig.
33. See M. Rübenstahl, '"Gedenket unsrer Landsleute, die fern der Heimat krank liegen!" – Der Deutsche Frauenverein für Krankenpflegen in den Kolonien', in *Kolonialmetropole Berlin*, 56–63; Wildenthal, *German Women for Empire*, 132–33.
34. The quote refers to correspondence concerning the establishing of a *Mädchenheim* (girls' home) in the South-West colony. Pierard, 'The German Colonial Society', 358.
35. BArch, R 8023/154, 247.
36. E. Altenloh, *Zur Soziologie des Kino. Die Kinounternehmen und die sozialen Schichten ihrer Besucher*, Jena: Eugen Diederichs, 1914, 89.
37. Wildenthal, *German Women for Empire*, 151.
38. *DKZ*, 17 January 1914, 44.
39. Similar efforts were made at universities. In 1899 the DKG's board of directors urged the introduction of courses in ethnology and geography at the universities so that students could acquire a better understanding of Germany's overseas possessions. Pierard, 'The German Colonial Society', 278.
40. See H.D. Schultz, 'Das "größere Deutschland" muss es sein! Der koloniale Gedanke im Geographieunterricht des Kaisserreichs und darüber hinaus', in R. Dithmar, and H.D. Schultz (eds), *Schule und Unterricht im Kaiserreich*, Ludwigsfelde: Ludwigsfelder Verlagshaus, 2006, 183–234.
41. See G. Schneider, 'Das Deutsche Kolonialmuseum Berlin und seine Bedeutung im Rahmen der Preußischen Schulreform um die Jahrhundertwende' in Mitarbeiter des historischen Museums (eds), *Die Zukunft beginnt in der Vergangenheit. Museumsgeschichte und Geschichtsmuseum*, Frankfurt am Main: Anabas Verlag, 1982, 155–99.
42. Ibid., 157.
43. Pierard, 'The German Colonial Society, 1882–1914', 279.
44. B. Clemenz, *Kolonialidee und Schule*, 2nd edn, Pädagogisches Magazin, no. 296, Langensalza: Hermann Beyer & Söhne, 1907, 39.
45. W. Sperling, 'Zur Darstellung der deutschen Kolonien im Erdkundeunterricht (1890–1914) mit besonderer Berücksichtigung der Lehrmittel', *Internationale Schulbuchforschung*, 1989, 11: 392.
46. 'Das Deutsche Kolonialmuseum', *DKZ*, 7 April 1904, 130–31.
47. Schneider, 'Das deutsche Kolonialmuseum Berlin', 171.
48. 'Das Deutsche Kolonialmuseum', *DKZ*, 131.
49. DKG, *Ausschuss*, 25 January 1904, 6.
50. Schneider, 'Das deutsche Kolonialmuseum Berlin', 174.
51. *General Anzeiger*, Essen, 26 October 1906.
52. Loiperdinger, 'Beginnings of German Film Propaganda', 311.
53. E. Perlmann, 'Die Kinematographen-Theater und der "Deutsche Flottenverein"', *Der Kinematograph*, 19 February 1908.
54. Benninghoff-Lühl, *Deutsche Kolonialromane 1884–1914*, 37.

55. W.C. Bach, *Unsere Kolonien im Schulunterricht,* Bielefeld: U. Helmichs Buchhandlung, 1907, 17.
56. *DKZ,* 16 March 1907, 112
57. *DKZ,* 9 March 1907, 100.
58. *Bergisch-Märkische Zeitung,* 19 September1906.
59. J. Köhler, *Schule und Kolonialinteressen,* Langensalza: Herman Beyer & Söhne, 1907, 19.
60. BArch, R 8023/1089, 40.

Chapter 6

RISE AND FALL OF THE KINEMATOGRAPHENKAMPAGNE

During the spring of 1907 the publicity committee of the DKG studied in detail the organization of film screenings in the DFV, and had initial exploratory talks with DFV's film exhibitor, the Deutsche Bioscop-Gesellschaft mbH. The Deutsche Bioscop was one of the most prestigious companies in Germany at that time and had been exhibiting films for the DFV since 1904.[1] One of the outcomes of the publicity committee's study was the idea of organizing three screenings a day and the creation of a special budget (*Garantiesumme*) to cover deficits and reduce the financial risk of film screenings in the branches. To save travel expenses the society planned to coordinate their screenings with those of the DFV. At the board's meeting in May 1907, the society's secretary, Dr Sander, enthusiastically presented the committee's motion and declared:

> With these screenings we should not only address our members, but also address broader circles, that until now have been outside our movement (Bravo!). Even if they cannot become members, we have to win them for our concepts, since all bigger movements require the mass. Since only a small or no admission can be taken from these circles, it has to be considered that financial losses might occur. That's why the executive committee … would like to establish a special budget.[2]

Without any discussion, the motion was unanimously approved. The booking conditions for a film screening were very similar to those of illustrated lectures. The branches had a choice between organizing a film screening on their own account or splitting the expenses with the head office. In the first instance the branch paid the Deutsche Bioscop via the head office and could keep all the income from ticket sales. Compared to what branches had to pay Carl Müller, the new payment agreement reduced the cost for a film screening by 40 per cent and could bring new money into the branches' coffers.

For the Berlin head office the new contract also was advantageous. The DKG was never a rich organization, so any chances for opening a new source of income must have had a considerable influence on the society's decision to start institutionalizing film screenings in the DKG's propaganda work. Müller's screenings were always based on exclusive contracts between himself and the individual branch. The second alternative of booking the Deutsche Bioscop provided the head office with one third of the proceeds from ticket sales for an evening screening and two thirds of the proceeds for an afternoon screening.[3] Besides the financial profit that the DKG expected from the screenings, another pragmatic consideration was to guarantee the fulfilment of each branch's request for a film lecture.

The entries on film screenings in the *DKZ* document how often Müller worked for the DKG's branches, but tell us nothing about how often he had to reject offers, either because of an already existing request from another branch or due to private commitments in Altenburg. Müller's main profession was not to show films in the DKG's branches but to run the Insel in Altenburg. In contrast, the Deutsche Bioscop's business was to screen films whenever a branch asked for it, and to fulfil as many engagements as possible. While Müller could do only one show at a time, the Deutsche Bioscop was able to send several projectionists to different branches at the same time and do parallel screenings with multiple copies of the same films. Having settled the financial aspect of film screenings in the branches, the DKG's task now was to augment the existing film material with new up-to-date films from the colonies.

New Films from the Colonies

Müller's films represented only an initial and limited film inventory for the DKG. The society did not yet have films from the Asian/Pacific colonies, and if the DKG wanted to offer colonial film screenings with a variety of films, sooner or later they would have to react to the branches' demand for new films and programmes. However, according to the

DKG, colonial film propaganda was in general a much more difficult task than naval film propaganda. Unlike the films of the German naval fleet, films from the German colonies were more expensive to produce and more difficult to shoot.[4] While the DFV's annual organized trips for schoolchildren to the harbours of the North and Baltic seas could easily give an impression of the navy's power, the DKG had to limit its efforts to the representation of the colonies in words and images. While a battleship after being built could be seen in its entirety, the colonies were a work in progress:

> and regarding the quite heavy circumstances, that we can show the subject of our efforts, the colonies, only in word and image to the Heimat, but the Navy League every year demonstrates directly the impressive sight of our powerful warships to a great number of its members, particularly the youth. And a warship is a finished whole, which in itself is completed and finished as soon as it floats fully equipped on the water. But our colonies are growing objects in which the stranger only sees the faults, similar to a growing child in which the one who does not know it only sees the mistakes, while the parents and educators can judge their aptitudes and progress. We are working therefore already from the outset under more difficult conditions than the Navy League.[5]

The disadvantageous conditions under which the DKG operated took a turn for the better during 1907. New films were provided by the German steamship line Norddeutscher Lloyd and the Deutsche Bioscop. Additional support in 'colonial film lecturing' came from the Leipzig ethnologist Karl Weule, who compiled for his lectures a film programme with films from his 1906 expedition to the south of the East-African colony, and from occasional screenings by Duke Adolf Friedrich zu Mecklenburg, the DKG president's brother, who showed films from his 1907/08 'Inner-Africa' expedition.

The Lloyd's material seemed to be identical with the film *Mit dem Norddeutschen Lloyd nach Neu-Guinea* (With the Norddeutschen Lloyd to New Guinea) that was released by the Internationale Kinematographen and Licht-Effekt-Gesellschaft mbH in the spring of 1907. The 350 m film was promoted as pictures from a scientific expedition, whose academic leader was identified in the advertisement only by the initial letters of his family name, 'Professor Sch...'.[6] *Mit dem Norddeutschen Lloyd* depicted in eleven parts a journey from Germany to the Pacific colony. It started with the departure from Bremerhaven and then showed social games on board the steamer, followed by pictures of stops in Marseille, Naples, the Arabian Coast and Ceylon, and the arrival in New Guinea. Pictures from New Guinea showed exercises of the German police troop and dances of the natives. The last part showed the Duk-Duk dance of a secret society, which, according to the advertisement, was the very first time that the dance had been filmed; foreigners and even natives that had previously tried to watch the dance had been killed. Reviews of screenings in other branches indicate that the material was included in the Deutsche Bioscop's programme.

The company's Africa material was shot by their operator, Georg Furkel, who travelled through the West African colonies on behalf of the Deutsche Koloniale Eisenbahn- und Betriebsgesellschaft (DKEB, German Colonial Railway and Operating Company). The company planned to use the films for promotion purposes at the Deutsche Armee-Marine- und Kolonialausstellung (DAMUKA, German Army, Navy and Colonial Exhibition), which opened on 15 May 1907 in Berlin. The DKEB was in charge of most of the colonial railway projects in the German colonies, and it was Furkel's job to document the construction work of the railways and to shoot phantom rides from the trains. Besides supporting Germany's colonial efforts, Furkel was also charged with shooting films about the colonies for which dances, market scenes and military exercises of the local troops were supposed to be arranged.[7]

The programme of the Deutsche Bioscop for the DFV's publicity campaign of 1907/08, which also included a small colonial section, gives some information about what Furkel shot during his travels in the African colonies. The short summary shows that, although scenes of the colonial railway made up a large part of the programme, Furkel covered many other aspects of colonial life:

> a) South-West-Africa: diving boys on the roadstead on Madeira (shot on the way to South-West-Africa), construction of the railway at Aus, Railway-Panorama of Aus (from the train station to the breach), a caravan passing Aus, German colonial forces, on horseback with military equipment, a squadron of a military transport, mules being led to the drinking trough, Halifax Island with inhabitants, surf at the Halifax island. b) Cameroon: railway construction in Cameroon, Scenic of the government building with park on the Josplateau, Post-office Duala. c) Togo: dance of the natives Bagida, Market in Lome, jetty in Lome, hustle and bustle at the Lome train station, swimming Negro children in the surf.[8]

The lack of information about the Deutsche Bioscop's programmes in the DKG's branches does not allow an exact comparison between the Deutsche Bioscop's material and that of Müller. However, the description of Furkel's films shows that they were not much different from those of Müller. Furkel, too, tried to vary shots that had more economic, military or political content with touristic sights. Reviews describe the

Deutsche Bioscop's films as clear, distinct and sharp (which was not always the case with Müller's), so one can assume that Müller's technically less-accomplished films were supplemented and probably partly replaced by better film material from the Deutsche Bioscop.

The new film material that was available at the beginning of their Kinematographenkampagne gave the DKG/Deutsche Bioscop the chance to compile a rather extensive colonial film programme.[9] Even if not all of it could be used for screening, together with the material from the Norddeutscher Lloyd and Müller's films, more than 10,000 m of colonial film were available around 1907/08. Calculating an average projection speed of between sixteen and eighteen frames per second, this made between nine to ten hours of film from the German colonies.

The most important difference between Müller and the Deutsche Bioscop is not to be found in the images but in a significant formal aspect: the separation of the exhibition of the films from the lecture. While the exhibition of the films during the Kinematographenkampagne was done by one of the Deutsche Bioscop's technical assistants, the lecturing was taken over by the DKG, namely by one of the branches' speakers, which made the DKG the only 'colonial expert' to provide comments and explanations to accompany the individual film pictures. Before each new part of the programme started, the speaker provided basic information about each colony, such as size, location, population and natural resources. After that, each 'view' was individually explained.[10]

The leaflet of Müller's Hamburg programme suggests that the audience either bought or received for free a programme with the films that were going to be screened, whereas posters and other publicity material were most likely provided by the branches. With the beginning of the Kinematographenkampagne standardized promotion materials, such as posters and so forth, were provided by the DKG head office.[11] Since the DFV and DKG coordinated some of their screenings for the publicity campaign of 1907/08, one can assume that film lectures in the individual branches of the two associations were not very different in organization and style. The analysis will refer in what follows, therefore, to the DFV's material.

The DFV's brochure 'Allerlei Fingerzeige für Flotten-Vereins-Abende' (All Sorts of Tips for Navy League Evenings) supplied the branches with detailed instructions on how to conduct an evening.[12] Different reprinted texts about the same topic made it possible for the lecturer to address either an adult audience, school children or soldiers, and explain the sea fleet's importance. The actual film screening was introduced by a second speech, which pointed out the financial and technical aspects and underlined the patriotic purpose of the screening. Before the film began, the audience joined in a cheer for the German emperor. The 1907/08 programme of the Deutsche Bioscop for the DFV was composed of three different segments plus an additional, optional part. Films about the naval fleet, including images of fleet manoeuvers at sea, made up the major part of the programme. This first part was followed by a colonial programme with images from South-West, Cameroon and Togo. The third segment included patriotic actualities of the German emperor and images of troop parades.[13] The additional part showed different humoristic shorts, which had been approved by the DKG beforehand.[14]

The DKG's programme structure was probably not much different from that of the DFV, except that it had a much stronger emphasis on the colonies so that parts one and two could change position with each other. Furthermore, the colonial film programmes started with an introductory speech by one of the branches' speakers, which was followed by the screening of the films. Reviews suggest that the major part of the programme at the beginning of the new publicity campaign was compiled from the Bioscop's colonial material. Besides Müller's films from the German East-African colony, which remained indispensable for comprehensive film coverage of the German colonies, the Durban material also remained in the Deutsche Bioscop's film programme. Like Müller, the Deutsche Bioscop also concluded a colonial film screening evening with some humorous shorts. To summarise, the DKG began its first cinematographic campaign with its new film exhibitor Deutsche Bioscop well prepared. Problems such as the booking procedure, new colonial films and the design of the programme had been solved, and the campaign was carefully organized. However, the results of the film screenings for the publicity campaigns of 1907/08 and 1908/09 show that the film campaign had a short life.

The End of the Kinemtographenkampagne

Between 15 October and 20 December 1907, the Deutsche Bioscop was successfully working as an exhibitor for the DKG. The company was booked for 120 screenings on forty-five days in thirty-nine different places.[15] The branches usually organized more than one screening per day; some branches even managed to organize four screenings a day. For 1908 the DKG reported on fifty-five screening days in fifty-two different places. In addition to the Bioscop, another commercial company, the Minerva, also exhibited films for the society.[16] The number of screenings per year suggests at first sight an increase in screenings at the branches. A more detailed analysis, however, shows that the number of screenings seemed to decrease in 1908 and probably came to an end during the publicity campaign of 1908/09. At the board's meeting in June 1908, the publicity committee's speaker reported about ninety-five screening days during the last publicity campaign.[17] Since forty-five screening days were already reported for the period October to December 1907, one has to assume that the rest of fifty screenings were organized in the second half of the publicity campaign, between January and April 1908. This would mean that the number of fifty-five screening days mentioned in the 1908 annual report was a significant decrease in film lectures during the publicity campaign of 1908/09. If fifty of fifty-five screenings had already been organized in the first half of 1908, only five screenings were organized between October and December 1908. Financially, film screenings also seem to have become an incalculable risk and confirm the hypothesis of the ending of the campaign. Although fewer screenings were reported, the claim on the special budget increased by almost 30 per cent from 1907/08 to 1908/09.[18]

The existence of only one report in the *DKZ* of a colonial film screening during the second half of the publicity campaign of 1908/09 supports the hypothesis of a sudden ending of colonial film screenings at the beginning of 1909. Although in none of its publications did the DKG comment on either the decrease or the ending of the film screenings, it is again the annual reports of the DFV that give some more information on this topic and show that, in the DFV's branches, film screenings were becoming less popular. After the publicity campaign of 1907/08 proved unprofitable for the Bioscop, the company did not renew the contract with the DFV.[19] As a consequence of the decreasing popularity of film screenings, the DFV decided that bookings for screenings should no longer be made through the head office but directly through the individual branches.[20] The Bioscop was replaced by Minerva, which became the DFV's new exhibitor for the second half of 1908 and agreed to tour through the league's branches until June 1909. The DKG seemed to follow the DFV's practice, and the Minerva became the DKG's new exhibitor in 1908. In contrast to the DFV, however, the DKG's 1908 annual report does not mention any problems with Deutsche Bioscop and introduces the Minerva as only an 'additional' exhibitor. It seems that the Minerva's real function was not that of second exhibitor but that of trustee in the DKG's failed project of institutionalizing colonial film screenings in their propaganda work.

The colonial film programmes that were shown to audiences in the branches reveal that the selection of films was rather heterogeneous, since they could include slapstick shorts as well as scenes of the German emperor. While this programme structure suggests that film screenings in the branches imitated those in commercial cinemas, the relationship between patriotic societies and commercial venues was more complex. For years travelling exhibitors criticized the DFV's film shows as a threat to their business.[21] Although the activities of the DKG were not mentioned in this context, the fact that the DKG and the DFV were cooperating with each other at this time, and that both had contracts with the Deutsche Bioscop, makes this criticism relevant for the general discussion of the relationship between the film business and associational film screenings. In an article in the *Kinematograph* in February 1908 exhibitors repeated their accusation and called for resistance against the DFV:

> Where it [the Navy League] has done a screening, private cinema owners' chances for business are without any doubt lost, since soldiers are ordered by company to the screenings, schools and other institutions usually have to line up and in fact everybody else with two pennies left in his pockets is mobilized. If a cinema owner tries to approach school directors concerning a recommendation of a very proper afternoon screening with the reference to a programme of a real academic interest, it is said that this would distract from work (!) or that the precious time had to be carefully weighed, but since for screenings of the German Navy League schools are even ordered to attend (!) in the morning hours (!), one may not doubt, that this kind of patriotic public entertainment is supported by the schools.[22]

The exhibitors' concern about associational film screenings at that particular time becomes even more plausible if one compares the size of the cities and towns in which colonial film screenings took place. The majority of reports of screenings in 1907 and 1908 did not come from big cities but small towns, where a local commercial cinema culture was probably not yet established. Associational film screenings may therefore have indeed posed an existential threat to local exhibitors that made their business mainly in small towns and rural regions. As travelling exhibitors argued, while they had to invest time and money in order to reach the audience, the DFV (and the DKG) relied on the patriotic commitment of the local institutions. Moreover, the exhibitors were in the difficult position of having to ask for permission for public screenings from local authorities, whose officials were often members of the local branch of a patriotic society. As the article reports, the DFV forced the owners of local lecture halls to cancel contracts with commercial exhibitors in favour of DFV's screenings. Exhibitors were therefore emphasizing their own patriotic commitment and promoted their cinemas as institutions of patriotic integrity. They considered their film programmes as an important contribution in the formation of the public's patriotic way of thinking: 'We are at least as good patriots as the Navy League and its members, we are paying no small fees for our cinema, without covering them up patriotically, and we present programmes in which the patriotic feelings of the citizen are continuously strengthened and consolidated'.[23]

As an article in *Die Flotte* from January 1907 shows, the Deutsche Bioscop did not necessarily benefit from its cooperation with the DFV. On the contrary, screenings for the DFV sometimes turned out to be financially unfavourable.[24] The article reports that three months after the Deutsche Bioscop started to organize film screenings for the DFV's branches, several screenings and whole tours had to be cancelled due to the uncooperative attitude of some branches. The DFV assumed that the reason for this situation was the branches' general mistrust of the company's commercial exploitation of a national patriotic interest. The Navy League underlined that this was not the case and reminded the branches that the contract between the DFV and the Deutsche Bioscop was made in order to minimize the financial risk for the DFV, which simply could not operate like a professional exhibitor. As the Deutsche Bioscop did not receive any financial compensation from the DFV's presidium for cancelled screenings, the Navy League reminded the branches to honour the conditions of the contract and support the Deutsche Bioscop in every way.

Whether a similar mistrust also existed or started to grow among the DKG's branches is difficult to say, but the Deutsche Bioscop was primarily a commercial film company that also sold colonial films to local exhibitors. It is therefore quite possible that the DKG's members, too, considered the Deutsche Bioscop merely a profit-making company. Rather than suggesting that it was the members' lack of trust in the company's patriotic respectability that caused the branches' decreasing interest in colonial film screenings, it is quite possible that the failure of the Kinematographenkampagne was largely related to the booming film business that competed with the patriotic societies for audiences around 1906/07. The release of various films from the colonies between 1907 and 1909 on the commercial film market suggests that travelling exhibitors became an attractive alternative to patriotic screenings and that the DKG was losing its 'monopoly' as the only exhibitor of films from the colonies.

Travelling exhibitors were starting to use the variety of their film programmes as their 'trump' to underline the quality of their cinematic fare. In contrast to the DFV's screenings, exhibitors argued that: 'undisputably we are presenting more thrilling performances than the Navy League, whose screenings of sea images, that offer only little variation, are tiring for the viewers'.[25] The exhibitors' vaunting of their more varied film programmes pointed to an issue of concern for the DFV. While travelling film exhibitors considered the screenings in the DFV's branches to be unfair competition, the DFV in turn realized that the variety in the programmes of commercial cinemas was a strong competitor to their screenings. As the annual reports of the DFV show, film screenings with exclusively sea fleet films became less effective in attracting members as well as the local public. In 1905 the DFV maintained that any changes in the composition of the programme would damage their patriotic commitment,[26] but by the following year they already had to adopt a more varied programme.[27] In 1907, the Deutsche Bioscop did not renew the contract with the DFV and explained that this decision was also due to the fact that even with new sea fleet films it became from year to year more difficult to compile a film programme that attracted an audience. According to the Deutsche Bioscop, the DFV had to abandon exclusively sea fleet programmes if the DFV's film shows were to remain competitive.[28] Even after increasing the variety in their film programmes for the following publicity campaign, the DFV's film shows continued to lose their attraction.[29]

The situation in the DKG's branches was similar. As reviews of film screenings in the branches show, colonial branches suffered as well from parallel film screenings of other exhibitors, which most likely had also colonial films in their programmes. In addition, the DKG's film screenings seemed to suffer from technical problems with regard to the films' quality. As the following example shows, audiences chose the best programme they could get for their money, and this was not necessarily the most patriotic one. In September 1906 the Velbert DKG branch organized three screenings on two successive days. The first screening was very well attended, and received a positive review in the local press. Few viewers came to the following two screenings. The newspaper attributed the fall off in attendance to the enormous rush the day before, but also pointed out that the images in the later screenings were not very clear. It is quite possible that the film screening on the first day already reached every viewer in a small town such as Velbert, but it is also possible that the audience preferred to save their money for the travelling film exhibitor who was coming to Velbert on the following

Sunday. This programme contained forty films and was publicized on Saturday in an advertisement that measured almost three times the size of the colonial film advertisement. The programme was covered in fifteen pictures of the German emperor and the German Navy and Army, and showed an additional twenty-five films from different genres. The programme attracted a very large audience and, according to the review, was clear, in focus and without any flickering.[30]

A similar incident was reported at the board's meeting in June 1908.[31] The representative of the Greiz branch reported on three screenings that had been organized by the branch in the latest publicity campaign. Due to the massive publicity for these screenings, all three were well attended. Despite the satisfying result for the branch, the audience nevertheless complained about the poor quality of the pictures and the exhibition: Some of the images were bad or difficult to recognize, and the screenings suffered from an annoying flickering during the projection. This, according to the representative, was especially unpleasant because another cinema in the city presented very good pictures. Supported by the approval of some of those present, the speaker of the Greiz branch emphasized that a continuation of the film campaign required the improvement of the film material. Complaints about the films' quality seemed to culminate in the year 1908; in November the Berlin branch forwarded a request to the executive committee, demanding the 'immediate purchase of new lantern slides and the immediate supply of extensive cinematographic records'. With reference to various complaints about the films' quality at the last general assembly, the Berlin branch argued:

> The average lantern slide series in question is not only technically backward compared to the modern illustrations that nowadays pass every week through numerous illustrated papers, but also from a neutral point of view it does not appear any longer lively enough to arouse enthusiasm for the colonial interest as is necessary for promotion purposes and even for the utmost lively stimulation of the broadest circles [*Volkskreise*], including women and children. However, the German Colonial Society's main emphasis in promotion and propaganda lies in the exhibition of lantern slides and – where finances do allow – in cinematographic representations. It does not just cause ideological losses but it is simply impractical if we let this medium of our promotion to become backward.[32]

The committee vehemently dismissed the complaint of the Berlin branch and considered the request a '*Mißtrauensvotum*' (vote of no confidence) against the DKG's office, which had always done its best in this respect. Although the committee turned down the request of the branch, the issue of whether the visual material for colonial propaganda such as lantern slides had become outdated nevertheless became a point of discussion at the board's meeting in December 1908. It was argued that 'the existing material no longer corresponds to modern demands' and could be shown 'at best in such working-class circles that have not yet listened to any slide lectures, whereas society members made higher demands. The new era has just simply raised the demands'.[33] Cinematographic recordings were not mentioned in this context, but the complaint about the low quality of the society's lantern slides that did not correspond to modern standards suggests that film screenings, too, were probably regarded rather critically and could not compete with commercial screenings in the long run. The DKG's turning away from film screenings in the branches finally became evident in May 1909, when the Rhineland regional association asked for the purchase of three-colour processed slides (*Dreifarbenverfahren*) and two-colour processed films (*Zweifarbenverfahren*).[34] One member of the publicity committee came to the conclusion that film screenings were no longer an appropriate medium for illustration. As it was often impossible to recognize details in the films, he preferred to improve the screening conditions in general and thus to turn down the motion.

The discussions about film at the DKG have shown that the society's attitude towards film screenings had changed. In contrast to 1905, when the society enthusiastically gave way to the branches' demand for the new medium film, it seems that the DKG was ultimately not able to continuously adapt their propaganda work to the changing cultural and technical standards of the time. Even though one may suppose that film screenings continued until the first half of 1909 and were also occasionally organized by individual branches in the following years, the lack of any explanation in any of the subsequent annual reports for the end of the Kinematographenkampagne may be read as the DKG's disappointment about the unfulfilled expectations regarding successful colonial film propaganda in the branches.

After the cinematographic campaign's failure the DKG returned again to 'traditional' media such as lectures and lantern slides. Even though the society would never again win as many new members as it had during the colonial elections' aftermath, the DKG grew continuously until the First World War. The idea of using film for propaganda purposes was never completely abandoned by the DKG, and efforts to use it to promote the colonies were not lacking after the cessation of colonial screenings by the DKG. Two Hamburg companies in particular seemed to exploit films from the colonies: Propaganda-Gesellschaft für die deutschen Kolonien (Propaganda Society for the German Colonies), founded in 1910, and the Deutschkoloniale Kino- Gesellschaft mbH (German Colonial Cinema Company), founded in January 1913. While no information could be found about the work of the latter company, the few reviews of film screenings of the Propaganda- Gesellschaft für die deutschen Kolonien in Hamburg, Stendal and Dessau suggest that this company had some success with colonial film screenings in the region between Hamburg and Berlin in the winter of 1910/11. There are no indications that the company was collaborating with the DKG or the society's local branches.

In contrast to the DKG's interest in promoting the colonies in general among the public, the Propaganda-Gesellschaft für die deutschen Kolonien seemed primarily interested in promoting the South-West colony, as an advertisement in the Dessau newspaper for a screening on 15 December 1910 illustrates.[35] The film show, which lasted more than an hour, was similar to the DKG's film shows: the audience learned about the history and the geography of the colony and viewed films that depicted the passage to and 'views' of the South-West African colony. However, the discovery of diamonds in South-West in 1908 opened a new aspect in colonial filmmaking that the Propaganda-Gesellschaft für die deutschen Kolonien seemed to be quite aware of: the Dessau screening was advertised with the subtitle 'Through the Diamond fields'.

For the local branches of the DKG, film screenings remained one of the possible propaganda techniques. The organization of film screenings in this case was no longer coordinated with Berlin but most likely with a local exhibitor in a fashion similar to the DFV's recommendation to their local branches.[36] From October 1911 onwards, the DKG's publicity commission was again discussing the use of film for colonial propaganda. The commission proposed approaching film companies to convince them of the advantage of producing films in the colonies.[37] Even if the society could not conclude any contracts, some companies seemed to be interested in this area, as the 1912 annual report notes. For the DKG it was just a question of the right moment for starting again with film screenings in the branches, whose success was beyond any doubt: 'In any case we will continue paying this matter the most active attention since we expect especially from cinematographic screenings in the individual branches greatest attraction and good successes, and as soon the society's means allow we plan to acquire colonial films or to look for other alternatives to make such screenings possible'.[38]

The DKG's interest in film around 1912 did not initiate a new film campaign, and the few screenings that were reported by the *DKZ* between 1909 and 1914 do not allow a detailed analysis of film's significance in the local propaganda work of individual branches. Notices of film lectures about aeroplanes and their use in the colonial service, colonial agriculture or the production of rubber, however, suggest that film remained a tool for instruction and information in colonial propaganda in the local branches. The example of a film screening at the Lorraine branch in Saint Avold in March 1914 shows that some branches did not even hesitate to show foreign film productions, such as Alfred Machin's *Reisen und große Jagden im Innern Afrikas/Voyage et grandes chasses en Afrique* (Pathé Frères, 1913)[39] to attract the local public to a patriotic endeavour in support of German colonialism. Films about big game hunting in Africa were clearly not what the DKG had in mind when trying to use film for colonial propaganda. As it remarked, hunting and adventure films from the colonial territories were rather romantic but produced a totally inadequate image of the colonial '*Neuräume*' (new spaces) and their economic significance for the Heimat.[40]

The DKG never officially commented on the end of the Kinematographenkampagne, but a major reason for the campaign's failure seemed to have been the increase of colonial film screenings on the commercial market. Film programmes of travelling exhibitors became an attractive alternative to the film screenings of the DKG, whose material was technically inferior. Although branches asked repeatedly for new film material, the DKG did not continue its colonial film propaganda work. Moreover, the financial situation of the society did not allow for the purchase of new films or for a continuous supply of new, technically superior films. In addition to technical problems and the growing competition with commercial cinemas as film became a rapidly growing entertainment industry, one can speculate on a third reason for the failure of the Kinematographenkampagne. Despite all its efforts to popularize colonialism among the German public, the DKG was finally incapable of considering colonialism as something other than just an economic and political issue. The DKG therefore could not imagine using film except as a means of conveying instructive, political information. From this perspective it should not be surprising that one of the most successful media in terms of promoting a more 'entertaining colonialism' did not come from the DKG but from its corporate organization the FDKG and its periodical *Kolonie und Heimat*. This journal offered readers an 'entertaining colonial programme', including travel accounts, colonial hunting stories, impressionistic descriptions, colonial novels, jokes and anecdotes.[41] Parallel to the role of colonial cinematography in commercial venues, where the notions of entertainment and the programme become paramount, German ethnography articulated its own interest in the colonies.

Notes

1. DKG, *Ausschuss*, 21 June 1907, 6. The Deutsche Bioscop GmbH, Berlin, was founded on 18 June 1902 by Julius Grünbaum, aka Jules Greenbaum. Along with Oskar Messter, Greenbaum is known to have been one of the first important German producers.
2. DKG, *Vorstand*, 22 May 1907, 32.
3. DKG, *Jahresbericht*, 1907, 46.
4. DKG, *Jahresbericht*, 1905, 11.
5. DKG, *Jahresbericht*, 1907, 6.
6. *Der Kinematograph*, 31 March 1907. The name's beginning refers to Hugo Schauinsland (1857–1937), director of the Bremen Übersee Museum. The Norddeutsche Lloyd supported several of Schauinsland's expeditions to the South Seas.
7. Except for a three-part article in the *Kinematograph* from 1926 in which Furkel describes the beginning years of cinematography in Germany and his work for the Deutsche Bioscop, there exists no further information about his stays in the colonies. G. Furkel, 'Film vor 30 Jahren', *Der Kinematograph*, 7 November 1926: 15–16; 14 November 1926: 1–12, and 21 November 1926: 11–12.
8. BArch-Militärarchiv (henceforth cited as BArch-MA), RM 3/9925,87.
9. The Deutsche Bioscop speaks of 8,000 m of negative material that Furkel carried during his journey. *Der Komet*, 1 June 1907, 16.
10. *Magdeburgische Zeitung*, 16 October 1907.
11. DKG, *Jahresbericht*, 1907, 47.
12. BArch-MA, RM 3/9914, 215–52.
13. BArch-MA, RM 3/9925, 85-87.
14. *Kinematographische Vorführungen des Deutschen Flotten-Vereins. Programm und kurze Erläuterungen der Bilder 1907/08*, BArch-MA, RM 3/9925, 83.
15. DKG, *Jahresbericht*, 1907, 47.
16. DKG, *Jahresbericht*, 1908, 33.
17. DKG, *Vorstand*, 11 June 1908, 21.
18. In June 1908 the special budget had a deficit of 1,100 marks, DKG, *Vorstand*, 11 June 1908, 21. In November 1909 the deficit was about 1,381. 61 marks, DKG, *Vorstand*, 9 November 1909, 27.
19. DFV, *Jahres-Bericht*, 1907, 7.
20. DFV, *Jahres-Bericht*, 1908, 17–18.
21. Anon., 'Der Deutsche Flottenverein als Schausteller', *Der Komet*, 20(927), 27 December 1902; anon., 'Flottenverein und Kinematograph', *Der Komet*, 23(1083), 23 December 1905.
22. Perlmann, 'Die Kinematographen-Theater und der "Deutsche Flottenverein"'.
23. Ibid.
24. Anon., 'Der Kinematograph', *Die Flotte*, 10(1), 9 January 1907.
25. Perlmann, 'Die Kinematographen-Theater und der "Deutsche Flottenverein"'.
26. DFV, *Jahres-Bericht*, 1905, 7.
27. DFV, *Jahres-Bericht*, 1906, 9.
28. DFV, *Jahres-Bericht*, 1907, 7.

29. Ibid., 18.
30. *Velberter Zeitung,* 24 September 1906.
31. DKG, *Vorstand,* 11 June 1908, 21–22.
32. DKG, *Ausschuss,* 27 November 1908, 8–9.
33. DKG, *Vorstand,* 4 December 1908, 78–80.
34. DKG, *Ausschuss,* 22 May 1909, 7; *Vorstand,* 8 June 1909, 128–29.
35. *Anhaltischer Staats-Anzeiger,* Dessau, 13 December 1910.
36. DFV, *Jahres-Bericht,* 1907, 7.
37. BArch, R 8023/1089, 52.
38. DKG, *Jahresbericht,* 1912, 35.
39. *DKZ,* 2 May 1914, 303.
40. Stuemer and Duems, *Fünfzig Jahre Deutsche Kolonialgesellschaft,* 103.
41. Warmbold, *Germania in Africa,* 92–94.

PART III

ETHNOGRAPHIC FILMMAKING IN THE COLONIES

Chapter 7

KARL WEULE IN GERMAN EAST AFRICA

The previous chapters have discussed colonial cinematography in the context of the German Colonial Society's propaganda work and the individual careers of semi-professional itinerant showmen such as Carl Müller and Robert Schumann. The following part shifts the focus to a group of films that was not necessarily used for propaganda purposes in the DKG's Kinematographenkampagne but nevertheless belongs to the colonial cinematographic repertoire – colonial ethnographic films. Emilie de Brigard's notion that 'ethnographic film began as a phenomenon of colonialism' reminds us not only of ethnology's origin in colonial imperialism but also that colonial territories usually provided the easiest access for ethnographers.[1] Very often the colonies were the first location for the filming ethnographer.

Research on early German ethnographic filmmaking is still in its early days.[2] The majority of surviving film prints come from German ethnographic expeditions to the South Seas, *Völkerkundliche Aufnahmen aus der Südsee aus den Jahren 1908–1910* (Ethnological Film Documents from the Pacific from the Years 1908–1910) of the Hamburg expedition or Richard Neuhauss's *Aus dem Leben der Kate auf Deutsch-Neuguinea. Aufnahmen aus dem Jahre 1909* (From the Life of the Kate in German New Guinea. Pictures from 1909). Almost no films exist that were shot in the African colonies. This part does not intend to give a comprehensive overview of ethnographic filmmaking in the German colonies but concentrates on the only known ethnographic footage from the African colonies. The films were shot by Leipzig ethnographer Karl Weule on his expedition to German East Africa in 1906/07. The small case study shows film's significance for Weule and his ideas of promoting film as a new research and didactic tool in ethnology and the museum. It ends with a more detailed discussion of ethnographers' and filmmakers' general problems when filming in the tropics.

Holding a doctorate in geography, Weule was an assistant to Adolf Bastian in the Africa section of the Königliche Museum für Völkerkunde (Royal Museum for Ethnology) in Berlin from 1893 until 1899. He became a lecturer in ethnology and geography at the University of Leipzig and assistant to the director of the Museum für Völkerkunde zu Leipzig (Leipzig Museum for Ethnography) in 1899. Two years later he was appointed to the chair for ethnology and prehistory at Leipzig University and promoted to vice director of the Leipzig museum. In 1907 he became the director of the Leipzig museum, which he made into the second major museum for ethnology in Germany and gained a worldwide reputation for this institution.

In the wake of such ethnographic filmmakers as Felix Regnault, Alfred Cort Haddon and Walter Baldwin Spencer, ethnographic filmmaking in the German colonies emerged parallel to the DKG's film propaganda and became widely known through the films of Austrian anthropologist Rudolf Pöch's 1904/06 expedition to the New Guineas and, less known in ethnographic film literature, Karl Weule's expedition to the south of German East Africa. Weule's ethnographic filmmaking certainly served colonial politics' interest but as an ethnographic scholar and the director of the second largest ethnographic museum in Germany he had his own personal political agenda: he aimed at addressing the academic community and the public at the same time. Exploring the new medium with regard to ethnographic observation, recording and study he also was aiming at promoting his discipline as a new social science among the German public and firmly establishing his museum with the help of his films within the competitive situation among German ethnographic museums.[3]

Ethnographic Film and the 'German tradition'

In her study of the origins of ethnographic film in North America, Alison Griffiths has shown that the introduction of the photo camera as a new research tool in ethnographic fieldwork led to a paradigmatic shift in ethnographic research in the second half of the nineteenth century.

The camera rendered the ethnographer's traditional draft book outmoded and became the new objective 'truth machine', which through anthropometric photographs could produce reliable and exact data on the native's body, for example. Unlike photography, however, film never gained the same degree of respectability due to a decreasing interest in the visual in the first two decades of the twentieth century.[4] In contrast to motion picture's growing popularity among the public, Griffiths concludes that very few anthropologists around the world were using a film camera at the beginning of the twentieth century.[5]

The situation in Germany seemed to have been part of this pattern. Though German scholars emphasized the importance of the new medium for science, film failed to become systematically applied in ethnographic fieldwork. However, while a history of the German ethnographic film and its beginnings still needs to be written – and very carefully researched – German ethnographers are usually referred to as having had a particular interest in using a film camera. According to Martin Taureg, German ethnographic film drew on two developments. Firstly, the application of the camera as a research tool in the natural sciences, and secondly, film as a new didactic medium, as was emphasized by the *Kinoreformbewegung* (cinema reform movement).[6]

The cameras as a research tool can be traced back to 1895, when Felix Regnault started to use the chronophotographe to make fast serial photographs of African people at the Exposition Ethnographique de l'Afrique Occidentale in Paris. Studying and analysing the movement of the African people, Regnault hoped to find in the specific movements and gestures a possible index of race. Though Regnault was not yet using film, in the sense of projecting sequences, Tobing Rony points out that Regnault's 'conception of ethnographic film as a positivist record to be stored in archives and examined repeatedly, frame by frame' remains the paradigm for dominant conceptions of ethnographic film.'[7] As Regnault remarked:

> Only cinema provides objective documents in abundance; thanks to cinema, the anthropologist can, today, collect the life of all peoples; he will possess in his drawers all the specials acts of different races ... He will study, when it pleases him, the series of movements that man executes for squatting, climbing trees, seizing and handling objects with his feet etc. He will be present at fests, at battles, at religious and civil ceremonies, at different ways of trading, eating, relaxing.[8]

Regnault's concept was especially relevant for theories in German ethnology. *Kulturkreislehre* (diffusionist theory), articulated in 1904 and dominating German ethnology for a long time, influenced the use of the film camera more in the German-speaking area of the discipline than, for example, in the British one. Diffusionism emphasized the significance of the comparative study of artefacts from different cultures to determine historical relationships. Film recordings could be an important ethnographic research tool to document the differences and similarities.

The second major development that influenced German ethnographic filmmaking came from the Kinoreformbewegung.[9] The reform movement was a heterogeneous group, including teachers, educationalists and jurists, as well as clerical and political circles. Common to all reformers was their fascination with the new technology. The belief in the camera's objective power of representing reality made some reformers consider the camera to be an expansion of human vision. According to the reformer Georg Melcher, the camera was a 'modern eye', which was able to look beyond the earth's surface, could cross time and space, and look backwards and forwards. Mental activities like memory 'have stopped being dependent on this dirty white mass that we call brain', and 'The modern human being does not remember any longer but collects and uses Kinogramme'. History was no longer written but produced by the camera's objectivity, and from now on Clio, the muse of history, was winding the crank of the camera and operating the phonograph.[10] Afraid of the moral and ethical decay of German society, especially German youth, through watching *Schundfilme* (trashy films), reformers emphasized cinema's educational and informational value. They favoured therefore nonfiction films such as geographic, folklorist, ethnographic, scientific and technical films.[11] German ethnographers 'most fully embraced Regnault's ideal of a scientific archive of ethnographic film'.[12] Filming material culture and seeing film as a new teaching aid framed German ethnographers' understanding of film for more than half a century, eventually leading to the 1953 establishment of the ethnographic film archive, the Encyclopedia Cinematographica at the Institut für den wissenschaftlichen Film (IWF), in Göttingen, an institution that considered film a 'non-corruptible document' that allowed for 'direct and unbiased observation'.[13]

German-speaking ethnographic filmmaking's historical embedding has become commonplace in ethnographic film literature, but there is little empirical evidence about when film's use in German ethnographic fieldwork exactly started, which ethnographers in particular favoured the film camera in the early years of cinema and how they collaborated, debated and disputed about the new medium.[14] In what ways are the two concepts, film as a medium for ethnographic study of material culture and film as a teaching aid, reflected in the individual work of the ethnographers? Against this background of the 'German tradition', Karl Weule's film expedition and his interest in film provide some preliminary information about the beginning of ethnographic filmmaking in Germany.

Ethnology and Colonialism

Very soon after Germany had become a colonial power, German ethnologists discovered the new colonial territories as a fresh research area.[15] While ethnology was not yet established as an academic discipline at German universities, most scholars considered colonial expansion as providing a chance to promote the new discipline in the academic field. While theories in German ethnology were of little practical use to colonial authorities, Woodruff Smith argues that 'colonialism enthusiasm gave ethnologists a very effective means of arguing for extensive government funding of museums, university seminars, chairs and expeditions, that were overtly anthropological in aim'.[16] Doing research in the colonies was for many scholars a unique chance to advance their academic careers and achieve national and international reputations. Ethnologists such as Adolf Bastian, the *Urvater* (forefather) of German ethnology, were quite sure that German colonial politics would increase the value of ethnology as a 'useful' science.[17] Colonial practice and colonial administration facilitated ethnographic research in the colonies that would otherwise have been much more difficult to conduct. In his case study on the Hamburg South Seas Expedition, Hans Fischer has shown that colonial rule created perfect research conditions for German ethnologists, and sometimes led to an ethnic group's trading, selling or otherwise losing most of its cultural heritage.[18] During the German colonial era ethnological museums were able to expand significantly their ethnographic collections. Consequently, Fritz Krause, Karl Weule's successor in Leipzig, could consider the collections of the Leipzig museum in 1926 to be the result of Weule's steady contacts with colonial circles and the scientific exploration of the colonies.[19]

Despite ethnology's embrace of colonialism, the relationship between ethnology and colonialism was rather ambivalent. German ethnologists such as Weule favoured ethnographic exploration of the colonies on the widest possible scale, but at the same time explicitly rejected any orientation of ethnological research towards colonial affairs.[20] This was no contradiction. Weule argued that scientific research existed for its own sake, and it was up to the authorities to draw consequences and practical applications from the results of this research.[21] In addition to his academic interest in studying the history of mankind in the colonies, Weule seemed to have had in mind that ethnography could create a kind of scientific database that could be used to support and improve the administration of the colonies. He suggested, for example, that the war with the Herero and the Nama could have been avoided had the colonial authorities had a better understanding of the African's mind, jurisdiction, customs and habits.[22]

The conditions for a sound and comprehensive exploration of the German colonies were created through the work of the Kommission für die landeskundliche Erforschung der deutschen Schutzgebiete (Commission for the Geographic Exploration of the German Protectorates), which coordinated, in large part, ethnographic expeditions in the German colonies after 1905. The commission, which was directed by Weule's friend and mentor Hans Meyer, saw its major task as the systematic exploration of the colonial territories.[23] The commission's founding concept went back to Meyer's lecture at the DKG's First Colonial Congress in 1902. In his speech, Meyer argued that economic success needed the combination of economy and sciences.[24] In contrast to the internationally famous German explorers of Africa in the nineteenth century, whose research had only 'metaphysical purposes', the new generation of explorers wanted to produce material results. Meyer emphasized that economic exploration of the colonies was possible only on the basis of a sound and comprehensive geographical exploration of the territories. The precondition for economic exploration was a 'spatial orientation' and a 'real geographic knowledge' about a new territory. This spatial knowledge had to include all information about a region, including that about the human beings in relation to their environment, such as the working space, work materials and tools. This could not be studied from the outside but only within the field of causal relations. To produce the necessary information Meyer planned to create an interdisciplinary network under the direction of geography. In the coordination and combination of topography, cartography, geology, meteorology, hydrography, botany, zoology and ethnology, Meyer planned the exploration of the colonies within the framework of a 'modern causative geography'.[25]

In July 1904, Meyer's theoretical considerations were translated into action. As a member of the Kolonialrat (Colonial Council), an advisory body of the KA and the RKA, Meyer submitted to this council a plan to establish a commission for the exploration of the German colonial territories.²⁶ The commission became a permanent one for the newly established RKA, and at the Third Colonial Congress in 1910 Meyer summarized the commission's concept as follows:

> In the centre of the working paper, that has been compiled at the beginning of the commission's activity, stands the geographic exploration of the protectorates in the sense of a modern causative geography, which is not satisfied with describing the objects and people in the countries, but seeks to understand the great causal connections between all appearances on earth and create lively illustrations of them ... From the study of mutual relations between nature's characteristics and the people will finally result the economic realities and possibilities that can be used and further developed by our colonial work.²⁷

Though Meyer shared with Weule the idea of a clear separation of scientific and colonial interest, Meyer finally emphasized that it was not science alone but practical colonization that the commission wanted and could support.²⁸ Weule's expedition became one of the first expeditions that was sent out by the commission to explore with the 'full equipment of modern ethnography' the material and mental culture of the people in the German East African colony.²⁹

Karl Weule's Film Expedition

Karl Weule arrived in the East African colony on 1 June 1906, where he planned to study the 'strange ethnic mixture' in a region southwest of Lindi.³⁰ Guarded by a small army troop, Weule's expedition did not give the usual impression of an ethnographic enterprise. As the head of an official expedition of the Colonial Office, Weule received every support from the local colonial administration and the subordinated African authorities, which made it quite easy to find the right motifs for his film camera as well as to recruit Africans for his different recording purposes.³¹

In Dar es Salaam the local administration organized especially for Weule a *ngoma*, a popular festivity with dancing and singing; in Lindi he was allowed to arrange a big *pombe*, a drinking party.³² Weule recorded these with both the phonograph and the film camera.³³ Weule's attitude, feelings and his opinion about African people were ambivalent. The rhythm of the drums at a ngoma, for example, almost led Weule to join the dancers, as he remarked, but his role as a representative of the '*Herrscherrasse*' (ruling race) finally reminded him of the need to keep his composure, so he continued following the party with the eyes of a scholar.[34] Weule used the phonograph on his expedition for pragmatic reasons: with the 'superb results'[35] of songs, poems or lectures, he planned to use the recordings for teaching purposes. Future colonial officials could either learn an idiom from the recordings or the recordings could be a first step for the production of idiomatic dictionaries.[36]

Not all recordings came out 'superbly', as his correspondence with Hans Meyer between June and October 1906 shows.[37] Very soon after his arrival, Weule encountered severe problems with the phonograph. By July it was impossible for him to record anything because the heat and humidity had destroyed the wax on the cylinders. Only in October did the cylinders recover so that he could continue with sound recordings. A second problem was that the phonograph was better suited for recording singing masses than individual people. He experimented therefore with recordings in closed rooms but soon realized that too many people in one room created disturbing background noises. Thirdly, according to Weule's correspondence many natives were not familiar with the phonograph and believed a rumour that was going around saying that the machine would steal their voice. Finally, many Africans were not always willing to collaborate with Weule and his interrogation marathon for his phonograms. As he reports, some Africans who were asked to repeat their traditional stories or poems for the phonograph in order to make a translation often told him the second time a version that was different from the first one.

Weule's decision to use a film camera on his expedition entered the expedition plan very late. Only after the expedition budget had already passed the major administrative stages did Weule buy the popular amateur model Ernemann-Kino, which by then he had to purchase with his own money. In his first report from Dar es Salaam to Meyer, Weule notes that he was successfully working with the photo camera, the phonograph and the film camera. Though as a beginner in shooting film he was still worried that the first films he had sent for processing to Ernemann in Germany might turn out to be poor in quality, his initial fear disappeared as the second report from Lindi shows. Weule reports enthusiastically about the easy handling of the film camera and remarks that it was just a matter of anchoring the tripod firmly in the sandy ground and, after having prepared everything for the shot, of cranking correctly and evenly. His initial enthusiasm did not last for long. Inexperienced in filming, Weule did not buy a special tripod for his film camera but planned to use the normal tripod of his photo cameras for this purpose. During his expedition he painfully regretted this decision because it turned out that the tripod was too light to absorb the jerky cranking of the camera. Weule had to improvise therefore and either used a heavy stone, a travel case or, if worse came to worse, one of his carriers as a heavy weight to secure the tripod.[38]

Weule's films have not yet aroused great attention by German visual anthropologists, which makes it difficult to contextualize the films into a broader ethnological context. He was not interested in using the film camera for anthropometric studies, which he considered an insufficient method for the production of ethnographic knowledge[39], but for shooting manufacturing techniques, dances, rituals and games that required a large performing space. Weule used the long take and shot his films in medium long shot, which allowed him – at least in theory – to cover a large space in front of the camera and not to miss any parts of the action performed within this space. The surviving prints of Weule's film material, however, show that it was not only the lack of a heavy tripod that made the results of some of his films rather unsatisfying; he also had considerable difficulties adjusting his camera to the performances.

The first film (no. I, copy from original positive print, henceforth cited as o.p.p.) depicts a dance performance in front of a crowd. Though dancers leave the frame for a short moment, the film gives a rather complete impression of this performance. Similarly successful is the shooting of a dance performed in the centre of a tribe's village (no. VI, copy from original nitrate negative, henceforth cited as o.n.n.) or a dance that he shot in the African bush (no. VII, o.p.p.). On the other hand, it is unclear what Weule planned to shoot in a film that shows a music trio together with a dancer (no. IV, o.p.p.); only at the end does the dancer enter the camera's field of vision from the right. Did the dancer disturb Weule's recording or was it Weule's or the dancer's bad timing? Similar to this film is the recording of an ecstatic dance, in which Weule may not have thought about the dancer's repertoire of extended movements (no. VIII, o.p.p.). During the dance, the dancer jumps out of the frame. Although he returns immediately into the camera's field of vision and starts again, Weule seemed to be unable to position his camera to take in all the space that was needed for the dance. The films suggest that Weule most likely could not pan the camera and in order to avoid incomplete performances like the one just mentioned, he seems to have directed some of the performances. Film no. VII (o.n.n.) could be one example of his directing: in this film dancers leave the frame but soon return into the camera field. Weule seems to have interrupted the performance at this stage and asked for a new beginning in order to record a complete scene. A very similar impression is given by the film in which Weule shoots his caravan (no. III, o.p.p.). To give a full impression of his military escort Weule stopped cranking the camera and ordered the troops to return to pass again in front of the camera's lens.

However, in one film Weule's technical inexperience created a remarkable aesthetic effect. Film no. II (o.p.p.) shows a group of musicians sitting in a row at some distance from the camera. People are standing behind them. After about thirty seconds, six women enter from the left of the frame. They are obviously dancing to the music and move rhythmically to the right. Their movements create a kind of a camera wipe. What gives this shot from today's perspective an aesthetic beauty is perhaps Weule's inability to control the depth of field. While the musicians are slightly out of focus, the women enter the frame clear and sharp, and in focus.

Despite the technical problems that are suggested by all the surviving film prints, reviews of his film lectures show that Weule had enough good film material to compile a film programme for his lectures.[40] The following quote from a review about a screening for the King of Saxony at the Leipzig museum in February 1907 gives an idea of the kind of film programme Weule offered:

> To give the King an impression of African technology, the lecturer showed first a blacksmith at his work. Beside the master squats the journeyman at the charcoal fire. With a fast beat he moves the pair of bellows up and down, while the master arranges the fire and only once in a while makes sure of the growing heat of the forging. Finally, it has reached a bright red heat. Picked by the pliers it quickly flies onto the (only) thorn-shaped anvil, and the hammer hastily rushes on the metal until it needs to be heated up again. Other pictures show dances and sing-along games from the male puberty festivities. Into the circle of squatting and standing spectators enters a masker dressed as a woman showing partly a festive, partly a funny solo dance. This is followed by a rhythmic heaving round dance of the women's choir that accompanies itself with its own singing. A third picture shows wild Men-Ugoma. Masked with leopard furs, feathers and dancing rattles they jump singing to the beat of the Ugoma drums onto the dancing square. They continue jumping, jump over each other, running on their hands. Suddenly resounds a marching song in verses, a dance, wedding and working song, also melancholic but all the more melodious.[41]

The review shows that Weule was using the camera to shoot primarily kinetic events, such as rituals or dances, quite similar to the work of the Austrian anthropologist Rudolf Pöch, who remarked that 'dances are the simplest and most effective subjects for cinematography and the best means for practicing the medium since they enable one to record what is most visual and effective when reproduced'.[42]

In her analysis of dance in early German ethnographic films, Valerie Weinstein points out the contemporary significance of dance for the understanding of primitive cultures.[43] Dance was considered the first human art form, and Wilhelm Wundt, Weule's colleague in Leipzig, regarded dance's original function as an expression of human spiritual life that has been lost to civilized man. Long shots of kinetic events such as dances therefore presented 'the royal road to the study of the heart of unique and the evolutionary origin of cultures'.[44] Shooting dances such as the Men-Ugoma from a certain distance, as is the case in a medium-long shot, turned dances into visual spectacles and invited the audience to study the image in all its detail.[45] Moreover, the lack of any critical remarks in the Leipzig review about blurred images or incomplete scenes in Weule's films suggests that the chance to see for the first time African people not in an artificial setting like in a Völkerschau but in their authentic environment compensated for any technical problems.

By the end of his expedition in November 1906, Weule had collected about 1,640 ethnographic objects, taken thirteen hundred photographs, recorded thirty-nine phonograms and shot forty films:[46]

> I have acquired not one piece in the collection without having seen a demonstration of its use, every archer showed his skill, every potter manufacturing her product before my eyes ... This way all crucial stages have been recorded with the pencil, the photo camera or on film, the name, method of production, the material ... I have been standing for hours in the heaviest crowds of people; songs, singing and dances textually recorded and interlinearily translated.[47]

Weule seemed to be rather satisfied with the cinematographic results of his expedition. In his book *Native Life in East Africa*, through which Weule addressed a more general public, he remarks:

> It certainly does not dispose one to cheerfulness, when Ernemann writes from Dresden that my last consignment of films has again proved a failure; but I have give over worrying over things of this sort ... Besides, I know, by those I have developed myself, that about two thirds of my thirty-eight cinematograph records must be fairly good, or at least good to use, and that is a pretty fair proportion for a beginner. Over twenty such imperishable documents of rapidly disappearing tribal life and customs – I am quite disposed to congratulate myself.[48]

In contrast to Weule's optimism regarding the quality of his films, records from his expedition show that during that time an intense debate about the films' quality had already arisen. In October Ernemann let Weule know that half of his twenty-nine films were overexposed and had not been smoothly cranked.[49] Weule did not blame himself for this poor result but the defective construction of the apparatus. According to him, amateur cinematography was still in its beginnings.[50] Back in Germany Weule tried to blame Ernemann for the company's lack of interest in improving the films' quality, but, according to Ernemann, only twelve films were of a quality suitable to be projected. Ernemann, however, offered to also develop those films that were of inferior quality.[51] Before March, Weule received another ten films from Dresden. He still disagreed with Ernemann's opinion about the quality of the rest of the films; Ernemann defended its judgment and explained in March:

> As for the films, you just have lower demands for your pictures than we (and our operator) have. Consequently, you like what we consider insufficient. It is just a matter of a point of view. We are sending back as you wished the rest of your negatives, which we think are not worth making into positives. In the pleasant hope that with this explanation your grim mood has calmed down[52]

The following day Weule received the package with seventeen undeveloped films. Unsatisfied with Ernemann's decision, Weule selected five films he considered acceptable and sent them back to Dresden. Though the outcome of the discussion between Weule and Ernemann about the films' quality is not known – the expedition file included only documents up until March 1907 – the correspondence shows that Weule tried hard to avoid the association of his film expedition with his personal failings as a filmmaker.

Ethnographic or 'Piquant' Films?

Weule's paying of large fees to Africans or the colonial authorities for 'assistance' could not always convince people to perform for Weule.[53] The Africans' fear of the film camera was quite similar to their fear of the phonograph. While many of the Africans were already familiar with the photo camera, the film camera was still considered a 'strange machine':

> The cinematograph is a thing utterly outside their comprehension. It is an *nchini*, a machine, like any other which the *mzungu*, the white man, has brought into the country – and when the said white turns a handle on the little black box , counting at the same time, in a monotonous rhythm,

'Twenty-one, twenty-two, twenty-one, twenty-two,' the native may be pleasantly reminded of the droning measures which he is accustomed to chant at his work; but what is to be the result of the whole process he neither knows nor cares.[54]

In addition to popular stories in which Africans believed that the camera would steal their souls, Weule was confronted with the problem that some Africans believed that the operator would see the people naked.[55] Although Weule expressed his anger about this 'rumor' that could be traced to a 'mean African' who, according to Weule, made the natives timid and reserved, the popularity of semi-ethnographic books in Germany at that time shows that the Africans' resistance to being photographed or filmed was not without reason. Photographers often demanded that the Africans get undressed in front of the camera. Max Weiss's *Die Völkerstämme im Norden Deutsch-Ostafrikas* (The Tribes in the North of German East Africa) (1910) or C.H. Stratz's *Die Rassenschönheit des Weibes* (Female Racial Beauty) (1901) are examples of the exploitation of African people for pornographic views.[56]

It is not known whether Weule demanded similar performances from African women, but he had an academic interest in the female African. One of the most important research projects on his expedition was the study of male and female puberty festivities, which he documented extensively with the film camera and the phonograph. On several occasions he had the chance to take photographs of the artificial modification of the female labia;[57] another time Weule was 'fixed to a spot by a sight' he had often heard of, the 'large keloids' on the women's thighs, which he could study during the traditional dance, the *ikoma*: 'With swift gestures the bright-coloured draperies fly up, leaving legs and hips entirely free, the feet move faster, and with a more vivacious and rapid motion the dancers now circle round one another in pairs'.[58]

In his study on anthropology in imperial Germany, Andrew Zimmerman points out the close relationship and narrow margin between the pornographic and the anthropological gaze of nude photographs in the collection of the Berlin Anthropological Society. The difference between the scholar's scientific interest and the public's *Schaulust* (voyeurism) was finally the scholar's ability to take 'all anthropological facts in a single, summarizing glance'[59] and to see nudity from an anthropological point of view rather than a pornographic one. Weule was certainly not interested in producing cheap pornographic pictures, but his films also seemed to be informed by this kind of double gaze and produced a surplus of erotic views that could be exploited commercially outside the academic field. A bill from Ernemann in Dresden for the development of three films called the films *'picante Diapositiv Films'* (piquant positive films).[60] This labelling was usually reserved for erotic films that were shown during so-called *Herrenabende* (gentlemen's evenings). It is possible that Ernemann was thinking of such films as well when it requested copies and the distribution rights for some of Weule's films?[61]

Notes

1. E. de Brigard, 'The History of Ethnographic Film,' in P. Hockings (ed.), *Principles of Visual Anthropology*, 2nd edn, Berlin, New York: Mouton de Gruyter, 1995, 13.
2. W. Fuhrmann, 'First Contact: The Beginning of Ethnographic Filmmaking in Germany, 1900–1930', *History of Anthropology Newsletter*, 2007, 34(1): 3–9; W. Fuhrmann, 'Ethnographic film practices in silent German cinema', in J.A. Bell, A.K. Brown and R.J. Gordon (eds), *Expeditions, Anthropology and Popular Culture: Reinventing First Contact (1914-1939)*, Washington, DC: The Smithsonian Institution Scholarly Press, 2013, 41–54.
3. Karl Weule seems to have offered his film lectures through individual contracts with the DKG's branches. Between 1907 and 1909 he held lectures at the following branches: Breslau, Hamburg, Braunschweig, Nuremberg, Munich, Strasbourg, Halle, Dresden and Düsseldorf. See entries in *DKZ* and Archiv des Museums für Völkerkunde zu Leipzig (henceforth cited as AMVL), file: C 17 AF.
4. Griffiths, *Wondrous Difference*, 128.
5. Ibid., 123.
6. M. Taureg, 'The Development of Standards for Scientific Films in German Ethnography', *Studies in Visual Communication*, 1983, 9(1): 19–29.
7. Tobing Rony, *The Third Eye*, 23.
8. Regnault quoted in Tobing Rony, *The Third Eye*, 48.
9. S. Hake, 'The Cinema Reform Movement', in S. Hake, *The Cinema's Third Machine. Writing on Film in Germany 1907–1933*, Lincoln: University of Nebraska Press, 1993, 27–42.
10. G. Melcher, 'Von der lebenden Photographie und dem Kino-Drama', *Der Kinematograph*, 17 February 1909.
11. H.H. Diederichs, 'Frühgeschichte deutscher Filmtheorie. Ihre Entstehung und Entwicklung bis zum Ersten Weltkrieg', Habilitationsschrift, Goethe University Frankfurt, 1996, 148. Retrieved 12 March 2014 from http://hb051.fh-muenster.de/subcollc/docs/fhdo/010402-000014-fruefilm.pdf.
12. Tobing Rony, *The Third Eye*, 69.
13. Günther Spannaus quoted in Tobing Rony, *The Third Eye*, 69. The IWF was closed in 2010.
14. Martin Taureg's article has in fact become the most quoted source for references on early German ethnographic film (e.g. in Tobing Rony; Griffiths and Oksiloff).
15. For a detailed discussion of the relationship between German ethnology and colonialism see A. Zimmerman, *Anthropology and Antihumanism in Imperial Germany*, Chicago, and London: University of Chicago Press, 2001.
16. W.D. Smith, 'Anthropology and German Colonialism', in A.J. Knoll and L.H. Gann (eds), *Germans in the Tropics. Essays in German Colonial History*, New York, Westport, CT and London: Greenwood Press, 1987, 45.

17. C. Essner, 'Berlins Völkerkunde-Museum in der Kolonialära', in H.J. Reichhardt (ed.), *Berlin in Geschichte und Gegenwart. Jahrbuch des Landesarchivs Berlin*, Berlin: Wolf Jobst Siedler Verlag, 1986, 67.
18. During the Hamburg South Seas Expedition members complained that some of their colleagues had bought the entire *Kulturbesitz* (cultural heritage) of a village. H. Fischer, *Die Hamburger Südsee-Expedition. Über Ethnographie und Kolonialismus*, Frankfurt: Syndikat, 1981, 98.
19. Krause quoted in M. Böhl, *Entwicklung des ethnographischen Films, Die filmische Dokumentation als ethnographisches Forschungs- und universitäres Unterrichtsmittel in Europa*, Göttingen: Edition Herodot, 1985, 55.
20. BArch, R 1001/5673–2, 95.
21. M. Gothsch, *Die deutsche Völkerkunde und ihr Verhältnis zum Kolonialismus. Ein Beitrag zur kolonialideologischen und kolonialpraktischen Bedeutung der deutschen Völkerkunde in der Zeit von 1870 bis 1975 (1945)*, Baden-Baden: Nomos Verlagsgesellschaft, 1983, 241.
22. K. Weule, *Wissenschaftliche Ergebnisse meiner ethnographischen Forschungsreise in den Südosten Deutsch-Ostafrikas. Ergänzungsheft der Mitteilungen aus den deutschen Schutzgebieten*, vol.1, Berlin, 1908, 140.
23. Hans Meyer (1858–1929) was a geographer, colonial politician and director of one of the biggest German publishing houses, the Bibliographische Institut in Leipzig.
24. H. Meyer, 'Die geographischen Grundlagen und Aufgaben in der wirtschaftlichen Erforschung unserer Schutzgebiete', in Deutscher Kolonialkongress, *Verhandlungen des Deutschen Kolonialkongresses 1902*, Berlin: Verlag Dietrich Reimer (Ernst Vohsen), 1903, 73–82.
25. H. Meyer, 'Übersicht über die Ergebnisse der Expeditionen der Landeskundlichen Kommission des Reichskolonialamtes', in Deutscher Kolonialkongress, *Verhandlungen des Deutschen Kolonialkongresses 1910*, Berlin: Verlag Dietrich Reimer (Ernst Vohsen), 1910, 5–10.
26. BArch, R 1001/6994, 14. After the dissolution of the KA in 1906 and the establishment of the RKA in 1907 the commission was renamed into Landeskundliche Kommission des Reichskolonialamtes (Geographic commission of the Imperial Colonial Office).
27. Meyer, 'Übersicht über die Ergebnisse der Expeditionen', 5.
28. H. Meyer, 'Die Landeskundliche Kommission des Reichskolonialamtes', *Koloniale Rundschau. Monatsschrift für die Interessen unserer Schutzgebiete und ihren Bewohnern*, 1910, 2(12): 724.
29. Ibid., 726.
30. Anon., 'Bericht der "Kommission für die landeskundliche Erforschung der deutschen Schutzgebiete" an den Kolonialrat über ihre Tätigkeit im Rechnungsjahre 1905/06', *Mitteilungen von Forschungsreisenden und Gelehrten aus den deutschen Schutzgebieten*, 1906, 19(4): 291–94.
31. G. Blesse, 'Karl Weule als Feldforscher. (Zur wissenschaftlichen Expeditionstätigkeit Karl Weules in Südost-Tansania 1906)', Sonderdruck aus *Jahrbuch des Museums für Völkerkunde zu Leipzig*, Münster and Hamburg: LIT Verlag, 1994, 40: 155–67.
32. Karl Weule's films have not yet been identified by an ethnologist; nor has the rediscovery of his films been considered important for the historical visual record. At least one of the surviving prints (no. I, 55 seconds) could show either the ngoma or the pombe in Dar es Salaam or Lindi.
33. BArch, R 1001/5673-2, 57–60.
34. K. Weule, *Native Life in East Africa. The Results of an Ethnological Research Expedition*, trans. A. Werner, New York: D Appleton and Company, 1909, 223 (originally pub-

lished in German: K. Weule, *Negerleben in Ostafrika. Ergebnisse einer ethnologischen Forschungsreise,* Leipzig: Brockhaus, 1908).
35. BArch, R 1001/5673-2, 92.
36. Anon., 'Bericht über die landeskundlichen Expeditionen der Herren Prof. Dr. Karl Weule und Dr. Fritz Jäger in Deutsch-Ostafrika', *Mitteilungen von Forschungsreisenden und Gelehrten aus den deutschen Schutzgebieten,* 1906, 19(4): 294–304.
37. Weule regularly reported about his work to Hans Meyer and the KA. BArch, R 1001/5637-2, 57–95.
38. Weule, *Native Life in East Africa,* 178.
39. F. Krause, 'Dem Andenken Karl Weules', in Museum für Völkerkunde (Leipzig), *Jahrbuch des Städtischen Museums für Völkerkunde zu Leipzig,* Leipzig: R. Voigtländers Verlag, 1928, 9:10.
40. It is quite possible that the only reason for the surviving film prints' existence was their low quality. They were therefore used less often by Weule and perhaps stored away.
41. *Leipziger Neueste Nachrichten,* 22 February 1907.
42. R. Pöch, 'Reisen in Neu-Guinea in den Jahren 1904–1906', *Zeitschrift für Ethnologie,* 1907, 39: 398. Translation from Tobing Rony, *The Third Eye,* 65.
43. V. Weinstein, 'Archiving the Ephemeral: Dance in Ethnographic Films from the Hamburg South Seas Expedition 1908–1910', *Seminar: A Journal of Germanic Studies,* 2010, 46(3): 223–39.
44. Ibid., 228.
45. A. Griffiths, *Wondrous Difference,* 142 ff.
46. BArch, R 1001/5637-2, 80.
47. Anon., 'Bericht über die landeskundlichen Expeditionen der Herren', 303–04.
48. Weule, *Native Life in East Africa,* 385.
49. BArch, R 1001/5637-2, 86.
50. After his expedition Weule revised his view and admitted that the films' failures were the result of his limited practical training before the expedition. Weule, *Wissenschaftliche Ergebnisse,* 2.
51. AMVL: Expedition, 8 February 1907.
52. AMVL: Expedition, 20 March 1907.
53. The act of paying or having people ordered to perform traditional rituals or games in front of the camera did not seem to render the recording inauthentic for Weule. As Rudolf Pöch remarked on similar problems during his expedition, staged scenes were not less authentic because they would include exactly the same actions as would be performed if the camera were not there. Pöch, 'Reisen in Neu-Guinea in den Jahren 1904–1906', 399.
54. Weule, *Native Life in East Africa,* 34.
55. BArch, R 1001/5637-2, 86.
56. See R. Steiger and M. Taureg, 'Körperphantasien auf Reisen. Anmerkungen zum ethnographischen Akt', in M. Köhler and G. Barche (eds), *Das Aktfoto. Ansichten vom Körper im fotografischen Zeitalter. Ästhetik, Geschichte, Ideologie,* Munich and Luzern: C.J. Bucher Verlag, 1985, 116–36.
57. Anon., 'Bericht über die landeskundlichen Expeditionen der Herren', 301 ff.
58. Weule, *Native Life in East Africa,* 223.
59. Zimmerman, *Anthropology and Antihumanism,* 175.
60. AMVL: Expedition, 2 March 1907.
61. AMVL: Expedition, 28 February 1907.

Chapter 8

THE EXPEDITION IN CONTEXT

Modern German Ethnography

Karl Weule never explained why he decided to use a film camera and remarked after his expedition that he did not know about any previous successful use of a film camera in the tropics[1] and considered himself therefore a pioneer in ethnographic film fieldwork.[2] Though there exists no evidence that Rudolf Pöch and Weule had personal contact before Weule's expedition, it seems most unlikely that Weule did not know about Pöch's expedition and his use of the film camera.[3] Moreover, Weule was a colonial enthusiast, member of the DKG's Leipzig branch and subscriber to the *DKZ*. It is almost impossible that he was not familiar with Carl Müller's films from the colonies and the success of his colonial film screenings within the colonial movement. Altenburg is near Leipzig, and Weule would have been able to consult Müller whenever he wanted. It is therefore quite possible that Weule realized that he could increase the public interest in his expedition and his museum by linking them to the recent popularity of films from the colonies. The chance to promote his expedition through film could have been one reason he decided to use a film camera.

A second important aspect was that Weule conceived of film as being the most modern research tool in ethnographic observation.[4] A year before Weule's expedition, Georg Thilenius, director of the Museum for Völkerkunde, Hamburg, emphasized in a memorandum on the goals of ethnographic research the crucial role film would play in future ethnographic research.[5] The film journal *Der Kinematograph* remarked in 1907 that photography had become insufficient when it came to the study of customs of natives in totally unknown or less explored regions. It was only the film camera that could show such events in all their detail.[6] Rudolf Pöch argued in a similar fashion: He had learned about ethnographic film in Cambridge in 1902, when Alfred Cort Haddon showed him his films from the Torres-Strait expedition. Impressed by the possibilities of cinema, Pöch emphasized that, in contrast to the traditional ethnographic work for which a scholar used a pen, a sketchbook and simple instruments, modern anthropology had become more complex. Modern technologies like film promised to produce valuable new results. Cinema was able to preserve the memory of cultures that were disappearing due to the encroachment of 'civilization'. His decision to use a film camera on his expedition was therefore also made in order 'to be entirely modern'.[7]

Weule, too, placed great expectations on the film camera, the use of which, as he remarked, had only been recently established in 'exotic ethnography'.[8] His repeated emphasis on the use of the film camera in his daily work suggests that Weule considered film to be the scientific research tool that offered the most advanced technological aid in supporting the ethnographer's daily work of collecting data and obtaining information on other cultures. He thus seemed to support the physiologist Oswald Polimanti's conclusion that, through film and the possibility it offered to compare different recordings of the same ethnic groups and their dances and rituals, ethnography will become ethnology.[9]

However, the chance of promoting ethnographic research and the possibility of showing true-to-life pictures, as Weule remarked, were also important aspects for the Geographical Commission. Meyer's strong emphasis on the broadest possible exploration of the colonies could be an indication that the commission was obviously experimenting with the new medium. The fact that at least three of the first four expeditions that were coordinated or supported by the commission used a film camera suggests that, especially in its early years, the commission did not want to miss a chance to demonstrate the success of its work. Weule's mention of a geographic archive at the RKA indicates the possibility that the commission initially planned to produce results other than just published reports.[10]

Whether the commission planned to establish its own film archive is not known, but critics such as the Leipzig geographer Alfred Kirchhoff warned the commission against creating an archive for the commission's results that was made only for civil servants and specialized scholars.[11] Though Kirchhoff was thinking of printed illustrated publications that were created for a scientific purpose but were nevertheless 'gripping' for any educated person, the range of Weule's film lecture activity after his return shows that Weule (and the commission) could successfully address a very heterogeneous academic audience, such as geographers, ethnologists, teachers, physicians, medical doctors and the colonial lobby.

While the academic results of his expedition on topics such as the different initiation rituals were presented at the congress of physicians and medical doctors in Dresden in September 1907, screenings in the DKG's branches were a chance to underline the commission's work for colonization. For such screenings, films of his military escort or the colonizer's punishment of African people were probably more appropriate to foreground the colonial character of his expedition.[12] On the other hand, his more ethnographic films could illustrate Weule's scientific recommendations for a practical colonization and emphasize that research and practice continued to go 'hand in hand'.[13] Scenes of dances, rituals, games and festivities could give a general impression of native life in the colonies and point out the characteristic features of the different events. More specifically, he could show moving images of the different ethnic groups in the colony and his evaluation of these groups with regard to their loyalty to the colonial government and their chances of becoming honest workers on colonial plantations.[14]

Film and the Construction of Human Cultural History

Weule could underline with his films the use value of his expedition for the administration of the colonies, but his films also had an important function with regard to his academic interests. Weule conceived of the film camera as an instrument for archiving the vanishing customs of primitive cultures.[15] This 'salvage ethnography' approach aligned Weule's interest with that of Regnault, Haddon, Spencer or Pöch. Weule emphasized that collection and preservation are the basic elements of the ethnographer's work, undertaken so that the material culture of *Naturvölker* (primitive cultures) could continue to be presented, even after the people have become 'civilized' or extinct.[16] Each characteristic feature of the East African culture, even if it appeared inconspicuous, carried information for the reconstruction of human cultural history that had to be carefully registered and archived.[17] Film was therefore not just simple illustration but provided the ethnologist with important ethnographic data.

His interest in collecting ethnographic objects and recording ethnographic data was not limited to the preservation of other culture's characteristics. Unlike many of his fellow scholars, Weule did not belong to a specific school in ethnology theory. Weule's academic training in Leipzig and Berlin brought him into contact with two rather opposed theories in early German ethnology. Interested in establishing ethnology as the foundation for a cultural history of mankind, Weule combined in his work the evolutionist perspective of Adolf Bastian, who considered African cultures as representatives of an earlier stage in human evolution, with Ratzel's diffusionist view in which human evolution was the result of migration and people's interaction with environmental factors such as climate, flora, fauna and so on.

Being familiar with both approaches, Weule did not consider it the ethnologist's main task to concentrate on the study of material culture as many scholars did by limiting their research to the study of ethnographic artefacts. According to Weule, material culture could not be researched without considering a culture's intellectual side. The intellectual and material cultures were not different expressions of the same culture, but they influenced and conditioned each other and therefore could not be studied separately. One way to make the intellectual side visible was the study of technology. Through technology a culture could transform its intellectual energies into 'extraphysical energies'.[18] Technology presented for Weule therefore the *leitmotiv* (theme) in a culture, a signifying characteristic in a cultural history of mankind through which it finally became possible to research, explain and describe individual cultures.[19] Weule's theoretical approach suggests that, for him, filming a broad range of manufacturing techniques like forging, weaving, food preparation and fire-making or dances, along with rituals and games, provided ethnographic data of the same value as written records. In this sense the application of film in ethnographic fieldwork could be considered another medium that supplied the ethnologist with 'bricks for the construction of human cultural history'.[20]

Looking at Leo Frobenius's concept of the 'kinematographic map' in this context might help us to understand in more detail Weule's interest in film.[21] Though nothing is known about the intellectual exchange between Frobenius and Weule, Frobenius was not only the most important collector for the Leipzig museum, one who received all possible support for his expeditions from Weule, he was also familiar with ethnographic filmmaking. At least two of his four expeditions, 1907 and 1913, were equipped with a film camera. Choosing cinematography as a metaphor for his alternative approach to traditional cartography,

Frobenius' kinematographic map indicates a paradigmatic shift in the perception of culture. In his contention that cultures are continuously in motion, Frobenius offered an elaborated approach, in which Weule's understanding of culture and the Geographical Commission's interdisciplinary concept of a 'causative geography' can be grounded.

Frobenius' use of the term kinematographic map did not mean that he was particularly interested in film as a new research tool. According to Oksiloff, filmmaking was not Frobenius' primary interest but he 'regarded film as one tool among many for achieving a "kinetic" view of culture, which implies a new way for the ethnographic eye to apprehend reality'.[22] Frobenius' kinematographic approach considered any given object as meaningful 'in relation to a shifting constellation of other objects and cultural elements'.[23] For Frobenius, the kinematographic principle was a continuous *Allbeziehlichkeit* (multi-referential oscillation) between all characteristics of culture, which could finally illustrate as a whole the 'full riches of life'.[24] Since culture was continuously in motion, or kinematographic, the map had to become kinematographic as well:

> The kinematographic representation of a group of cultural forms ideally aims at summarizing all the essential characteristics of a culture. It is not a particular figure, nor any particular cultural relations, but a general relevance, in other words the full riches of life, which can intimate the meaning of the whole as an integral fabric to the reality of the human imagination, which is statically restricted by logic and abstraction.[25]

With this approach Frobenius turned against traditional approaches in ethnology, in which cultures were described in fixed classification and categorizations and represented by huge ethnographic collections in a museum's showcases. The traditional approach to cartography can be seen in the work of the Kolonial-Kartographische Institut (Colonial Cartographic Institute), for example. In 1899, in an effort to achieve a systematic registration of the colonies, it produced an enormous output of topographic maps of the colonial territories.[26] While the traditional function of maps was 'to select from the totality of the world those aspects that can serve to depict it through ordering, classifying and constructing pictures of reality',[27] Frobenius considered the map merely as a way of circumscribing culture but insufficient to describe it.[28]

Frobenius' *Atlas Africanus* is a voluminous study in the form of more than two hundred maps and commentaries that attempt to include and to preserve a fundamentally dynamic interaction between all of the major disciplines, 'including the natural sciences, theology, law and philology, and to preserve a fundamentally dynamic interaction between these different fields without privileging one over the other', as Oksiloff notes.[29] Though Frobenius' approach aimed at more than the representation of material culture and, as mentioned above, he did not consider film as the key medium to understand other cultures, the 'kinetic view' of culture seemed to be informed by an interest very similar to Meyer's multi- and interdisciplinary approach of a causative geography. Understanding culture as a continuous progression and interaction between internal and external characteristics meant that culture was no longer perceived as a permutation of ethnographic artefacts but as the dynamic interrelation of a people's intellectual and material sides.

Similar to Frobenius's emphasis on the kinetic moment in culture and the representation of culture in graphic series that made the invisible 'perceptible as a cartographic adventure',[30] film was considered a new research tool said to offer an objective view of all aspects of culture. Weule drew on this approach in his address to an academic audience at the Verein für Erdkunde (Geographic Society) in Leipzig. Aside from the emphasis on the novelty of having used a film camera in his ethnographic fieldwork, he pointed out the ethnological intentions of his expedition. Photography, phonographic recordings and filming were part of the production of an overall ethnological picture of the research area, in which all material and intellectual cultural possessions were recorded.[31] As important to Weule as film's significance for ethnology was the specific role of his films with regard to his interest in promoting his museum as a scientific but nevertheless popular institution of ethnological knowledge.

Popular Ethnology

Weule's role in German ethnology has been only marginally studied in ethnology history, but his academic reputation was based less on his role as a theoretical leader in his discipline than on his practical efforts in establishing ethnology as a new academic discipline. For this reason he had a major interest in promoting public recognition of ethnology, which also meant presenting ethnology to the broad public in a popular way. In this sense, Weule considered film to be a perfect teaching aid for the lecture hall and felt that the wide circulation of film should be supported by all means: 'Film is the demonstration tool of the lecture hall; at the same time it is the archive of the vanishing customs of our primitive races. As such, its use and circulation should be supported with all means as a long as there is still time'.³² During his expedition Weule had already reflected on the possibility of filming these peoples and combining film and phonograph recordings for making the non-East African public familiar with African customs: 'If the films are good, we will have the chance to show the non-East African through the simultaneous exhibition of film and phonograph recordings the overall picture of such a ngoma, moreover, the characteristic singing performances are thus preserved for posterity'.³³ Weule seemed to know that his films represented a unique demonstration tool that was very different in kind from the ethnographic artefacts that could usually be looked at in a museum. The exhibition of his films became an integral part of his lectures, and reviews show that wherever Weule showed films his lectures were a success.

While the success was partly the result of the spectacular character of his films, which represented the only chance for many people to see real Africans, Weule also did not seem to mind going popular in order to attract the public's interest. Weule's films included more than just ethnographic shots as the surviving print of his the military escort illustrates. His draft lecture notes reveal that other films showed his caravan as well as himself working as the *'zünftige Professor'* (proper professor) in 'wild Africa'.³⁴ A film in which Weule shot an African clown was certainly interesting from an ethnographic perspective as it represented a traditional figure in the region, but the film could also have been used as a funny intermission in a popular lecture about a scientific topic. As notes in the (incomplete) draft for Weule's lecture at the Geographic Society in Leipzig show, his lecture was a carefully structured performance of his films, slides and phono-recordings, which created a loose chronological order and narrative. The lecture finished with a phono-film exhibition showing the expedition on its return journey. Though Weule varied his film lectures according to the type of audience present, the success of his film lectures was mainly due to the fact that he did not mind presenting his scientific ethnographic expedition within a more popular framework. It therefore is not surprising that his lecture at the DKG's local branch in Nuremberg became a well-attended *'Familienabend'* (family evening).³⁵ His fascination with film as the perfect demonstration tool was noted by a reviewer of his lecture in Düsseldorf, in which the only point of criticism was that Weule showed too many films.

The reception of early ethnographic film as a phenomenon somewhere between ethnographic spectacle and popular sensationalism also characterized the films from Duke Adolf Friedrich zu Mecklenburg's first Africa expedition of 1907–09. Mecklenburg's expedition included ten scholars from eight different disciplines and corresponded to the Geographical Commission's goal of a systematic exploration. In contrast to the expedition's research results, which were published in a multi-volume publication, Mecklenburg's films were first of all a compilation of shots that foregrounded the sensational aspects of his expedition, such as jumping Watusi, cannibals, pygmies and the expedition members' ride on the Congo's dangerous rapids.

Unlike Mecklenburg, who did not tour as extensively as Weule through the German Reich, Weule was quite busy as a film lecturer, and, as records suggest, was not interested in sharing his films with other institutions, which would have meant giving control over them into the hands of others. Correspondence between the director of the Rautenstrauch-Joest-Museum for Ethnology in Cologne, Wilhelm Foy, and Weule illustrates that Weule was aware of how exceptional his material was at this time and how he wanted to keep the control over his films. In this correspondence Foy asks Weule for copies of his films to be used for screenings in the Cologne museum.

The correspondence between the two museums started in November 1905 and dealt with the organization of a lecture by Weule at the Cologne museum. After Weule's return from his expedition, he started to use his film recordings as a strong argument to renegotiate his lecture fee. While before his expedition Weule had accepted that the museum would cover travel expenses and pay a fee of one hundred marks, after his expedition Weule argued that, having spent so much money on his technical equipment, 'I must demand to my own chagrin half a blue note more'.[36] Foy was not pleased to learn about Weule's new claim of an additional fifty marks for his lecture, but Weule insisted that, if Foy did not agree to the increased fee, he either would limit his lecture to the projection of lantern slides or refuse to lecture in Cologne at all.

The continuous back and forth between Leipzig and Cologne shows the stubbornness and, as Weule remarks, Foy's 'tenaciousness' in the negotiation of getting Weule and his films to Cologne. Weule's emphasis on the 'new situation' created by his expensive technical equipment shows that he was quite aware of his position as an exceptional lecturer among his colleagues. This status was also acknowledged on the day of his lecture. The notes for the introductory speech about Weule's expedition underlined: 'The lecturer is able to show these dances in living pictures, while the phonograph reproduces the songs that were sung at this moment, for Völkerkunde this is something brand new and of high interest'. Weule's lecture at the museum was a success, but this did not put an end to the correspondence between Foy and Weule. On the contrary, it entered into a second, even more confusing, round, which was characterized by Weule's tactic of wearing Foy down in his attempts to obtain copies of the films.

According to a resolution of the Geographical Commission, other German museums could purchase Weule's films at cost price.[37] This apparently simple transaction, however, was complicated by a long and confusing correspondence between Weule in Leipzig, where the films were archived, and the RKA in Berlin, which held the rights to the films. Foy seemed to be impressed with Weule's films and considered using films for exhibition purposes in addition to the museum's phonographic listening hours. Right after Weule's lecture he contacted the RKA and asked about the conditions for obtaining copies of Weule's films.[38] While Meyer advised Weule to follow the commission's resolutions concerning the purchase of the films, Weule referred Foy back to the RKA in Berlin. In response to Foy's inquiry the RKA contacted Weule and asked him about *his* vending conditions and advised him to put the copies at Foy's disposal.[39] This time Weule could not refuse this official request, but obviously he wanted to draw the sale out for as long as possible. Weule answered a new letter from Foy by asking for more details. Foy became indignant about these delaying tactics:

> Since we do not want to use your phono- and film recordings for scientific studies but exclusively for museum purposes, we are not asking for detailed comments but are satisfied with correct information on the content and origin, quite similar to your lectures in which you presented phonograms and films without extensive explanations. With reference to the decision that we received from the colonial office we ask therefore again for the conditions and the sending of a list.[40]

Weule again did not comply with this request but only sent a list of his phonograms. In July 1908 the correspondence between Leipzig and Cologne came to an end. In a last letter, Foy indicates that the museum was just thinking about the possibility of future film screenings in the museum and wanted therefore to obtain information about the price of an apparatus and the running costs. The museum had not yet decided about the purchase of Weule's films but would reflect on this later. The reason for Foy's sudden restraint and the abrupt ending of the correspondence is not known, but Weule certainly made his contribution to the confusion that also might have influenced Foy's declining interest in Weule's films. The question that must be asked about the confusing correspondence between Foy and Weule is what interest Weule had in keeping control over his films. A possible answer is to be found in the competition between ethnological museums in Germany around 1900.

A Leipzig Ethnographic Filmarchive?

According to a resolution of the Bundesrat (Federal Council), from 1889 all ethnographic collections from expeditions to the German colonies financed by the Reich had to be handed first to the Berlin museum.[41] The resolution put the Berlin museum in a privileged hegemonic position with regard to other ethnological museums, especially non-Prussian museums like the Saxon museum in Leipzig.[42] In spite of the lack of support from Berlin, however, Weule made the Leipzig museum into the second major ethnological museum in Germany. Since 1904 it had been in the hands of the city of Leipzig, which made generous donations and gifts to the museum. The museum's continuous growth was due not only to Weule's talent in finding private investors and donors for his museum but also to the support received from the local academic environment and Saxon politics. By the turn of the century Leipzig University had developed into an intellectual centre of cultural sciences, where Karl Lamprecht, Wilhelm Wundt and Friedrich Ratzel formed the 'Leipzig Circle', the academic counterbalance to Berlin.[43] After Ratzel's death, Weule assumed his position and became the leading figure in cultural anthropology at the university, establishing the first Ph.D. programme for ethnology in Germany in 1904. Through Hans Meyer's financial support, historian Karl Lamprecht could create in 1914 the König-Friedrich-August-Stiftung, which combined Wundt, Weule and his own institute under one roof. The foundation was designed as a humanities counterbalance to the natural sciences that were grouped at the Kaiser-Wilhelm-Institute in Berlin. The Leipzig activities reveal that, as Woodruff D. Smith concludes, 'the elites of Saxon politics, business and intellectual life were usually ready to support anything that would show Saxony to advantage in comparison with Prussia'.[44] From this strong position Weule tried to fight the Berlin museum's hegemonic position. With the founding of the Geographical Commission, Weule saw the chance that the commission would change the existing resolutions in favour of a more balanced distribution of ethnographic collections.[45] His expectation was not fulfilled. Berlin maintained its hegemony, and a third of the ethnographic artefacts from his own expedition went to Berlin.[46]

While the Berlin museum certainly benefited from the requirement that expeditions hand over a certain portion of their ethnographic artefacts, the museum also suffered from the abundance of exhibition objects. It was often impossible for visitors to understand the ethnological meaning of the collections. By the turn of the century the museum's director, Adolf Bastian, noted that 'the cases are overfilled so that every instructive arrangement of the collection remains impossible'.[47] Many visitors considered the museum's disorganized display as a deliberate neglect of the public by the museum's curators, but as Zimmerman notes, the Berlin museum was actually never intended to be an institution of popular instruction or for visitors with no prior anthropological knowledge: 'If the museum were to educate the public, anthropologists maintained, it would be only by instructing teachers and other already educated people who would in turn transmit this knowledge to a wider population'.[48]

Weule was also concerned with the limited exhibition space and the continuous growth of the collections in the Leipzig museum, although the situation in Saxony did not approach the 'terrible conditions' in Berlin.[49] In contrast to the Berlin concept, Weule was very much interested in establishing a close and vivid contact with the public and fighting the image of ethnological museums as archives for curiosities.[50] In his museum he wanted to show that the 'so-called savages' that many Europeans still considered to be 'half animals' had a broad range of manufacturing techniques and a rich culture. To make the museum more popular, Weule experimented with new exhibition concepts, organized specific thematic exhibitions and offered museum tours. Revolver-stereoscopes with ethnographic pictures could be used by the viewer in the exhibition halls and were permanently occupied. Furthermore, the museum established a slide archive that could be used by local institutions.

Film screenings in the museum were another chance to get the local public interested in the museum and ethnology. Although Leipzig may not have had the advantage of being the first to choose from collections of recent expeditions, the situation seemed to be different in regard to the exploitation of Weule's films. Though the RKA held the rights to his films and the negatives were with Ernemann in Dresden, the positive prints were with Weule in Leipzig, where he could show his films whenever he liked and use them for lecture purposes. After the Geographical Commission's second expedition equipped with a film camera failed to produce useful films, Weule was the only scholar who could show ethnographic films from his expedition. After his return from Africa, Weule explained in his lecture to the city council of

Leipzig that he planned to employ his phonographic recordings and his films for lectures and courses as a part of the utilization of the museum by the general public.[51] Weule showed his films at several occasions, such as at the previously mentioned visit of the King of Saxony in February 1907. Instead of guiding the king through the museum's exhibition halls, Weule preferred to show his films. As his drafts indicate, he used the museum's ethnology courses that were open for all classes as a chance to experiment with his films for teaching purposes among the local public.[52] The museum inaugurated this new concept with two courses on the German colonies in the winter of 1908/09 and continued the offer in the winter of 1909/10.[53] The courses were rather successful and, in particular, the percentage of participants from the working class increased in these two years. Officially, film screenings were not planned to be organized for the courses but only in the future, as Weule declared at the annual conference of the German Anthropological Society in Cologne in 1910. With reference to the Cologne museum, which organized daily phonogram listening hours, Weule downplayed the role of modern media in his museum and emphasized that Leipzig was more concerned with important tasks like the making of an inventory of the ethnographic collections:

> More in the background for us are performances of phonograms and kinematograms. As far as I know, Cologne has daily performances of phonograms at a certain hour, something we cannot do in Leipzig, due to our immense expansion whose management requires all of our energies. Therefore we are satisfied to perform our cylinders and films only at lectures and in meetings of the Verein für Völkerkunde [Association for Ethnology]; as soon as times have become more calm, we will not neglect to pay more attention to this part of the programme.[54]

It is quite possible that Weule no longer planned to use film screenings in his courses, but his holding back information concerning his film experiences once again in his museum could also suggest that it was his purpose not to share his experiences with other museums and to explore the possibilities of film exclusively for the Leipzig museum. This might also explain his continued interest in film that could have been the basis for the idea of establishing a film archive for ethnographic films.

Weule never went on another ethnographic film expedition, but ethnographic films remained a major concern in his work. Weule expressed confidence in film's important role in ethnology.[55] In October 1907 the city of Leipzig supported Leo Frobenius' second German Inner Africa research expedition (*Deutsche Inner-Afrikanische Forschungsexpedition*, DIAFE) with thirty-five thousand marks. The contract with Frobenius stipulated that the museum receive prints and copies of his films, as well as photographs and phonographic recordings for the cost price.[56] In the following year, Weule's assistant, Friedrich (Fritz) Krause, went on a one-year expedition to Brazil, equipped with two photo cameras, a phonogram and a film camera. In 1909, the museum's assistant, Ernst Sarfert, was part of the expedition crew of the Hamburg South Seas Expedition. Finally in 1913, Weule sent his assistant, Paul German, to accompany Frobenius' fourth Africa expedition. On that occasion Weule emphasized in particular the significance of film on the expedition, as the exhibition of ethnographic films was 'so to speak in the air'.[57] He referred to German and Austrian museums that were going to establish a *kartell* (alliance) at the annual assembly of the German Society for Anthropology. Though the minutes of the assembly give no indication of an official initiation of this alliance, the event did not do without films.[58] On the evening of the second day, the assembly participants saw in the local cinema films from the Freiburg Molucca Expedition of 1910–12. Since Rudolf Pöch, Richard Neuhauss (Neuhauß), Karl Weule and one of the Freiburg expeditioners, Odo Deodatus Tauern, attended the annual meeting, one can suppose that these 'experienced' ethnographic filmmakers were doing more than just watching the films.

After the loss of the colonies following the First World War, Weule additionally pursued the systematic use of cinematography in ethnographic research. After the founding of his research institute for ethnology in 1914, Weule used his international contacts with scholars in the colonies and asked them to collect, photograph and film. For this he distributed questionnaires and instructions, and supplied the scholars with photo and film cameras.[59] Without having further information on Weule's relation to film one can only speculate on his influence on the growing importance of film in German ethnology, but it is possible it was his collection of ethnographic films and his anticipation of the medium's significance in ethnology that led Fritz Krause, Weule's successor in Leipzig, to call for the establishment of an ethnological and anthropological film archive at the annual meeting of the German Society for Anthropology in 1928.[60] Ethnographic films, according to Krause, represented the 'most outstanding cultural documents' and were therefore needed by ethnology as a research tool.[61] Producing cultural documents, however, required at least some technical training, a fact that most ethnographers simply ignored.

Notes

1. Weule, *Wissenschaftliche Ergebnisse*, 2.
2. Weule, *Native Life in East Africa*, 385.
3. Pöch mentions the first experiments with film in his third expedition report, which was published in May 1906. R. Pöch, 'Dritter Bericht über meine Reise nach Neu-Guinea (Neu-Süd Wales, vom 21. Juni bis 6. September 1905, Britisch-Solomoninseln und Britisch Neuguinea bis zum 31 Jänner 1906)' in *Sitzungsberichte der kaiserlichen Akademie der Wissenschaften*, 1906, 65(6): 601–15.
4. Weule, *Negerleben in Ostafrika*, 466.
5. Thilenius quoted in Fischer, *Die Hamburger Südsee-Expedition*, 94.
6. H. Ste, 'Der Kinematograph im Dienst der Völkerkunde', *Der Kinematograph*, 11 December 1907.
7. Pöch, 'Reisen in Neu-Guinea in den Jahren 1904–1906', 394.
8. Weule, *Negerleben in Ostafrika*, VII. The English translation does not include Weule's foreword but points out that so many of his films 'proved a disappointment'. Weule, *Native Life in East Africa*, XII.
9. O. Polimanti, 'Die Anwendung der Kinematographie in den Naturwissenschaften der Medizin und im Unterricht', in F.P. Liesegang (ed.), *Wissenschaftliche Kinematographie. Einschliesslich der Reihenphotographie*, Leipzig: Liesegang, 1920, 270.
10. BArch, R 1001/5637-2, 167–68.
11. *Deutscher Kolonialkongress. 1906. Verhandlungen des Deutschen Kolonialkongresses 1905*, Berlin: Verlag Dietrich Reimer (Ernst Vohsen), 30.
12. Correspondence between Weule and a medical doctor, Dr Krusius, from Berlin in 1912/13 shows that Weule at least once documented the whipping of an African on film. Krusius wanted to use Weule's films for lecture purposes. Weule agreed and advised Krusius to contact Ernemann in order to make prints. However, he would not allow the exhibition of the film about the whipping of the African. BArch, R 1001/5637-2, 180.
13. Weule, *Wissenschaftliche Ergebnisse*, 140.
14. AMVL: Expedition. Draft for the lecture at the Geographic Association Leipzig, 12 March 1907.
15. BArch, R 1001/5673-2, 57.
16. Weule, *Negerleben in Ostafrika*, 21. The English translation skips Weule's second chapter, in which he outlines his study plan. Parts of it are integrated into chapter one.
17. Weule, *Wissenschaftliche Ergebnisse*, 145–46.
18. The following discussion refers to an unfinished draft for a book project, *Völkerkunde auf dynamischer Grundlage*, which due to Weule's death in 1926 was never completed. See C. Schütze, 'Karl Weule und die Völkerkunde', master's thesis, Ludwig-Maximilians-Universität Munich, 1993, p. 20.
19. Ibid.
20. Weule, *Wissenschaftliche Ergebnisse*, 145.
21. L. Frobenius, *Karten als Sinnbilder der Kulturbewegung: Einführung in den Atlas Africanus und in das Verständnis der kinematographischen Karte*, reprint from *Atlas Africanus*, Munich, 1922. Frobenius's approach is discussed in more detail in Oksiloff, *Picturing the Primitive*, 99–116.
22. Ibid., 100. I will continue using the German spelling 'kinematographic' in order to avoid a misunderstanding with film or cinema and to emphasize Frobenius's focus on the kinetic aspect of culture.

23. Ibid., 103.
24. Frobenius, *Karten als Sinnbilder der Kulturbewegung*, 25.
25. Ibid.. Translation as quoted in Oksiloff, *Picturing the Primitive*, 100.
26. See I.J. Demhart, *Die Entschleierung Afrikas. Deutsche Kartenbeiträge von August Petermann bis zum Kolonialkartographischen Institut*, Gotha: Klett Perthes, 2000.
27. E. Hooper-Greenhill, *Museums and the Interpretation of Visual Culture*, London: Routledge, 2000, 17.
28. Frobenius, *Karten als Sinnbilder der Kulturbewegung*, 23.
29. Oksiloff, *Picturing the Primitive*, 109.
30. Frobenius, *Karten als Sinnbilder der Kulturbewegung*, 24.
31. AMVL, C 17 AF: draft for the lecture at the Verein für Erdkunde, Leipzig, 12 March 1907.
32. Weule, *Negerleben in Ostafrika*, VII.
33. BArch, R 1001/5673-2, 57.
34. Ibid., 86.
35. *Fränkischer Kurier. Nürnberg*, 10 March 1908.
36. The correspondence between Karl Weule and Wilhelm Foy from 1905 until 1908 is archived at the Historical Archive of the City of Cologne, file 614, no. 364.
37. This is mentioned in a letter from Meyer to the director of the Rautenstrauch-Joest-Museum. BArch, R 1001/5637-2, 141.
38. Ibid., 140.
39. AMVL: Expedition, RKA to Weule, 4 May 1908.
40. AMVL: Expedition, Foy to Weule, 27 May 1908.
41. Cf. Essner, 'Berlins Völkerkunde-Museum', 65–94.
42. The Deutsche Kolonialmuseum was no real competitor to the Berlin Völkerkunde Museum since it received no subsidies from the state. See Essner, 'Berlins Völkerkunde-Museum', 84.
43. I am borrowing this term from Woodruff D. Smith, who points out that the label 'Leipzig Circle' implies a degree of coherence and organization that is not really justified. W.D. Smith, *Politics and the Sciences of Culture in Germany 1840–1920*, New York and Oxford: Oxford University Press, 1991, 204.
44. Ibid., 205.
45. K. Weule, 'Der Stand der ethnographischen Forschung in unsern Kolonien', in Deutscher Kolonialkongress, *Verhandlungen des Deutschen Kolonialkongresses 1905*, Berlin: Reimer, 1906, 25.
46. Blesse, 'Karl Weule als Feldforscher', 166.
47. Adolf Bastion quoted in Zimmerman, *Anthropology and Antihumanism in Imperial Germany*, 191.
48. Zimmerman, *Anthropology and Antihumanism in Imperial Germany*, 191.
49. K. Weule, 'Die praktischen Aufgaben der Völkermuseen auf Grund Leipziger Erfahrungen', *Korrespondenzblatt der Deutschen Gesellschaft für Anthropologie, Ethnologie und Urgeschichte*, 1910, 41(9–12): 74.
50. K. Weule, 'Die nächsten Aufgaben und Ziele des Leipziger Völkerkundemuseums', in Städtisches Museum für Völkerkunde (Leipzig), *Jahrbuch des Städtischen Museums für Völkerkunde zu Leipzig*, Leipzig: R. Voigtländers Verlag, 1910, 3: 151–74.
51. AMVL: C 17 AF, lecture to the Rat und Stadtverordnete der Stadt Leipzig, 3 April 1907.
52. AMVL: C 17 AF, draft for ethnology course 1908/09.
53. Weule, 'Die nächsten Aufgaben und Ziele des Leipziger Völkerkundemuseums', 169.
54. Weule, 'Die praktischen Aufgaben der Völkermuseen auf Grund Leipziger Erfahrungen', 76.

55. The correspondence with Krusius shows that Weule was also generally interested in collecting films (see footnote 12). Krusius proposed an exchange of films to Weule; if Weule sent him his expedition film, Krusius would send him his films from Latin America. BArch, R 1001/5673-2, 180.
56. Stadtarchiv Leipzig, Akten des Museums für Völkerkunde, 1907, Kap. 31., No. 12(5), 120.
57. Stadtarchiv Leipzig, Akten des Museums für Völkerkunde, 1903, Kap. 31., No. 12(8), 200.
58. K. Hagen, 'XLIV. Allgemeine Versammlung der Deutschen Anthropologischen Gesellschaft in Nürnberg', *Korrespondenz-Blatt der Deutschen Gesellschaft für Anthropologie, Ethnologie und Urgeschichte*, 1913, 44(8/12): 61–134.
59. O. Reche, 'Karl Weule', in O. Reche (ed.), *In Memoriam Karl Weule. Beiträge zur Völkerkunde und Vorgeschichte*, Leipzig: R. Voigtländers Verlag, 1929, 10.
60. G. Thilenius (ed.), *Tagungsbericht der deutschen anthropologischen Gesellschaft. Bericht über die 50. Allgemeine Versammlung der Deutschen Anthropologischen Gesellschaft in Hamburg vom 1.-13. August 1928,* Hamburg: Friederichsen, de Gruyter & Co. 1929, 67.
61. Fritz Krause quoted in Böhl, *Entwicklung des ethnographischen Films*, 79.

Chapter 9

FILMING IN THE COLONIES

Training and Improvisation

Karl Weule's experiences with the film camera show that making films in the colonies was not an easy task. In contrast to fiction filmmaking in a safe studio setting, outdoor filming was more difficult and even more so when filming in the tropics, where extreme climate conditions made it almost impossible to predict the positive outcome of a shoot.[1] Reports in technical articles, instructions and first-hand information from 'colonial filmmakers' illustrate that early filmmaking in the tropics was a complex technical endeavour. Shooting under extreme climate conditions not only required the proper technical equipment but often the operators' talent for improvisation.

The study of filmmaking in the colonies suggests that most of the filmmakers were familiar with the films of their filmmaking colleagues. They often knew each other and exchanged their experiences. The discourse that started among colleagues was designed to improve filmmaking in the tropics, shifting towards the use of professional film equipment and overcoming the initial problems of the amateur. In March 1904 the *DKZ* reported the advantages of using a film camera on a trip, which would soon become as popular as the photo camera. Filming was much closer to life and thus considered to have a greater value for the traveller and the audience; the film image conveyed a much fuller idea than did a photograph.[2] The type of camera that was recommended for the travelling film amateur was the Ernemann Amateur-Aufnahme-Kino. The model existed in two different versions at this time. The 1903-produced Amateur-Aufnahme-Kino I used a 15 m magazine for forty seconds recording time. It had a claw mechanism and could also be used as a projector. The 1904 Kino II ran with a 50 m magazine and had a Maltese cross gear. Like the earlier model it could also be used as a projector.[3] Both cameras were made for 17.5 mm film (frame size 10x15 mm), with centre perforation. The small size, weight and the easy handling of the Kino I were important features that convinced Weule to choose this type of camera. The price of 150 marks for the camera was moderate and not more expensive than a normal photo camera. Though the Amateur-Aufnahme-Kino was often mentioned and recommended by different camera handbooks, the camera nevertheless had the disadvantage that the 17.5 mm film material could not be projected in public cinemas.[4]

The correspondence between Weule and Ernemann shows that the projection of his films was indeed a problem. The Amateur-Aufnahme-Kino was not designed for projection in large lecture halls; the 27 mm lens was designed for home use only. Only a week after Weule received his projection equipment, he had to order a stronger lens (75 mm) and a lamp that would project an image of 3.60 m in diameter over a distance of 20 m.[5] However, even with the new lens, Weule could not produce satisfactory images to accompany lectures in large halls. In December 1907 a report in *Der Kinematograph* on one of Weule's lectures at the Breslau concert hall notes that even though his projection created a sharp and brilliant image that could be seen by everybody in the hall, a larger image would have been better.[6] The review in *Der Kinematograph* concludes by indicating that Richard Neuhauss was also going to use the Ernemann model on his next expedition. Neuhauss, however, was not convinced by film cameras that were using the unusual format of 17.5 mm. The centre perforation created an unstable image during the recording and the projection.[7] Without naming the Ernemann camera or commenting on Weule's problems, Neuhauss warned against buying *Schundware* (cheap trashy products) for expedition purposes, which were not even worth the transport.[8] This does not mean that photographers considered Weule's achievements insignificant. The *Photographische Unterhaltungsbuch*, a technical guide that was mainly addressed to the photographic amateur, explicitly referred to Weule's presentation at the congress of scientists and physicians in 1907. It underlined that Weule's research results with his films could have never been achieved in the same way with photographs.[9] The limited projection capacity of the Ernemann Kino was not necessarily a disadvantage, but the camera-projector function was sufficient only for home entertainment. However, this was not what Neuhauss or Weule had in mind. In conveying ethnological knowledge to the public, professional cameras offered better chances for the film's exploitation in non-private circles.

Neuhauss favoured 35 mm cameras that guaranteed smooth projection and therefore were more comfortable to the viewers' eyes.[10] A camera that met these requirements was the Kine-Messter, which had been produced since 1900 by Oskar Messter. Due to its size, 20x14x14 cm, and a weight of 3 kg, the camera was still handy for an amateur but required professional 35 mm film material. The Kine-Messter was used by Carl Georg Schillings in 1903, by the Duke of Mecklenburg on his first Inner Africa expedition in 1908 and by Neuhauss himself on his expedition to New Guinea in 1908–10.[11] The Kine-Messter had a magazine for only 20 m of film that made around one minute of recording time, but, according to Neuhauss, it was sufficient for the traveller's needs. Rudolf Pöch argued similarly, considering shorter films the better choice. The 'choreographic motif' of dances and songs were in most cases so short that longer filming would just record the repetition of the same element.[12]

The decision to become more professional also was a question of money. In contrast to the Ernemann Aufnahme-Kino, the Kine-Messter was no cheap camera. The price for the tropic model, made of teakwood instead of mahogany, was 415 marks.[13] Additional costs included a good lens and the film processing.[14] These combined costs show that even the basic film equipment cost around forty-five hundred marks, a sum that was a considerable investment for an amateur. However, money and good equipment did not guarantee the success of a film shooting in the tropics.

In contrast to Karl Weule's initial opinion that filming did not need much practice, Richard Neuhauss strongly recommended that one practice filming under different lighting conditions and test the material before the trip in order to avoid unexpected surprises later. Like Neuhauss, filmmaker Hans Schomburgk reports that it was the lack of training that produced the disappointing results of his first film expedition and the small output of usable film from the Duke of Mecklenburg's first inner-Africa expedition, although he was using the best equipment available at that time.[15] That even photography required some technical training and experience can be seen from an anecdote about the Duke of Mecklenburg's training with flashing powder in the spring of 1907. While experimenting with 500 g of flashing powder on a barracks square, Mecklenburg blew out sixty windows in the barracks.[16]

Filming was more than pointing the camera at the scene and cranking. Neuhauss emphasized the importance of counting the revolutions while cranking the camera in order to know how many metres of film were left in the magazine. For example, it took 125 revolutions to unroll the 20 m magazine of the Kine-Messter.[17] Weule did not seem to know this simple rule and only realized after his expedition that every shooting needed at least a minimum of orientation, timing and staging. Due to his lack of practice and timing he often missed important actions and complained that 'with a devilish malice the last end of film whirred off exactly at that moment when something thrilling at festivities and dances of the Negroes was expected'.[18] As a consequence he often had to stop in the middle of an action in order to crawl into his changing bag and switch films, which, as he adds, nevertheless was an interesting and strange ritual for the Africans to watch. As important as counting the revolutions was learning to adjust the recording speed to the lighting conditions and the movements of the recorded object. Slow-moving objects could be recorded with fewer revolutions than fast-moving objects.[19] For this the operator had to control the field of vision. To avoid unexpected surprises Neuhauss did not recommended following movements but filming movement within the camera's field. Even panning with a tripod had to be learned.

A final important preparation that would increase the chances of obtaining suitable films was to carry sufficient film stock on an expedition.[20] Neuhauss suggested that the operator of a Kine-Messter should at least carry one hundred films – about 2,000 m. A large amount of exposed material increased the chance of being able to edit afterwards only the best shots.[21] While an amateur might carry 2,000 m of film, professional operators travelled with thousands of metres and more than one camera. Octave Fière, Paul Graetz's operator, who will be discussed in the following chapter, carried two cameras, two tripods, five lenses and 10,000 m of film, a quantity that due to its weight was spread over fourteen different stops on the expedition route.[22] Almost the same amount of film was used by Georg Furkel, the operator of the Deutsch Bioscop in the DSWA.[23]

Technical training could solve many problems beforehand, but the tropical climate could hardly be controlled and often demanded the operators' talent for improvisation on location. For all filmmakers the extreme climate conditions represented a major problem and presented a constant risk for the camera and the sensitive film material. Furkel reports that he had to constantly clean his camera because of the fine desert sand in DSWA.[24] Since early film cameras were primarily made of wood, they often started to warp and crack from heat and humidity. Unprofessional packing totally destroyed the camera that was to have been used on the third expedition of the Geographical Commission to Cameroon.[25] Schomburgk remembered that cracks in the cameras were repaired with sealing wax, and the cameras were wrapped in banana leaves in order to protect them from the sun. The wrapping, however, heated the cameras up during daytime so that the lacquer started melting.[26] The wrapping of the camera was particularly dangerous as it affected the precision working of the lens. It was therefore necessary that the operator always control the focus. Schomburgk warned against filming against the horizon or at high noon since the shimmering of the hot air on the horizon was often misunderstood during projection as a defect of the films. Secondly, shots that were taken at high noon did not provide enough contrast and shadows for the image.[27]

Another major problem was that the tropics do not always have the same light intensity throughout the year. The light was much weaker during the drought than during the rainy period. For that reason Schomburgk advised the use of a small aperture and long exposure time. This was not a contradiction but resulted from his experience with the fading effect in the tropical heat. In this case it was almost impossible to develop the films back home because the images on the negative had been erased through the weeks of transport in the humid heat.[28] According to Schomburgk, the films could be reused a second time for shooting. To compensate for the fading effect, Schomburgk on his second expedition to Togo in the summer of 1913 started to overexpose the material by up to 50 per cent.[29] For the long transport, Schomburgk constructed cooling boxes by pouring ashes between double-bottom boxes. At night the boxes were opened in order to trap the cold air to combat the daytime heat.[30]

Low quality was not necessarily a reason for limiting a film lecture only to the best films. Reviews of Carl Müller's film lectures show that not all his films were perfect, and the review of *Eine Expedition in Deutsch-Ost-Afrika* (An Expedition in German East Africa) (Eclipse, 1911), which was shown in German cinemas, suggests that the content could often make up for the poor quality of the film:

> An expedition in German East Africa. It should be mentioned beforehand, that through the decaying influences of the tropical climate the film has not turned out as it should have given the film's relevance. The spots on the positive are from the negative and are due to the effects of bacteria and the weather. Nevertheless the film that depicts the march of a frontier survey expedition to Ruanda shows extremely interesting im-

ages from the life on such an expedition in our oldest colony. In Indian file the convoy of porters, of which every single porter can carry an enormous load, has to move through a very rough ground covered with grass and bushes as high as a man and it is no surprise to hear that on a daily march one does not cover more than ten to twelve kilometres. The film shows other scenes from camp life, African wrestlers and women preparing flour. Despite the defects we are convinced that due to its interesting content the film will find good friends.[31]

The review shows that the more the operator left the safe infrastructure in order to explore the interior of the continent, the greater the risk he would return with faded or damaged negatives. One strategy to avoid this risk was to develop the films on location, which also had the advantage of providing immediate feedback about the film's quality. This was, for example, recommended by Weule after his expedition.[32] As he remarked, storing the films in boxes for a long time, the transportation of the films over a long distance, bacteria or electric discharge represented too many risks. Even if the processing of films on the spot was not without problems, the operator still had the chance to repeat the shot on the following day if necessary. A laboratory in Africa could have a variety of guises. Schomburgk used a double-walled tent as a darkroom; Octave Fière, Paul Graetz's operator, a hut made of grass; and Robert Schumann a cold cellar. But even with perfect conditions like those in a cold cellar, a positive outcome in film processing was not guaranteed, as Schumann's experiences show. In one of his books Hans Schomburgk remembers that Schumann could not prevent the emulsion layer from coming off the nitrate:

> Here at the coast Schumann has equipped a small print lab in an old Arab-cellar with thick walls. The room was relatively cool and as ice was available the water could be cooled down to a quite low temperature. That way the processing could be done quite well. The film was soaked and then stretched on the drying drum [*Trockentrommel*]. Two calm and skilled moors started to turn the drum and then the tragedy happened before my eyes and happened again with almost every repetition of the turning of the drum. Pieces of the coating came loose from the film and slapped against the wall. In nightmarish dreams I still hear this ugly sound: 'Slip-slop' and see the pieces of the coating flying.[33]

Similar to Schumann's experiences with developing his films, Neuhauss remarked that the task of film development was the only work on his expedition that he often physically was not up to.[34] However, Schumann seems to have learned from his mistakes. Reviews of films that he shot between 1911 and 1913 and sold later through his film com-

Figure 9.1. Robert Schumann and his operator in German East Africa (after 1911). Source: Deutsche Jagdfilm-Gesellschaft. 1916. *Aus der afrikanischen Wildnis: Jagd- und Reisestudien des Forschungsreisenden Robert Schumann*. Berlin, p. 8.

pany, the Deutsche Jagd-Film-Gesellschaft (DJFG, German Hunting Film Company), do not mention any technical problems.

Ethnographic filmmaking in the colonies is part of the history of colonial cinematography. The colonies provided an important research area for German ethnographers that scholars hoped to explore with the most modern research tools available at that time. Using a film camera increased the public reception of such expeditions and promised to be the most accurate technique in ethnographic observation. Even though ethnology tried to downplay the discipline's active involvement in German colonialism, ethnographers considered their research an important contribution to the better administration of the colonies, and film was used to support this discourse.[35] The case study on Karl Weule, his ethnographic film expedition to the German East African colony and his continued interest in film is only a first provisional case study for a historiography of German ethnographic filmmaking, in which Weule must be considered a key figure. Though Weule was not a typical representative of the diffusionist school in German ethnology, his academic training suggests that he also conceived of film as an important medium for the exploration of foreign cultures. Similar to the cinema reform movement's emphasis on film as a didactic medium for public education, Weule's efforts to promote ethnological knowledge among the public seem to confirm German ethnographers' particular interest in film as a didactic medium. From today's perspective it is hard to imagine why anyone would go through all the moments of disappointment, technical drawbacks and unexpected surprises that were inherent to the experience of filming in the tropics a century ago. However, a sound knowledge of the apparatus and a solid training in filming were the most important prerequisites for success, and good films were guaranteed an eager public back home.

Colonial propaganda, amateur footage or ethnographic film: the last three parts have touched on rather different representations of the colonies and aspects of colonial cinematography. Though different in what they depicted, common to all of these films was their exhibition in the context of voluntary colonial or academic associations. The non-commercial exhibition context characterizes an important aspect in the history of colonial cinematography. Many other colonial films that were produced in the colonies were shot by commercial film companies and shown in commercial cinemas. The following parts, therefore, consider the role of colonial films in commercial venues and the development of colonial cinematography up to the end of the First World War.

Notes

1. This is corroborated by Hans Sachers' accounts of his expedition in 1913. Many film companies did not want to support his expedition because the money required for a single expedition to Africa was enough to produce several more profitable studio-filmed dramas. H. Sachers, 'Der Kolonialfilm', *Afrika Nachrichten*, 14 May 1921, 94. Sachers's expedition will be discussed in the next chapter.
2. Hübner, 'Der Kinematograph in der Ausrüstung des Reisenden', *DKZ*, 24 March 1904, 113–14.
3. P. Göllner, *Ernemann Cameras: Die Geschichte des Dresdener Photo-Kino-Werks*, Hückelhoven: Wittig Fachbuchverlag, 1995, 245.
4. Later camera books recommended the Ernemann Model A and Model B, which both used 35 mm material and were produced in 1908 and 1910 respectively. The Model A was later used by Hans Schomburgk on his expedition to Togo. Cf. H. Schomburgk, *Von Mensch und Tier und etwas von mir*, Berlin: Wijomkow-Verlagsanstalt, 1947, 134.
5. AMVL: Expedition, Ernemann to Weule, 4 March 1907.
6. H. Ste., 'Der Kinematograph im Dienste der Völkerkunde', *Der Kinematograph*, 1907, 3.

7. R. Neuhauss, 'Der Kinematograph', *Photographische Rundschau und Photographisches Centralblatt*, 1907, 21: 273.
8. R. Neuhauss, 'Der Kinematograph auf wissenschaftlichen Reisen', *Photographische Rundschau und photographisches Centralblatt*, 1906, 20: 291. In this respect Weule was a rather inexperienced filmmaker compared to Carl Müller, who had had some practice in filming and travelled with technical equipment whose value exceeded the expenses of a normal film amateur.
9. A. Parzer-Mühlbacher, *Photographisches Unterhaltungsbuch*, Berlin: Verlag Gustav Schmidt, 1910, 277.
10. Neuhauss, 'Der Kinematograph', 273.
11. O. Messter, *Mein Weg mit dem Film*, Berlin: Max Hesse, 1936, 47.
12. Pöch, 'Reise in Neu-Guinea in den Jahren 1904–1906', 396.
13. C. Ilgner and D. Linke, *Unsichtbare Schätze der Kinotechnik. Kinematographische Apparate aus 100 Jahren im Depot des Filmmuseums Potsdam*, Berlin: Parthas, 2001, 31.
14. Neuhauss recommended a Zeitz lens, 7.5 mm with an aperture of f/3:5. The price for such a lens was 100–120 marks. Neuhauss, 'Der Kinematograph', 275. The film processing of 2,000 m of film cost about four thousand marks (two thousand for the negative print and two thousand for the positive print). R. Neuhauss, 'Neuere Photographische Hilfsmittel für den Forschungsreisenden', *Zeitschrift für Ethnologie*, 1907, 39(4): 970.
15. H. Schomburgk, *Zelte in Afrika. Eine autobiographische Erzählung*, Berlin: R. Hobbing, 1931, 365.
16. Neuhauss, 'Neuere Photographische Hilfsmittel für den Forschungsreisenden', 969.
17. Ibid., 970.
18. Weule, *Wissenschaftliche Ergebnisse*, 2.
19. Neuhauss, 'Der Kinematograph', 275.
20. Schomburgk's first expedition shows that this was no guarantee of success. Inexperienced as he and his colleagues were, only one sixth (500 of 3,000 metres) of the material proved satisfactory. H. Schomburgk, *Mein Afrika*, Leipzig: Verlag Deutsche Buchwerkstätten, 1928, 271.
21. Neuhauss, 'Der Kinematograph', 275.
22. P. Graetz, *Im Motorboot quer durch Afrika. Vom Indischen Ozean zum Kongo*, Berlin: Braunbeck & Gutenberg Aktiengesellschaft, 1912, 76. All of the film equipment was supplied by Éclair.
23. Furkel, 'Film vor 30 Jahren', 12.
24. Ibid., 11.
25. K. Hassert, 'Vorläufiger Bericht über Einige Ergebnisse der Kamerun-Expedition 1907/08 des Reichs-Kolonialamtes', *Geographische Zeitschrift*, 1908, 14(11): 628.
26. Schomburgk, *Von Mensch und Tier und etwas von mir*, 138.
27. Ibid., 137.
28. R. Neuhauss, 'Kinematographische und photographische Aufnahmen aus Deutsch-Neuguinea', *Zeitschrift für Ethnologie*, 1911, 43(1): 136.
29. H. Schomburgk, *Von Mensch und Tier und etwas von mir*, 135–37.
30. Ibid., 138. Paul Graetz, on the other hand, reports that the film cans, in which the negatives were wrapped in silver foil, were embedded in cork in soldered pewter cases that had to be opened with a can opener. The cases in turn were stored in wooden boxes. Graetz, *Im Motorboot quer durch Afrika*, 79.
31. *Der Kinematograph*, 8 November 1911.
32. Weule, *Wissenschaftliche Ergebnisse*, 3.
33. Schomburgk, *Von Mensch und Tier und etwas von mir*, 133.

34. Neuhauss, 'Kinematographische und phonographische Aufnahmen aus Deutsch-Neuguinea', 136.
35. In this respect, Manfred Gothsch considers ethnology's emphasis on its usefulness for German colonialism as merely a marketing strategy. Gothsch, *Die deutsche Völkerkunde,* 268. Hans Fischer makes the same point. Ethnology used colonialism's interests for its own purposes rather than vice versa. Fischer, *Die Hamburger Südsee-Expedition,* 12.

PART IV

TOURISM, ENTERTAINMENT AND COLONIAL IDEOLOGY

Chapter 10

COLONIAL FILMS IN PUBLIC CINEMA

The failure of the DKG's Kinematographenkampagne was connected to the boom in Germany's film industry around 1906/07 and the DKG's structural incapability of offering a competitive alternative to screenings in public cinemas. Together with the increase in the number of cinemas from forty in 1905 to more than three thousand in 1912, film viewing became a new public leisure activity.[1] The initial shop cinema (*Ladenkino*), usually a former shop or pub converted into a projection room, became replaced by more comfortable film theatres that offered a luxurious ambience to the film-viewing audience.

Film programmes in public cinemas at that time were still copying the variety's programme structure with a loose dramaturgy of tension and relief, but by the First World War audiences had become familiar with watching longer films and longer programmes. The growing popularity of cinema as a new cultural industry demanded a continuous supply of new films that resulted in an increase in film production, including colonial films. However, in contrast to previous years, fiction films started to dominate the film programmes. The reason for this was primarily economic: fiction-film production was easier to control and could be planned and calculated in advance. To give the films a distinctive feature, fiction films increased in length, which had significant influence on two major aspects: the emphasis on the narrative, the story and the actor who, within the budding star system, was used to promote a film in public.[2] The increasing proportion of longer fiction films in the programmes had drastic consequences for nonfiction films. From 1910/11 the films were marginalized within the film programmes, and they assumed the role of a supporting act rather than being a constitutive element of a programme's success.[3] Colonial films that were shown in public cinemas corresponded to the average length of nonfiction films between 1906/7 and 1910/11: *Land und Leute in Deutsch-Südwest-Afrika* (Land and People in German South-West Africa) (Deutsche Mutoskope- und Biograph, 1907) measured 150 m, *Leben und Treiben In Tanga (Deutsch-Ost-Afrika)* (Hustle and Bustle in Tanga [German East Africa]) (Deutsche Bioscop, 1909) 140 m and *Fortschritte der Zivilisation in Deutsch-Ostafrika* (The Progress of Civilization in German East Africa) (Pathé Frères, 1911) 110 m.[4] Watching the films in commercial venues, however, was different from attending screenings in the DKG's branches.

Viewers were not dependent on a branch's decision to hire a film exhibitor for an evening screening. With the growing number of local cinemas and film shows through travelling exhibitors, viewers could often choose between different cinemas that were all offering weekly changing programmes and could be attended every day at various times. In commercial cinemas viewers could usually watch a varied programme of *Naturaufnahmen,* (natural spectacles), *Reisebilder* (travelogues), *Aktualitäten* (topicals), animations, *Tonbilder* (sound pictures), scientific pictures and dramatic or slapstick shorts. We have almost no information about how colonial films were exactly programmed in the public cinemas (one example will be given later in this chapter), but it is hard to imagine that profit-oriented cinema owners had a strong interest in programming their films in combination with long, patriotic speeches designed to win the audience for colonialism. Thinking of the film programme as a vehicle to attract a wide audience, exhibitors had to weigh up colonial euphoria and interest against variety and commercial benefit. The programme's variety was a chance to address viewers seeking political and educational information as well as viewers who wanted to be entertained with amusement, emotion, thrills and visual spectacles. It was the variety and the quality of the programme that determined the cinema's acceptance among the public and its economic survival in a competitive market. Last but not least, the popularity of the new medium and the variety of topics to be viewed in a film programme called critics into action. The cinema reform movement considered the nonfiction film form, including colonial films, as a didactic medium to educate the German public, especially the German youth.

An example that illustrates the intersection of the various aspects involved in the discussion of colonial cinematography in public cinemas is the film *Leben und Treiben in Tanga,* which will be discussed in more detail later in this chapter. The release advertisement for this film emphasized its German origin and called the film 'a German colonial film'. To draw the readers' attention to the film, the advertisement delivered a rather detailed summary of the film's content, which gave potential customers an idea of what the film was about and maybe in what way this film could be made part of their film programme. In the form of a travelogue the film showed the African quarter and the European part of Tanga, a German school and military exercises of the Askari soldiers. The Bioscop underlined that due to the total lack of German colonial films, the film would be a *Schlager* (hit) for every film theatre.[5]

Although the Deutsche Bioscop's advertisement seemed to address the patriotic spirit of each customer, the emphasis that the film would be a 'hit' for every film theatre indicates that it was not only patriotism that would convince customers to order this film. *Leben und Treiben in Tanga* addressed the colonial film viewer, but the representation of the colony in form of a travelogue corresponded to the most popular viewing convention in early cinema through which film audiences explored foreign territories. The generic form of the travelogue made colonial films far from exclusive, esoteric items for a handful of colonial enthusiasts. Colonial travelogues offered a range of alternative readings that situate the films at the intersection of colonial instruction and the modern experience of film travelling the world. The strong emphasis on the German origin of the film and the remark about the total lack of German colonial films lead us to question how the demand for colonial films was articulated in Germany, who supported the production of the films and what discourses framed their reception.

The Kinoreformbewegung and Colonial Discourse

Colonial films did not seem to be a topic worthy of extensive discussion in the early German film trade press. In February 1907 *Der Kinematograph* carried a short note about the illustrated lantern slide lectures at the colonial museum, but did not mention Schumann's screenings at this time. Colonial films were never discussed in articles, and reviews of colonial films became even rarer with the growing popularity of fiction films in the cinemas' film programmes. However, references to colonial cinematography can be found in the writings of cinema reformers, who had a major influence on early film journalism. Cinema reformers could use the apparent lack of colonial films in the cinema programmes to support their demand for transforming cinema into an instrument for national education and national renewal by replacing 'bad fiction films' with 'good nonfiction films'. The reformers were following the still popular ideas of Romanticism, in which the *heimatliche Natur* (the nature of [one's] Heimat), gave every nation its individual character;⁶ by combating the *Verschlampen des deutschen Empfindens* (the ruin of German natural sentiment), as one advocate put it, national colonial films could become part of the formation of a national German identity.⁷

One of the first discussions about colonial films was published in the film journal *Der Kinematograph* in April 1907.⁸ Apparently unaware that films from the colonies already existed and were successfully shown at the DKG's branches at that time, the article included some of the movements' characteristic demands and complained that cinematography has not 'yet understood using the interest of the day for its purpose'. Obviously written under the influence of the recent changes in German colonial policy, the article emphasized the German public's strong demand for films from the colonies and the public's interest in what the colonies looked like:

> I am unaware that even one filming from our colonies exists or that steps have been taken for the production of such 'filming' even though because of the widely known happenings there exists the utmost interest among our people, regardless of which political point of view one may hold. Since the 'Southwesterners' in their uniforms have been seen in all parts of Germany, the sympathy with our colonies has increased. And there will not be many Germans that do not like to see how cities, settlements, the farms and plantations, the mountains and the plains, in one word, how the South African 'desert' there actually looks. And one is not limited to Southwest because East Africa has perhaps even more to offer.⁹

Even though the article did not demand explicitly the official production of colonial films by the German government, it argued for the government's support and fostering of such productions that could popularize the colonial impulse among the public. Much more explicit were cinema reformers, who demanded state-run film productions and suggested that state and communities 'should turn the tables and use cinema's suggestive power according to today's state-supporting social order' (*staatserhaltende Gesellschaftsordnung*).¹⁰ Walther Conradt, a clerical reformer, considered film a medium that made politics transparent to the public. Films about military exercises, the navy and the emperor and his family were perfectly suited for the formation of a patriotic national identity that also included the depiction of the colonies: 'Well, perhaps His Excellency Dernburg decides to send a photographer to our colonies and distribute the images. After all, every tax payer wants to see what will be done with his money over there'.[11] Likewise, the reformer Konrad Lange considered film a tool for communication and education. In contrast to Conradt, Lange seemed to be familiar with the DKG's lecture activities, even though not with the society's film lectures.[12] He envisioned the government as a future producer of colonial films and proposed what aspects of colonial life should be shot:

> Lectures about the essence of colonialism [*Kolonialwesen*] already belong to the major attractions of smaller cities. How much more interest for our colonies could be aroused, if one would show the work on the plantations and the diamond fields, the life of our civil servants, the farmers and the Schutztruppe in moving images? ... How interesting and at the same time of a general interest were instructions about the opportunities for emigration and the necessity of railways in the colonies, about the life of farmers, about the work of women and the need for females to move to the colonies. Here you can combine the pleasing with the useful, present instruction and entertainment at the same time. I see the time coming when the government will take care of this genre and produce political films for public information.[13]

In contrast to Gaupp and Lange, who considered film primarily a means of communication through which colonial films could be used for the nation's political education, the reformer Hermann Häfker focused on film's aesthetic possibilities, a position that represents a second major approach in the reform movement. His writings confirm Scott Curtis's general observation that German 'Kinoreformers' seized on the constellation of taste, nation and education and shared a belief that 'education *through* art was a way of building a distinctly national art, while education *to* art was designed to build consensus and therefore national unity'.[14]

In opposition to a cinema that was dominated by the fiction film, Häfker established his own concept of cinema, the so-called Kinetographie, which 'offered the best possibilities for studying nature and the beauty of movement, for overcoming time and space, and for understanding the world's secret rhythm'.[15] For Häfker, knowing the world was closely linked to knowing one's own Fatherland – two sides of the same coin. He therefore considered geography the 'real aesthetic' among all natural sciences, which made the geographic film a key genre in Häfker's approach.[16] Playing with the meaning of the German word *Aktualität*, Häfker argued that it was impossible to shoot *Aktualitäten* (topical films) because topicality was not predictable. Instead the geographic film could illustrate *Aktualität* (relevance) with regard to thoughts, movements and interests that had a long temporal influence.[17] Films that taught the viewer about the Heimat were so relevant as they provided excellent illustrations of the meaning and activities of the nation. To this body of films Häfker added films from the colonies, as they could make the audience feel enthusiastic about the territories and connected to the different German *Volksstämme* (tribes) everywhere in the world. To coordinate the production of geographic films, Häfker proposed the establishment of a Deutsche Erdkundliche Kinogenossenschaft (German Geographical Cinema Co-Operative).[18] The films had to be made by experts, as would be the case, for example, with colonial films made on behalf of colonial authorities.

The cinema reform movement's complaints about the lack of colonial films and its demand that government take over colonial film propaganda indicates the reform movement's ignorance not only of the DKG's film lectures during the preceding years but in general of any film activities in voluntary associations. In 1913 the reform journal *Bild und Film* proposed to organize a special screening for voluntary associations.[19] The model screening the author presented also included one for a colonial association. The film titles, however, had little to do with the German colonies. After an overture and a slide lecture on the German colonies, the film list included: *Am Kongo* (At the Congo), *Industrie auf Borneo* (Industry on Borneo), *Spiel and Sport und in Sumatra* (Games and Sports in Sumatra), *Leben und Treiben auf einer afrikanischen Farm* (Hustle and Bustle on an African Farm), and *Baumwollernte* (Cotton Harvest).

The reform movement's concepts were hard to combine with the film industry's commercial interests. In 1913, cinema reformer O.T. Stein came to the conclusion that much had been said about the reformation of the cinema in theory, but practice and practical understanding were still lacking.[20] The movement's strong prejudices 'against the narrative film and their underlying belief in film as an educational tool' left reformers standing 'at the margins of a film culture primarily concerned with entertainment'.[21] However, the film industry did not avoid all contact with the reform movement. Industry representatives were willing to use the reform movements for their own needs since 'the reformers were still a legitimating presence – they were, after all, educators, clergy, journalists and otherwise pillars of their respective communities'.[22] The following examples of colonial film productions show how the film industry tried to address reformers' concerns by underlining the respectability of their projects.

Commercial Colonial Film Production: Between Support and Reservation

There exists no evidence of the reform movement's direct influence on the production of colonial films, but, as records and correspondence of two colonial film projects show, a reformist claim was not uncommon in the promotion of the production of such projects. In February 1913, Hans Schomburgk organized a film expedition to the colonies that he claimed would rehabilitate cinema's reputation that had been tarnished by 'blood soaking dramas and implausible gangster stories'.[23] Schomburgk planned to visit Liberia, Togo and Cameroon and considered his expedition as part of the fight against the *Kinounwesen*, the nuisance of (commercial) cinema, and as part of the effort to create the necessary expansion of colonial understanding and interest among the public. The expedition was well prepared. Besides serving colonial interests, it also had the ethnographic task of documenting disappearing primitive cultures. For this Schomburgk received the support of scientific institutes and well-known ethnologists, as well their attention afterwards.[24] Schomburgk's advisor on aesthetic questions was Kay Nebel, a German painter, who shot 'extremely effective objects' to present the beauties of the tropical landscape to the German audience.[25]

With an intention quite similar to Schomburgk's emphasis on the 'noble endeavour' character of his expedition, the Lübeck travel novelist and chief editor of the local Lübeck newspaper *Lübecker Nachrichten*, Heinz Sachers and Lieutenant Wilhelm von Gusmann respectively, organized their expedition in April 1914.[26] The expedition was called Mit Film und Feder rund um Afrika (With Film and Pen Around Africa), and had as its primary purpose promoting knowledge about the colonies among the German public. The first films from their expedition were shown in July 1914 and included images of railways, German settlers, mining and scenes of the beauty of the South-West colony.[27] The exploitation of Sachers's and Gusmann's films was in the hands of the reformist Zentrale für wissenschaftliche und Schulkinematographie (Centre for Scientific and School Cinematography), whose aim was to use film for education in schools and for the *Volksbildung* (popular eudcation) of the German public.[28] To emphasize the respectability of the centre on the one hand and, on the other, the expedition film's significance for the national interest in improving the public's knowledge about colonies, Sachers and Gusmann included a testimonial about the centre written by the most nationalist of the reformers, Karl Brunner.

In contrast to the above-mentioned individual German film expeditions, little is known about the work of production companies in the German colonies. Release advertisements show that German colonial topics were not exclusively shot by national film companies. In 1911 Pathé Frères released a film about a state vocational school in Tanga, *Die Fortschritte der Zivilisation in Deutsch-Ostafrika*, which seemed to be the only film about this rare topic and supplied the German audience with information about the colonial education system in the East African colony. Similarly exclusive coverage was offered by the film company Eclipse, with a film about the opening of the DAMUKA in May 1907 in Berlin, *Eröffnung der Kolonialausstellung in Berlin am 2. Mai durch S. Kaiserliche Hoheit den Kronprinzen* (Opening of the Colonial Exposition on 2 May in Berlin by his Imperial Majesty the Crown Prince). Eclipse underlined that it had exclusive marketing rights to shoot on the grounds of the Berlin DAMUKA, and promoted the film as a service of information to all the viewers who could not personally attend the exposition. According to the promotional text, interesting moments such as 'Negro dances', a Bedouins' camp, navy spectacle, military presentations or the flying of a hot air balloon were planned to be shot in the following weeks.[29]

The reform movement's strong interest in establishing a decent cinema in which German youth would not be exposed to films that would corrupt their minds made reformers particularly interested in effective censorship laws. Consequently, film companies had to be interested in trying to convince censors of the educational and important aesthetic character of their films. In this regard, the emphasis on the German origin of the film *Leben und Treiben in Tanga* was an effort to call to the attention of the censors the patriotic importance of the film. Likewise, the film company Raleigh & Robert used images of the colonial troops to recommend a particular kind of colonial film to their customers. *Unsere Schutztruppe in Deutsch-Süd-West-Afrika* (Our Colonial Troops in German South-West Africa) (Raleigh & Robert, 1911) showed the condition of the colonial troops in DSWA, military and riding exercises, artillery and the preparation of an air balloon. In the release advertisement Raleigh & Robert addressed, in particular, cinemas that were frequented by army personnel and underlined that the film would generate splendid income for any theatre that had a military audience.[30] The film *Im Reich der Diamanten* (In the Land of the Diamonds) (Raleigh & Robert, 1907) was supposed to be of particular educational and instructional interest due to the colonial powers' general interest in exploiting the colonies for their natural resources. In their sales advert Raleigh & Robert remarked that the 'intelligent cinema owner' was right in demanding no comic scenes but instead choosing interesting, instructional *Naturaufnahmen* (nature recordings).[31]

Colonial films were often considered as having educational value and had few problems in passing censorship. The reformist Kommission für 'Lebende Photographie' (Commission for 'Living Photography') that was set up by the Gesellschaft der Freunde des vaterländischen Schul- und Erziehungswesens (Society of Friends of National Schools and Education) included the film *Die Wilden beim Eisenbahnbau* (The Savages Constructing a Railway) (Raleigh & Robert, 1907) on a list of films with educational interest.[32] But not every topic that came from Africa or the colonies was automatically approved. The film *Quer durch Zentral-Afrika* (Across Central Africa) (Eclair, 1912) was allowed only after a scene that showed sleeping sickness was cut. Films about hunting generally had little chance to be screened uncut: *Giraffenjagd in der Massaisteppe* (Giraffe Hunting in the Massai Steppe) (Pathé Frères, 1913) was prohibited for children, and *Eine Elefantenjagd am Viktoriasee in Afrika* (An Elephant Hunt at Lake Victoria) (Pathé Frères, 1913) could be shown only after a scene of a dying elephant looking right into the camera was cut. Nudity was another point that provoked the censors to intervene: when it came to *In Afrika, der schwarze Kontinent* (In Africa, the Black Continent) (Express-Film, 1915), Munich censors were particularly concerned about the depiction of an African woman breastfeeding her baby and a scene in which some women's breasts 'conspicuously protruded'.[33]

The film industry emphasized their patriotic service to the viewer and most likely pleased cinema reformers in their efforts to create an educational cinema, but colonial officials had a rather ambivalent attitude towards the production of colonial films and often remained sceptical about such projects. Surviving correspondence between film companies and the RKA shows that producers often used a reformist rhetoric in order to give their projects a certain respectability with colonial authorities, who were often less enthusiastic about supporting such projects. In October 1913, the film company Iris Film in Munich approached the RKA and asked for support for the company's plan to shoot films in the German colonies. Iris described the film project as the recording of 'historical-cultural-natural and industrial cinematographic films' that were the best guarantee for exact scientific and first-class artful images.[34] The result of this trip with film and photo cameras, according to Iris, would 'certainly contribute to the perfect design of official colonial publications and ought to promote significantly the colonial interest'. The RKA, however, refused this request, underlining that no official budget existed for these kinds of enterprises.

While the RKA refused to support the Iris' intention to produce films in the colonies that could have been used as a promotion for the colonial idea, the RKA also seemed to know – or care – little about the reform movement's concepts and their interest in using film for national education, which included the promotion of colonialism among the German public, as is evident from the correspondence between Leo Stachow and the RKA in July 1907. Stachow, who was the owner of the Aar Kinematographen-Werk, a company which sold projectors, and owner of a reform cinema, asked the RKA for permission to exhibit Karl Weule's films in the programmes of his reform cinema.[35] He planned to open his 'educational institution' in Berlin at the end of July and described the cinema as an 'absolutely decent' enterprise with sufficient ventilation, good musical contributions, supervision and a programme that did not show cruel serials but educational, entertaining and amusing films. Stachow expected in this way to uplift cinema's image among the public and to turn the educated circles' growing aversion to cinema into goodwill. Weule's films were planned to become part of the evening programme for an adult audience and should familiarize the audience with foreign countries, their people and customs. Officially the RKA expressed no objection to Stachow's project, but indicated that Weule probably intended to exploit the films first for his scientific work. The RKA's rejection of Stachow's request at the end of July may have therefore come as no surprise for Stachow. However, an informal note on the RKA's first letter to Stachow indicates that the RKA was rather concerned about a too close cooperation with the film business:

> In my opinion I would recommend to make first an official inquiry about the applicant. Regarding the not always perfect productions of the cinematographic enterprises one should be cautious. It is not pleasant to see our images used by other people who have a bad reputation. Moreover, I propose we consider refusing altogether. Such [unidentified word] are not pleasant towards other enterprises. It is not our task to get other people an income through our [help? unidentified word], which normally would only be possible through considerable means. Besides, obligingness from our side could be taken amiss by the competitors.[36]

It is difficult to conclude from this short remark that the RKA disapproved of colonial filmmaking in general, but apparently the RKA felt they should be cautious towards colonial film projects or the exploitation of colonialism by people of questionable reputation. By July 1907 colonialism had only recently regained a new respectability among the public, and the RKA had to be concerned about avoiding anything that would again publicly discredit colonialism. This was even more important since the colonies attracted not only serious academic scholars like ethnographers, geographers or biologists, but all kinds of self-appointed colonial experts, who made their living by marketing their patriotic expeditions; for which the film camera was one more chance to promote their hazardous endeavours to the public. As the RKA's remark indicates, the colonial office's support of one project, even a serious one, would encourage others to address the RKA as well, which would make it almost impossible to check each project for its colonial respectability.

The most enigmatic figure in this area of 'colonial adventure tourism' was Paul Graetz, a former officer of the colonial troops. Graetz's fame started with his first expedition, crossing Africa from Dar es Salaam in German East Africa to German South-West Africa between 1907 and 1909 in an automobile. Graetz's second expedition was no less spectacular. Graetz exchanged the car for a motorboat and crossed the African continent from east to west by using different African rivers as a connecting water route. On his arrival on the west coast of Africa in December 1912, Graetz announced his plans for a third expedition even more spectacular than his earlier trips: the exploration of New Guinea with an airship.[37]

Graetz's expeditions were well-organized publicity events that were widely covered in the German press and received nationwide attention. Popular adventure accounts of his expeditions were published, and his lectures became rather successful events in the DKG's branches. German industries such as Ernemann, whose photo cameras were used by Graetz, and food producers such as Oetker and Knorr supported his motorboat expedition; the vessel itself was named after the well-known chocolate company Sarotti.[38] The organizing committee of Graetz's airship expedition included a range of well-known politicians, merchants and scholars, such as Richard Neuhauss, who was also one of the expedition members and responsible for scientific photographic recordings. It is not known whether Neuhauss also planned to shoot films on this expedition, but Graetz's adventurous expeditions had attracted the attention of film companies. On his motorboat expedition Graetz was accompanied by the Frenchman Octave Fière, a filmcamera operator of the Eclair company, who was killed on the expedition while trying to film a buffalo hunt.[39]

News about spectacular expeditions in the colonies certainly drew the public's attention to the possible cinematographic results, but also caused a problem for colonial authorities who did not automatically consider every colonial endeavour a positive promotion of the colonial idea. This was particularly the case with Graetz's extraordinary expeditions. With reference to his airship expedition, a confidential paper that circulated among the DKG's presidium and board expressed concern about pseudo-scientific 'discovery frauds' (*Entdeckungsschwindel*), as such expeditions only damaged Germany's national reputation.[40] Reservations and negative experiences might not have been the only reason to be cautious in supporting colonial film projects; it is quite possible that the RKA also harboured concerns about the exploitation of colonialism for a private individual's personal prestige and also took this into consideration when articulating their reservations about Leo Stachow's request.

All the examples show that it was rather difficult for filmmakers and film companies to receive official support, but it was not impossible as the following anecdote about the production history of the film *Staats-Sekretär Dr. Solf in den Kolonien (Togo im Film)*/ (State Secretary Dr. Solf in the Colonies [Togo on Film]) (Hans Schomburgk, 1914) shows. In April 1913 the Express-Films Co. GmbH from Freiburg contacted the RKA, offering to film the 'most important parts' of state secretary Solf's trip through the West African colonies Togo and Cameroon in the autumn of 1913 by putting one of the company's operators at the RKA's disposal.[41] The office refused the company's offer and explained that it had to keep the travelling group as small as possible. However, Solf's stay in Togo was finally documented by a film camera and shot by Hans Schomburgk and his operator Jimmy Hodgson, who were staying in Lomé at that time, preparing their expedition into the Togo hinterland.[42] The film shows Solf's visit to Togo, starting with his arrival at the jetty in Lomé and his reception by the colony's governor Duke Adolf Friedrich zu Mecklenburg, as well as his different activities during his stay in Togo, such as attending a parade of the Togo police troop or taking the small colonial railway to reach Atakpame. As one of the very few existing prints from the colonial era the film perfectly sums up aspects that will be discussed in more detail below. There is almost no shot that does not show Solf in motion: on horseback, in a rickshaw or with the railway, Solf hurries from one meeting to another. The film gives the impression that every corner of the colony has already been explored and can easily be reached. Images that show Solf mostly standing in a colonized setting, such as colonial buildings, emphasize the impression of a 'modern colony'.

Figure 10.1. State Secretary Solf arriving in a Riksha. Still from *Staatssekretär Dr. Solf besucht im Oktober 1913 Togo* (1913). Reproduced courtesy of Bundesarchiv-Abteilung Filmarchiv.

Staats-Sekretär Dr. Solf in den Kolonien was distributed in Europe by British Motion Pictures Sales Agency and the Lichtbild-Vertrieb GmbH in Germany. For the promotion of the exclusive material the Lichtbild-Vertrieb asked Solf for a statement confirming the authenticity of the material. It became part of the advertising strategy of the Lichtbild-Vertrieb, which promoted the film as an 'ethnographically and culturally unique film'.[43]

The examples of the Iris film company, Greatz's publicity and the Lichtbild-Vertrieb show the RKA's ambivalent attitude towards colonial film projects. While the RKA did not want to become associated with colonial adventurers like those of Graetz, and rejected Iris Film's offer and turned down Stachow's request, they finally approved Schomburgk's unique film. The RKA's ambivalence was obviously based on their general concern over how the colonies would be represented. The RKA did not mind supporting a colonial film as long as it presented the official side in a flattering way, but it was very sceptical about projects whose outcome was uncertain and bore the risk of damaging colonialism's image. The notion of ambivalence also characterizes the historical reception of colonial films in the public cinemas. Colonial authorities may have been concerned about the correct representation of the colonies, but viewers went to see films for different reasons. Programmes with colonial films certainly addressed the colonial viewer who was interested in colonial politics, but the films also offered an entertaining viewing experience for those not interested in political instruction at all.

Notes

1. A. Jason, *Der Film in Ziffern und Zahlen,* Berlin: Deutsches Druck- und Verlagshaus, 1925, 22–23, quoted in J. Garncarz, 'Über die Entstehung der Kinos in Deutschland 1896–1914' in *KINtop: Jahrbuch zur Erforschung des frühen Films,* 2002, 11: 145–58.
2. Müller, *Frühe deutsche Kinematographie,* 143.
3. C. Müller, 'Variationen des Kinoprogramms. Filmform und Filmgeschichte', in C. Müller and H. Segeberg (eds), *Modellierung des Kinofilms. Zur Geschichte des Kinoprogramms zwischen Kurzfilm und Langfilm 1905/06–1918,* Munich, 1998, 60.
4. Exceptional in length for this period is the 1907 *Mit dem Norddeutschen Llyod nach Neu Guinea.* At 350 m the film clearly stood out in a programme.
5. *Der Kinematograph,* 10 November 1909.
6. W. Mühl-Benninghaus, 'Der dokumentarische Film in Deutschland zwischen erzieherischen Anspruch und wirtschaftlicher Realität', in U. von Keitz and K. Hoffmann (eds), *Die Einübung des dokumentarischen Blicks,* Marburg: Schüren, 2001, 81–102.
7. Cf. W. Rath, 'Emporkömmling Kino', in J. Schweinitz (ed.), *Prolog vor dem Film. Nachdenken über ein neues Medium 1909–1914,* Leipzig: Reclam, 1992, 86.
8. L. Montagne, 'Naturaufnahmen für Phono- und Kinematographen', *Der Kinematograph,* 14 April 1907.
9. Ibid.
10. W. Warstatt and F. Bergmann quoted in Schweinitz, *Prolog vor dem Film,* 60.
11. W. Conradt, *Kirche und Kinematograph. Eine Frage,* Berlin: Hermann Walther Verlagsbuchhandlung GmbH, 1910, 43.
12. The same goes for reformer Victor Noack, who referred to the Navy League's film shows. V. Noack, *Der Kino. Etwas über sein Wesen und seine Bedeutung,* Gautzsch b. Leipzig: Dietrich, 1913, 16.
13. R. Gaupp and K. Lange, *Der Kinematograph als Volksunterhaltungsmittel,* Munich, 1912, 42.
14. S. Curtis, 'The Taste of a Nation. Training the senses and Sensibility of Cinema Audiences in Imperial Germany', *Film History,* 1994, 6(4): 460.
15. H. Häfker, *Kino und Kunst,* M. Gladbach: Volksverein-Verlag, 1913, 13. Unlike many of his colleagues, Häfker did not remain on a theoretical level but drew practical consequences from his theoretical approach. In so-called '*Mustervorstellungen*' (model projections) he presented his concept of Kinetographie, in which the combination of lecture, sound and the moving image created an artistic *Gesamtwirkung* (efficiency).
16. H. Häfker, *Kino und Erdkunde,* M. Gladbach: Volksvereins-Verlag, 1914, 7.
17. Ibid., 50.
18. Ibid., 55.

19. A. Rosenthal, 'Kinovorstellungen in Vereinen', *Bild und Film*, 1913/14, 3(8): 198–200.
20. Diederichs, 'Frühgeschichte deutscher Filmtheorie', 154.
21. Hake, 'The Cinema Reform Movement', 27.
22. Curtis, 'The Taste of a Nation', 451.
23. H. Schomburgk, 'Der Kinematograph im Dienste der kolonialen Propaganda', *Koloniale Zeitschrift*, 4 April 1913, 219.
24. For instance, Georg Thilenius of the Hamburg museum and the custodian of the Royal Zoological Museum in Berlin, Paul Matschie.
25. Schomburgk, 'Der Kinematograph im Dienste der kolonialen Propaganda', 219.
26. Probably as one of very few, this expedition received a grant of a thousand marks from the RKA and had the official support of colonial secretary Solf. BArch, R 8023/232, 44.
27. Anon., 'Die Kino-Expedition durch Deutsch Südwest-Afrika', *Lichtbild-Bühne*, 11 July 1914, 40.
28. BArch, R 8023/232, 45.
29. Though Eclipse underlined that it had the exclusive rights, Pathé Frères also released images from the Berlin exposition. *Der Präsident der Republik, Fallières, in der Kolonial-Ausstellung* (1907) showed the French president visiting the exposition.
30. *Der Kinematograph*, 11 October 1911. The DKG had already organized special film screenings of colonial films for military personnel, which indicated the significance of film for military education.
31. *Der Kinematograph*, 15 May 1907.
32. Gesellschaft der Freunde des vaterländischen Schul- und Erziehungswesens zu Hamburg, *Bericht der Kommission für 'Lebende Photographie' erstattet am 17. April und im Auftrag des Vorstandes bearbeitet von C. H. Dannmeyer*, Hamburg, 1907, 8.
33. H. Birett, *Verzeichnis der in Deutschland gelaufener Filme*, 541.
34. BArch, R 1001/6630, 3.
35. BArch, R 1001/5673-2, 113. Stachow had earlier contacted Hans Meyer, the head of the Landeskundliche Kommission. It was Meyer who recommended that Stachow contact the RKA regarding this matter.
36. Ibid., 114.
37. BArch, R 8023/232, 240.
38. Graetz, *Im Motorboot quer durch Afrika*, 216.
39. Graetz, *Im Motorboot quer durch Afrika*, 95. See also *Lichtbild-Bühne*, 30 September 1911, 22; *Von Zambesi zum Kongo*, Prod: Deutsche Motorboot Gesellschaft mit Eclair, Länge 205 m, 1927.
40. BArch, R 8023/232, 77–78.
41. Schomburgk, *Zelte in Afrika*, 385.
42. The film suggests that Hans Schomburgk accompanied Solf on his travels with the camera, so he seems to have been much more involved in the official visit. Solf reports that after dinner at the Kamina station, where a telegraph station had been built, a film evening was organized with films about the station. Wilhelm Solf quoted in R. Klein-Arendt, '*Kamina ruft Nauen'. Die Funkstellen in den deutschen Kolonien 1904–1918*, Ostheim: Wilhelm Herbst Verlag, 1996, 205. It is quite possible that some of the footage is identical to *Dokumentaraufnahmen vom Bau der Telefunken-Großstation, Kamina/Togo (Afrika) für die drahtlose Verbindung des ehemaligen deutschen Schutzgebiets Togo mit Berlin* (archive title), which is archived at the Deutsches Technikmuseum in Berlin. I would like to thank Jutta Niemann for this valuable information. The film is archived at the Bundesarchiv-Abteilung Filmarchiv as *Staatssekretär Dr. Solf besucht im Oktober 1913 Togo*.
43. *Lichtbild-Bühne*, 3 January 1914.

Chapter 11

THE COLONIAL TRAVELOGUE

A close examination of surviving films, titles, reviews, advertisements and summaries of films from the colonies reveals that the most satisfactory form of travelling the colonies was the colonial travelogue. Composed of different emblematic shots, travelogues belonged to one of the most popular genres in early cinema for illustrating foreign places or regions and served 'as vicarious travel, as a substitute for actual travel that could be experienced by those without the financial means to tour around the globe'.[1]

The aesthetic of the travelogue was largely based on the aesthetic of the 'view', which, according to Tom Gunning, is the *'Urform'* (prototype) of early nonfiction film.[2] With this term Gunning highlights 'the way early actuality films were structured around presenting something visually, capturing and preserving a look or a vantage point'. The 'view' forms part of the cinema of attractions that 'directly solicits spectator attention, inciting visual curiosity, and supplying through an exciting spectacle – a unique event, whether fictional or documentary, that is of interest in itself'.[3] Gunning emphasizes that the line between 'view' and act is hard to draw, so both could function as attractions, but in contrast to an attraction he considers the 'view' as having 'greater claim to recording an event of natural or social history':[4]

> 'Views' tend to carry the claim that the subject filmed either pre-existed the act of filming (a landscape, a social custom, a method of work) or would have taken place even if the camera had not been there (a sport-

ing event, a funeral, a coronation), thus claiming to capture a view of something that maintains a large degree of independence from the act of filming it.[5]

In film, according to Gunning, 'views' do not simply unfold a landscape in front of the viewers' eyes, but mime the act of looking. The camera 'literally acts as tourist, spectator or investigator' and the audience's pleasure 'lies in the surrogate of looking'.[6] The primary indication for this 'mode of observation' lies for Gunning in the acknowledgement of the camera's presence: a look or gesture, a demonstration of a work process or custom of the people filmed. Secondly, the camera observes the action from the best viewing position.

'Views' in the travelogue are exploring, what Peterson calls, a 'central obsession of Western visual culture from the nineteenth century through the First World War: images of the Other and of other places and images of the changing modern world'.[7] While viewers explored the foreign exotic world of the cultural and ethnic Other, the convention of the travelogue genre contained the ambivalence of 'fascinating yet potentially threatening moving images'. In other words, while the travelogue's formulaic structure offered the chance to present a wide range of exotic 'views', this exploration was also secured by 'the familiar confines of the travelogue genre'[8]: For Peterson the travelogue is characterized through a 'delicately balanced polarity', a tension between the 'different' and the 'normal': 'the place presented must merit the curious filmgoers' gaze; therefore the place must be (constructed as) exotic, yet in this presentation there is at the same time a certain disavowal of that exoticism, a desire to mark what is Other and then contain it, to keep it at arm's length'.[9]

As Peterson points out, this tension has been highly efficient and adaptable, and characterized films of colonial and exotic landscapes as European locales. However, although travelogues refer to places that exist in the real world, the representation of these places in film is something different. Travelogues present an 'idealized cinematographic geography'[10] that exists only on the screen. The travelogue's ambivalence of containing the exotic and its geographic idealization within a strict set of conventions needs therefore to be complicated with regard to the representation of the colonies. Colonial travelogues addressed the audience through the display of colonial locations and visual novelties, but it was not just the convention of the genre that contained the experience of the exotic Other. Colonial travelogues tried explicitly to overcome the exoticism by emphasizing aspects and events in the colonies that were not exotic but quite familiar for Western audiences. In keeping with colonial ideology, colonialism did not want to scare but to attract people.

Attracting the audience involves another ambivalent characteristic of the colonial travelogue – the visual experience of unity. John Noyes considers the appropriation of space a key issue in German colonial discourse, one closely related to the way of looking. The colonizer's surveying gaze at the arrival in a new territory 'is an initial appropriation of space. It defines spaces of objectivity and establishes relations between these spaces'.[11] Though the organization of colonial space into structures and a 'functional network of discreet spaces' supported the functioning of the colony, there remains a contradiction of spatiality in colonial discourse, as 'an ever increasing segmentation and fragmentation of space on almost every level' runs counter to the concept of the colony as a unity:

> The colony must, however, present itself as a unity, not only for the purpose of ideology, but also (and perhaps this is a more important consideration), for the purpose of communication – its very ability to function as a colony. It is the myth of mobility which establishes an itinerary of colonial discourse, granting the individual a mythical ability to join all various spaces and spatial qualities which colonization is in the process of fragmentation[12]

Exotic and familiar, fragmented and united – the colonial travelogue was a rather perfect medium with which viewers could experience the 'myth of mobility'. On film they experienced the colony not as a fragmented exotic Other but as a comprehensive familiar unity under the control of the viewer's eyes.

Travelling the Distant Heimat

The foundation of the Koloniale Verkehrsverein (Colonial Tourist Office) in 1911 was one of the first efforts to promote and organize tourism in the colonies.[13] The DKZ remarked about 'pleasure trips' (*Vergnügungsreisen*) in Africa that, after the brave explorer and the passionate hunter, it was now up to the tourist to explore the colonies.[14] Likewise the first tourist guidebook for the East African colony emphasized that 'be it in the vastness of Siberia, the South American Pampas, or the African plains' there were more and more people in Germany who considered the world as their Heimat.[15] However, Africa was not Egypt or India, and people were still mixing up the East African Tanga with the Tunisian Tanger and moved the East African Dar es Salaam to the South-West African colony. Travelling in the colonies meant therefore also getting to know better the 'bigger Germany' and learning how valuable this territory was for the German nation.[16] The transformation of the African colonies into a mirror image of Germany was not only a significant feature in colonial literature but also characterized the rhetoric in the tourist guides. Travelling in the Usamabara mountains was considered as easy as travelling in the German Harz.[17] The Pugu mountains recalled Thuringia; the Amani region was a tropical *Vogesenbild*, picture of the Vosges; Dar es Salaam the African Potsdam; and since the Kilimanjaro was the tallest mountain in the German Reich, it was only natural that the Kilimanjaro Mountain Club planned an association with the Austrian Alp Club.[18]

Films from the colonies had a very similar function. Studying film reviews in the trade press shows that the films often were less concerned about the dangers of the African jungle or the incalculability of life in the tropics but rather tried to depict the colonies as an extension of the German Heimat. The notion of Heimat with regard to the German colonies appears odd because the distance between Germany and its colonies suggests exotic otherness rather than a common semantic topography. However, Heimat is a key word in German history, which serves as a 'bonding agent between the local and the national'.[19] In their historical studies, Celia Applegate and Alon Confino have shown that 'Heimat has been at the centre of a German moral – and by extension political – discourse about place, belonging and identity'.[20] Based on Applegate's and Confino's studies, which both involve a conceptualization of space, Johannes von Moltke has shown how the *Heimatfilm* genre of post-Second World War German cinema is situated within a 'contradictory cinematic construction of Heimat as a refuge from modernity'.[21] For Moltke, the modern-industrial is as much a part of the Heimatfilm genre as the pastoral; they are two sides of the same coin: '[T]he genre continually produces ideological compromise formations aimed at "harmonising" the contradictions between the local and its variously defined "others". A closer look at the genre reveals that the spaces of Heimat remain profoundly ambivalent, bearing traces of both the pastoral and the industrial, the local and the global, the traditional and the modern.'[22] While Moltke identifies the formations in the individual fiction films, his approach is also very useful for the understanding of colonial films in imperial Germany. Studying the dominant motifs in colonial films, one notes that the harmonization of the modern with the traditional does not occur in a single film but through the change from nonfiction to fiction. The representation of profitability and progress as a significant characteristic of the nonfiction colonial film before the First World War changes into the representation of the pastoral life in the colonies, the life of farmers and settlers, in fictional dramas, which were produced during the First World War and will be discussed in the last chapter.

As they were produced before the war, nonfiction films from the colonies did not present the territories as being different from Germany but stressed the similarities by emphasizing the modern, urban character of the colonies. As was argued about film screenings at the DKG's branches, the use of moving images was perfectly suited to demonstrate technical progress and mobility in the colonies. In addition, the depiction of 'beautiful European buildings', a German hotel or the existence of a modern advertisement pillar in the streets of Swakopmund were for reviewers the proof that 'the pioneers of Germandom are beginning slowly but surely to put their mark of German characteristics on land and country abroad'.[23]

Remarks like these show that film travels to the 'black Germany' were not a nostalgic or idyllic view into a pre-industrial time. Films from the colonies included 'views' of farms and farmers, but these were never discussed at length in any of the surviving reviews. In other words, although farming and settling was an important aspect in German colonial ideology, there exists no indication that film companies and private filmmakers were particularly interested in this topic. Cinema's cultural-epistemological rooting and emergence in the context of modernity, that is, the city and urban life, aimed instead at representing the colonies as progressive modern and urban spaces. The representation of the colonies as the modern, civilized Africa adds an important aspect to Assenka Oksiloff's notion of the colonies as a setting for 'picturing an epic Ur-encounter with the primitive body of the Other'.[24] It is important to note that exclusively ethnographic films played only a marginal role in the film reception of the German colonies. Such films were very rarely promoted in the trade press and were not part of regular film programmes. Even the DKG, wich could have easily articulated an educational interest in the screening of ethnographic films for its members, was rather reserved about including ethnographic material in its colonial film programmes. If Africans were presented in the films, the setting was either urban or they were positioned in a context where modern Western technology was in use.

One of the first travelogues from the German colonies to reach the German screens in 1907 was *Südwest-Afrika* (South-West Africa), shot by

Georg Furkel during his stay in the colony and released by the Deutsche Bioscop in June 1907.[25] The different 'views' in the film, which are listed in the film's release advertisement, still show the influence of the recent political events in the colony. While the shot order in travelogues often appears scattered and loose from today perspective, as Peterson points out, *Südwest-Afrika* seems to follow a dramaturgy, in which the recent events in DSWA are integrated into the process of colonization and progress. The violent past becomes softened and toned down by the film's sequential logic. The film starts with three shots of railway construction workers, the properties of the railway construction company and a panorama shot of Lüderitzbucht: 1. 'Workers constructing the railway shafts at Aus'; 2. 'Administration buildings of Lenz & Co. in Lüderitzbucht'; 3.'Panorama of Lüderitzbucht, taken from Diamant Mountain'. The following nine shots are dedicated to the Herero and Nama prisoners, the 'Hottentots'. In this second series of shots, number eleven, printed in bold letters in the advertisement, was supposed to be the film's highlight, showing the main chiefs of the Nama warriors: 4. 'Samuel Isaak, sub-captain of Hendrik Witboi'; 5. 'Dance of the Hottentot women'; 6. 'Service of the missionary in Lüderitzbucht'; 7. 'Camp of the Hottentots and captured Herero'; 8. 'Continuation, camp of prisoners in Burenkamp, Lüderitzbucht'; 9. 'Overall view of the camp'; 10. 'Captured Hottentots and Herero women returning from collecting water'; 11. 'The main leaders of the Hottentots: David, son of Isaak – Lazarus of Britain – The small Jakob – Eduard'; 12. 'Group of the main leaders and the head people'. After this visual climax the following seven shots show Nama children playing in the concentration camp, a panorama of Swakopmund, life on the jetty, roads and shore and finally passengers boarding a steamer: 13. 'Playing Hottentot children in the prison camp'; 14. 'Panorama of Swakopmund'; 15. 'Hustle and Bustle on the jetty'; 16. 'Jetty, taken from the boat'; 17.' Roadstead and surf in Swakopmund'; 18. 'Passengers boarding the 'A. Wörmann', Swakopmund'.

The film can be divided into three main clusters of shots: the Aus region and Lüderitzbucht, prison camp and Swakopmund. All three establish rather different spaces of the same territory. The visual climax in *Südwest-Afrika* is obviously the depiction of the prisoners, but this climax is integrated in a context that presents the colony as no longer threatened by uprisings and rebellions but as a safe place for travelling and living. In contrast to the prison camp, the shots at the beginning and the end, panoramas of colonial cities and the progress that has been made emphasize the picturesque aspects of the colonies. Starting and ending with the construction of infrastructure and the boarding of an ocean cruiser, the film recommends the colonies as a place that is worth visiting. The beginning and ending of the film again demonstrate technical progress quite similar to films shown at the DKG's branches. *Südwest-Afrika* can be considered an example of colonization's creation of discrete spatial units that facilitated control and administration of the geographic territory.[26] With the African placed in the confined space of the prison, traces of the Other have become erased from the colonial territory so that it can be filled with the colonizers' presence.[27]

A more detailed look at the shot order reveals a careful composition. The different clusters resemble a narrative fade in/fade out of a flashback into the history of DSWA. With the switch to the prison camp, the viewer is reminded of the war that has only recently come to an end. The different 'views' in the prison camp cluster recall de Certeau's division of space as a panoptic practice.[28] The different 'views' function like a controlling camera that is monitoring the prisoners: observing, measuring and controlling them. Following the aesthetic of the 'view' in which the camera 'literally acts as tourist, spectator or investigator'[29], the panoptic practice originates from the place from which the practice proceeds – the colonizer's cinema hall. The prison cluster is not entirely presented in a form of documenting punishment. *Südwest-Afrika* is intercut with the missionary's work in the prison. In this way the prison has become a place in which the enemy's conversion is performed. The transition from the prison camp to more pleasing 'views' such as the panorama of Swakopmund is smoothed by the depiction of playing children. However, the children shot, like the dancing women shot in the beginning of the film, is ambivalent. Does the shot order of prisoners and children intend a humiliation of the brave warriors, who are compared to children, or does the shot stand for a new generation of innocent colonized Africans and therefore refers to the missionary's work? Was the editing that placed the dancing women before the missionary to illustrate the African women's intemperateness and therefore the missionary's necessity in the camp or was it supposed to indicate that camp life is less barbarous as it might appear to some viewers? The whole film seemed to be bracketed by the picturesque panorama shots in the beginning and the end, which master the reminiscence of the colonial war so that the most violent period in German colonial history becomes integrated into a discourse of unstoppable progress and peaceful colonial everyday life.

While *Südwest-Afrika* introduces the colony as a peaceful region that was going to become 'blessed' with Western infrastructure in the future, the advertisement text of the travelogue *Leben und Treiben in Tanga* from 1909 demonstrates what life in the colony was about:

> In perfect excellent photography, supported by differently coloured, effective tinting and toning, this interesting recording shows among other things the quarter of the natives with the picturesque, strange mud huts, a street in the native quarter with the vivid hustle and bustle of Negroes, Mohammedans, Indians and so on., the arrival of the train at the small but clean train station, the interesting traffic in the main street with trolleys, rickshaws, baby carriages, distinguished Europeans, black urchins [*Gassenjungen*] and so on, well, even the music arrives (the school children marching band of the German School), happily surrounded by young and old, exactly as in Germany, a children's party on Bismarck Square with the pretty Bismarck monument, Europeans sitting at the coffee table, amused by an extremely funny chimpanzee, a gym lesson at the German school with round dances, vaulting and so on., exercises of the native Askari military troop, whose uprightness [*Strammheit*] and dashing character [*Schneidigkeit*] almost equal that of their German comrades.[30]

The summary suggests that the film depicted colonial life as rather joyful and entertaining. Living in the colony did not involve making any sacrifices or giving up habits or traditions. The marching band, a children's party and a laid coffee table almost remind one of a family's Sunday activities or a holiday. The party on Bismarck Square 'with the pretty Bismarck monument' leaves no doubt that even if the location were African, the setting was German. The most significant message of the film is therefore that life in Tanga was 'exactly as in Germany'.

The synopsis of *Leben und Treiben in Tanga* makes it difficult to conclude that there was a spatializing of the colony similar to that in *Südwest-Afrika*, but the film seemed to emphasize difference. At the time of its production, the film could not foresee projects that planned segregated cities with separate native and European quarters due to concerns about racial hygiene[31]; it contrasts the African quarter, with its 'picturesque, strange mud huts', with the European part of the town and its 'clean train station', main street and Bismarck Square. Unfortunately, no copy of the film has survived, so one can only speculate about what the images looked like. The mentioning of a differently coloured effective tinting/toning indicates the possibility that the contrast between the clay-coloured mud huts and the white colonial architecture was even more emphasized in the film.[32]

Peterson has pointed out that travelogues did not present the real world, but 'created a world that does not exist: an idealized cinematographic geography'.[33] *Leben und Treiben in Tanga* is an example par excellence of an idealized colonial life. It presents German East Africa as a preferred place for living. The summary gives no indication that the film audience is watching a particular day or event, and the film is not inventing anything that did not exist in Tanga: contemporary travellers' reports show that concerts of the marching band on Bismarck Square were one of Tanga's main attractions. Looking at the production of the film, however, we see that *Leben und Treiben in Tanga* did not show everyday life. The local *Usambara-Post* reports that the film was carefully staged so that the joyful afternoon was the result of three days of shooting.[34] Nevertheless, the film's hustle and bustle presents itself in the timeless present and assures the viewer that the one is watching life just as it is and that everything that is happening in the film could happen again any time and any day. It is the abundance of different 'views' in the film that creates the idealized colonial life that stands in sharp contrast to the people's complaints and their frustration about the monotony of the reality of colonial life. *Leben und Treiben in Tanga* wants to suggest that at least life in Tanga was anything but a 'palm-desert tropical treadmill'.

Technology and Colonization

The representation of the colonies as a modern space of living was not possible without the emphasis on and the demonstration of modern technology in the colonial territories. Through understanding technology not only as a practice of using machines and tools but also as knowledge in the sense of organization and administration, the representation of technology stood for the new beginning in German colonialism, as it justified the colonizers' presence in the foreign territory. In this respect, colonial films that were produced after the Herero War started where Frenssen's novel *Peter Moor* finishes. While the lieutenant at the end of Moor's stay in South-West remarks that Africans 'have earned their death before God and man ... because they never built houses and dug wells', reviews of Robert Schumann's film from the South-West colony indicate that the colony was at the beginning of a more prosperous period in German colonialism: 'German South-West Africa is by no means the worthless sand desert that some non-experts have slurred it as; with our highly developed technology we will manage to open the country and make its treasures useful for the German fatherland'.[35] Traces of the war had been erased by 1912, as suggested by the shot order of *Bilder aus Deutsch-Süd-West-Afrika* (Scenes from

German South-West Africa) (Raleigh & Robert, 1912), which seemed to present the colony as a place where colonizer and colonized were living together in harmony: 'Railway journey from Luederitzbucht to Keetmanshoop'; 'Fort and Panorama Views of Keetmannshoop'; 'Hottentot Houses'; 'The German School System in the Colonies'; 'Ostrich Farm in Keetmanshoop'.[36] A significant element in almost all colonial travelogues was the depiction of the railway. The construction of a colonial railway infrastructure had priority in German colonial policy and was driven by two major economic concerns. The exploration of the hinterland and its cultivation with cotton and other plantations would make Germany independent of the world market in the future. This was possible only through an efficient connection to the coast. Secondly, a railway infrastructure would increase the trade in the colonies and give Africans the chance to sell their products on the market and to purchase new ones. Between 1894 and 1912 the colonial German railway system grew from 14 to 4176 km.[37] Images of the railway, therefore, were the most visible and complex signs of colonization and stood for the colonizer's efforts of civilizing the territory according to Western standards. The railway was the colonizing machine that reminded the audience of its technological superiority, represented modernity and showed how far civilization had progressed. Images of trains and railways turned Africa into a commodity – real estate that could be entered and left at any time. The following remark in a review of the 1907 film *Die Wilden beim Eisenbahnbau* (The Savages Constructing Railway) emphasizes once more that Africa was explored for the Western traveller's needs and pleasures:

> and so we civilized people would surely not stand still before we cannot enter and leave Africa, the continent that has been up until now explored the least, indeed hardly explored at all, like other continents. ... That way culture moves more and more forward and each mile towards Cairo means progress. It will not be too long, then before also the 'dark continent' will be explored for us, to the utmost satisfaction of all that intend to visit this continent.[38]

The shot of the railway was also prominently placed in *Leben und Treiben in Tanga*. The 'view' of the arriving train at the Tanga train station in the film shows that Tanga was connected with the world and could already be reached on the African continent. As important is the moment in which the train seemed to have entered the film. It marked the transition from the native quarter to the European part of the town and initiated the subsequent presentation of a whole range of mobile vehicles that establish Tanga as a modern urban space.

'Views' of machines and their application in the colonial territory were powerful images, not only to show that civilization had reached the last corners of the world but also to emphasize the difference between colonizer and colonized as is done in the first shots of *Aus dem Innern Afrikas* (From Inner Africa) (Raleigh & Robert, 1911). The film starts with the intertitle 'African Industry' and then shows three shots of Africans who are doing craft work: 1. Seven men sitting together in a half circle, grinding crop for the making of flour; 2. Three women weaving carpets; 3.Three women making pottery. All three shots are obviously staged for the camera. Shot in medium long shot, the people are facing towards the camera. This 'ethnographic exposition' is followed by scenes from a diamond mine: 4. An excavator is loading a tipper wagon, the sun bounces off the steel excavator, the wagon is pushed off-frame; 5. The smashing and cleaning of the diamond-laden earth in a labyrinthine system of steel and conveyor belts. The following two shots show the manual sorting of the diamonds: 6. A pan from right to left shows workers sitting at tables, trying to spot diamonds amid the crushed earth; 7. A close-up of one of the tables, a diamond is carefully picked out of the earth and put into a small can. The film then switches to a set of shots of African animals: 8. 'Gnus'; 9. 'Zebras'; 10. 'Antelopes'; 11. The film ends with a 'view' of Victoria Falls.

Aus dem Innern Afrikas obviously played with the viewer's associations with the term 'industry' and mocks traditional crafts, as depicted in the first three shots, as technologically retarded.[39] It is the display of steel, machines and steam power in *Aus dem Innern Afrikas* that finally delivers what the first intertitle promised. With regard to the other 'views' to be seen in the film, the diamond mine sequence is the only one that points to the colonizer's presence. In addition to the demonstration of Africa's mineral abundance for the benefit of Western luxury, the shots function to show off Western technology and knowledge. A similar effect is suggested by the shot order mentioned in a review of *Der Kongo* (The Kongo). A shot of two African griots is contrasted in the review with shots of two white scientists doing medical research:

> Of almost overwhelming comic force is a scene in which two black singers glorify the fame of their tribe's deeds and vie with each other in face-pulling. – The shots of two German scientists showing how by testing the blood of a Negro suffering from sleeping sickness they are able to identify the pathogen that caused the sickness (germs that have the medical term 'Typanosomes') deserve particular attention. The last scene is filmed microscopically and shows clearly how the pathogens are moving through the blood.[40]

The contrast in the film between the natives and the scientists seems even to be further emphasized by the mirroring of the two shots. The two griots are described as laughable 'face-pullers' who recount Africa's past, while the two scientists are dealing with a serious present and future problem in Africa, sleeping sickness. The direct switch to the technical device of the microscope, as described in the review, seemed to have been a common aesthetic to create a cultural gap between tradition and modern science. The Pathé Frères production *Moderne Landwirtschaft* (Modern Agriculture) from 1912 demonstrates that the showing off of Western technology was not always presented in a simple contrast but could even be presented in a quite subtle way. The film starts with the intertitle: 'Threshing with the flail is slow and monotonous work'. The first shot shows men on a field threshing the corn. Then the film switches to North Africa. Five camels drive a kind of a threshing mill and the intertitle informs us that in North Africa camels are used for this work: 'In the Algerian Oasis camels are used for this work'. The following intertitle informs us: 'The threshing machine is one of the best inventions of our time' and the film switches back to Europe. The switch from Africa to Europe comes as a surprise. Why this switch at this moment? One is tempted to believe that 'Modern Agriculture', promised in the film's title, is the depiction of the North African people's cleverness in overcoming the hard physical work in the fields. However, the switch of location is just a visual detour. The film cuts back to Europe and introduces a modern threshing machine. The last intertitle makes it clear that Africans stay one step behind modern European technology and probably will never be up to date with it. Through its shot order the film visually ridicules the African and emphasizes colonial thinking that usually considered colonized cultures as living in the past. Putting things right in the colonies, therefore, became a *Kulturmission*, a cultural mission.

A Cultural Mission

Travelogues usually focus on specific geographic regions, and it was a visual tour through the region that structured the film. In this respect the shot order of *Südwest-Afrika*, or the one suggested by the summary of *Leben und Treiben in Tanga*, is not a narrative in the classical sense as the 'views' do not give the impression that they were motivated by one another. However, with regard to the discursive context in which colonial films were placed, colonial ideology provides the films with a kind of meta-narrative in which the implicit story in the films was that of civilizing the colonized.

One of the most distinctive features of German colonial ideology that was used to morally justify colonial rule was the emphasis on the evolutionary difference between colonizer and colonized. Consequently, it was the colonizer's duty to fulfil a Kulturmission in the colonies. In the reformist colonial discourse, colonization was considered a mutual give and take in which the exploitation of the natural resources was counterbalanced by giving the colonized the chance to benefit from the colonizers' higher culture, moral ideas and better methods.[41] Because colonization required that the colonizing society itself first be disciplined, productivity and the society's disciplining became the colonizing principles according to which civilization could be measured.[42] From this perspective, the shot of the missionary in the prison camp in *Südwest-Afrika* indicated the possible conversion of the Nama and Herero warriors into the same industrious workers that could be seen in the expositional 'view' of workers laying railways.

The disciplining of the colonized body also marks the first and last 'views' in *Leben und Treiben in Tanga*. In terms of physical movement, the description of the 'vivid back and forth' in the natives' quarter implies a certain degree of chaos and unpredictability. In contrast, the Askari soldiers are described as dashing and upright, almost equalling their German comrades. By 1909 the Askari had the reputation of a 'skilled, loyal but brutal force', not least due to the defeat of the Maji-Maji Rebellion two years before.[43] The ending of the film pays tribute to the image of the 'loyal African', an image that later would be exploited in colonial revisionism in Weimar politics.[44] *Leben und Treiben in Tanga* juxtaposes African disorganisation against Prussian discipline and illustrates, indeed concludes with, the successful civilization of the colonized body. Oksiloff sees a quite similar 'evolutionary line of progress ... from the most assimilated to the least' in the closing shots of a parade in *Staats-Sekretär Dr. Solf besucht die deutschen Kolonien*, in which African soldiers, the Togo police troop, follow the Europeans 'in seemingly direct imitation of their colonizers'.[45] Focusing on the African soldier Oksiloff notes:

> According to the evolutionary humanist discourse, he [the African soldier] is clearly on the proper path for attaining the Western civilized ideal ... Despite their subservience to the higher ranking white officials – evident in the bare feet and lack of proper uniform – these figures provide proof that the body can be tamed as part of the one ostensibly universal system benefiting 'mankind'[46]

Figure 11.1. The marching Togo police troop. Still from *Staatssekretär Dr. Solf besucht im Oktober 1913 Togo* (1913). Reproduced courtesy of Bundesarchiv-Abteilung Filmarchiv.

The moral duty of the cultural mission to educate the African became even more apparent in the comparison of the colonized with children, as discussed by Solf himself in the German Reichstag: 'The natives are ignorant – they have to be taught. They are lazy – they have to learn to work … All in all … they are big children, who need education and guidance'.[47] Films on the colonial school system and training were the best way to show the colonized in the role of the obedient student. *Die Fortschritte der Zivilisation in Deutsch Ost-Afrika* is a compilation of different practical lessons at the vocational school in Tanga.[48] Under the supervision of white instructors, African students are laying bricks, turning wood, printing and producing books, using the typewriter and being instructed in medical research and medical care. The film is striking for the strongly performative character of all of its scenes. Since lighting conditions made it impossible to shoot inside buildings, almost every demonstration is carefully staged for the camera outside the school. In a shot of a student working with a typewriter one notes that papers are pinned on the table and move vigorously in the wind.

The notion of performance is important as it unintentionally undermines the goal of the film to show the functioning of colonial training. The scene 'Heilkunde' (medicine) shows three older students standing behind a table on which three microscopes are placed. One student is wearing a shirt and takes notes. The other two appear a little bit helpless as they are looking at each other. The first shot of this scene suggests that all three are trained in medical research and supports the positive image of Germany's educational efforts. This impression also characterizes the following shot, a medium close-up of one of the students, who is looking through his microscope. The next shot, however, fractures the positive image the film was trying so hard to conjure up. A vignette shot pretends to reveal what the student is looking at. The shot frames small spots and suggests we are looking at a microscopic shot in which one can see dangerous pathogens, for example. But if we look carefully at the shot, we recognize that the shot is fake, as one can clearly see a salamander suddenly entering the image. The cut back to the student re-establishes the medical research situation, and the film moves on to a scene in which students learn how to apply bandages.

The scene poses many questions: were all these students trained in medical research? Are some just acting, performing 'doing science'? Maybe all of them were trained but were embarrassed by the camera. Is it possible that German colonial officials did not have enough students to demonstrate successful progress in colonial education and therefore had to stage the scene? Maybe the filmmaker was just trying to create an aesthetically balanced image. Most importantly, what did the contemporary audience make of this colonial educational scene? Did it see through the faked vignette shot and was it amused by it? Were some viewers scared of African pathogens that had the size of salamanders? Did the film confirm existing prejudices about the Africans' ignorance that demanded education and guidance? It is impossible to give satisfying answers, but it is the catalogue of questions that challenges the consistency of colonial ideology as presented in this colonial educational film. The image of the three students produces an awkward feeling of watching people who feel uncomfortable with the given situation. The faked microscope shot emphasizes the artificial, staged character of the scene. 'Heilkunde' aims at demonstrating Germany's benevolent Kulturmission, but the clumsy and failed representation of it only reveals the mission as a colonial farce.

The idea that colonial education is being 'playacted' in the film also characterizes the scene 'Tischler und Holzdrechsler' (carpenter and wood turner). The majority of people in this scene are Africans who

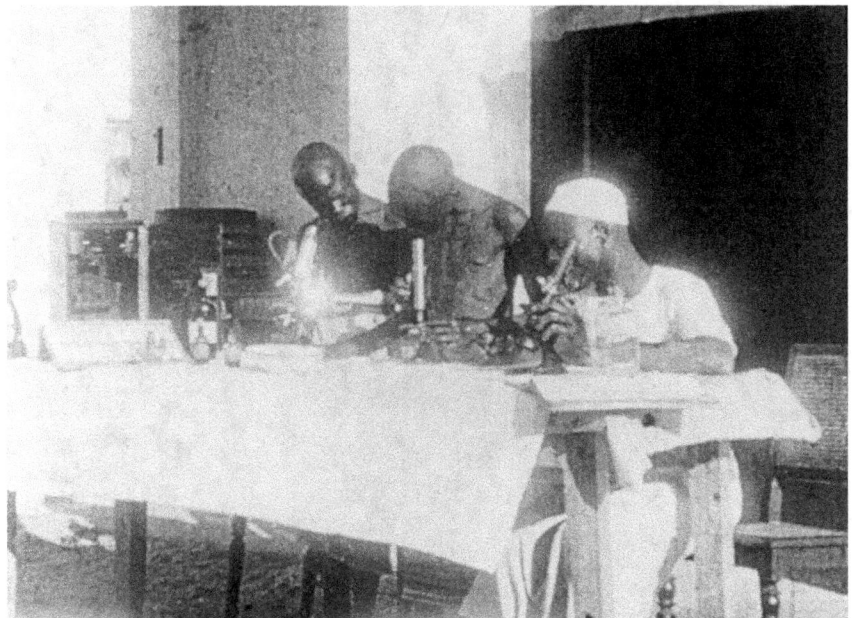

Figure 11.2. Performing science. Still from *Die Fortschritte der Zivilisation in Deutsch-Ostafrika* (1911). Reproduced courtesy of Stiftung Deutsche Kinemathek.

are sawing and planning. A white person controls the work and the products, which resemble window shutters. In the centre of the image, however, one can see an African sitting on the ground, who is handling antlers of African animals. Considering the intertitle, the shot is a contradiction in itself; while most of the image follows the intertitle's idea of presenting students working with wood, the African in the centre works on the transformation of African resources into a European décor – the production of 'imperial kitsch as consumer spectacle'.[49]

The film ends with a propagandistic message. An insert shows a telegram saying: 'The students of the Tanga School send greetings to their comrades in Europe'. The very general address to the European comrades indicates that the film was not aimed at a specific audience, but as a French production, the fraternizing gesture was not without problems in the German context. The telegram text corresponds more to the concept of assimilation in French colonial ideology than to German colonial ideology, in which the colonized 'instead of becoming a bad novelist' might much better be suited to becoming a 'diligent plantation worker',[50] as Adolf Bastian put it, who could never reach the same step

208   *Imperial Projections*

Figure 11.3. Handcraft and imperial kitsch. Still from *Die Fortschritte der Zivilisation in Deutsch-Ostafrika* (1911). Reproduced courtesy of Stiftung Deutsche Kinemathek.

on the evolutionary ladder as the colonizer, not to mention becoming an equal comrade.

The notion of the physical qualities of the colonized points out that the aim of colonialism's 'cultural mission' was not to uplift the Other to a higher level but rather the exploitation of the Africans' work for colonial projects, as *Der Kinematograph* commented in its review of the film *Die Wilden Beim Eisenbahnbau*:

> One has to consider, that nothing else is available for laying railways except for black workers whom nature has designed for a different purpose. … The first experiments have shown, however, they are excellently suited for this kind of work and carry it out with such a skill that is equal to that of our white German workers. That is why a strong will is required that forces them and knows how to achieve a discipline, which is absolutely and blindly followed, then also the savage power is useful for modern labour! … And everything in an unparalleled order. There is no futile standing around, but everybody knows his work and does it untiringly and skilled. One mile of railways laid in one hour, think of it what it means! That is enormous! One can count oneself lucky to have such working material [*Arbeitsmaterial*] as the blacks.[51]

'First experiments', 'savage power' or 'working material' – the dehumanizing remarks about the colonized population stand in sharp contrast to films that were promoting benevolent colonial education. In the same way that the quote reveals colonialism's racism, African students were not trained to conduct serious medical experiments as was suggested in *Die Fortschritte der Zivilisation in Deutsch-Ostafrika*: they were the object under scientific scrutiny; their systematic exploitation for the colonizer's interest.[52]

Surviving film prints and reviews show little interest in colonized people as individuals and usually conceive the colonized as a stereotype. A striking example in which the technical apparatus itself is manipulated for proving the stereotyped image of the 'lazy African' can be found in a review of one of Carl Müller's screenings in Stuttgart in November 1905:

> Particularly successful was the screening of the life of the natives, their dances, their work on the plantations, the hustle and bustle on the markets etc. First one was astonished by the extreme industriousness of the blacks while they were working and one was asking oneself if they finally have given up for a short time, for the camera and their good reputation in Europe, their traditional apathy. However, soon one discovered that only the accelerated projection speed of the films has caused this active bustle.[53]

What could have been a powerful demonstration of the African workers' productivity in the territories was turned into its opposite by manipulating the projection speed: not admiration but laughter was the effect on the audience.

According to Homi K. Bhabha, the colonial stereotype is a 'form of knowledge and identification that vacillates between what is always "in place", already known, and something that must be anxiously repeated'.[54] The construction of the colonial Other is therefore based in a 'paradoxical mode of representation: it connotes rigidity and an unchanging order as well as disorder, degeneracy and daemonic repetition'.[55] The process of ambivalence of the colonial stereotype seemed be present in many colonial films. The synopsis of *Leben und Treiben in Tanga* ends with images of the Askari soldiers' uprightness and dashing character, which almost equal that of their German comrades. The review of *Die Wilden beim Eisenbahnbau* reports that the skilfulness of the African railway workers equals that of white German workers. Remarks like these illustrate the oscillation between a fascination for the physical strength and skilfulness of the African workers on the one hand, and, on the other, the effort to conceive of them only as the product of the colonizer's strong will. But do these remarks eventually prove the success of the colonization and education of the colonized Other?

Reviews' emphasis on the similarity between colonizer and colonized point to what Bhaba calls the mimicry in colonial discourse: the desire for a reformed, recognizable Other as the subject of a difference that is nearly but not completely the same.[56] The ambivalence of the mimicry, 'almost the same/but not quite', also contains a moment of resistance and uproar that threatens colonial power.[57] Studies of the German ethnologist Julius Lips show that the colonizers' presence and work had already been picked out as a central theme in the arts of colonized people. Illustrations and carvings show that German discipline was clearly understood as a characteristic of the obedient German and underline the colonized's analytical take on the ridiculousness of the aspiring 'serious' colonial official.[58] This subversiveness and the implied threat to colonial authority also seemed to be present in colonial films. While films try to contain their fascination within the authoritative colonial discourse, they express at the same time the impossibility of this containment.

An example of the possibility of a de-authorization of colonial power is the film *Deutsch-Ostafrika. Eine grosse öffentliche Schule der Provinz Usambara* (German East Africa. A Big Public School in the Usambara Province) (Pathé Frères/Germania Film, 1912).

The film starts with a geography lesson. The teacher asks the children to show on a map of the colony some parts of the Usambara region. Several children come up to the teacher and demonstrate their geographical knowledge.

During the break all the students come out of the school building and line up to form two different groups, which walk off-frame. In a total shot we see two people holding a long stick as a hurdle. The children are waiting in the background and start running and jumping over the hurdle towards the camera. A new shot shows the same street as before. A marching band is approaching, accompanied by dancing children. The band passes the camera from right to left. Then the film continues with the depiction of the same lively atmosphere, as in *Leben und Treiben in Tanga*. The last two shots are introduced by the intertitle 'The phonograph of the Pathé company takes care of the entertainment'. The film shows Europeans sitting at a table (on a public square?) where wine, champagne and cigars are served, and a phonograph is placed. The table is surrounded by musicians of the marching band and children who are pushing each other in order to catch a glimpse into the phonograph's horn.

Figure 11.4. Geography lesson in a German East African public school. Still from *Deutsch-Ostafrika: Eine große öffentliche Schule in der Provinz Usambara* (1912). Reproduced courtesy of Bundesarchiv-Filmarchiv.

The two clusters, education for the colonized African public and entertainment for the colonizer, suggest the clear separation of roles in colonial public life. However, the film can also be read as undermining the colonial order. According to the film title, the film deals with a school in the Usambara region. It focuses on the school, the lessons, the children and the marching band after school. Until this stage, a film about a school in Germany would not have been much different: school children behave well during the lesson and are joyfully running and jumping when class is over. More difficult to understand is the combination with the final shots of the Europeans sitting at a table, where champagne, wine and cigars are served, and children surround the phonograph. These shots do not make any sense in the sequential logic of the images that were shown before. No additional information about the school system is given in the shots of the Europeans: compared to the sequential logic of the earlier images the final shots seem awkwardly placed.

The first part of the film shows an African school system that functions perfectly without any intervention from the colonizer. But what

Figure 11.5. Listening to the phonograph. Still from *Deutsch-Ostafrika: Eine große öffentliche Schule in der Provinz Usambara* (1912). Reproduced courtesy of Bundesarchiv-Filmarchiv.

would the film have been like without the visible presence of the white colonizers in the final shots of the film? Is it possible that in this case the film would be an example of the possibility of an independent administration that did not require the colonizers' benevolent help? A film like this could break the 'rule of colonial difference' and threaten the whole colonial project by destabilizing the desired difference between the colonizer and colonized, which is a prerequisite for colonial power.[59] From this perspective the final shots function to re-establish the colonial order that the film's structure threatened to undermine. In this context and for this specific reading of the film's ending, the shot of the phonograph assumes significance. The encounter of Western technology and the colonized population was a common topos in colonial visual culture. Oksiloff calls Rudolf Pöch's film *Buschmann spricht in den Phonographen* (Bushman Speaks into the Phonograph) (1908) a 'dramatic encounter between the two ends of the evolutionary line: the *most* primitive and the most advance specimens of culture'.[60] A colourful illustration of Weule and his phonograph adorns the German edition of his popular publication *Native life in East Africa*, which immediately triggers the association of a magician's show. Numerous adverts in specialized journals like the *Phonographische Zeitschrift* (Phonographic Journal) used colonial Africa as a backdrop for demonstrating the wonder of such voice-recording tools as gramophones and records.[61] *Deutsch-Ostafrika. Eine grosse öffentliche Schule der Provinz Usambara* is no exception. It is not the presence of the African marching band performing live music but the technical device of a phonograph that produces delight among the people and leaves the colonized in incredulous disbelief. In other words, it is Western technology that makes the difference. Like the establishing 'view' of railway construction and the final shot of a steamer in *Südwest-Africa* and the arrival of the train, which functions as the symbolic border between the native quarters and the European part of the town in *Leben und Treiben in Tanga*, it is the phonograph that characterizes the colonizer as the civilized among the 'uncivilized children'.

The Aesthetic Experience

The previous examples of colonial travelogues have shown how the colonies could be represented as an extension of the German Heimat and how they legitimized colonial rule. Peterson reminds us that 'though colonial ideology underlies many travelogues, there are other contexts in which to place travel films, such as that of landscape and the actual cultural practice of tourism and travel'.[62] Likewise, Martin Loiperdinger suggests that we need to distinguish two modes of looking that are at work in films from the colonies, the colonial gaze and the tourist gaze: 'The colonial gaze is connected with the interest of the nation, exploiting and civilizing a foreign country to profit from it, both economically and militarily. The tourist gaze is related to an individual who wants to have the world within reach, to see what interesting things the world offers him, whether it is tradition or exoticism'.[63] Loiperdinger points out the danger of discussing colonial travelogues exclusively in categories of colonial propaganda, education and ideology, and in that way missing film's significance as an aesthetic event within a film programme.[64] As has been discussed above, most screenings at the DKG's branches featured a combination of colonial and non-colonial film material. What might have been a concession on the part of the DKG to its members was a 'must' in public cinemas: in early film programmes a film from the colonies was only one film among many others. A film programme was no randomly assembled melange of films but usually followed a formula designed to attract the audience from the very first to the very last minute.[65]

The following example of a film programme at a cinema in February 1907 shows how a colonial film could be programmed:

> *Nilpferdjagd in Deutsch-Südwest-Afrika* [Hippo Hunt in German South-West Africa], *Falscher Alarm* [False Alarm], *S.M.S 'Sleipner' im Sturm* [S.M.S 'Sleipner' in Storm], *Der neue Laufbursche* [The New Office Boy], *Rheinfall bei Schaffhausen* [The Rhine Falls at Schaffhausen], *Der Photograph* [The Photographer], *'Tor die* [sic] *Quinto' (die Centauren der Gegenwart)* [Tor di Quinto (The Centaurs of the Present)], *Der Traum des Feinschmeckers* [The Gourmet's Dream], *Durchgehende Pferde* [Runaway Horses], *Das Rollende Fass* [The Rolling Barrel], *Rundfahrt durch den Kieler Hafen* [Trip through the Kiel Harbour], *Das Theater des kl. Bob* [Little Bob's Theatre], *Schön ist ein Zylinderhut* [Nice is a Top Hat], *Eine Reise durch die Schweiz* [A Journey Through Switzerland][66]

Given the recent event of the election of the Reichstag just the week before, one could consider the programme's first film as an adequate patriotic prelude. The second title suggests a short comedy; the film does not continue the serious or thrilling mood of the first, but offers comic relief before another patriotic film follows, depicting a torpedo boat of the imperial sea fleet in a storm. Looking closely at the programme one notes that many films address the 'view' aesthetic: the African colony, the ocean, the Rhine falls on the Swiss border, the Kiel harbour and Switzerland. Considering the beginning and the end of the programme, what did viewers make of the hippo hunt in Africa in combination with a journey through Switzerland? One explanation is that it was the programmer's intention to bracket the programme through the extreme contrast between these typical elements of the two continents: the African hippo and the Swiss mountains. The difference also implies a climatic contrast between the heat and the cold. The contrast of geographic distance, topographic or climatic, seemed to be one of the most attractive programming strategies for exhibitors. In the following weeks other cinemas programmed the hippo-hunt film in combination with the Switzerland film.

Too few primary sources exist to discuss the strategies of programming of colonial films and their internal dynamics with other parts of a programme. The idea of the programme, however, indicates that audiences could contextualize a film very differently. Technology could be viewed as a modern colonizing tool, but it also played on the viewer's fascination with the machine as a visual spectacle, such as the gleaming steel in *Aus dem Innern Afrikas*, the construction work in *Südwest-Afrika* or the display of various moving vehicles in *Leben und Treiben in Tanga*. For a viewer watching films from far away regions for the pleasure of virtual travel, films from Africa or the South Seas could highlight the beauty of the unfamiliar flora and fauna or the height of an African waterfall. In this sense, the 1907 production *Die Viktoriafälle* (The Victoria Falls) was, on the one hand, an example of how German industry was planning 'very soon to use the enormous power of water for bringing electricity into the Interior of Africa' and, on the other, a visual aesthetic experience produced by the cinematographic apparatus and the tinting and toning of the film, which showed 'wonderful changing scenes, the cataracts at sunrise, sunset and by moonlight, the beautiful colourings when the enormous mass of water crashes down the abyss'.[67]

Film's ability to bridge geographic distance and simulate a real travel experience made colonial travelogues into vicarious journeys that were affordable for everybody. Aiming at an audience that could not afford a trip to Africa but should not have to miss anything was the idea of the travelogue series *Quer durch Afrika* aka *Von Cairo zum Kap* (Across Africa aka From Cairo to the Cape). The series, of which *Die Viktoriafälle* was part, was the result of an expedition of the film company Raleigh & Robert through Africa from the south to the north between 1906 and 1907. It covered almost every aspect of what viewers expected to see in 'the whole black part of the world, from one end to the other',[68] and the film journal *Der Kinematograph* remarked that the series allowed the audience 'to make a whole journey ... that they think, they were really in the country that was shown'.[69] Film's possibility to explore the world for the viewer was linked to an emerging mass tourism and the way in which modern transportation systems took the tourist to formerly unknown places. This symbiotic relation is felt almost physically by the so-called phantom ride films in which the camera was mounted on a moving vehicle. The most popular exhibition mode of this kind of 'filmic railway travel' was the Hale's Tours, in which film simulated the travel experience by screening 'railway films' in a real, but stationary, railway carriage.[70] The co-operation between railways and film companies was quite common because railways perceived film as a useful form of publicity.

The popular mode of simulating the travel experience was also adopted by the organizers of the Berlin exposition DAMUKA in May 1907. There had been a plan to provide and operate a real colonial tropical railway on the exhibition grounds and to run a film theatre that was designed to imitate the Lomé station in Togo, showing Georg Furkel's films from the colonies. Even though the original idea of screening colonial films for exhibition goers who had just travelled on a real colonial railway could not be realized, the train station-cinema became one of the exposition's main attractions.[71] In the review of the *Berliner Tageblatt* the colonial context is shifted into the background in favour of the filmic experience of crossing the African desert without really being there. It was the pleasure of travelling through the 'drifting sand dunes, undergrowth and the enemy's territory without suffering from thirst', as the reviewer put it, that made the viewing of the films an outstanding experience at this exposition.[72]

The emphasis on the travel experience also characterizes *Fahrt durch den Urwald* (Trip Through the Jungle) (Archive Title, 1910?), which was shot in the Usambara region of the East African colony. The film begins with a phantom ride, probably taken from the Sigi railway. The train passes Africans. After the train has been loaded with coal by Africans, the train arrives at a jungle station. Before the viewer arrives in a camp where a European man and woman are having dinner, the film shows a journey through a dense forest, passing a native hut. An intertitle announces the 'Sigi-Fälle' of which one can see several shots, one showing an African posing by the falls with an umbrella. The intertitle 'The famous Pangani-Waterfalls' is followed by shots of a rope bridge across the river, a 'view' across the bridge and natives crossing the bridge.[73] The film's images of the dense forest, waterfalls and the rope bridge refer to the late eighteenth-century aesthetic of the picturesque in its function of rendering beauty and the sublime, but Peterson underlines that travelogues are less rooted in the 'world of high art or aesthetic theory', as they refer to more popular art forms.[74] In this respect *Fahrt durch den Urwald* does not invite the viewer to engage in a contemplative study of the colony's untouched nature, but the travelogue's generic form makes the film appear as a visual tourist guide that presents particularly interesting sights for the tourist. Comparing the individual shots of the film with descriptions in the official tourist guidebook from 1914 makes the film almost a promotional film for the Usambara region:

> The railway cuts first of all through the fertile and beautiful Bondei that, like the Magrotto Mountain that comes soon into sight, is densely settled with natives ... Behind the Kwamkuyubridge at the bridle path's first curve forks another path, that gives one the chance after ten minutes on the jungle path to see the Sigi falls. ... A tropical Vosges picture! ... the Margarete–Falls of the Pangani, which no traveller should miss. The Pangani will be crossed on a primitive rope bridge that could make frightened souls nervous but which is absolutely safe.[75]

In contrast to *Fahrt durch den Urwald,* in which the travel through the colony's present natural beauty was more important than the focus on the African people, other travelogues established a different travel experience. Travelling the colony through film-going could become not only a chance to visit a geographically distant location but also simulate a thrilling time travel into the past, encountering people still living in a prehistoric time, or triggering associations with adventure and Africa's exploration. Raleigh & Robert emphasized that their 1907 film *Ein Afrikanisches Idyll* (An African Idyll) was not a farce performed by a 'half civilized travelling gang of Negroes' but an authentic recording of the Masha-Kulumbi tribe made by eavesdropping on their over-a-hundred-year-old traditions.[76] The triple motif of travel, distance and time characterizes *Mit dem Norddeutschen Lloyd nach Neu-Guinea.* The arrival in New Guinea is presented as the arrival in a primitive age, in which war dances, secret societies and lethal rituals are part of everyday life.[77] The travel from Germany to the South Seas starts with the departure from Bremerhaven: 1. 'Departure from Bremerhaven'; 2. 'Parlour Games [*Gesellschaftsspiele*] on Board of the Norddeutschem Lloyd Steamer 'Preußen'. Shuffle – Broom Dance'; 3. 'At the Marseille Harbour'; 4. 'Musical welcome at the Harbour in Naples'; 5. 'At the Arabian Coast. Camel Riders – Parade of the Natives'; 6. 'At the Coast of Ceylon. Bathing Beach – Laundry – 5 Minutes Before End of Work'; 7. 'Arrival in New Guinea – Friedrich-Wilhelmshafen'; 8. 'Exercises of the German Police Troop in New Guinea'; 9. 'Festival Dances of the Natives in New Guinea'; 10.' War dances of the natives in New Guinea'; 11. 'Duk-Duk-Dance, a Secret Society Dance. Photographed for the first time, foreigners and even natives who had previously tried to see these dances had been sentenced to death'.[78]

The film documents carefully the viewer's departure from the familiar European territory to the Arabian coast and finally to the exotic world of New Guinea, whose inhabitants were still described at the 1896 colonial exposition in Berlin as 'just sprung from stone ages'.[79] In New Guinea the viewer has finally arrived back in the Stone Age. 'Views' of festive and war dances – not to mention the secret society's dance, unauthorized participation in which was punished with death – were supposed to give the viewers an impression of the dangers of the colony. The contrast between the two cultures at this moment could not be more intense. While the 'modern' shuffle-broom dance was part of the tourist's entertainment on board the steamer, the traditional dances in New Guinea retain a mysterious, deadly quality. In the film the admission to the secret society, the Duk-Duk society, which was the precondition for marriage for young people on the Bismarck Archipelago,[80] loses its scientific relevance. Compared to European wedding traditions the strange initiation rituals on the island were an uncanny encounter. However, similar to *Südwest-Afrika,* in which the prison camp shots are placed within the tourist shots and softened through 'pleasing' prison shots such as the playing children, *Mit dem Norddeutschen Lloyd nach Neu-Guinea* situates the police troop between the shot of the tourist's arrival and the natives. In this way the natives appear to be living on a reservation guarded by the police troop. The contrast between tourist and the natives thus becomes less drastic, and the film adventure becomes a quite safe form of travel.[81]

The example *Mit dem Norddeutschen Lloyd nach Neu-Guinea* shows that although travelogues could hardly be called narratives in the sense of a classical storytelling strategy, patterns of narrativity were not absent from early nonfiction films. Most simply, the travel can be considered a narrative in itself. In contrast to the previous examples in which the popularity of the travelogues was discussed with regard to the 'view' aesthetic, the emphasis on the temporal aspects in a travelogue address the narrative dimension of the films.

Tom Gunning points out that 'view' films are open to a variety of approaches. The depiction of industrial processes, for instance, gives way to temporal strategies. Such process films usually depicted the manufacturing of a particular good in which the different steps in the production process are broken down in a logical sequence of several shot clusters. Filming of the harvesting, processing and transport of coffee or production processes of other traditional colonial goods, such as cotton, sugar or cacao, were perfect examples to be discussed with reference to the national colonial economic context. Watching a production process in a colonial travelogue could be an exotic viewing experience in the double sense: while the production process was already interesting in itself, it was the processing of an unfamiliar, exotic good that made the film even more spectacular.[82] Process films often ended with the 'consumption of the manufactured good, within a comfortable or even glamorous bourgeois interior', which placed the goods at the intersection of desire and lack.[83] *Wie ein Brief von den grossen Seen Zentral-Afrikas zu uns gelangt* (How a Letter Travels from the Great Lakes of Central Africa) (Pathé Frères, 1911), which shows the different stages of the transport of a letter from Africa to Europe, is an interesting example of blending different viewing experiences. It combines the characteristic features of a process film with the travelogue's interest in the exploration of foreign places and suggests a small narrative that intertextually refers to the numerous adventure stories about Africa's discovery.

The film starts with an African paddling in a reed canoe through the swamp, somewhere near the source of the River Nile. A letter is attached to a stick in the middle of the canoe. He hands over the letter to a canoe paddled by three Africans. They reach a felucca that accepts the letter and sails with it to a European colonial outpost. Two large bags of mail are handed over to two Arabs, who mount their camels. The men are seen crossing the desert and arriving at a town. A paddle steamer transports the mail to Upper Egypt. The mail is then put onto a train that arrives later in Alexandria, where it is loaded onto a steamer. The steamer arrives in a European port. A postman delivers the letter to a woman, who takes it to her daughter who is playing in the house, to read.

The film's main topic is the transport of the letter that is paralleled by a kind of history of transportation: from the primitive canoe to the modern ocean steamship liner. The film, however, also shows that a colonial travelogue could attract the audience's attention by offering more than just a virtual travel experience. As was typical for the process film, it ends with a small narrative closure that contextualizes the film in a real life experience: the letter from the interior of Africa arrives at the home of a family, a mother and her child. Though the viewer does not learn anything about the author of the letter, the film triggers the questions about its addressor: who wrote the letter? Is it a message from the husband and father for which the family has already been waiting a long time?

When films from Africa entered early film programmes, the era of Africa's exploration was nearly finished and Africa as a geographic unity had ceased to exist. However, until the nineteenth century the source, course and direction of the great African rivers remained a mystery, which was supported by the legend of the 'dark mysterious' continent.[84] The search for the River Nile's source became a prestigious quest for Western explorers, whose reports about successful or failed expeditions made the river the most prominent topic for popular representation in the second half of nineteenth century. The film's appeal lies in its intertextual challenge of linking the film's closure to the film's beginning: where does the canoe come from? The film seems to refer to the discovery of the Nile's source, a place that was considered the heart of Africa. With this reading, the film receives a historical dimension and recalls John Hanning Speke's historic telegram to the Royal Geographical Society: 'The Nile is settled'. The film shows that colonial travelogues offered a range of different readings to the audience. The possibility of triggering associations of adventure and exploration, as was suggested in this last film, was an alternative that characterizes Robert Schumann's second film career.

Notes

1. J. Peterson, '"Truth is Stranger than Fiction": Travelogues from the 1910s in the Nederlands Filmmuseum', in D. Hertogs and N. de Klerk (eds), *Uncharted Territory. Essays on Nonfiction Film*, Amsterdam: Stichting Nederlands Filmmuseum, 1997, 78.
2. Gunning, 'Before Documentary', 14.
3. T. Gunning, 'The Cinema of Attractions. Early Film, its Spectator and the Avant-Garde', in T. Elsaesser (ed.) *Space-Frame-Narrative*, London, 1990, 56–62.
4. Gunning, 'Before Documentary', 14.
5. Ibid., 15.
6. Ibid.
7. Peterson, 'Truth is Stranger than Fiction', 76.
8. Ibid.
9. Ibid., 81.
10. Peterson, 'World Pictures', 1.
11. J. Noyes, *Colonial Space. Spatiality in the Discourse of German South West Africa 1884–1915*, Chur et al.: Harwood Academic Publishers, 1992, 163.
12. Ibid.
13. Anon., 'Kolonialer Verkehrsverein', *DKZ*, 20 May 1911, 338.
14. Richelmann, 'Etwas über Vergnügungsreisen in Afrika', *DKZ*, 1 April 1911, 206; *DKZ*, 15 April 1911, 249–51.
15. O. Karstedt, *Deutsch-Ostafrika und seine Nachbargebiete. Ein Handbuch für Reisende*, Berlin: Dietrich Reimer (Ernst Vohsen), 1914, VII.
16. Ibid., IX.
17. Arbeitsausschuss der II. Allgemeinen Deutsch-Ostafrikanischen Landesausstellung in Daressalam (ed.), *Wohin reise ich im Sommer 1914?*, Berlin, 1914.
18. Karstedt, *Deutsch-Ostafrika und seine Nachbargebiete*, 227, 172, 210, 205.
19. J. Jäger, 'Colony as Heimat? The Formation of Colonial Identity in Germany around 1900', *German History*, 2009, 27(4): 470. In the same way, Germans living in the colonies considered the colony as their Heimat. Cf. D. Rowen-Steinbach, 'Defending the Heimat: The Germans in South-West Africa and East Africa during the First World War', in H. Jones, J. O'Brien and C. Schmidt-Supprian (eds), *Untold War. New Perspectives in First World War Studies*, Leiden, Boston: Brill, 2008, 179–208.
20. C. Applegate, *A Nation of Provincials: The German Idea of Heimat*, Berkeley. University of California Press, 1990, 4; A. Confino, *The Nation as a Local Metaphor: Württemberg, Imperial Germany, and National Memory, 1871–1918*, Chapel Hill: University of North Carolina Press, 1997.
21. J. von Moltke, *No Place Like Home. Locations of Heimat in German Cinema*, Berkeley: University of California Press, 2005, 13.
22. J. von Moltke, 'Evergreens: The Heimat Genre', in T. Bergfelder, E. Carter and D. Göktürk (eds), *The German Cinema Book*, London: BFI, 2008, 19.
23. *Darmstädter Tageblatt*, 16 March 1908.
24. Oksiloff, *Picturing the Primitive*, 50.

25. *Der Komet*, 20 June 1907. Parallel to this, the film company Deutsche Mutoskop-und Biograph released *Leute in Südwest Afrika* (People in South-West Africa) with 'original scenes from the theatre of war [*Kriegsschauplatze*]'.
26. Sometimes the units were spatially not differentiated but at least assigned to different places within the same image, as was shown by the scene 'Armenian fighters' in *Der Kongo*. According to a review, two Europeans are seated in an elevated special viewing place in order to observe the fight.
27. This does not mean that films about prisoners in the colonies were no longer produced. The Pathé Frères catalogue for example lists the film *Un bagne en Afrique orientale allemande* (A Penitentiary in German East Africa) (Pathé Frères 1910). According to the brief summary the film showed 'the rude and miserable life of a prisoner in Africa: putting chains on the prisoners' neck, visit of the director, the labour duties with wood, water and stones, the meals and the punishments'. There is no evidence that the film was officially distributed or sold in Germany. H. Bousquet (ed.), *Catalogue Pathé des Années 1896 á 1914, 1910–1911*, Bures sur Yvette, 1994, 282.
28. M. de Certeau, *The Practice of Everyday Life*, trans. S. Randall Berkeley, Los Angeles, London: University of California Press, 1984, 36.
29. Gunning, 'Before Documentary', 15.
30. *Der Kinematograph*, 10 November, 1909.
31. See A. Eckart, 'Koloniale Stadtplanung und europäischer Rassismus: Die Enteignung der Duala', in W. Wagner (ed.), *Rassendiskriminierung, Kolonialpolitik und ethnischnationale Identität*, Referate des 2. Internationalen Kolonialgeschichtlichen Symposiums, 1991, Münster and Hamburg: Lit Verlag, 1992, 206–16.
32. Too few prints exist to discuss the role of colour in colonial films. For a discussion of colour in early cinema see D. Hertogs and N. de Klerk, *'Disorderly Order'. Colours in Silent Film. The 1995 Amsterdam Workshop*, Amsterdam: Stichting Nederlands Filmuseum, 1996.
33. Peterson, 'World Pictures', 1.
34. Anon., 'Kinematographische Aufnahmen in Tanga', *Usambara-Post*, 4 September 1909.
35. *Gränzbote Tuttlingen*, 6 May 1907.
36. *Der Kinematograph*, 17 January 1912.
37. Schinzinger, *Die Kolonien und das Deutsche Reich*, 63. Shots of railway construction are numerous in the colonial film repertoire. Other films that focused on construction in the colonies or Africa were: *Die Wilden beim Eisenbahnbau/Quer durch Afrika III* (The Savages Constructing a Railway) (Raleigh & Robert, 1907), *Die Wilden beim Brückenbau, Quer durch Afrika IX* (The Savages Constructing a Bridge) (Raleigh & Robert, 1908), *Bau einer Eisenbahnlinie in Afrika* (Construction of a Railway in Africa) (1908) and *Eisenbahnbau bei Kindu* (Railway Construction near Kindu) (Cinéma des Colonies, 1911).
38. Anon., 'Der Fortschritt', *Der Kinematograph*, 10 February 1907.
39. This rhetorical strategy was also used in *Der Kongo*, in which the reviewer uses the same intertitle to refer to a wood carver who produces 'with the most primitive instruments, household tools'. *Der Kinematograph*, 19 February 1913.
40. Ibid.
41. See also Dernburg, *Zielpunkte des deutschen Kolonialwesens. Zwei Vorträge*, Berlin: Verlag Ernst Siegfried Mittler und Sohn, 5.
42. See also H. Melber, 'Rassismus und eurozentrisches Zivilisationsmodell: Zur Entwicklungsgeschichte des kolonialen Blicks', in N. Räthzel (ed.), *Theorien über Rassismus*, Hamburg: Argument Verlag, 2000, 131–63.

43. M. Moyd, 'Askari and Askari Myth', in P. Poddar, R. Shridhar Patke and L. Jensen (eds), *A Historical Companion to Postcolonial Literatures: Continental Europe and Its Empires*, Edingburgh: Edinburgh University Press, 2008, 209.
44. T. Morlang, *Askari und Fitafita: 'Farbige' Söldner in den deutschen Kolonien*, Berlin: Ch. Links Verlag, 2008, 92.
45. Oksiloff, *Picturing the Primitive*, 77.
46. Ibid., 78.
47. Solf quoted in H. Melber. '"…dass die Kultur der Neger gehoben werde!" – Kolonialdebatten im deutschen Reichstag', in *Kolonialmetropole Berlin*, 69.
48. *Die Fortschritte der Zivilisation in Deutsch-Ostafrika* probably was identical to *Erste staatliche Fachschule in Tanga* (First vocational school in Tanga) (Pathé Frères, 1911), which was released a week before and had the same length (110 m). Other films on colonial schools that were shown in the German cinemas were: *Eine Schule in Neu-Guinea* (A School in New Guinea) (Pathé Frères, 1909) and *Deutsch-Ostafrika. Eine grosse öffentliche Schule der Provinz Usambara* (Pathé Frères/Germania Film, 1912), probably identical to *Eine öffentliche Schule in Ostafrika* (A Public School in East Africa) (Pathé Frères, 1912).
49. A. McClintock, 'Soft-Soaping Empire. Commodity Racism and Imperial Advertising', in N. Mirzoeff (ed.), *The Visual Culture Reader*, 2nd edn, London: Routledge, 2002, 508.
50. A. Bastian quoted in Gothsch, *Die deutsche Völkerkunde und ihr Verhältnis zum Kolonialismus*, 59.
51. Anon., 'Der Fortschritt'.
52. Though colonization's civilizing efforts were usually considered a serious issue, it probably was not always treated seriously in film. The Raleigh & Robert production *Die Sittenverbesserung eines Negers* (The Moral Improvement of a Negro) (1911), for example, seemed to be a comical short that showed the 'funny picture of a Negro' trying to become 'civilized'. *Der Kinematograph*, 18 January 1911.
53. *Schwäbische Chronik*, 4 November 1905.
54. H.K. Bhabha, 'The Other Question. Stereotype, Discrimination and the Discourse of Colonialism' in *The Location of Culture*, London: Routledge, 1994, 66.
55. Ibid.
56. H.K. Bhabha, 'Of Mimicry and Man: The Ambivalence of Colonial Discourse', in *The Location of Culture*, London: Routledge, 1994, 86.
57. Ibid., 89
58. J. Lips, *The Savage Hits Back*, London: Lovat Dickson Limited Publishers, 1937, 90 (fig. 42), 213 (fig.19).
59. See P. Chatterjee, *The Nation & Its Fragments: Colonial & Postcolonial Histories*, Princeton, N.J.: Princeton University Press, 1993.
60. Oksiloff, *Picturing the Primitive*, 46
61. See, for example, Beka Records (illustration): 'Ein Koloniales Ereignis!' (A Colonial Event!), *Phonographische Zeitschrift*, 1908, 9(26): 635. The illustration shows a German salesman who is selling records and gramophones to African people. In the background one African bites into a record.
62. Peterson, '"Truth is Stranger than Fiction"', 84.
63. Martin Loiperdinger, 'The Eye of the Beholder', CD-Rom, Filmmuseum, Amsterdam, the Netherlands (eds), 3rd Amsterdam workshop, 1998, Discussion Session 2.
64. See M. Lewinsky, 'The Best Years of Film History: A Hundred Years Ago', in M. Loiperdinger (ed.), *Early Cinema Today: The Art of Programming and Live Performance*, New Barnet, Herts: John Libbey Publishing, 2011, 28.

65. Corinna Müller quotes the following formula for a film programme around 1910: '1. Music, 2. Actuality, 3. Humoristic, 4. Drama, 5. Comical Break, 6. Scenic, 7. Comical, 8. The Big Attraction, 9. Scientific, 10. Strong Comedy'. Müller. 'Frühe deutsche Kinematographie', 12.
66. *Der Kinematograph*, 3 February 1907.
67. *Der Kinematograph*, 10 July 1907. *Die Viktoriafälle* was simultaneously distributed in different lengths by Raleigh & Robert for The Continental Warwick Trading Co. Ltd (140 m), *Der Komet*, 20 July 1907, 1; Charles Urban Trading Company (128 m), *Der Komet*, 27 July 1907, 4. It suggests that the Raleigh & Robert film team probably was one amongst others that contributed to the British Urban Africa expedition that was produced by the Charles Urban Trading Company, 'Great Victoria Falls, Zambesi River', retrieved 20 March 2013 from http://colonialfilm.org.uk/node/503.
68. *Der Komet*, 5 January 1907, 1.
69. Anon., 'Der Fortschritt'. The German reviews do not mention the cooperation with the Urban-Africa expedition, see footnote 65.
70. C. Musser, 'The Travel Genre in 1903–1904. Moving Towards Fictional Narrative', in T. Elsaesser (ed.), *Early Cinema: Space, Frame, Narrative*, London: British Film Institute, 1990, 127.
71. L. Brauner, 'Der Kinematograph als Ausstellungsattraktion', *Der Kinematograph*, 13 July 1910.
72. *Berliner Tageblatt*, 1 March 1907.
73. It is quite possible that the film is identical to *Die Sigifälle in Deutsch-Ostafrika* (The Sigi Falls in German East Africa) (Deutsche Bioscop GmbH, 1910).
74. Peterson, 'World Picture', 213.
75. Karstedt, *Deutsch-Ostafrika und seine Nachbargebiete*, 170–79.
76. *Der Kinematograph*, 7 August 1907.
77. Hans Fischer points out that for many people the correct differentiation between Polynesia, Melanesia and Micronesia was less important than the simple dichotomy between the enchanting exoticism of the South Seas (Tahiti, Hawaii, Samoa) and the visit to the Stone Age in New Guinea. Fischer, *Die Hamburger Südsee-Expedition*, 14.
78. *Der Kinematograph*, 31 March 1907.
79. Arbeitsausschuss der Deutschen Kolonial-Ausstellung (ed.), *Offizieller Katalog und Führer der Deutschen Kolonial-Ausstellung 1896*, Bearbeitet von Gustav Meinecke, Berlin, 1897, 15.
80. P. Ryan (ed.), *Encyclopedia of Papua and New Guinea*, Carlton: Melbourne University Press, 1972, 554.
81. The police troop in the New Guinea colony was made up not of German policemen but of local people, which means that the shot order can also be read in terms of the cultural mission argument and the successful civilizing of the colonized.
82. Similar production-process films were: *Goldindustrie in Afrika* (Raleigh & Robert, 1911), *Im Reiche der Diamanten/Die Diamanten von der Erde zum Juwelier* (Raleigh & Robert, 1907), *Diamantensuche am Vaalfluss* (Empire, 1912) and *Diamantenfelder in Deutsch-Südwestafrika* (Hansafilm, 1914).
83. Gunning, 'Before Documentary', 17.
84. A. Honold, 'Flüsse, Berge, Eisenbahn: Szenarien geographischer Bemächtigung', in A. Honold and K.R. Scherpe (eds), *Das Fremde. Reiseerfahrungen, Schreibformen und kulturelles Wissen*, Beiheft 2 der Zeitschrift für Germanistik, N.F., 2000, 149–74.

Chapter 12

COLONIAL FILMS IN TRANSITION

Robert Schumann's Comeback

Film-viewing culture changed significantly around 1910/11. Short films had become cheap, mass products, so the production of long fiction films was considered a chance for consolidation in the film market. Longer films made producers pay more attention to aspects of storytelling and the actors' acting. The growing popularity of fiction films in the programmes had consequences for nonfiction films; in contrast to the entertaining character of longer fiction films, the production of long nonfiction films was costly and sometimes hardly entertaining for the viewer. A film about Scott's South Pole expedition, *Scott's Südpolexpedition* (Elge-Deutsche Gaumont, 1912), was criticized for just showing the same iceberg for one and a half hours.[1] Robert Schumann's films from Africa, which represent his 'comeback' in the German film business, seemed to be different in kind.

Schumann had enormous success with his own film company Deutsche Jagd-Film-Gesellschaft (DJFG), which released three hunting films and one fiction film that he had shot during his stay(s) in the East African colony between 1908 and 1913. His films, especially their reediting and rerelease during the First World War, indicate the beginning of a transformation of the 'view' aesthetic, so characteristic for the colonial travelogue, into a new nonfiction film form in which the material became dramatized and embedded in a larger argument – the documentary film.[2] Schumann's hunting film repertoire, however, also points to an alternative reception context, the rise of the wildlife protection movement.

Nothing is known about Schumann's activities after he lectured for the DKG in the 1907 election's aftermath. The few findings that are summarized in what follows illustrate his success with films about big game hunting in Africa; one can conclude that Schumann remained somehow linked to filmmaking and was able to make important contacts with film companies. In December 1908, Robert Schumann began his film expedition to the East African colony. As was common in the preparation for such an expedition, Schumann contacted the DKG and the RKA offering his professional skills and knowledge as a ranger.[3] As with the colonial projects discussed above, Schumann emphasized the colonial political interest of his expedition. He intended to film colonial industry, plantations, farms and the infrastructure in order to illustrate colonial life for teaching purposes and for colonial friends at home. Furthermore, he mentioned his interest in new cinematographic techniques. For this purpose, he planned to shoot African wildlife at long distance and conduct entomological studies of African insects with his film equipment.

Though Schumann did not present filming big game hunting as his main intention in the colonies, it was for his hunting films that Schumann became famous following his return to Germany in 1913. The colonial office did not enlist Schumann's services but supported his project by recommending it to the colonies' governor. Schumann's expedition was not a one-man project, but at least partly coordinated with the French film company Pathé Frères.[4] One can only speculate how the contact originated, but a possible explanation could be Pathé's interest in increasing the production of films on big game hunting. The company had already some experience in this area. Between December 1907 and August 1908, Alfred Machin, together with the Swiss zoologist Adam David, shot several hunting films on their expedition to the Sudan.[5] Schumann reached the East African colony with a certain Livier at the end of December, where he started his expedition from Dar es Salaam to Morogoro across the Massai Steppe to Lake Victoria and, on his way back, to Moschi (Moshi), the Kilimajaro and to Tanga.[6] There exists no information about the expedition or about Schumann's life in the colony in the following years. In his autobiography, Hans Schomburgk reports about his first meeting with Schumann in Morogoro, an encounter that represented his first contact with cinematography and his inspiration to start filming. In his book *Zelte in*

Afrika, Schomburgk describes how he met Schumann when he arrived in town:

> There stood a shapeless box on three legs, covered by a black cloth and underneath obviously was the head of a man. A slim face covered in sweat became visible, his bearer gave us a sign that we should continue walking and not, Europeans and Africans, thrilled by this unusual view, pay attention to this strange appearance at the edge of the African Steppe. As we continued walking, a little bit embarrassed and sneaking to the box, the man started like one possessed to wind a rasping crank. This was my first encounter with film.[7]

Although Schumann's first film expedition did not bring the expected results and suffered from the technical problems of processing the films in the African climate, as Hans Schomburgk reports, some of his films seemed to turn out well and probably entered commercial distribution. A small article in the *Usambara-Post* describes Schumann as someone to whom one 'owed most interesting Kinemato-images'.[8] It is, therefore, possible that Schumann returned to Europe and set up his own film expedition before he returned to DOA in summer 1911. He moved to the northern region of the East African colony, where he and his camera operator, Bergmann, were joined by Christoph Schulz of the Hamburg Hagenbeck Stellinger Zoo. Schulz published his adventures on this expedition in his book *Film- und Jagdabenteuer in Afrika* (Film and Hunting Adventures in Africa), in which he presented himself as the film expert and demoted Schumann to his guide.[9]

Schumann returned to Germany in 1913 and, together with his brother-in-law Carl Steaker, founded the DJFG in Berlin.[10] The company's purpose was the commercial exploitation of Schumann's Africa films and different film technical inventions. With the films the company wanted to address professional hunters and connoisseurs of high quality pictures. It underlined that the films were expert recordings that had been produced in accordance with 'hunting principles' (*waidgerecht*).[11] The sharpness and artistic photography of the images made the films not only thrilling and interesting documents of big game hunting but also the most noble films of the contemporary cinema, the company claimed. Schumann's films lacked the 'usual African mist and electric discharge'[12] and, compared to other hunting films, were in 'a class of their own'.[13] Though Schumann seemed to be specialized in hunting films, the company's repertoire included at least one short comedy. *Das gestörte Liebesidyll im afrikanischen Laubenurwald oder: Ein Freibad im Urwald* (The Disturbed Love Idyll in the African Jungle or: A Public Bath in the Jungle) from 1914 was advertised as the 'first African comedy' with the 'first African actors', which would depict 'extremely funny scenes'.[14] All that is known about the story of the film was that it included a black dandy who is made into a laughing stock by some swimmers. The film was shot during one of Schumann's expeditions and performed by two of Schumann's male companions. In a short report in the advertisement Schumann presented himself almost like a circus director who was rehearsing the African actors as one would train animals:

> More than two months I was rehearsing with the extremely mistrustful and inaccessible natives from the region of Usucuma (German East Africa) before I was satisfied with mimic, gestures etc. Only due to my patience, good knowledge of the language, and colonial experience did we make the extremely funny scenes. At the beginning the black gentlemen [Herrschaften] were stiff like sticks. Only the dressage [Dressur], almost the correct word, made them cinematic, so that every viewer will enjoy this film.[15]

Reading the remark one could easily consider the film another example of Schumann's colonial domestication: in the same way he presented himself as the master of African nature, he knew how to train his African companions to produce an 'enjoyable' film. However, one must question Schumann's self-portrayal. An official booklet of his film company states that the original idea for the story goes back to the African members of Schumann's expedition team.[16] In this case the film was not possible without a very close collaboration between Schumann and his expedition team. Schumann took over the role of the director because the creativity of his African team, responsible for both the idea and acting, made it possible. Like no other film before, *Das gestörte Liebesidyll* indicates an agency of the colonized African that makes the film to an important example of early Tanzanian film culture.

With the outbreak of the First World War in August 1914 Schumann's career as a filmmaker and popular film lecturer came to an unexpectedly sudden ending. In patriotic euphoria Schumann joined the German army immediately, and by 14 September he was missing in action. Without Schumann's reputation and experience in the film business, his brother-in-law could not continue the work of the DJFG. The company was disbanded in November 1915. Producer Hans Neumann purchased the rights for the commercial exploitation of the company's films and re-released some of the material, such as *Aus der Afrikanischen Wildnis*, in July 1916, a film that became a splendid success. Neumann rereleased the film again in October of the following year.[17]

There is little information about the success of Schumann's films in local cinemas,[18] but his popularity in Berlin is quite well documented.

With the release of his films Schumann quickly became a prominent figure in Berlin's film culture.[19] The German emperor and the crown prince were both passionate hunters, and their interest in hunting films made Schumann a well-known guest in the local 'high society.' In February 1914 Schumann presented his films of hunting scenes of gnus, eland, elephants and rhinos to the German emperor, the empress, Chancellor Bethmann-Hollweg and other high-ranking personalities at the Reichskanzler Palais in Berlin.[20] After the screening Wilhelm II met Schumann for a private conversation about hunting, which made the whole evening, according to the *Lichtbild-Bühne,* an outstanding event and the DJFG 'the most successful film company of the recent past'.[21] Schumann would strengthen his reputation as an excellent lecturer and filmmaker in the following days. Only four days after the screening for the German emperor, Schumann was invited to a reception for state secretary Solf at the Hotel Adlon, where he again showed his films to members of the Berlin colonial movement, such has the DKG's president.[22] In a personal thank you letter from Solf to Schumann that was published a few days later in the *Lichtbild-Bühne,* Solf expressed his confidence that Schumann's artistic hunting films would surely become a success in public cinemas.[23]

Schumann's success in Berlin was partly the result of his film lectures for the Kinematographische Studiengesellschaft (Cinematographic Study Society), which also became a popular venue for anyone who was interested in watching colonial films. The Studiengesellschaft was founded at the Treptower Sternwarte (Treptow Observatory) in Berlin in February 1913 and devoted itself to the application and improvement of cinematography in sciences, culture and education.[24] With regular programmes and free screenings in the winter of 1913/14, the Studiengesellschaft very soon became a new attraction in Berlin film culture. Anyone interested in watching films from the German colonies had good chances to see some of them in one of the society's programmes. The Studiengesellschaft held its first free film screening at the Mozartsaal on the Nollendorfplatz in December 1913.[25] In their programmes, usually lasting two hours in the afternoon (3.30–5.30 pm), the society wanted to show films addressing a scientific, educational or cultural interest. These could be either new films or films that were already in distribution. During the screening each film was judged by the audience on a scale from one (very good) to five (unsatisfactory), which would give the film companies a direct response about the quality of their films.[26] Even though it is impossible to say how the audience judged Schumann's films, the fact that he was personally invited to show his films at one of the Studiengesellschaft's screening events suggests that his films must have been rather popular. The programmes of the Studiengesellschaft became an immediate success in Berlin and a chance for Schumann to promote the DJFG's first films. The promotion for *Nashornjagd in Deutsch-Ost-Afrika* started in October 1913 and it was offered for sale in December, followed by the release of *Jagd auf Riesenschlangen* (Hunting Boa Constrictors) in January 1914. Both films were also part of the Studiengesellschaft's first screening in December and became the major attraction at this event. The success made the Studiengesellschaft a new competitor in the local film culture, whose free screenings were especially popular among the Berlin youth. In order to avoid a conflict with commercial exhibitors, the society decided at the end of January to bar young viewers from the fourth screening, which again included films from the colonies, *Diamantenfelder in Deutsch-Südwestafrika* (Diamond Fields in German South-West Africa) (Hansafilm, 1914) and *Schwarze Truppen in Dar-es-salam* (Black Troops in Dar-Es-Salaam), as well as a lecture by R. Neuhauss on the film expedition to New Guinea.[27] The lack of young viewers did not mean a smaller audience. In February the society's screenings were so crowded that the Mozartsaal, with a capacity of 950 seats, was too small to offer seats for all to see *Das Hinterland von Tanga* (The Tanga Hinterland) (Hansafilm, 1914).[28] Two weeks later hundreds of viewers had to stay outside the cinema, which had become overcrowded long before the screening started. On this afternoon Schumann was welcomed with 'thunderous applause' and lectured on his film *Die Gnu- und die Onixjagd* (sic) (Gnu and Oryx Hunting).[29] For the last programme in the society's first screening period, the Studiengesellschaft finally moved from the Mozartsaal to the Cines-Palast at the zoo, which offered seats for 1,750 viewers and an additional five hundred standing places.[30] On the 23 March, a day after the last public screening, the Studiengesellschaft organized a reception for Paul Graetz in the auditorium of the Treptow Sternwarte, where Graetz showed films and slides from his motorboat expedition of 1912.[31] While the Berlin audience was in a privileged position to see Schumann live at his lectures, the larger German audience could see Schumann on a film lecture tour throughout Germany from April until the summer of 1914.

'We are in Africa! Jungle! Aha!'

Even though the DJFG's repertoire included some colonial studies, Schumann seemed to have little interest in representing the colonies in a way that characterized most of the colonial travelogues.[32] Schumann's films presented the colony as a place for dramatic adventure, as the following description of his film *Nashornjagd* shows. The description is based on a copy with French intertitles: 'Chasse aux Rhinocéros en Afrique Orientale prise par l'explorateur d'Afrique Robert Schumann' (Rhino Hunt in East Africa by the African Explorer Robert Schumann).

The film starts with an intertitle: 'Orientation using binoculars in the pathless bush in order to reach the Mutjek Forest, the Eldorado of the biggest rhinoceros'.[33] 1. The first shot introduces Schumann and his African companion standing on a hill. Schumann is looking through his binoculars at the valley below. 2. The expedition headed by Schumann and his assistant crosses the plain, continuously watching out for rhino spoor; intertitle: 'A panic breaks out among the bearers, and suddenly bang! Three rhinos are in the undergrowth in front of us'. 3. The spoor of a rhino is discovered; the African bearers panic and escape, some are climbing up a nearby tree. 4. Two rhino that look like a mother rhino and her young one are hidden in a bush. 5. Schumann enters from the left side of the frame and kills the rhino. 6. A close-up shows the animal's death throes. 7. The film cuts back to Schumann, who waits and stares at the rhino as if he were unsure whether the rhino needed a second bullet, then he approaches the rhino; intertitle: 'The second rhino is right on a native's heels. The native would be lost if the hounds did not throw themselves in front of the furious animal, and one dog is caught by the rhino's horn and thrown six metres into the air and killed'. 8. The camera shows a second rhino; it defends itself from the hunting dogs; suddenly it gores one of the dogs and throws it up in the air; Schumann enters from the right, points his rifle at the rhino and shoots it. 9. Schumann examines the rhino; his assistant approaches, and they congratulate each other; intertitle: 'If the savage rhino in its rage wants to seize you, climb up a tree in time or you will regret it'. 10. The film cuts back to the expedition group, some come out of the bushes, others climb down the tree. 11. They come to the dead rhino, climb over it and start celebrating the killing with a dance; intertitle: 'The upper lip of the pachyderm protrudes in the form of a finger; it is a vestige of a trunk from prehistoric times. The beast uses it to strip off the leaves and crush the branches in its mouth'. 12. A close-up of the rhino's head is used to describe the animal's peculiar muzzle and how it eats. 13. Then the group turns the rhino over, and Schumann explains how to cut up the animal; intertitle: 'The horns, the skin, the feet and the meat are of great value to the hunters'. 14. Schumann demonstrates to one African how to cut off the horn with an axe; he instructs another how to cut off the skin with the knife; on the side he calms down one of his dogs that is nervously jumping up on him; intertitle: 'You remove the skin that, dried and cut into slices, is used to make whips'. 15. A close-up shows how the skin is cut off in a big slice; one African holds the skin and looks into the camera; he is obviously communicating with the cameraman or somebody who controls the shooting; he follows the instructions and tries to offer a better view of the slice. 16. In the following shot some Africans are standing with their backs to the camera so that one does not see what is happening; suddenly they all move to the right; together they have ripped off a big slice of the rhino's skin; a mass of intestines comes out of the rhino; intertitle: 'Blessed with a night of full moon, the roasting of the meat is quickly carried out to the joyful singing of the natives. For the next two weeks the dried meat offers a pleasant supplement to the expedition's provisions'. 17. The final shots show Schumann's group preparing a huge barbecue. 18. Two Africans eating and drinking.

Tom Gunning points out that nonfiction films' interferences with reality include their centring 'on the act of looking and describing' and the acknowledgement of the camera by the filmed people.[34] In contrast, the

Figure 12.1. Robert Schumann at the set in German East Africa. Source: Deutsche Jagdfilm-Gesellschaft. 1916. *Aus der afrikanischen Wildnis: Jagd- und Reisestudien des Forschungsreisenden Robert Schumann*. Berlin, p. 3.

documentary film is 'a more rhetorical and discursive form', in which 'individual shots lose much of their independence as separate 'views' and become instances of evidence or illustration within an argument or story'.[35] *Nashornjagd* still follows the definition of early nonfiction films. The film is rooted in the 'view' aesthetic and the cinema of attraction, which satisfies the viewers' visual curiosity. Several shots in the film are emblematic and need no further contextualization. The killing of the rhino and the goring of one of Schumann's dogs are spectacles that viewers had not seen before in such detail. The African's look into the camera and the way he worked to present the slaughtered rhino to the camera illustrate early nonfiction's efforts to offer viewers the best vantage point. In contrast to conventional travelogues, *Nashornjagd* makes use of editing within the shot composition: the cut in to a close-up of the dying rhino (shot 6) or the rhino's head to show the rudimentary horn (13). The cut from a medium long shot when Schumann approaches the second rhino (8) to a long shot allows the large group of the bearers to enter the frame (9). The cut does not happen abruptly but uses Schumann's movement towards the animal. However, in contrast to editing strategies in documentary film, the editing in this film does not dramatize the action but is still subsumed under the camera's privileged view. The discovery of the rhino in the beginning of the film and the final shot of the Africans eating the roasted rhino illustrate the sequential logic of early process films, in which the narrative culminates in a scene of consumption.

Although the film corresponds in many ways to the conventions of early nonfiction filmmaking, the film indicates a subtle step away from nonfiction as 'view' towards an argument. Schumann used the colony as a setting for the depiction of a rudimentary dramatic story. This novelty was understood, for example, by the *Berliner Tageblatt*, which welcomed the film because it did not show again for the 'sixty-seventh time Dar es Salam and greasy Negro villages and the extremely boring tobacco harvesting and such things that are pompously put in front of the viewer'.[36] The reviewer was obviously thinking of a colonial travelogue in which different 'views' of German East Africa were presented together with a lecture that emphasized the economic aspects of the colony. In this regard Schumann's film was different as he made only 'dramatic remarks to a dramatic film' in his film lectures in the cinemas:[37]

> Yesterday he stood in his frock coat on the lecture podium and pointed with a long stick to himself, who was marching on the screen through

> undergrowth and jungle. And he made nothing but dramatic remarks to the dramatic film; nothing long-winded that cannot already be found in Livingstone and Emin Pascha and Roosevelt and Schillings. No, we were simply with him in Africa. Thousands of gnus were running over the drought plain. 'Pay attention to the turning buck in the upper right corner' shouts Mr. Schumann, who jumps out of the lower right corner in a firing position. 'Now – ! Ho!' The buck collapses under the fire. A moment of darkness. Then the half-lying animal, caught, barked at by the dogs (marvelous lads!). 'Ho!' the coup de grâce.[38]

The review indicates that Schumann fascinated his audience by integrating his films within a thrilling spoken narrative. Live lecture made it easy to authenticate the film through one's own personal accounts, but the first intertitle of the French copy also indicates that in national distribution *Nashornjagd* emphasized that it was not the depiction of any hunt but a particular one, which can be identified by its protagonist, the 'African explorer Robert Schumann'. Even though the film's editing does not create a dramatic progression in the film, the first intertitles try to create a certain suspense before the film becomes rather instructional and formal. The film introduces the region as the 'Eldorado of the biggest rhinoceros'. That this region is probably also the most dangerous is suggested by the second intertitles, which tells the viewer of the panic among the bearers when three rhinos are discovered. Having established the region as a territory inhabited by the biggest rhinos, wild and cruel animals, the killing of the rhino can be justified, and Schumann becomes the hero who has protected his expedition group from the beasts. Although the *Berliner Tageblatt* underlined that in Schumann's 'Kintopp' (flicks) 'clearly nothing was staged'; what people believed they were seeing as the real Africa was a very carefully planned and arranged filming.

Colonial hunting reality was rather different from what one sees in the film. Strict hunting laws and high fines for their violation made a successful hunt the result of an administrative act, including paying for a hunting license and fees for each animal killed by the hunter.[39] Filming a hunt, therefore, was difficult, too. It required a certain logistic so that everybody on the expedition was familiar with the shooting of a scene and knew what to do to in order to guarantee the best outcome.[40] *Nashornjagd* obviously does not present the colony in terms of illustrating the political stability or economic prosperity. These aspects are excluded in favour of the dramatic action of the hunt. The use of stereotypes such as the 'cowardly African' versus the 'cold-blooded white hunter' is important in establishing Schumann as the main character in the film. His position as the group's leader is emphasized by the fact that in contrast to the panicking bearers he remains calm and kills the beast. Moreover, he seems to be the only one who knows how to carve the skin of a rhino, which makes him the real Africa expert. Shifting his persona as the colonial adventurer to the foreground, his films gave viewers a chance to identify with an authentic protagonist, the intrepid hunter and the adventurous explorer. The question to what extent Schumann's films were a direct reaction to the marginalization of nonfiction films in cinemas is difficult to answer. Schumann's single hunting films were obviously too short to compete with an hour-long fictional feature film in the cinemas' programmes. With a length of 276 m, *Nashornjagd* had an approximate running time of twelve minutes; however, Schumann's films played for a month in a sold-out Berlin cinema in May 1914. The re-release of his collected films in 1916 and 1917, as *Aus der afrikanischen Wildnis,* was about 1,757 m long, which made an approximate running time of almost one and a half hours (eighteen frames per second) and indicates that Schumann's material was able to produce a competitive, long colonial nonfiction film.

Films about hunting big game represented a substantial part of the overall production of films from Africa. The films' ideological purpose was to visualise in a racial manner the white hunter's mastery of the African jungle, but concentrating exclusively on this aspect means to miss the films' semantic ambivalence. Intended or not, hunting films such as those of Robert Schumann played an important role with regard to the establishment of the national and international wildlife protection movement, and provoked a discussion of the ethics of killing animals for fashion purposes.

Big Game Hunting and Wildlife Protection

Not every viewer welcomed films on big game hunting in the same way. An anonymous letter that was passed to the RKA in March 1913 denounced a film that depicted the slaughtering of giraffes in the German East African colony and questioned this kind of public entertainment, which did not contribute to the colonies' honour.[41] In July 1914 the *Lichtbild-Bühne* noticed that films on hunting were losing sympathy among the audience,[42] and film journals were reporting about 'faked' film hunts, in which the animals were deliberately made aggressive so that they could be killed for a film recording.[43]

Figure 12.2. Still from *Löwenjagd in Afrika* (before 1914). Reproduced courtesy of Bundesarchiv-Abteilung Filmarchiv.

The film fragment *Löwenjagd* (Lion Hunt) (archive title, before 1914) is an example of such a faked hunt. The film shows a lion lying under a bush. When the first shot hits the lion, the creature is obviously hindered by a shackle from escaping a second bullet. This lion gets shot, and the German hunter celebrates his triumph. In his book *Mit Blitzlicht und Büchse,* C.G. Schillings complained about the practice of faking hunts for commercial purposes. Pictures of wild animals in the wilderness, according to Schillings, were often little more than fakes. Cinematography achieved 'amazing' results by tying an animal's hind leg so the beast could be shot by a 'marksman' and his 'infallible' bullet. Schillings referred in this context to a film in which a hunting dog was killed by a rhino before the rhino was shot by the hunter. According to Schillings, the rhino obviously had one of its feet tied up.[44] The scene that Schillings describes in his book was undoubtedly Robert Schumann's *Nashornjagd,* and watching the film carefully one realizes that Schilling was correct in his observation.[45]

While hunting films were for many viewers examples of the perils of the (colonial) jungle, they initiated a discussion about the ethics of killing of animals for pleasure or export purposes. For many viewers films about hunting were not the same as 'documents of nature', such as wildlife photography. A film that illustrates the oppositional discourses in hunting film is *Jagd auf den Silberreiher in Afrika* (Shooting Egrets in Africa) (Pathé Frères, 1911).

The film starts with a shot of a white hunter and his two African helpers, who are sneaking through the African bush. The hunter points to a tree. The following shots show an egret colony perched in the tree. The hunter and his helpers are some distance from the tree and shoot some birds. They shoot a third and fourth time at the birds. They run to the tree and disappear underneath the tree's large projecting branches. At least fifteen birds are killed. The birds are collected; the helpers string up the egrets on sticks and put them on their shoulders. The hunter carries two other large birds on a stick. On a boat two white men are plucking the birds for their valuable feathers. In a close-up one sees two hands that hold a dead egret. They show where to find the valuable feathers. Suddenly the hands pluck the feathers from the bird's body and show the little bunch of egret feathers. The intertitle informs us that every year thousands of these beautiful birds are killed to adorn

Figure 12.3. Still from *Jagd auf den Silberreiher in Afrika* (1911). Reproduced courtesy of Gaumont Pathé Archives.

the ladies' hats. The last shots were not filmed in Africa. A female hand presents a bunch of egret feathers to the camera. A chic young lady tries on a feather hat. In a medium close-up one sees the young lady smiling at the camera. She is moving her head so that the feathers can be seen in the most flattering way.

Combating the hunting of egrets and birds of paradise for their precious feathers was one of the first major campaigns of the Bund für Vogelschutz (BfV) (League for the Protection of Birds), which was internationally coordinated with the Audubon Society in the United States and the British Royal Society for the Protection of Birds (RSPB). Carl Georg Schillings became one of the main speakers and lobbyists in this campaign and gave a vehement speech about '*Moderne Damenhüte als Vernichter der Vogelwelt*' (fashionable ladies' hats as the exterminator of the ornithological world) at the first national *Vogelschutztag* (bird-protection day) in May 1910 in Berlin. The German public was asked to enlist in so-called *Federnverzichtslisten* (feather waiver lists), in which the signatory declared his/her renunciation of buying feathers from birds of paradise, egrets or the humming bird.[46] Feminist associations joined the campaign. The 'Board of the Bavarian Association for Women's Right to Vote' considered the 'feather fashion' to be unworthy of the modern woman, and wearing such items would put her on the same evolutionary step as wild and childish primitive cultures.[47] Prices between eight hundred and fifteen hundred marks for an egret feather made the trade a flourishing industry, and gave it every reason to oppose the BfV's campaign. Berlin's flower and feather industry alone employed eight thousand people and made almost twenty million marks with the production of the fashionable feathers.[48] In their 1910/11 annual report, the BfV reports that the protection of wildlife 'concerned the German public as it had never done before'.[49] The society's tireless efforts had wide-reaching consequences. In November 1913 the DKG set up a commission for the protection of egrets and birds of paradise, and in 1914 state secretary Solf, himself a member of the BfV, put a ban on the import of feathers.

Watching the film against the background of the BfV's campaign positions *Jagd auf den Silberreiher* in a different discursive context. The film that starts as an ordinary film about hunting birds in Africa turns into a visual accusation against the senseless slaughter of helpless birds. The film's ending becomes ambivalent in its meaning. Does the film care about wildlife protection or does it support the feather fashion? Should women feel guilty when watching the film? Does the beauty of the egret justify the hunting of the birds or is the film's ending a cynical comment on some ladies' perverted fashion pleasure?

Figure 12.4. Illustration criticizing the slaughter of paradise birds for fashion purposes. Source: Jahresheft 1915 des Bundes für Vogelschutz, p. 13. Reproduced courtesy of Naturschutzbund Deutschland. e.V (NABU).

The importance of film in the BfV's campaign is shown by an illustration in the society's 1915 annual report, in which the relationship between films about the killing of egrets and birds of paradise and the ignorant audience is thematized. The illustration shows a luxurious film theatre in which among the audience watching a film about the hunting of birds of paradise are several women wearing expensive feathers. On the screen one sees a grim-looking hunter who almost squeezes a small bird with one of his hands. The beginning of a verse from Goethe's *Faust II* comments on the illustration: '*Missgestaltete Begierde...*' (Misshapen dwarfish passions... ['steal the egrets' noblest gems']), and points out the abuse of the cinema for the 'glorification of the pernicious devastation of feather trimming, especially the extermination of the egret and the marabou'.[50]

Film was not just a medium that was viewed with suspicion by wildlife protectionists and the BfV; it also became an important medium for the association's own propaganda work. Film screenings that demonstrated the current disgrace of the lack of protection of wildlife were used to reach the broad public, to draw the press' attention to the situation and make the associations' influence felt among high-ranking officials. The BfV's activity is one more example of the significant relationship between early film and voluntary associations:

> Also the events and meetings that are organized by us are used to draw the attention to the disgrace and through cinematographic screenings to give an insight into the conditions. These screenings we were allowed to show on the occasion of our general meeting to Her Majesty the Queen of Württemberg, who, as is known, has gained particular merits for the fight against the egret fashion, and at the general meeting of the German Society for the Protection of Birds to His Majesty King Friedrich August of Saxony.[51]

The BfV's campaign at the time Schumann's films became popular, and the role that film played for the BfV, lead us to ask to what extent film were companies such as Pathé Frères aware of the worldwide campaign to ban feather imports, and whether this campaign had any influence on the editing of hunting films such as *Jagd auf den Silberreiher in Afrika*. Was the initial idea of this film to document the hunt and the feathers' beauty, or did Pathé change the plans at short notice to join the growing antipathy for the killing of animals for fashion purposes? Whatever the answer might be, the great number of hunting films that were produced in early cinema and the critique of their production show that the films could address even opposed film audiences.

The end of colonial film screenings in the DKG's branches did not mean the end of watching films from the colonies. Colonial films in commercial venues in the years between 1907 and 1914 were open to a number of different, sometimes even conflicting, readings. While cinema reformers emphasized the necessity of producing colonial films for the national education of the public, colonial officials were rather reluctant to support their production. They were afraid of becoming associated with the spectacular and entertaining side of cinema and preferred to promote films that left no doubt about the 'correct' representation of the colonies. The ambivalence that characterized the RKA's attitude towards film was a significant feature of the colonial travelogue. The films addressed patriotic issues while also serving as joyful film travels to exotic regions. A characteristic feature of colonial films was the representation of the colonies as modern territories in which viewers encountered living conditions similar to those in Germany. While images of the railway assured viewers of the modernity of the colonies, railway journeys through the colonies also triggered associations with adventurous tourism and sightseeing. Finally, the example of Robert Schumann's hunting films has shown in what ways colonial cinematography developed when cinemas started to increase the number of fiction films in their programmes. The films made by Schumann show that his use of the colony not as the location where German colonialism takes place but as a setting for dramatic adventures offered audiences a new way of watching colonial films. The last part focuses again on the relationship between colonial cinematography and colonial propaganda during the First World War. In contrast to the previous chapters, in which propaganda was identified with nonfiction films, the main centre of attention will be the colonial fiction film.

Notes

1. K. Bleibtreu quoted in Müller, 'Variationen des Kinoprogramms', 64.
2. Cf. Gunning, 'Before Documentary', 20.
3. BArch, R 1001/6621, 120–23.
4. Schumann's address in France where he could be contacted was 'L'Avenue du Polygone à Vincennes'. That was the address of Pathé Frères. I would like to thank Stephen Bottomore for this important information.
5. In October 1908 the *Basler Nachrichten* (Switzerland) published a series of ten articles about Adam David's first expedition. In 1916 David published his 'film adventures' under the title *Jagden und Abenteuer in den Gebieten des Oberen Nil*, Basel: Friedrich Reinhart.

6. *DOAZ*, 24 December 1908. Schumann's companion, Livier, was most likely Pathé Frères's operator M. Livier.
7. Schomburgk, *Zelte in Afrika. Fahrten-Forschung-Abenteuer in sechs Jahrzehnten*, Berlin: Verlag der Nationen, 1957, 258–259.
8. *Usambara-Post*, 19 August 1911.
9. C. Schulz, *Jagd- und Filmabenteuer in Afrika*, Dresden, 1922. Hans Schomburgk writes that the expedition was led solely by Schumann and accuses Schulz of shameful historical misrepresentation. H. Schomburgk, *Bwakukama. Fahrten und Forschungen mit Büchse und Film im Unbekannten Afrika*, 2nd edn, Berlin: Deutsches Literarisches Institut, 1922, 176–77.
10. The planning for the establishment of the DJFG had begun a year before. In November 1912 the *Usambara-Post* reports in a small article about the preparations for founding such a company. For this reason several hunters were in the Arusha and Mansua regions filming their hunts. Anon., 'Deutsche Jagdfilm-Gesellschaft', *Usambara-Post*, 2 November 1912.
11. *Lichtbild-Bühne*, 8 November 1913, 45.
12. Anon., 'Eine neue Filmfabrik', *Der Kinematograph*, 15 October 1913.
13. Anon., 'Streiflicher aus der deutschen Filmmetropole', *Der Kinematograph*, 25 February 1914.
14. *Lichtbild-Bühne*, 24 January 1914, 5.
15. *Der Kinematograph*, 21 January 1914.
16. Deutsche Jagdfilm-Gesellschaft, *Aus der afrikanischen Wildnis: Jagd- und Reisestudien des Forschungsreisenden Robert Schumann*, Berlin, 1916, 8.
17. *Lichtbild-Bühne*, 29 July 1916, 37; *Lichtbild-Bühne*, 20 October 1917.
18. A successful run is reported from Hagenbeck's Kino in Hamburg in 1914. The film *Aus der afrikanischen Wildnis* (From the African Jungle), a production of Schumann's collaboration with Christoph Schulz, was made specifically for screenings at Hagenbeck's Kino. Ames, *Carl Hagenbeck's Empire*, 209.
19. See also W. Fuhrmann, '"Nashornjagd in Deutsch-Ostafrika"- Die frühe Kolonialfilmindustrie', in Heyden and Zeller, *Kolonialmetropole Berlin*, 184–87.
20. BArch, R 1001/6632, 41.
21. Anon., 'Ein großer Erfolg der Deutschen Jagdfilm-Gesellschaft', *Lichtbild-Bühne*, 21 February 1914, 48.
22. *Vossische Zeitung*, 20 February 1914.
23. Anon., 'Ein großer Erfolg', 48.
24. Anon., 'Die Gründung der "Kinematographischen Studiengesellschaft"', *Lichtbild-Bühne*, 1 February 1913, 16–21.
25. Anon., 'Eine wissenschaftliche und belehrende Filmschau', *Lichtbild-Bühne*, 27 December 1913, 38.
26. Anon., 'Kinematographische Studiengesellschaft', *Lichtbild-Bühne*, 17 January 1914, 30.
27. Anon., 'Wochen-Rundschau über neue Films', *Lichtbild-Bühne*, 31 January 1914, 36.
28. Anon., 'Kinematographische Studiengesellschaft', *Lichtbild-Bühne*, 14 February 1914, 55.
29. Anon., 'Die Film-Schau der Woche', *Lichtbild-Bühne*, 28 February 1914, 44.
30. Anon., 'Die Kinematographische Studiengesellschaft', *Der Kinematograph*, 1 April 1914.
31. Anon., 'Kinematographische Studiengesellschaft', *Lichtbild-Bühne*, 14 March 1914, 45.
32. For the title quotation see anon., 'Aus der afrikanischen Wildnis', *Lichtbild-Bühne*, 29 July 1916, 55–56.

33. In her study on pre-colonial fantasies in Germany, Susanne Zantop points out the sexual connotations of such tropes as the conquest of the 'virgin' territory by the male conqueror or the 'impenetrable jungle', which were again activated by Schumann's adventure films. Cf. Zantop, *Colonial Fantasies*.
34. Gunning, 'Before Documentary', 18.
35. Ibid., 22.
36. *Berliner Tageblatt*, 1914, quoted in Anon., '"Aus der afrikanischen Wildnis"', *Lichtbild-Bühne*, 29 July 1916, 55–56.
37. Anon., '"Aus der afrikanischen Wildnis"', 56.
38. Ibid., 55.
39. Reichs-Kolonialamt (ed.), *Jagd und Wildschutz in den Deutschen Kolonien*, Jena: Verlag Gustav Fischer, 1913.
40. Cf. Schulz's description of a Gnu hunt. Schulz, *Jagd-und Filmabenteuer in Afrika*, 19.
41. The film mentioned here is probably *Giraffenjagd in der Massaisteppe* (Pathé Frères, 1913). BArch, R 1001/7779, 246. A handwritten remark on the letter suggests that the RKA suspected Carl Georg Schillings to be its author.
42. Anon., 'Die Tierdressur für Kino-Aufnahmen', *Lichtbild-Bühne*, 25 July 1914, 63–64.
43. C. Mordhorst, 'Wie eine Löwenjagd gestellt wird', *Lichtbild-Bühne*, 25 October 1913, 18.
44. C.G. Schillings, *Mit Blitzlicht und Büchse im Zauber des Elescho*, Leipzig: R. Voigtländers Verlag, 1922, 34–35.
45. In a vein similar to Schillings's position, politician and pacifist Hans Paasche implicitly attacked Schumann's films in the article 'Der Jagdfilm', *Ethische Rundschau: Monatsschrift zur Läuterung und Vertiefung der ethischen Anschauungen und zur Förderung ethischer Bestrebungen*, 1914, 3(5–6): 85–87.
46. A list was enclosed in the February issue of the *Ornithologische Monatsschrift*, 1912, 37(2).
47. BArch, R 1001/7771, 34–38.
48. 'Wider den Paradiesvogelmord. Lobby-Arbeit anno 1910: die ersten Naturschutzkampagnen'. Retrieved 20 March 2014 from http://www.nabu.de/nabu/portrait/geschichte/00346.html.
49. *Ornithologische Monatsschrift*, 1912, 37(2): 129.
50. Anon., 'Bericht über die Tätigkeit vom 1. Oktober 1913 bis 1. Oktober 1914', *Jahresheft 1915 des Bundes für Vogelschutz*, 1915, 13. In Goethe's *Faust II* the German verse goes: 'Missgestaltete Begierde, raubt des Reihers edle Zierde'.
51. Anon., 'Bund für Vogelschutz E.V.. Jahresbericht für die Zeit vom 1. Oktober 1911 bis 1. Oktober 1912', *Ornithologische Monatsschrift*, 1913, 38(2): 131.

PART V

COLONIAL FILM PROPAGANDA DURING THE FIRST WORLD WAR

Chapter 13

SETTING UP COLONIAL WAR PROPAGANDA

The outbreak of the First World War on 1 August 1914 marked the end of filmmaking in the colonies. The immediate sea blockade by the British navy cut off Germany from its colonial territories and made any supply of films from the colonies impossible. Except for East Africa, all the colonies were lost by the end of the year. The military actions limited cinema owners' possibilities to react with new films to the fighting in the colonies and to the colonial loss. Although the trade journal *Der Kinematograph* emphasized that in 'agitated times' (*aufgeregten Zeiten*) audiences mainly wanted to watch topicals, few new colonial films were available.[1] At the end of August, Carl Rudolph Monopol Film GmbH in Berlin offered two films from the colonies. Under the title 'Our Threatened Colonies' the company released *Kiautschau im Film* (Kiaochow on Film), which was said to show the only existing original shots, and *Süd-West-Afrika* (South-West Africa), which showed the German black troops in battle.[2] The films were most likely the last original footage from the colonies that reached Germany before the blockade. After the initial successful screening, *Kiautschau* was banned in August by Berlin censors following the instructions of the naval ministry.[3] The ban was lifted and the film allowed for screening, including to children, after the loss of Kiaochow in November. The film was sold as 'the cheeky robbing of our East-Asian colonial pearl' and showed the 'captor of the English fleet', the German battleship *Gneisenau* in the colonial harbour.[4]

To overcome the shortage of films, film critic Josef Aubinger suggested that old material be re-edited and re-released: one simply had to use available material from old *Wochenschauen* (news reels) and edit these parts with new intertitles.[5] Following this strategy, the Deutsche Bioscop released new copies of films from the company's archive in October, such as *Leben und Treiben in Tanga (Deutsch-Ostafrika)* and *Die Sigifälle in Kamerun*.[6] Emphasizing that the films were 'interesting especially at this moment', the Deutsche Bioscop did not seem to pay much attention to geographic accuracy at this stage and relocated out of hand the East African Sigi Falls to Cameroon.

Programming became a difficult task for German cinema owners. While foreign productions had dominated the film programmes until the war, during it these films became banned from the German screens. Cinemas expressed their national patriotic commitment by excluding foreign films from the programmes, and police authorities started to confiscate foreign films and close down foreign film companies or put them under the control of German *Zwangsverwaltung* (compulsory management). At the beginning of 1915 the government finally imposed a ban on the importation of foreign films.[7] The lack of foreign films did not mean exhibitors had a free hand in compiling a film programme. Authorities reminded cinema owners that their programmes should reflect 'the seriousness of the time' and the 'patriotic mood of the nation'; otherwise films would be confiscated and cinemas closed.[8] Government directives left little margin: while humorous films were viewed with suspicion for their frivolous indulgence, other films were banned as they inflicted spiritual and moral damage. Restriction and censorship measures nevertheless had a positive influence on the domestic film industry. The number of national productions grew, and during the four years of war the number of national film companies increased fivefold. In the first months of the war the film industry started to produce 'melodramatic *kitsch* films known as the "field-gray" genre'.[9]

By the end of 1914 officials realized that the war could not be won in a short time, and the situation at the front became rather unfathomable. German media considered every move at the front a victory, but real successes were few. With the prolongation of the war, resistance grew among the German public. While the interest in patriotic films decreased, the German government was quite cautious in directing public propaganda campaigns during the first two years of war.[10] The public turned towards other, more entertaining, genres. Instead of fighting the low morals of a popular cinema, 'the government was forced to recognize that the commercial cinema would not be suppressed but could be used to bolster morale'.[11]

In 1916 the situation began to change. Almost in parallel, the German military and German industry each started to set up its own individual propaganda machinery. On 19 November German industry set up the Deutsche Lichtbild-Gesellschaft (DEULIG, German Cinematographic Company), whose aim was to produce and distribute films and to promote German industry and culture abroad.[12] However, the private character of the DEULIG and the political demands that were made by the Oberste Heeresleitung (High Command) led to irreconcilable differences between industry and the military. As a consequence the military set up its own film section; in January 1917 the Film-und Photostelle (Film and Photo Service), which had started its work in November 1916, was transformed into the Bild und Filmamt (BUFA, Photography and Film Office) and extended its operations to more than just the production of military films. As David Welch notes: 'Conscious of the need to counter enemy propaganda abroad and to bolster flagging public morale at home. BUFA's task was to refashion the whole German film industry into a fighting propaganda machine that would make a vital contribution to the war effort'.[13]

At the time when the German military and German industry were organizing film propaganda on a broad national level, the colonial side also started to discuss the efficacy of film propaganda. Until 1916 no significant efforts were made to bring the colonial territories back into the film audience's mind. It was the filmmaker Hans Schomburgk and the Deutsche Kolonial-Filmgesellschaft (DEUKO, German Colonial Film Company), specialized in the production of fictional colonial propaganda films, who became the main protagonists in the production of colonial films. Colonial filmmaking now became essentially a matter of producing colonial look–a-like-films that were shot not in the colonial territories but in and around Berlin.

Colonial Film Propaganda at the DKG

The outbreak of the First World War brought the DKG's plans and project of a German colonial empire to a premature ending. The society reached its membership peak of 43,244 in October 1914, but the numbers gradually decreased in the succeeding months and years as members were drafted and killed in the war.[15] The executive committee put the DKG 'on a war footing'[16] and developed in the following years propaganda activities that emphasized through war bulletins and leaflets the significance of the colonies for the German empire, their restoration to Germany after the war and Germany's colonial extension through the creation of a German 'Middle-Africa', which reached from the west to the east coast of the African continent.

The suggestion to use film for the DKG's colonial propaganda in wartime was brought up for the first time in March 1917, when the executive committee received two requests asking for support for colonial film projects. The first colonial project came from director and actor Dr Hans Oberländer, who planned to set up a colonial film company for the production of a colonial film drama. The film aimed to illustrate the problems of settlers and the value of the territories for the fatherland. The committee did not agree to support this project but became interested in the second project, which was submitted by Emil Zimmermann, a well-known author of colonial publications.[17] Zimmermann planned to organize in public cinemas and the DKG's branches screenings of films that were made by Hans Schomburgk. The project aroused the executive committee's interest; they accepted suggestions to contact the BUFA in this matter and to pass the project for further evaluation to the society's Aktionsausschuss (AA, Action Committee), which coordinated all actions concerning the reclaiming of the colonies during the war. The executive committee recommended that the society consider acquiring a financial stake in this project. In the committee's subsequent meetings the 'Zimmermann-Schomburgk project' shifted into the background in favour of general discussion about the setting up of a colonial film company and the DKG's financial share in it. Members hotly debated the pros and cons of such a project that was the only non-organizational topic at the meetings. At the first meeting in April, advocates of the 'colonial film project' emphasized that lantern slide shows no longer had the same effect as they had had in the past. Nowadays film was the best tool for propaganda, so it was a pity that such a film company did not already exist.[18] The 'pro-film group' in the committee was supported by the BUFA's positive response, agreeing to include colonial films in the office's programme, and the AA's positive response of setting up a film company in which the DKG and other investors would become the company's shareholders.[19] After the AA's positive evaluation, members argued that it was less a question of what films were suitable for propaganda but of the committee quickly raising the initial capital without asking for the permission of the board.

Not all members agreed on this topic. The most prominent voice on the opposing side was the DKG's president, the Duke of Mecklenburg. Though he was not personally present at the committee's meetings, his opinion in this matter was read out to all the members at the beginning of the meeting and was obviously aimed at keeping the committee's members toeing the party line: 'However lovely it might be to have nice film screenings for entertainment, I think that we should keep our money at this moment. We don't get back the colonies through film screenings. When we have them back again, it will be the time to get the audience interested in the old and new territories through new images'.[20]

Mecklenburg's opinion did not fail to have the desired effect.[21] In the course of the discussion most of the members followed his policy of 'wait and see'. Members questioned whether the Zimmermann/Schomburgk films were the right films for 'the colonial matter' and referred to the financial risk of such an endeavour. The committee decided therefore to postpone a final decision in this matter until the next meeting and to wait until the final report of the AA was available. It is impossible to say what influence the president's opinion in this matter had on the AA's final decision, but at the following meeting the society's party line was re-established. Similar to the president's attitude, the AA now suggested that the society wait until a private colonial film company was set up and had contacted the DKG. Without mentioning its experience with film ten years before, the DKG now considered itself too large an organization and at the same time too inexperienced in film matters to take up this proposal. It concluded that it would be better to join a company that knew how to operate on the film market and could assume the financial risk of film production that the DKG was not willing to take. Under the condition that it be granted influence on the production of the films, the society could then support the company through its name and a small financial stake. Reversing the AA's positive reaction two weeks before, in which it voted unanimously for the project, it now turned down the project in its final report.[22] The DKG's decision did not prevent others from starting their own colonial film project. The same day that the executive committee turned down colonial film plans, 27 April 1917, the DEUKO was set up in Berlin, and also on this day the BUFA had its first screening of propaganda films in Berlin. Cinematographic colonial war propaganda was on its way.

Hans Schomburgk

Unlike Robert Schumann, who became rather successful with films he had shot in the German East African colony, Hans Schomburgk became known to most German viewers through films that were shot in Togo, 'the German Sudan'. The inspiration for producing films in Africa, however, was Robert Schumann, whom Schomburgk had met in German East Africa in 1908.[23] His first own film expedition to Liberia in 1912/13 turned out to be a failure. More successful was his second expedition to Togo between August 1913 and March 1914, from which he released in 1917 the film *Im Deutschen Sudan* (In the German Sudan). On this expedition Schomburgk was working on behalf of the British MP Sales Agency and was accompanied by the British camera operator James S. Hodgson, the painter and amateur actor Kay Nebel and the amateur actress Emma Augusta 'Meg' Gehrts. Together they shot several fiction films and ethnographic shorts.[24] The outbreak of the First World War made Schomburgk return, via London, to Germany, where Schomburgk started work as a freelance writer for the Hamburg newspaper *Hamburger Fremdenblatt*. Most of the film material was confiscated by British authorities and must be considered lost.

In wartime Schomburgk was drafted as the head of a motorcycle troop in France and later a motor vehicle troop in Russia. Due to an injury he returned to Berlin, where he was assigned to the *Kommando der Schutztruppen* (command of the colonial forces), for which he started to give propaganda lectures to accompany his film, *Im Deutschen Sudan*, all over Germany; these lectures also made him an important figure in the DKG's colonial propaganda work in 1917.[25] Although most of his film material remained in London, the available amount of material with which he arrived in Germany was sufficient to make him the only one who could release new film material from one of the African colonies. The continuous demand for new films gave him the chance to release several films in 1916: *Der Bau der nördlichsten Station in Togo* (The Construction of the Northernmost Station in Togo), *Unsere Polizeitruppe in Togo* (Our Police Troops in Togo) and *Unsere Schutztruppe im Krieg* (Our Colonial Troops in Wartime) were belated colonial topicals that reminded the German audience of their African 'model colony' shortly before the war. German film journals did not review Schomburgk's releases, but the titles suggest that *Der Bau der nördlichsten Station in Togo* displayed the construction of the northernmost control post in Togo and was supposed to demonstrate Germany's 'positive' efforts in making Togo a modern colony. *Unsere Polizeitruppe* and *Unsere Schutztruppe* seemed to be colonial versions of newsreels that corresponded to the audience's interest in authentic footage of the German military forces. Moreover, because the East African colony would resist allied invasion until 1916, the films were also seen as having a certain topical quality.

In addition to the ethnographic film *Frauenleben in Westafrika* (Women's Life in West Africa) (1916), Schomburgk also released in 1916 the fictional adventure film *Der Raub in den Sudu-Bergen* (The Outlaw of the Sudu Mountains) and in 1917 *Die Weisse Göttin der Wangora* (The White Goddess of the Wangora).[26] In her book, *A Camera Actress in the Wilds of Togoland,* a project that also was written 'to win friends for the colonial cause',[27] Meg Gehrts provides some information about the production of the individual films. The decision to shoot scenes for a film depended either on the availability of Togolese people or a particular exotic location. This could explain why Schomburgk preferred to develop his stories on location; only for the Wangora film did he prepare a script. Echoing Schumann's derogatory remarks about African actors, Schomburgk did not consider the Togolese as real actors; they could only react (*handeln*) but not act (*spielen*).[28]

In German film journals only *Die Weisse Göttin der Wangora* was reviewed: it tells the story of a white baby found by an African tribe in the jungle. The baby is brought up by the tribe and worshiped as a goddess. Years later, a young white male is captured. The 'goddess' falls in love with him, liberates him and both escape.[29] The Wangora film does not indicate any specific colonial reference, though a film like *Der Raub in den Sudu Bergen* refers to the Sudu mountains in the colony of Togo. In all his publications Schomburgk makes little or no mention of this part of his filmmaking career. It is difficult to say to what extent Schomburgk's fiction films were viewed with regard to colonial propaganda that demanded the return of the colonies. More likely these films reflect Schomburgk's entrepreneurial intuition for the novelty of shooting fiction films on location in Africa – *Die Weisse Göttin der Wangora* was critically acclaimed at its premieres in London and Berlin.[30]

More important for colonial propaganda was Schomburgk's feature-length nonfiction film, *Im Deutschen Sudan.* In addition to British MP Sales Agency's interest in producing fictional adventure films in an authentic African setting, Schomburgk's second focus was on shooting nonfiction material in Togo. This part of his film work was probably based on a joint venture between Schomburgk and the RKA. Reviews of his lectures accompanying *Im Deutschen Sudan* mention that the expedition was commissioned by the Deutsch-Afrikanische Film-und Vortragsgesellschaft (German-African Film and Lecture Company), which was working for the RKA.[31] This official aspect of Schomburgk's film work must have facilitated the contact between the DKG and Schomburgk, who started with film lectures in the summer of 1917 at events for the so-called Kolonialkriegerdank, whose purpose was to collect money for German prisoners of war in the colonial territories and colonial war invalids.[32] A nationwide event within this campaign became the *Opfertage* (sacrifice days) for colonial soldier donations on 17 and 18 August 1918. During these two days cinemas and theatres were asked to screen and perform primarily patriotic films or plays. The DEUKO offered for this special occasion a short animated film that was 'very appropriate for these days'.[33] Everyone who agreed to participate in this event donated a certain percentage of the income to the colonial war donation. In preparation for these days the DKG sent a leaflet to the local branches with instructions concerning the organization of the days. Branches were required to contact local cinema and theatre owners and negotiate contracts for the event. According to the contract, eight days before the event film programmes had to carry the slogan 'Sacrifice days for the Colonial War donation on 17 and 18 August. Donate – Donate generously.' Parallel to this, cinemas could receive on request a slide that reminded the audience of the sacrifice days.

The most prominent lecturer in Berlin was Hans Schomburgk, who, between 2 and 18 August 1918, lectured fourteen times as accompaniment to *Im Deutschen Sudan*.[34] Like Robert Schumann's compilation of an adventurous, long, nonfictional hunting film, *Im Deutschen Sudan*, at 1,370 metres in length, was designed to become an evening's entertainment. Assenka Oksiloff describes the film as a 'pastiche of changing perspectives and set-ups… a lengthy version of the earliest multi shot films, which did not employ continuity editing and often appeared as a string of juxtaposed shots rather than a series of visually and thematically interlaced views'.[35] Tobias Nagl similarly considers the film as standing in the tradition of a tourist home movie due to the lack of any anthropological contextualiation.[36] Schomburgk's film appears in large part as a lengthy early travelogue, introducing all kinds of 'views' and attractions to the viewer: picking cotton, weaving and iron-making, an ostrich and hippo hunt, fishing and horse-riding games (*Reiterspiele*). The film has no story in the classical sense, but scenes of camp life and intertitles give the film a loose expedition narrative.

With regard to the DKG's interest in using film to present a flourishing colony that attracted potential investors, *Im Deutschen Sudan* is rather uncolonial and an inappropriate film. It does not show the achievements of German colonization or urban colonial life in Lomé. Images of the colonial railway are missing, as are scenes from German plantations, and the expedition members are the only Westerners in the film. However, the film's success and value as colonial propaganda seemed to be based exactly on the absence of any visual colonialism. Following the expedition, members on their trip through Togo gave colonial officials the chance to create a rather 'innocent' and positive image of Germany as a colonizing nation. This image justified the demand for an even bigger colonial empire after the war as it disproved the allies' accusation of Germany's failure in colonial civilization, which made the film also important for colonial revisionism after the First World War.[37] Ethnographic shots such as iron-making were important as they illustrated the colony's significance for Germany's economic future, but they also gave the film an apolitical look. The focus on Togolese people and their daily life in the villages, with their traditions, customs and habits, rather than on Africans doing hard labour on German plantations emphasized Germany's serious scientific interest in African culture and its diversity. *Im Deutschen Sudan* was a perfect vehicle to demonstrate Germany's respect for its colonies and their people.

Although Schomburgk's film might have initially not corresponded to the DKG's idea of film propaganda, it nevertheless showed that *sujets* other than colonial economy and political stability could sell colonialism to the German public. As with Robert Schumann's identification as the intrepid German hunter in Africa's dangerous jungles, Schomburgk could be presented as the prototype of the cosmopolitan German explorer and African expert.[38]

Parallel to Schomburgk's expedition film, it was the film company DEUKO that became the most important film company for the production of fictional colonial films. Their films had little in common with the travelogue-expedition character of *Im Deutschen Sudan*. The DEUKO represents the colonial side's efforts to establish film propaganda parallel to and largely independent of such propaganda institutions as the DEULIG or the BUFA, which are usually associated with German film propaganda in the First World War. In contrast to the DKG's early film propaganda, which usually emphasized the political and economic significance of the colonies, the DEUKO put its emphasis on the colonist's personal drama. Colonialism became linked to addressing the emotions of the viewer, and patriotism was embedded in a dramatic story that reminded the viewer of the suffering of Germans in the colonies or German virtues (*Tugenden*) in Africa. The DKG's growing interest in the DEUKO's work indicates that the DKG seemed to move from 'serious colonialism' to colonial propaganda in the form of entertaining events.

Notes

1. J. Aubinger, 'Der Kinematograph in Kriegszeiten', *Der Kinematograph*, 12 August 1914.
2. *Lichtbild-Bühne*, 29 August 1914, 14–15.

3. Birett, *Verzeichnis der in Deutschland gelaufenen Filme*, 188, 192.
4. *Lichtbild-Bühne*, 14 November 1914, 31.
5. Aubinger, 'Der Kinematograph in Kriegszeiten'.
6. *Der Kinematograph*, 7 October 1914.
7. D. Welch, *Germany, Propaganda and Total War, 1914–1918. The Sins of Omission*, London: The Athlon Press, 2000, 45.
8. Ibid., 44.
9. Ibid., 45.
10. See also R. Rother, 'Bei unseren Helden an der Somme. Eine deutsche Antwort auf die Entente-Propaganda', *KINtop: Jahrbuch zur Erforschung des frühen Films*, 1995, 4: 123–42.
11. Welch, *Germany, Propaganda and Total War*, 48.
12. Deutsche Lichtbildgesellschaft e.V. (eds), *Der Film im Dienste der nationalen und wirtschaftlichen Werbearbeit*, Berlin.
13. Welch, *Germany, Propaganda and Total War*, 54.
15. Pierard, 'The German Colonial Society', 106.
16. Ibid., 365.
17. BArch, R 8023/328, 97–98. Emil Zimmermann's own role in colonial filmmaking is unclear. The records of the DKG include two letters from Zimmermann in which he reminds the society to return forty-six films he sent to the DKG. BArch, R 8023/232, 243, 245.
18. BArch, R 8023/328, 92.
19. The AA proposed that the film company should be set up with investments by the DKG and the KWK of twenty thousand marks each and by the two private investors of five thousand marks each. BArch, R 8023/328, 90.
20. Ibid.
21. It does not mean that Mecklenburg was against film in general. Like the German emperor or other members of the royal families, Mecklenburg, too, was flattered by film recordings of his persona that were shown in public cinemas. *Der Film*, 4 March 1916, 32.
22. BArch, R 8023/328, 87.
23. H. Schomburgk, *Zelte in Afrika. Fahrten*, 260.
24. For a detailed introduction of Gehrt's and Schumburgk's films see C. Alexander, 'Annals of Exploration, "*The White Godess of the Wangora*"', *The New Yorker*, 8 April 1991, 43–76. Retrieved 14 March 2014 from http://www.newyorker.com/archive/1991/04/08/1991_04_08_043_TNY_CARDS_000359730.
25. Schomburgk, *Zelte in Afrika*, 394–403. An overview of Schomburgk's later film activities is given by G. Waz, 'Auf der Suche nach dem letzten Paradies. Der Afrikaforscher und Regisseur Hans Schomburgk', in J. Schöning (ed.), *Triviale Tropen. Exotische Reise und Abenteuerfilme aus Deutschland 1919–1939*, Munich: edition text + kritik, 1997, 95–109; also Nagl, *Die Unheimliche Maschine*, 227–308.
26. The production *Odd Man Out* was not released in Germany. With the exception of *Frauenleben in Westafrika*, which was prohibited for children in Berlin (but allowed in Hamburg), Schomburgk's films passed all censorship. *Die Heldin von Paratau* was probably not exhibited before 1918.
27. M. Gehrts, *A Camera Actress in the Wilds of Togoland*, London: Seely, Service & Co. Ltd, 1915, x.
28. Schomburgk, *Zelte in Afrika*, 378.
29. Anon., 'Fetischkönigin der Wangora', *Der Kinematograph*, 4 April 1917. A lucid analysis of the film is given in Nagl, *Die unheimliche Maschine*, 283–86.

30. Alexander, 'Annals of Exploration', 66.
31. The Film and Lecture Company is also mentioned as the precursor of Schomburgk's the Übersee-Film AG and the Übersee-Film GmbH, BArch, R 8023/329, 91.
32. The Kolonialkriegerdank organized special donation events that became known as the *Kolonialkriegerspende*, e.g. 21 October 1917 in Berlin; 9 November 1917 in Rostock.
33. BArch, R 8023/1048a, 179.
34. Besides Schomburgk, many more lecturers were using film to illustrate their talks. At least in Berlin the audience could actually choose which colonial film lecture they would like to attend: on 9 August Lieutenant Hans Schomburgk at the Urania theatre about *Im Deutschen Sudan*, Captain Gruner at the Sternwarte Treptow on 'Our Colonial Future' and Captain Roscher 'Adventures from Togo during the War and in Captivity in Dahomey' at a second Urania theatre. Other film lectures were 'War Adventures from Cameroon', 'The Heroic Fight in German East Africa' or 'Our Schutztruppe'. A list of the different screenings can be found in: BArch, R 8023/1048a, 93–96.
35. Oksiloff, *Picturing the Primitive*, 81.
36. Nagl, *Unheimliche Maschine*, 255.
37. The image of Germany as a benevolent colonizing nation was heavily attacked by the victorious allied powers after the war. It was argued that Germany was not able to colonize and had lost therefore the right to have colonies. On the German side the discussion became known as the *Koloniale Schuldlüge* (colonial guilt lie), and colonial revisionists demanded the return of the colonies to German administration.
38. The success of Robert Schumann's hunting films for colonial propaganda was also realized by the DKG's propaganda commission in 1920, when they recommended that Schumann's films be used to revive the colonial spirit in the German public. BArch, R 8023/1089, 3.

Chapter 14

THE DEUTSCHE KOLONIAL-FILMGESELLSCHAFT (DEUKO)

The DEUKO presented a coherent concept for colonial film production, which was put on a solid financial ground with an initial capital of sixty thousand marks. According to the DEUKO's statute, the company's purpose was 'the production and exploitation of colonial and other films'.[1] As one of its directors, Martin Steinke, explained in an article to the readers of the DKZ, the company had been set up in reaction to British and French propaganda films that depicted German soldiers as gruesome killers.[2] The DEUKO wanted to instruct the public about the colonies and produce colonial film dramas with thrilling content and a 'healthy tendency'. After the DEUKO had succeeded in making the colonies a common good among the German public, it planned to produce colonial *Kulturfilm,* films for the German youth and schools as scientific lecture films.

The DEUKO immediately became known within the colonial movement. In May Steinke and his colleague Karl Karalus personally introduced the company to the DKG and joined the society by becoming members of the Berlin branch. There is no information about in what ways the DEUKO collaborated with the RKA, but the company had very good contacts in the office, which seemed to support the production of the films in every way.[3] After opening their office on the Friedrichstrasse in Berlin, the company organized a competition for colonial screenplays to supply it with 'effective, dramatic screenplays, that reflect the history and culture as the hustle and the bustle in the colonies in order to show in this way their value and significance for the fatherland'.[4] The purpose of the competition, however, was not just to award the first two winners but also to purchase those scripts that could be used for later projects. The composition of the prize jury illustrates the DEUKO's good standing in the colonial movement: two representatives from the DKG and its subdivision, the Kolonialwirtschaftliches Komittee (Colonial Economic Committee), Major Göring from the headquarters of the Schutztruppen at the RKA, Karalus from the DEUKO and the scriptwriter Carl Boese. To reach potential colonial script writers, the competition was publicized in the *DKZ* in July 1917.[5]

In May the DEUKO had already begun production of its first film, which was to be part of a larger film cycle called 'Freedom of the World'. While first film was supposed to have been directed by Hans Oberländer,[6] the film *Der Verräter* (The Traitor) was finally directed by Georg Alexander, who also played one of the main parts in the film.[7] In March 1918 the company released the second colonial feature, *Farmer Borchardt* (Carl Boese, 1917), which was followed by one short animated propaganda film, *Opfertag für die Kolonial-Kriegsspende* (Sacrifice Day for the Colonial War Donation) and two non-colonial films: the social crime drama *Der letzte Augenblick* (The Last Moment)[8] and the 'sensational' film *Die Heldin von Paratau* (The Heroine of Paratau).[9] No information exists about a fifth feature film called *Das Ende der Alma Bonar* (The End of the Alma Bonar). In October 1918 the DEUKO released the last colonial feature film, *Der Gefangene von Dahomey* (The Prisoner from Dahomey) (Hubert Moest, 1918). Only the company's colonial dramas, *Der Verräter*, *Farmer Borchardt* and *Der Gefangene von Dahomey* were reviewed in the trade press. All three have to be considered lost.

Three Colonial Film Dramas

Der Verräter tells the story of the young Englishman Smith, who falls in love during peacetime with the daughter of a German businessman and owner of a farm in the South-West colony. Smith marries the girl, moves to DSWA and becomes the manager of his father-in-law's farm. Having moved to Africa, Smith neglects his young wife but intensifies the contacts with his British neighbours. The farm's German assistant telegraphs to Germany and reports on the strange goings-on at the farm. The father's nephew is sent to check on Smith's work. When the war breaks out, Smith's cover as a spy is blown, and the reason for his strange behaviour discovered. He was trying to transfer his father-in-law's property to the British side. Smith dies in a motorboat chase on the Oranje River.[10]

Farmer Borchardt was a South-West drama set during the Herero War in 1905. A young man breaks off his engagement with his fiancée, Agnes, after her father dies. The young woman eventually marries the farmer Borchardt and moves with him to DSWA. Though they live a carefree life, the young woman cannot forget her first fiancé. After the death of her first child she feels lonely and falls in love again with her old love, who is now working as a state official for the government in the colony. Borchardt discovers the secret love and sends both away. Meanwhile the Herero War has started and the young woman realizes that life has changed. Now in love with Borchardt she returns to the farm. Shortly after her return, Herero warriors attack the farm. Borchardt wants to save his wife from the enemy's atrocities and decides to shoot her. German Schutztruppen approach and rescue the farm. Borchardt believes that he has killed his wife and becomes depressed. His wife recovers, and they start a new life together.[11]

Der Gefangene von Dahomey, the DEUKO's last film, was based on a script by the colonial novelist Lene Haase. The film tells the story of a German planter, Burgsdorf, who becomes a prisoner of the French army at the beginning of the war. In the prison camp at Dahomey Burgsdorf and his comrades suffer especially from the sadistic excesses of the French captain, who does not even hesitate to beat a priest. Burgsdorf does not revolt. He tries to make the best out of his situation and demands fair treatment. For his decent attitude an African is ordered to punish Burgsdorf with a hippo whip. The African disobeys the order and is killed by the captain. On another occasion Burgsdorf is tortured with thumbscrews until he faints. Burgsdorf receives help from an old African woman, who works for the French captain's wife. She gives Burgsdorf a mysterious drink that makes him appear to be dead. After he is buried, the African woman takes his 'dead' body and revives it with an antidote. From now on Burgsdorf lives a double life. Every night he returns to the prison camp and kills one of the guards. One night the French captain sees Burgsdorf. He gets in a panic and orders the exhumation of the body. When he sees an already decaying corpse – a substitute – he is relieved. Meanwhile, Burgsdorf and the captain's wife have fallen in love. The French captain discovers the relationship and wants to kill Burgsdorf. Chasing Burgsdorf in a swamp the French captain gets killed. Burgsdorf and the captain's wife leave for Switzerland and start a new life.

Little is known about the shooting of the films, except for *Der Gefangene von Dahomey*. All three films were produced under the patronage of the RKA, and the stories suggest that colonial authorities supplied the DEUKO with props, technical equipment and real troops.[12] In contrast to the DEULIG and the BUFA, which were both interested in the production of colonial films but considered producing them in the colonies, the DEUKO's plan from the beginning was to produce fictional 'lookalike' colonial dramas in Germany. Interior shots were made in Berlin studios and exterior shots in the Berlin area. These home sequences were edited together with real footage of natives, African villages and so on, which were taken from authentic film footage from the colonies.[13] The quality of this kind of faked colonial reality seemed to be very convincing, and reviews underlined the producers' talent in finding the correct location to counterfeit colonial reality. Reviews of the DEUKO films were divided. The *Kinematograph* suggested that a better director would have made more of the 'rich material' in *Der Verräter*;[14] the *Lichtbild-Bühne* argued that the propagandistic aim in *Farmer Borchardt* had swung to the other extreme: what was left was just a touching love story.[15] The crude story of death, 'transanimation' and revenge of *Der Gefangene von Dahomey* was attributed to Lene Haase's fantasy rather than to any real events.[16] Despite the critique the trade press welcomed in general the company's colonial commitment and considered the colonial background a promising *sujet* for future films supportive of the colonial idea. *Farmer Borchardt* had a successful run in the Berlin cinemas in April 1918 and became a major financial success for the DEUKO and abroad.[17]

The DKG's executive committee's members had differing opinions about the quality of the DEUKO films. Some still were thinking in terms of colonial travelogues and films that were shot in the colonies when talking about colonial film propaganda. A film like *Farmer Borchardt*, for example, was considered far from being able to support the colonial idea. The 'unfavourable' impression regarding the film's morality was criticized. Instead of showing the 'hustle and bustle' in the colonies, the film was addicted to a *Kinoton* (cinema tone), which simply meant that the film entertained rather than informed the viewer.[18] In other words, to use films that were produced according to commercial standards was inconceivable for some of the DKG's members, who seemed to follow a cinema reformist discourse in colonial propaganda. Other members argued that moralistic concerns should not be overemphasized in the film, but that it was important to produce what the audience wanted to see.

Fictional colonial dramas were rather different in style, and content from the films that had been shown in the DKG's branches in earlier years. The DEUKO films were not about civilizing efforts or depicting German progress in Africa, but showed a side of colonial life that nonfiction films generally were not able to penetrate. Heide Schlüpmann's remark that 'early fiction films were fuelled by the same interest as the documentary films, and that they also represent a kind of documentation, albeit by other means' is important in this context.[19] The individual's private fate in the colonies was something that did not belong to the film repertoire in the DKG's screenings and was not part of colonial travelogues, but could now be shown in the colonial fiction dramas.[20] *Der Verräter* presents the colony as a second Heimat and persuades the viewer by the example of a personal story that the new colonial Heimat was as worth fighting for as the original European one.[21] While the thrilling story of love and betrayal appealed to the audience's preferences and patriotism, the inserted nonfiction images offered the chance to establish another aspect of colonial ideology. Scenes of natives in their villages, on the farms, at work and displaying their 'affection' towards the colonizer were, according to a review, impressive and educational at the same time. The demonstration of a peaceful life in which the colonized were glad to live under German administration supported the image of Germany as a good colonizing nation and buttressed the demand for the colonies' return after the war. The commercial success of *Farmer Borchardt,* a film that focused on the individual life and love of a German settler in the colonial Heimat, suggests that viewers identified with the personal drama that had little to do with the colonial economic achievements as they were shown in colonial travelogues.

Unlike the pre-war nonfiction colonial travelogues, the DEUKO films retreated from the image of the modern colony. Given the impossibility of producing any more nonfiction films in the colonies, the DEUKO films added an important aspect of what had been missing from earlier colonial films – the colony as the pastoral Heimat, the native soil. With the resemanticization of the colonies in the films of the DEUKO, the company's productions present a complementary aspect of the Heimat film discourse, which is characterized by the ambivalence of the traditional and the modern.

From this perspective a film like *Farmer Borchardt* could successfully support the government's official war propaganda. In contrast to the focus on technology in earlier colonial travelogues, colonial dramas addressed the emotions of the audience and thus fulfilled one of the main goals of the war propaganda that official institutions like the

BUFA aimed at but never successfully achieved. With the mixture of thrilling drama, touching love story and ideological nationalist elements, the DEUKO films reflected the changing attitude towards film propaganda in the First World War. For the BUFA, the private initiative of the DEUKO was therefore a good chance to cover one aspect of film production that could not be done entirely by the BUFA alone.[22] Though the office produced fiction feature films such as *Jan Vermeulen, der Müller aus Flandern* (Georg Jacoby, 1917) or *Der Feldarzt/Das Tagebuch des Dr. Hart* (Paul Leni, 1917), BUFA authorities were primarily concerned with military propaganda and had little idea of film as an entertainment industry. Military and government authorities came to the conclusion that the audience was watching films not only with their eyes but also with their 'minds and feelings' (*Gemüt und Empfindung*).[23] People went to the movies to see films in which the dramatic elements stood in the foreground, so that short instructional films could only support a film programme that was dominated by the feature film. In this combination cinema was a useful propaganda tool that even offered the advantage of being a place for instruction *and* distraction.[24] The BUFA's offerings could not compete with the Italian, French or U.S. productions;[25] audiences did not want to see films from the front but were asking for long feature films, such as those offered by the DEUKO.

In a secret aide memoire at the end of 1917 the BUFA reflected on what a propaganda film was supposed to be: 'the propaganda film must beat the pure entertainment film [*reinen Unterhaltungsfilm*] not just by aiming at the instincts that the propaganda is trying to arouse but also by aiming at the masses' legitimate desire for entertainment and "visual desires" [*Schaubedürfnis*], without which the cinema simply cannot exist'.[26] The financial success of *Farmer Borchardt* shows that the DEUKO's eclectic mix of genre forms and apparent ideological ambiguity was particularly suited to find success with the public. On the one hand, the adventurous melodramatic story made the film a reinforcement of a 'stand-by-your-man-ideology', which addressed the female audience whose husbands were fighting at the front. On the other hand, the dramatic recourse to colonial history indirectly corresponded with crucial elements of German war ideology by reminding the German audience of the value of their German Heimat, while to calling for a patriotic commitment. The comparison with another colonial drama that had been released six years earlier shows the ideological value of the DEUKO films during war time.

In 1911 the Deutsche Bioscop released the 'romantic exotic' two-act drama *Zwei Welten* (Two Worlds). The film recounts a dramatic love story set during the Herero War. A pastor's daughter, Maria, falls in love with Lieutenant Colonel Max von Raven. Gambling debts lead Max to get married to another woman. At his wedding day Max realizes that he actually loves Maria. His wife learns about her husband's real love and takes comfort in the arms of another man. Max finds out about his wife's cheating and heads for the South-West African colony. In a battle Max gets wounded and finally dies in Maria's arms, who meanwhile has become a volunteer nurse in the colony. The film was promoted by emphasizing the 'scenically charming setting' and the realistic fighting against rebellious 'real Negroes' in the African desert. Max's leaving for Africa is described as a seeking of 'distraction and forgetting on the colony's battlefields'.[27] The review suggests that the colony's only function was to trigger a dramatic narrative sequence, a place for male adventure and a tragic ending. The film showed little interest in establishing the colony as a German living space that was worth defending.

In contrast to *Zwei Welten, Farmer Borchardt*'s reference to the Herero War articulates an important analogy to propaganda rhetoric. Colonial ideology was characterized by a strong social Darwinist worldview in which the 'superior German culture' and virtues stood against a culture whose 'inferiority' did not need any proof. Consequently the public reception of the Herero and Nama wars, which ended with the quasi-genocide of both ethnic groups, was that of a battle between 'black' and 'white', between '*Kultur*' and '*Unkultur*'.[28] In a similar tone, German war rhetoric emphasized the battle between German culture and foreign civilization: German culture as the quasi-natural life stood in contrast to civilization as an expression of the human beings' alienation from tradition and interpersonal relations. The DEUKO underlined that the company did not want to become associated with foreign *Hetzfilme* (malicious films) that addressed only the lower human instincts but, 'in keeping with German nature', to operate in the field of *Kulturarbeit* (cultural work).[29] With this 'noble' task the DEUKO joined the official propaganda rhetoric in which Germany was a nation of heroes defending their superior culture against the foreign *Unkultur*.[30]

Following the BUFA's propaganda instructions, which recommended cultivating and eliciting only those 'favourable moments' that were still 'dozing in the viewers' unconscious' but not those creating 'concern and worry' in the viewers' mind, *Farmer Burckhardt* avoided a direct equation of 'cultureless' Herero with the Entente, but the film seemed to have hit one of the 'favourable moments'.[31] The drama emphasized the values and virtues of Germanness like idealism, heroism and self-sacrifice – everything for which German culture stood in German war ideology.[32] Where else could German virtues better be defended than on soil that was cultivated through German hands or, to use an etymologically related term, that had been *colonized* through German virtues – the German colonial Heimat.

The work and the success of the DEUKO attracted the attention of colonial, military and government officials. The surviving correspondence suggests that the contact between the DEUKO and the DKG must have been more regular, as the cooperation between the two sides became more intense in early 1918. In February Steinke reported to the DKG about the company's success in signing contracts with five 'Monopol-Inhaber' cinemas for eight to ten colonial films for 1918/19. The society acknowledged the success of the DEUKO by putting Carl Müller's amateur recordings from 1904 to 1906 at the company's disposal, and invited Steinke to report personally about the DEUKO at one of the executive committee's meetings. At this meeting in April Steinke could refer to the recent successful press screenings of *Farmer Borchardt* in Hamburg and Berlin, and emphasized that, with the contracts it had signed, the DEUKO had access to all three thousand cinemas in the country, and films could be screened simultaneously in eleven different cities for the year 1918/19.[33]

Steinke's presentation was successful in two ways. The DKG awarded a unique grant of two thousand marks and agreed, after a more detailed evaluation of the company, to reorganize the DEUKO in order to support more fully the production of colonial propaganda films.[34] The plan for a reorganization of the DEUKO was advantageous for the company and the DKG; while the DEUKO received access to the whole system of branches that increased the chances of promoting the films on local and regional levels, the films put the DKG in contact with millions of film viewers and potential new members.[35] Before the committee's next meeting, Steinke had already come up with a clear outline of the company's future development. Steinke presented the DEUKO as a profit-making company whose balance would be improved through more contracts abroad. To become independent from the market he planned to have a film studio and processing section, which could be rented out to other companies to make additional profit. In contrast its current capital of half a million marks, the DEUKO required capital of between one and one and a half million marks for the time after war. To start immediately shooting films in the colonies after the return to peacetime, Steinke underlined the necessity of buying good film scripts and contracting a good staff now. The preparations for the reorganization of the DEUKO continued until the summer of 1918. In June the

DKG decided to take a stake in the DEUKO and to increase the company's capitalization with the support of new shareholders.[36] The preparations for the DEUKO's reorganization continued during the summer. Pre-screenings for the company's third colonial drama, *Der Gefangene von Dahomey*, were welcomed by colonial authorities. State secretary Solf acknowledged the production of the film that illustrated the suffering of German prisoner of war in French captivity and was therefore 'perfectly suited' to find a wide reception in the German nation.[37] While the BUFA planned to show the film at every general command,[38] the DEUKO planned to organize special screenings in every major German city to show the film in an extravagant style.[39]

The film, however, which was announced as a 'colossal and magnificent colonial work of film'[40] and took almost a year in production, could not change political reality. Since the beginning of the allied counteroffensive in July 1918, Germany's chances of winning the war started to dwindle and disappeared by the end of September. Instead of becoming a new highlight in the company's short history of operation, *Der Gefangene von Dahomey* marked the ending of colonial film propaganda and the DEUKO's existence as a film company.

Of all the DEUKO films, *Der Gefangene von Dahomey* elaborates least a discourse on the notion of Heimat. As a propaganda film for the recovery of the lost colonies it had almost no use. Burgsdorf is a displaced person who ends up in Switzerland, which gives little support for the idea of a new colonial Heimat. Reviewers were disturbed by the film's depiction of excessive violence, which made it into a desperate 'die-hard' slogan at a time when a German victory was no longer to be expected. Considering Germany's approaching defeat and the loss of the colonies, the film rather stands for a nation's frenzied collapse as a world and colonial power. Burgsdorf's revenge is not on any particular enemy but a general payoff aimed at everyone who crossed his plans. The shooting of *Der Gefangene von Dahomey* indicates a disturbing inversion of reality and fiction.

The film's intention was to demonstrate French atrocities against German internees in African camps. The collaboration with the RKA made it possible to shoot the film in a real prisoner- of-war camp in Berlin-Wünsdorf, which had been set up by the Oberste Heeresleitung for coloured Muslims to prepare a jihad against the French and British powers.[41] Stills from the shooting of the film suggest that the coloured prisoners were part of the cast and had to play the role of the African troops, a fact unmentioned in the reviews. Thus, the production of the film was based on a perverse logic: the real German camp near Ber-

Figure 14.1. Still from *Der Gefangene von Dahomey* (1918). Reproduced courtesy of bpk/Museum Europäischer Kulturen, SMB/Otto Stiehl.

lin became a fictitious French camp in Africa. Under the conditions of real detention the African internees were ordered to play the camp's guardsmen, while the German protagonist plays a prisoner of a camp that actually was under German control.

The sparse information on the film in the reviews does not allow a close textual analysis, but the story seems to be based on a combination of African witchcraft, resistance, revenge and love story.[42] The suggested alliance between the colonizer and the colonized forecloses in a way a historical discussion that was yet to come. After the war, the image of Germany as a benevolent colonizing nation was heavily attacked by the victorious allied powers. It was argued that Germany was not able to colonize and had therefore lost the right to have colonies. On the German side the discussion became known as the *koloniale Schuldlüge* (colonial guilt lie), and colonial revisionists demanded the return of the colonies to German administration.[43] In *Der Gefangene von Dahomey* the guilt is shifted to the French enemy. Germans and Africans are suffering from French atrocities, and it is Burgsdorf who is the defender of human rights. The relationship between Germans, French and Africans, however, is more ambivalent. The suggested alliance between the African woman, who plays the noble savage, and Burgsdorf must suppress a characteristic element of colonial ideology, according to which Western culture is superior to that of the colonized. In the film the colonizer can survive only because of the powerful witchcraft of the colonized employed to take revenge on the French captain, who is described in reviews as a *'Deutschenfresser'* (German-Eater), making not the African but the Frenchman the real cannibal. The film, however, has an interesting twist regarding the power relationship between black and white. African and Asian soldiers for the French and British military in the First World War caused a heated debate in Germany, which considered the use of such troops as a threat to the racial order. According to Karl Weule, a coloured, lower race would lose the respect for and awe of the 'adored white', which would make it impossible to rule the colonized in future.[44] The discussion finally reached its peak with the occupation of the Rhineland in 1919, in which the presence of black French soldiers resulted in a campaign that was called *Die Schwarze Schmach* (The Black Shame).[45]

It is noteworthy that while the French captain does not die at Burgsdorf's hands but drowns in the swamps, the African guards are felled by Burgsdorf night by night, one by one. Though the review suggests a common front of Germans and Africans against the enemy, Burgsdorf actually exterminates everyone who stands in his way, primarily African soldiers. Almost as a consequence, the film's happy ending must take place neither in Germany nor Africa, but on innocent, neutral ground: Switzerland.

According to the *Kinematograph, Der Gefangene von Dahomey* was a 'malicious' film, whose purpose was no longer relevant. Though the film had good acting, it included cruel moments that drove people to leave the theatre before the film's ending.[46] The propagandistic aim to represent the 'typical' fate of a German colonialist as a prisoner of war failed. People did not want to see the cruelties of war that already had become reality for most of them. Reviews chose to see the film as the depiction of the fate of an individual German and not interpret the French captain's sadism as standing for the entire French nation.[47] Though initially prohibited only for children, *Der Gefangene von Dahomey* was ultimately banned from German screens. For the DEUKO the censorship decision was a financial disaster from which the company never recovered. The film was sold all over Germany but could not be shown in the cinemas. In the following months the company became involved in several court cases, and the lack of any available capital made the declaration of bankruptcy inevitable.[48] The DEUKO's uncertain future meant the end of the DKG's interest in reorganizing the DEUKO into a financially strong colonial film company. In March 1919 the DEUKO ceased operation and gave up its expensive office in Friedrichstrasse the following month.[49]

The Versailles peace treaty between Germany and the allies in 1919 put an official end to the German colonial era and to colonial cinematography in imperial Germany. In the course of colonial revisionism in the 1920s, however, Germany's colonial history continued to be present on the screen and for the most part received broad critical acclaim.[50] Conrad Wiene's film *Ich Hatte einen Kameraden* (I Had a Comrade) (1926) premiered on the eve of the *Hamburger Kolonialwoche* (Hamburg Colonial Week) in July 1926 and had considerable success at the box office.[51] As pointed out by Christian Rogowski, Wiene's film aimed at combating the colonial guilt lie by emphasizing in a melodramatic story the 'benefits of German *Kulturarbeit* (civilizing work)'.[52] Wiene's film remained the only colonial revisionist fiction film of Weimar cinema, which does not mean that colonial Africa had lost its popularity on the screen.

Hans Schomburgk strengthened his reputation as a filmmaker for African *sujets* with feature films such as *Tropengift* (Tropical Poison) (1919) and *Goldfieber* (Gold Fever), both starring his wife, Meg Gehrts. With the support of the DKG he founded in 1921 the Übersee–Film AG and released *Im Kampf um Diamantenfelder* (In the Battle over Diamond Fields) and *Eine Weisse unter Kannibalen (Fetisch)* (A White among Cannibals [Fetish]) in 1921, a remake of his 1916 feature film *Weisse Göttin der Wangora*. Schomburgk's films did not make references to the former German colonies, but it was one of the company's purposes to re-establish Germany's image as a benevolent colonizing nation and to keep up the colonial spirit in the German public.[53]

Schomburgk's film project met broad enthusiasm in the colonial lobby, and in 1924 he could present the first German expedition film to Africa, *Mensch und Tier im Urwald* (Man and Animal in the Jungle). In 1925 he released *Verlorenes Land* (Lost Country), a compilation of old film material he had shot in Togo before the war. The film conjured up colonial nostalgia, but it was not the only one of its kind. In his discussion of colonial revisionist films of the Weimar period, Tobias Nagl points out that the pathos of colonial conquest gave way to the trauma of defeat, and provided Weimar cinema with a touch of the surreal.[54] German expedition films of the 1920s, such as *Das Kolonialland Afrika* (The Colonial Land Africa) (Roebel-Kulturfilm, 1924) and its sequel *Vom Kilimandscharo zum Nil durchs verbotene Afrika* (From the Kilimanjaro to the River Nile Through Forbidden Africa) (1925), or *Zum Schneegipfel Afrikas* (To Africa's Snow Peak) (Carl Heinz Boese, 1924), addressed the public at large with their mélange of colonial nostalgia, which lamented the loss of Germany's colonies along with images of African fauna and flora, underlining the significance of the *Kulturfilm* as a 'moral institution' for the German public. The DKG's film work, the Kinematographenkampagne and the interest in the DEUKO's expansion have been excluded from the society's apologetic official histories, but film remained for them an important propaganda medium. In their annual report of 1926, the DKG proudly announced that the number of film screenings had increased compared to the previous year.[55] No fewer than six film companies were again distributing films from the former colonies.[56]

Notes

1. BArch, R 8023/328, 37.
2. M. Steinke, 'Koloniale Propagandafilms', *DKZ*, 20 September 1917, 137.
3. The archive of the Schutztruppen was totally destroyed in the Second World War, thus little is known about the cooperation between the DEUKO and the RKA in the production of the films. However, in cooperation with the Navy League the command of the Schutztruppen supported the production of another film. *Die Seele des Kindes* (The Mind of the Child) (Walter Schmidthässler, 1918) was shot in Lübeck and edited together with scenes from East Africa. *Der Kinematograph*, 12 June 1918.
4. BArch, R 8023/328, 85–86.
5. *DKZ*, 20 July 1917, 107. The prize jury decided not to award the first prize to any of the scripts and declared that none of them met the competition's requirements. *DKZ*, 20 October 1917, 156.
6. *Lichtbild-Bühne*, 5 May 1917, 42. The mentioning of Oberländer is interesting in this context as he contacted the colonial society's executive committee in March requesting support for a colonial film project (see p. 248).
7. *Der Kinematograph*, 8 August 1917.
8. *Der letzte Augenblick* is the only film that seems to have survived. A copy is archived at the EYE Film Institute Netherlands. Unfortunately the last reel is missing.
9. According to an advertisement, the actress in *Die Heldin von Paratau* was 'Meg Gehns' [sic]. *Der Film*, 1918, 37. This was Meg Gehrts, which suggests that either the DEUKO released the film Schomburgk had shot in 1913/14 or re-shot the film and edited it with footage from Schomburgk's expedition.
10. *Der Kinematograph*, 29 August 1917.
11. In December 1917 it was planned to call the film '*Der Liebe Macht*' (The Power of Love). The melodramatic title, however, does not trigger immediately a colonial association, which was probably one reason the film's title was changed.
12. The RKA actively supported the production of *Der Verräter*. *Der Film*, 4 August 1911, 60.
13. In February 1918 the head of the executive committee informed the other members that Carl Müller's film material had been put at the company's disposal. It is therefore possible that some of the authentic footage in *Farmer Borchardt* came from Müller's material or that the company had purchased films from Africa or colonies elsewhere.
14. *Der Kinematograph*, 29 August 1917.

15. *Lichtbild-Bühne*, 16 March 1917, 92.
16. *Der Film*, 12 October 1917, 42.
17. Farmer Borchardt also had success in Amsterdam and elsewhere in the Netherlands in October 1918. H. Barkhausen, *Filmpropaganda für Deutschland im Ersten und Zweiten Weltkrieg*. Hildesheim, Zürich and New York: Olms Presse, 115.
18. BArch, R 8023/328, 61.
19. H. Schlüpmann, 'The Documentary Interest in Fiction', *Uncharted Territory*, 1997, 33–36.
20. The reviews of colonial film screenings in the DKG's local branches suggest that a farmer's life was not particularly interesting to them. It tried primarily to depict the colonies as an extension of an industrial modern Germany and not as its pre-industrial agrarian refuge, which was one of the major arguments in colonial ideology. The only exceptions are films of the Propaganda-Gesellschaft für die deutschen Kolonien (see Chapter Six).
21. *Der Film*, 4 August 1917, 60.
22. The special screenings of *Der Verräter* at the BUFA in August 1917 and of *Der Gefangene von Dahomey* in the summer of 1918 show the BUFA's interest in the DEUKO's productions. *Der Film*, 25 August 1917, 46; BArch, R 8023/328, 13.
23. W. Mühl-Benninghaus, 'Exemplifikation des militärischen zwischen 1914 und 1918. Die Darstellung des Ersten Weltkrieges im Nonfictionfilm', in Müller and Segeberg, *Modellierung des Kinofilms*, 292.
24. Barkhausen, *Filmpropaganda für Deutschland*, 105.
25. Ibid., 156. The shortcomings of the BUFA eventually led to the setting up of a much more effective film organization in December 1917. The Universum Film AG (Ufa) was an amalgamation of several film companies whose shares were purchased by private investors acting on behalf of the German government. At one of the first meetings on 30 January 1918 Major Göring from the RKA mentioned that the DEUKO was considering joining the Ufa. BArch-MA, RM 9901, 197.
26. Bild- und Filmamt (1917), 'Bild- und Filmamt: Der Propagandafilm und seine Bedingungen, Ziele und Wege', in W. von Bredow and R. Zurek (eds), *Film und Gesellschaft in Deutschland. Dokumente und Materialien*, Hamburg: Hoffmann und Campe, 1975, 77. I would like to thank Philipp Stiasny, who drew my attention to this document.
27. *Der Kinematograph*, 23 August 1911.
28. M. Brehl, '"The drama was played out on the dark stage of the sandveldt". The destruction of the Herero and Nama in German (popular) Literature', in J. Zimmerer and J. Zeller (eds), *Genocide in German South-West Africa: The Colonial War of 1904–1908 and Its Aftermath*, London: The Merlin Press Ltd, 2008, 101.
29. Steinke, 'Koloniale Propagandafilms', 137.
30. See R. Chickering, *Das Deutsche Reich und der erste Weltkrieg*, München, 2002, 163–70.
31. 'Bild- und Filmamt', 81–82.
32. Chickering, *Das Deutsche Reich und der erste Weltkrieg*, 165.
33. BArch, R 8023/328, 65.
34. Ibid., 60.
35. Ibid., 73–74.
36. Ibid., 17–18.
37. BArch, R 8023/328, 14.
38. Ibid., 13. The correspondence between the DEUKO and the DKG regarding colonial film propaganda ends with this letter.
39. *Lichtbild-Bühne*, 31 August 1918, 124.
40. *Der Kinematograph*, 21 August 1918.

41. On Black Muslim prisoners in Germany see G. Höpp, *Muslime in der Mark – Als Kriegsgefangene und Internierte in Wünsdorf und Zossen, 1914–1924*, Berlin: Das Arabische Buch, 1997, 41.
42. Lene Haase, the scriptwriter, was married to a medical doctor working in Cameroon. It is quite possible that Haase was inspired by a witchcraft practice known as *liemba*, in which the witches 'leave their bodies at night and "eat" people so that they become ill and die'. E. Ardener, 'Witchcraft Economics, and the Continuity of Belief', in M. Douglas (ed.), *Witchcraft, Confessions and Accusations,* London et al.: Tavistock, 1970, 145. I would like to thank André Walter for this information.
43. Gründer, *Geschichte der deutschen Kolonien,* 217.
44. B. Lange, 'Die Welt im Ton – In deutschen Sonderlagern für Kolonialsoldaten entstanden ab 1915 Einzigartige Aufnahmen', *iz3w. Informationszentrum 3.Welt,* 2008, 307, 22–25. Retrieved 25 February 2014 from http://www.freiburg-postkolonial.de/Seiten/Lange-Welt-im-Ton.htm#_ftn2.
45. See Nagl, *Die unheimliche Maschine,* 154–99.
46. *Der Kinematograph,* 9 October 1918.
47. *Der Film,* 12 October 1918.
48. Landesarchive Berlin (LAB), A Rep. 342-02, no. 2476.
49. In December 1927 the Berlin court decided to strike the company from the register of companies.
50. Nagl, *Die unheimliche Maschine,* 309.
51. C. Rogowski, 'The "Colonial Idea" in Weimar Cinema', in V. Langbehn (ed.), *German Colonialism, Visual Culture, and Modern Memory,* New York: Routledge, 2010, 223.
52. Ibid., 232
53. R 8023/329, 141–43.
54. Nagl, *Die unheimliche Maschine,* 311.
55. Deutsche Kolonialgesellschaft (ed.), *Jahresbericht der Deutschen Kolonialgesellschaft,* Berlin: Deutsche Kolonialgesellschaft, 1926, 11.
56. Anon., 'Kolonial Film und Lichtbilderreihen', in Kolonialkriegerdank e.V., *Koloniales Hand- und Adreßbuch 1926–27,* Berlin: Verlag Kolonialkriegerdank, 1926, 98–102. The companies were Roebel-Kulturfilm, Institut für Kulturforschung, Universum-Film-Aktiengesellschaft (Ufa), Die Vaterländische Film-Gesellschaft mbH, John Hagenbeck Film GmbH and Walther Dobbertin.

CONCLUSION

Beyond the Colonial Era

'Although we are still far from understanding what kind of life the cinema used to lead among its audiences when it was dominated by travelling showman or made its entry into the urban centres of the fast growing German Reich, it is clear that from 1896 onwards a lively and diverse awareness of cinema developed in Germany just as it did in other European countries'.[1]

German colonial cinematography has no forgotten masterpieces or great filmmakers to offer, but it underlines once more Thomas Elsaesser's observation that the 'very first decades of innovation and experimentation' tell more 'about this cinema as a "national" cinema than any symptomatic masterpieces'.[2] *Imperial Projections* has shown that German colonialism initiated a diverse and lively activity among amateur and professional filmmakers whose films met the different preferences of the audience.

According to historian Winfried Speitkamp, imperial colonialism was the expression of a crisis that shook and shocked the people's self-understanding and their daily life in the nineteenth century. The growing consolidation of the world through industrialization and modern infrastructure resulted in an increasing demand for orientation, order and a fatal incomprehension of non-Western civilizations that virtually provoked the colonial grab for colonies.[3] Orientation and order also describe the DKG's initial motivation around 1905 to integrate film shows into its colonial propaganda. At the time German cinema developed a distinct national image, between 1909 and 1914, the DKG had just finished a period of intense examination of the new medium. Film screenings presented an attractive way to address its members, to recruit new members among the German public and to create an individual profile for the society, which would make it competitive with other associations. The films presented the colonies as economically prospering territories and therefore worth defending. Even if the DKG's experience with film encompasses only a short period in the society's history, film significantly changed the character of the DKG's propaganda work at this time.

As articles in the DKZ show, national colonial movements knew, observed and corresponded with each other. Even though no records regarding film could be discovered in the DKG's archive files that document the exchange of propaganda strategies related to film, the movements must have been aware of the other groups' successes and failures. Convents reports about a Belgian pendant to the DKG's film campaign that proved rather successful. Le Cinématograph des Colonies (The Cinematograph of the Colonies) was a private company founded in Brussels in December 1908, which aimed at popularizing everything linked to the Belgian colony. The company ran its own cinema and released films between 1909 and 1914.[4] John MacKenzie notes that in United Kingdom the 'Colonial Office Visual Instruction Committee', set up in 1902, was rather unsuccessful precisely because it took up techniques of the lantern slide when this medium had already become obsolete. As MacKenzie reports, a fateful decision was taken in 1908 when the committee decided not to use film for their propaganda purposes.[5] Finally, as the small 1916 booklet *Le Cinéma Colonisateur*, written by a member of Pathé Frères's Algerian branch with a preface by Charles Lutaud, governor of Algeria between 1911 and 1918, shows, discussion about cinema's significance for colonial interests also can be found in French colonial discourse.[6] Demonstrating to the audience at home the extension of the French colonial empire, using film for colonial education and fostering colonial tourism or displaying France's power to the colonized population were strategies quite similar to those of the DKG.

At the 1994 Amsterdam workshop on early nonfiction film, historian Ben Brewster remarked that early nonfiction film 'did not seem to exist in the regime of stylistic pressure that was clearly there for fiction filmmakers'.[7] In response to Brewster's observation, Tom Gunning has argued that one of the reasons for the lack of motivation for transformation was that 'existent modes of film style remained entirely *effective* for the genres then practiced'.[8] The analysis of the colonial travelogue indicates that the reason for the efficacy of the travelogue could have been its ambivalence of meaning for the audience. While the exhibition context – town hall, museum and film theatre – suggest reading modes such as propaganda, science and entertainment, the film *Südwest-Afrika* illustrates best the colonial travelogue's ambivalence regarding political domination and control of the colonized Other, and its surrender to exotic scenes, reverie and adventure.

To understand early colonial films, the analysis of colonial cinematography has demonstrated the importance of studying early nonfiction cinema in alternative exhibition contexts such as voluntary associations. Numerous local cinema studies have produced a considerable amount of empirical data on early cinema, which shape the understanding of the medium's impact on social and cultural life. However, too often the studies focused on film screenings in commercial venues and less on those in private ones. Further research into the distribution and exhibition practice of film in and for voluntary associations can make an important contribution to the 'very first decades of innovation and experimentation' and will hopefully give us a more accurate view of nonfiction's significance in early cinema in general.

Imperial Projections has focused on colonial cinematography from the perspective of the German film viewer in the German Reich, rather than on what cinema meant to people who were actually living in the colonies and what film culture was like in the colonies. The study of colonial newspapers show that, at least in DOA and DSWA, travelling exhibitors regularly organized film screenings in the colonies. The German Bundesarchiv offers too few records from the colonial governments that could provide a basis for even a crude analysis of cinema's role in colonial life, but it is worth thinking about in what ways film may have shaped the colonizers' identity as Germans and to what extent film screenings were a common entertainment for the colonized population. Questions like these also refer to a much broader filmhistorical context. In contrast to the twenty thousand Germans who were living in the German colonies on the eve of the First World War, many times that number had migrated to other countries and continents and were living, for example, in the United States, Chile, Argentina or Brazil. What role did film play in their immigration process? Did it preserve the immigrant's old identity or did it contribute to a new one? Did it mediate between the old and the new? The enormous range of topics that define early nonfiction cinema, but as well documentary and fiction filmmaking, and the variety of exhibition contexts could be a starting point to investigate aspects of continuity and change in traditions, institutions and biographies from a transnational perspective.[9]

Having outlined in detail the history of German colonial cinematography in this book, a final question comes into mind. How do film and television report today about Germany's colonial past? One might expect that under the influence of postcolonial thinking a more critical discussion of Germany's colonial history would characterize today's film narratives. Wolfgang Struck's lucid analyses of recent TV dramas shows that 'the representational system of German popular culture … has not changed much since the time of colonialism'.[10] In his analysis of *Wüstenrose* (Desert Rose) (Hans Werner, 2000), a historical melodrama set in the South-West African colony, Struck shows how the film's narration still employs the dubious link between colonial fantasy and sexuality, 'a figure already at work in the "original" colonial situation of the late nineteenth and early twentieth centuries'.[11] Though, as Struck assumes, the colonial setting was not intended but rather randomly chosen; the film is an 'intolerable narration' as it excludes the evidence of genocide, violence and oppression in favour of a happy ending.[12] Martin Baer's extraordinary compilation film *Befreien Sie Afrika* (Free Africa) (1999) supports Struck's observation in an entertaining, instructive and at times polemical way. The compilation of hundreds of clips from films, interviews, comics, television spots and television reportages, Baer's film is a critical inventory of the continuity of derogatory images of Africa in the German media, east and west, from the end of the Second World War up to the mid 1990s.

In contrast to a range of private local initiatives that critically inform the public about the colonial past[13] and the growing interest in German colonialism and postcolonial issues in schools and universities, the examples of recent television productions like *Die deutschen Kolonien* (The German Colonies) (G. Graichen, P. Prestel, T. Hies, 2005) or *Das Weltreich der Deutschen* (The German's World Empire) (S. Dehnhardt, R. Schlosshanon, 2010) show that German media still have a troubled relationship with its colonial history.[14] The documentaries were criticized for their Eurocentrism, 'banalizing' and 'exoticizing' Germany's colonial past.[15] Exoticization and banalization are terms that also could be applied to the aesthetics of the early colonial travelogue *Südwest-Afrika*. More than a hundred years later, do German media still need a history lesson?

Notes

1. T. Elsaesser and M. Wedel (eds), *A Second Life. German Cinema's First Decades*, Amsterdam: Amsterdam University Press, 1996, 10.
2. Ibid., 9.
3. W. Speitkamp, *Deutsche Kolonialgeschichte*, Stuttgart: Reclam, 2005, 14.
4. Convents, *A la recherche des images oubliées*, 93.

5. J. MacKenzie, *Propaganda and Empire. The Manipulation of British Public Opinion*, Manchester: University Press, 1985, 165.
6. G. Medieu, *Le Cinéma Colonisateur*, Alger: Typographie Adolphe Jourdan, 1916.
7. Hertogs and de Klerk, *Nonfiction from the Teens*, 32.
8. Gunning, 'Before Documentary', 13–14.
9. See generally S. Conrad and J. Osterhammel (eds), *Das Kaiserreich Transnational: Deutschland in der Welt 1871-1914*, Göttingen: Vandenhoeck and Ruprecht, 2004; for a transnational perspective in film history see W. Fuhrmann, 'Deutsche Kultur- und Spielfilme im Brasilien der 1930er Jahre Eine Transnationale Perspektive', in I. Schenk, M. Tröhler and Y. Zimmermann (eds), *Film – Kino – Zuschauer: Filmrezeption / Film – Cinema – Spectator: Film Reception*, Marburg: Schüren, 2010, 399–418.
10. W. Struck, 'Reenacting Colonialism: Germany and Its Former Colonies in Recent TV Productions', in V. Langbehn (ed.), *German Colonialism, Visual Culture, and Modern Memory*, New York: Routledge, 2010, 260–77.
11. W. Struck, 'The Persistence of (Colonial) Fantasies', in M. Perraudin and J. Zimmerer (eds), *War, Genocide and Memory. German Colonialism and National Identity*, New York: Routledge, 2010, 229.
12. Ibid.
13. The Freiburg initiative *freiburg-postkolonial.de* is one example out of many others that gives detailed information about the city's colonial past on its website. Retrieved 28 March 2014 from http://www.freiburg-postkolonial.de.
14. Cf. M. Perraudin and J. Zimmerer (eds), *German Colonialism and National Identity*, New York: Routledge, 2011, 1.
15. J. Zeller, 'Spurensuche Light. ZDF-Historiker Guido Knopp Scheitert an der Deutschen Kolonialgeschichte', *iz3w. Informationszentrum 3. Welt*, 2010, 319: 41; T. Wahl, 'Barbusig baden', *Berliner Zeitung*, 6 April 2010. Retrieved 28 March 2014 from http://www.berliner-zeitung.de/archiv/ein-zdf-dreiteiler-ueber-die-deutsche-kolonialgeschichte-setzt-vor-allem-auf-exotik-und-dramatik-barbusig-baden,108 10590,10709114.html.

FILMOGRAPHY

The majority of the films mentioned in the book have not survived. The following filmography includes exclusively surviving film prints of German colonial films and of films that are discussed in the book.

Aus dem Leben der Kate auf Deutsch-Neuguinea. Aufnahmen aus dem Jahre 1909 (From the Life of the Kate in German New Guinea. Pictures from 1909). Director/Operator: Richard Neuhauss. Archive: Bundesarchiv-Abteilung Filmarchiv (BArch-FA).

Buschmann spricht in den Phonographen (Bushman speaks into the Phonograph). German South-West Africa. 1908. Director/Operator: Rudolf Pöch. Archive: Österreichische Mediathek.

Deutsch-Ostafrika: Eine grosse öffentliche Schule der Provinz Usambara (German East Africa. A Big Public School in the Usambara Province). German East Africa. 1912. Production: Germania Film/Pathé Frères. Archive: BArch-FA.

Die Fortschritte der Zivilisation in Deutsch-Ostafrika (The Progress of Civilization in German East Africa). German East Africa. 1911. Production: Pathé Frères. Archive: Stiftung Deutsche Kinemathek.

Dokumentaraufnahmen vom Bau der Telefunken-Großstation, Kamina/ Togo (Afrika) für die drahtlose Verbindung des ehemaligen deutschen Schutzgebiets Togo mit Berlin (Images of the Construction of the Telefunken-Großstation, Kamina/Togo [Africa] for the Wireless Transmission of the Former Colony Togo with Berlin). Togo. 1913. Director: Hans Schomburgk. Archive: Deutsches Technikmuseum.

Ethnographische Aufnahmen aus Deutsch-Ostafrika. Sixteen films/fragments from Karl Weule's German East Africa Expedition. 1906–07. Director/Operator: Karl Weule. Archive: Museum für Völkerkunde zu Leipzig.

Fahrt durch den Urwald (Trip Through the Jungle). German East Africa. 1910 (?). Archive: BFI National Archive.

Im Deutschen Sudan (In the German Sudan). Togo. 1914. Director: Hans Schomburgk. Operator: Jimmy Hodgson. Archive: BArch-FA.

In Deutsch-Ostafrika während des Ersten Weltkrieges. Aufnahmen aus den Jahren 1914–16 (In German East Africa during the First World War. Images from the Years 1914–1916). German East Africa. 1914–16. Director/Operator: Walther Dobbertin. Archive: BArch-FA.

Löwenjagd in Afrika (Lion Hunt in Africa). Fragment. German East Africa. Before 1914. Archive: BArch-FA.

Nashornjagd in Deutsch-Ost-Afrika / Rhinoceros Hunting in Africa. German East Africa. 1913. Deutsche Jagd-Film-Gesellschaft. Director: Robert Schumann. Operator: Bergmann (?). Archive: BFI National Archive.

Neu-Guinea 1904–1906 – In memoriam Professor Dr. Rudolf Pöch (New Guinea 1904–1906 – In memoriam Professor Dr. Rudolf Pöch). German New Guinea. Director/Operator: Rudolf Pöch. Archive: Österreichische Mediathek.

Ost-Afrika/Östliches Afrika (East Africa). This title is mentioned by Gosfilmfond (Russia). The film was probably made in the 1910s. It has German intertitles.

Staatssekretär Dr. Solf besucht im Oktober 1913 Togo (State Secretary Dr. Solf visits Togo in October 1913). Togo. 1913. Director: Hans Schomburgk. Operator: Jimmy Hodgson. Archive: BArch-FA.

Völkerkundliche Aufnahmen aus der Südsee aus den Jahren 1908–1910 (Ethnological Film Documents from the Pacific from the Years 1908–1910). Melanesia and Micronesia. Archive: BArch-FA.

Other Colonial Films

Aus dem Innern Afrikas (From Inner Africa). Production: Raleigh & Robert. 1911. Archive: EYE Film Institute Netherlands.

Die Viktoria-Fälle (Great Victoria Falls, Zambesi River). Production: Raleigh & Robert/Warwick Trading Company. 1907. Archive: BFI National Archive.

Jagd auf den Silberreiher in Afrika. Director: Alfred Machin. Production: Pathé Frères. 1911. Archive: BArch-FA.

Moderne Landwirtschaft/L'agriculture Moderne (Modern Agriculture). Gaumont. 1912. Archive: EYE Film Institute Netherlands.

Shooting Egrets in Africa. Director: Alfred Machin. Production: Pathé Frères. 1911. Archive: BFI National Archive (the English release title of *Jagd auf den Silberreiher in Afrika*).

Wie ein Brief von den grossen Seen Zentral-Afrikas zu uns gelangt/Comment une lettre nous parvient des grands lacs de l'Afrique Centrale (Post from Africa to Paris). Director: Alfred Machin. Production: Pathé Frères. 1911. Archive: BFI National Archive.

Bibliography

Books

Abel, R. 2005. *Encyclopedia of Early Cinema*. New York: Routledge.
———. 2006. *Americanizing the Movies and 'Movie-Mad' Audiences, 1910–1914*. Berkeley, Los Angeles and London: University of California Press.
Abel, R., G. Bertellini and R. King (eds). 2008. *Early Cinema and the 'National'*. London: John Libbey Publishing.
Allen, R., and D. Gomery. 1985. *Film History: Theory and Practice*. New York and St. Louis, MO: McGraw-Hill.
Altenloh, E. 1914. *Zur Soziologie des Kino. Die Kinounternehmen und die sozialen Schichten ihrer Besucher*. Jena: Eugen Diederichs.
Ames, E. 2009. *Carl Hagenbeck's Empire of Entertainments*. Seattle and London: University of Washington Press.
Ames, E., M. Klotz and L. Wildenthal (eds). 2005. *Germany's Colonial Pasts*. Lincoln: University of Nebraska Press.
Anderson, B. 1991. *Imagined Communities: Reflections on the Origin and Spread of Nationalism*. Rev. edn. London: Verso.
Applegate, C. 1990. *A Nation of Provincials: The German Idea of Heimat*. Berkeley: University of California Press.
Arbeitsausschuss der Deutschen Kolonialausstellung. 1897. *Deutschland und seine Kolonien 1896. Amtlicher Bericht über die erste Deutsche Kolonialausstellung*. Berlin: Verlag Dietrich Reimer.
Arbeitsausschuss der II. Allgemeine Deutsch-Ostafrikanische Landesausstellung in Daressalam. 1914. *Wohin reise ich im Sommer 1914?*. Berlin.
Augustin, G. 2009. *Gruß aus Deutsch-Südwest: Ansichtskarten erzählen. Ein Bild-Lesebuch*. Halle: Projekte-Verlag Cornelius GmbH.
Axster, Felix. 2014. *Koloniales Spektakel in 9x14. Bildpostkarten im Deutschen Kaiserreich*. Bielefeld: Transcript.
Bach, W. C. 1907. *Unsere Kolonien im Schulunterricht*. Bielefeld: U. Helmichs Buchhandlung.
Barkhausen, H. 1982. *Filmpropaganda für Deutschland im Ersten und Zweiten Weltkrieg*. Hildesheim, Zürich and New York: Olms Presse.
Barnes, J. 1997. *The Beginnings of the Cinema in England, 1894–1901*. Exeter: University of Exeter Press.
Barnouw, E. 1993. *Documentary. A History of the Nonfiction Film*. 2nd edn. New York: Oxford University Press.

Barsam, R.M. 1992. *Nonfiction Film: A Critical History*. Bloomington: Indiana University Press.
Barth, D. 1974. 'Zeitschrift für alle. Das Familienblatt im 19. Jahrhundert. Ein sozialhistorischer Beitrag zur Massenpresse in Deutschland', Ph.D. dissertation. Münster: Universität Münster.
Bechhaus-Gerst, M., and M. Leutner (eds). 2009. *Frauen in den deutschen Kolonien*. Berlin: Ch. Links Verlag.
Bechhaus-Gerst, M., and S. Gieseke (eds). 2007. *Koloniale und postkoloniale Konstruktionen von Afrika und Menschen afrikanischer Herkunft in der deutschen Alltagskultur*. Frankfurt: Peter Lang.
Becker, M. 2008. *Bwana Simba. Der Herr der Löwen. Carl Georg Schillings. Forscher und Naturschützer in Deutsch-Ostafrika*. Düren: Hahne & Schloemer.
Belgum, K. 1998. *Popularizing the Nation. Audience, Representation, and the Production of Identity in 'Die Gartenlaube' 1853–1900*. Lincoln: University of Nebraska Press.
Benali, A. 1998. *Le cinéma colonial au Maghreb*. Paris: Éditions du Cerf.
Benninghoff-Lühl, S. 1983. *Deutsche Kolonialromane 1884–1914 in ihrem Entstehungs- und Wirkungszusammenhang*. Bremen: Im Selbstverlag des Museums.
Bergfelder, T., E. Carter and D. Göktürk (eds). 2002. *The German Cinema Book*. London: BFI.
Berman, R.A. 1998. *Enlightment or Empire. Colonial Discourse in German Culture*. Lincoln and London: University of Nebraska Press.
Beta, O. (aka Ottomar Bettziech). 1908. *Das Buch von unsern Kolonien*. 4th edn. Leipzig: Ferdinand Hirt & Sohn.
Bezirksamt Treptow von Berlin. 1997. *Die Berliner Gewerbeausstellung 1896 in Bildern*. Berlin: Berliner Debatte.
Bhabha, H.K. 1994. *The Location of Culture*. London: Routledge.
Birett, H. 1980. *Verzeichnis der in Deutschland gelaufenen Filme. Entscheidungen der Filmzensur 1911–1920*. Berlin, Hamburg, Stuttgart and Munich: Saur Verlag.
———. 1991. *Das Filmangebot in Deutschland 1895–1911*. Munich: Filmbuchverlag Winterberg.
Böhl, M. 1985. *Entwicklung des ethnographischen Films. Die filmische Dokumentation als ethnographisches Forschungs- und universitäres Unterrichtsmittel in Europa*. Götttingen: Edition Herodot.
Bollig, M. and J.B. Gewald (eds). 2000. *People, Cattle and Land: Transformations of a Pastoral Society in Southwestern Africa*. Cologne: Rüdiger Köppe Verlag.
Bopp, P., P. Märker and M. Wagner (eds). 1981. *Mit dem Auge des Touristen. Zur Geschichte des Reisebildes*. Tübingen: Eberhard-Karls-Universität.
Bottomore, S. 2007. 'Filming, Faking and Propaganda: The Origins of the War Film, 1897–1902', Ph.D. dissertation. Utrecht: Utrecht University. Retrieved 20 February 2014 from http://dspace.library.uu.nl/handle/1874/22650.
Bousquet, H. (ed.). 1994. *Catalogue Pathé des Années 1896 á 1914, 1910–1911*. Bures-sur-Yvette.
———. 1995. *Catalogue Pathé des Années 1896 á 1914, 1912–1913–1914*. Bures-sur-Yvette.
Braun, M., C. Keil, R. King, P. Moore and L. Pelletier (eds). 2012. *Beyond the Screen: Institutions, Networks and Publics of Early Cinema*. London: John Libbey Publishing.

Bredow von, W. and R. Zurek (eds). 1975. *Film und Gesellschaft in Deutschland. Dokumente und Materialien.* Hamburg: Hoffmann und Campe.
Bund für Vogelschutz e.V. 1915. *Jahresheft 1915 des Bundes für Vogelschutz.* Stuttgart: Geraer Verlagsanstalt.
Calhoun, C. (ed.). 1992. *Habermas and the Public Sphere.* Cambridge, MA: MIT Press.
Charney, L. and V. Schwartz (eds). 1995. *Cinema and the Invention of Modern Life.* Berkeley: University of California Press.
Chatterjee, P. 1993. *The Nation & Its Fragments: Colonial & Postcolonial Histories.* Princeton, NJ: Princeton University Press.
Cherchi Usai, P., and L. Codelli (eds).1998. *Before Caligari: German Cinema, 1895–1920.* Venice: Edizioni Biblioteca dell'Immagine.
Chickering, R. 1984. *We Men Who Feel Most German. A Cultural Study of the Pan-German League 1886–1914.* Boston: Goerge Allen & Unwin.
———. 2002. *Das Deutsche Reich und der erste Weltkrieg.* Munich: C.H. Beck.
Ciarlo, D. 2011. *Advertising Empire: Race and Visual Culture in Imperial Germany.* Cambridge, MA: Harvard University Press.
Clemenz, B. 1907. *Kolonialidee und Schule.* 2nd edn. Langensalza: Hermann Beyer & Söhne.
Confino, A. 1997. *The Nation as a Local Metaphor: Württemberg, Imperial Germany, and National Memory, 1871–1918.* Chapel Hill: University of North Carolina Press.
Conrad, S. 2008. *Deutsche Kolonialgeschichte.* Munich: Beck.
Conrad, S. and J. Osterhammel (eds). 2004. *Das Kaiserreich Transnational: Deutschland in der Welt 1871-1914.* Göttingen: Vandenhoeck and Ruprecht.
Conradt, W. 1910. *Kirche und Kinematographie: Eine Frage.* Berlin: Hermann Walther Verlagsbuchhandlung GmbH.
Convents, G. 1986. *A la Recherche des Images oubliées: Préhistoire du Cinéma en Afrique: 1897–1918.* Brussels: Organisation Catholique Internationale du Cinéma et de l'Audiovisuel (OCIC).
Cosandey, R., and F. Albera (eds). 1995. *Cinéma sans frontières 1896–1918, Images Across Borders.* Lausanne: Nuit Blanche Editeurs/Edition Payot.
Crothers, G.D. 1941. *The German Elections of 1907.* New York: Columbia University Press.
David, A. 1916. *Jagden und Abenteuer in den Gebieten des Oberen Nil.* Basel: Friedrich Reinhart.
De Certeau, M. 1984. *The Practice of Everyday Life,* trans. S. Randall. Berkeley, Los Angeles and London: University of California Press.
Debusmann, R., and J. Riesz (eds). 1995. *Kolonialausstellungen-Begegnungen mit Afrika?.* Frankfurt: IKO-Verlag für interkulturelle Kommunikation.
Demhart, I.J. 2000. *Die Entschleierung Afrikas. Deutsche Kartenbeiträge von August Petermann bis zum Kolonialkartographischen Institut.* Gotha: Klett Perthes.
Dernburg, B. 1907. *Zielpunkte des deutschen Kolonialwesens. Zwei Vorträge.* Berlin: Verlag Ernst Siegfried Mittler und Sohn.
Deutsche Jagdfilm-Gesellschaft. 1916. *Aus der afrikanischen Wildnis: Jagd- und Reisestudien des Forschungsreisenden Robert Schumann.* Berlin.
Deutsche Kolonialgesellschaft. 1888 (1889)–1928 (1929). *Jahresbericht der Deutschen Kolonialgesellschaft: bearb in d. Geschäfsstelle.* Berlin: Deutsche Kolonialgesellschaft.

———. 1889–1936. *Berichte über die Sitzung des Vorstandes der Deutschen Kolonialgesellschaft*. Deutsche Kolonialgesellschaft.
———. 1893–1914. *Berichte über die Sitzung des Ausschusses der Deutschen Kolonialgesellschaft*. Berlin: Deutsche Koloniagesellschaft.
———. 1895. *Material zur Ausarbeitung von erklärenden Vorträgen zu den Lichtbildern der Deutschen Kolonialgesellschaft über Deutsch-Ostafrika*. Berlin: Julius Sittenfeld.
———. 1901. *Wanderung durch unsere Kolonien*. Berlin: Deutsche Kolonialgesellschaft.
Deutscher Kolonialkongress. 1903. *Verhandlungen des Deutschen Kolonialkongresses 1902*. Berlin: Verlag Dietrich Reimer (Ernst Vohsen).
———. 1906. *Verhandlungen des Deutschen Kolonialkongresses 1905*. Berlin: Verlag Dietrich Reimer (Ernst Vohsen).
———. 1910. *Verhandlungen des Deutschen Kolonialkongresses 1910*. Berlin: Verlag Dietrich Reimer (Ernst Vohsen).
Deutscher Flottenverein. 1902–1918. *Jahres-Bericht des Deutschen Flottenvereins e.V.* Berlin.
Deutsche Lichtbildgesellschaft e.V. 1918. *Der Film im Dienste der nationalen und wirtschaftlichen Werbearbeit*. Berlin.
Diederichs, H.H. 1996. 'Frühgeschichte deutscher Filmtheorie. Ihre Entstehung und Entwicklung bis zum Ersten Weltkrieg'. Habilitationschrift, Goethe University Frankfurt. Retrieved 12 March 2014 from http://publikationen.ub.uni-frankfurt.de/frontdoor/index/index/docId/4924.
Dithmar, R., and H.D. Schultz (eds). 2006. *Schule und Unterricht im Kaiserreich*. Ludwigsfelde: Ludwigsfelder Verlagshaus.
Douglas, M. (ed.). 1970. *Witchcraft Confessions and Accusations*. London: Tavistock.
Dreesbach, A. 2005. *Gezähmte Wilde. Die Zurschaustellung 'exotischer' Menschen in Deutschland 1870–1940*. Frankfurt: Campus Verlag.
Eckert, A. 2006. *Kolonialismus*. Frankfurt: Fischer Taschenbuch Verlag.
El-Tayeb, F. 2001. *Schwarze Deutsche. Der Diskurs um 'Rasse' und Nationale Identität 1890–1933*. Frankfurt: Campus Verlag.
Eley, G. 1980. *Reshaping the German Right. Radical Nationalism and Political Change after Bismarck*. New Haven, CT and London: Yale University Press.
Elsaesser, T. (ed.). 1990. *Early Cinema: Space, Frame, Narrative*. London: BFI.
———. 1996. *A Second Life. German Cinema's First Decades*. Amsterdam: Amsterdam University Press.
Engelhard, J.B., and P. Mesenhöller (eds). 1995. *Bilder aus dem Paradies. Koloniale Fotografie aus Samoa 1875–1925*. Cologne: Rautenstrauch-Joest-Museum für Völkerkunde.
Erll, A., and S. Wodianka (eds). 2008. *Film und kulturelle Erinnerung. Plurimediale Konstellationen*. Berlin and New York: de Gruyter.
Fell, J.L. (ed.). 1983. *Film Before Griffith*. Berkeley, Los Angeles and London: University of California Press.
Fischer, H. 1981. *Die Hamburger Südsee-Expedition. Über Ethnographie und Kolonialismus*. Frankfurt: Syndikat.
Frenssen, G. 1906. *Peter Moors Fahrt nach Südwest. Ein Feldzugbericht*. Berlin: Grote'sche Verlagsbuchhandlung.

———. 1909. *Peter Moor's Journey to Southwest Africa. A Narrative of the German Campaign*, trans. M. Ward. London: Archibald Constable/Boston and New York: Houghton Mifflin.

Friedrichsmeyer, S.L., S. Lennox and S. Zantop (eds). 1998. *The Imperialist Imagination. German Colonialism and its Legacy*. Ann Arbor: University of Michigan Press.

Frobenius, L. 1922. *Karten als Sinnbilder der Kulturbewegung: Einführung in den Atlas Africanus und in das Verständnis der kinematographischen Karte*. Sonderdruck aus dem Atlas Africanus, Munich, C.H. Beck'sche Verlagsbuchhandlung.

Fuhrmann, W. 2003. 'Propaganda, Sciences, and Entertainment. German Colonial Cinematography: A Case Study in the History of Early Nonfiction Cinema', Ph.D dissertation. Utrecht: Utrecht University.

Fullerton, J., and A. Soderbergh-Widding (eds). 2000. *Moving Images: From Edison to Webcam*. Sydney: John Libbey Publishing.

Garncarz, J. 2010. *Masslose Unterhaltung. Zur Etablierung des Films in Deutschland 1896–1914*. Frankfurt and Basel: Stroemfeld.

Gaupp, R., and K. Lange. 1912. *Der Kinematograph als Volksunterhaltungsmittel*. Dürerbund 100. Flugschrift zur Ausdruckskultur, Munich.

Gehrts, M. 1915. *A Camera Actress in the Wilds of Togoland*. London: Seeley.

Gesellschaft der Freunde des Vaterländischen Schul- und Erziehungswesens zu Hamburg. 1907. *Bericht der Kommission für 'Lebende Photographie' erstattet am 17. April und im Auftrag des Vorstandes bearbeitet von C. H. Dannmeyer*. Hamburg.

Göllner, P. 1995. *Ernemann Cameras. Die Geschichte des Dresdener Photo-Kino-Werks*. Hückelhoven: Wittig Fachbuchverlag.

Gothsch, M. 1983. *Die deutsche Völkerkunde und ihr Verhältnis zum Kolonialismus. Ein Beitrag zur Kolonialideologischen und kolonialpraktischen Bedeutung der deutschen Völkekunde in der Zeit von 1870 bis 1975 (1945)*. Baden-Baden: Nomos Verlagsgesellschaft.

Graetz, P. 1912. *Im Motorboot quer durch Afrika. Vom indischen Ozean zum Kongo*. Berlin: Braunbeck & Gutenberg Aktiengesellschaft.

———. 1913. *Im Motorboot quer durch Afrika. Zweiter Teil: Durch den Kongo und Neu- Kamerun*. Berlin: Braunbeck & Gutenberg Aktiengesellschaft.

Grieveson, L., and C. MacCabe (eds). 2011a. *Empire and Film*. London: Palgrave Macmillan.

———. 2011b. *Film and the End of Empire*. London: Palgrave Macmillan.

Griffiths, A.M. 2002. *Wondrous Difference: Cinema, Anthropology, and Turn of the Century Visual Culture*. New York: Columbia University Press.

Grosse, P. 2000. *Kolonialismus, Eugenik und bürgerliche Gesellschaft in Deutschland 1850–1918*. Frankfurt: Campus Verlag.

Gründer, H. 2004. *Geschichte der deutschen Kolonien*, 5th edn. Paderborn: Schönigh.

Guggisberg, C.A.W. 1977. *Early Wildlife Photographers*. Newton, Abbot, London and Vancouver: David & Charles.

Guibbert P. (ed.). 1985. *Les premiers ans du cinéma français*. Perpignan: Institut Jean Vigo.

Gutsche, T. 1972. *The History and Social Significance of Motion Pictures in South Africa 1895–1940*. Cape Town: Howard Timmins.

Habermas, J. 1991. *The Structural Transformation of the Public Sphere: An Inquiry into a Category of Bourgeois Society.* Cambridge: MIT Press.

Häfker, H. 1913. *Kino und Kunst.* Mönchen-Gladbach: Volksvereins-Verlag.

———. 1914. *Kino und Erdkunde.* Mönchen-Gladbach: Volksvereins-Verlag.

Hake, S. 1993. *The Cinema's Third Machine. Writing on Film in Germany 1907–1933.* Lincoln: University of Nebraska Press.

Hansen, M. 1991. *Babel and Babylon, Spectatorship in American Silent Film.* Cambridge, MA: Harvard University Press.

Hartmann, W. (ed.). 2004. *Hues between Black and White. Historical Photography from Colonial Namibia 1860s to 1915.* Windhoek: Out of Africa Publishers.

Hartmann, W., P. Hayes and J. Silvester (eds). 1998. *The Colonizing Camera: Photographs in the Making of Namibian History.* Cape Town: University of Cape Town Press.

Heidtmann, Frank. 1984. *Wie das Photo ins Buch kam.* Berlin: Verlag Arno Spitz.

Hertogs, D., and N. de Klerk (eds). 1994. *Nonfiction from the Teens. The 1994 Amsterdam Workshop.* Amsterdam: Stichting Nederlands Filmmuseum.

———. 1996. *'Disorderly Order'. Colours in Silent Film. The 1995 Amsterdam Workshop.* Amsterdam: Stichting Nederlands Filmmuseum.

———. 1997. *Uncharted Territory: Essays on Early Nonfiction Film.* Amsterdam: Stichting Nederlands Filmmuseum.

Hiery, H.J. 2002. *Die deutsche Südsee 1884–1914 – Ein Handbuch,* 2nd edn. Paderborn: Schöningh.

———. 2004. *Bilder aus der deutschen Südsee. Fotografien 1884–1914.* Paderborn: Schöningh.

Hockings, P. (ed.). 1995. *Principles of Visual Anthropology,* 2nd edn. Berlin and New York: Mouton de Gruyter.

Höpp, G. 1997. *Muslime in der Mark – Als Kriegsgefangene und Internierte in Wünsdorf und Zossen, 1914–1924.* Berlin: Das Arabische Buch.

Holman, R. (ed.). 1982. *Cinema 1900–1906: An Analytical Study. Proceedings of the FIAF Symposium held at Brighton, 1978.* FIAF, vols 1 and 2.

Honold, A. and K.R. Scherpe (eds). 2000. *Das Fremde. Reiseerfahrungen, Schreibformen und kulturelles Wissen,* Beiheft 2 der Zeitschrift für Germanistik, N.F..

Honold, A., and O. Simons (eds). 2002. *Kolonialismus als Kultur: Literatur, Medien, Wissenschaft in der deutschen Gründerzeit des Fremden.* Tübingen and Basel: Francke Verlag.

Hooper-Greenhill, E. 2000. *Museums and the Interpretation of Visual Culture.* London: Routledge.

Ilgner, C. (ed.) 2001. *Unsichtbare Schätze der Kinotechnik. Kinematographische Apparate aus 100 Jahren im Depot des Filmmuseums.* Potsdam and Berlin: Parthas Verlag.

Jaikumar, P. 2006. *Cinema at the End of Empire: A Politics of Transition in Britain and India.* Durham, NC: Duke University Press.

Jason, A. 1925. *Der Film in Ziffern und Zahlen.* Berlin: Deutsches Druck- u. Verlagshaus.

Jones, H., J. O'Brien and C. Schmidt-Supprian (eds). 2008. *Untold War. New Perspectives in First World War Studies.* Leiden and Boston: Brill.

Jung, U., and M. Loiperdinger (eds). 2005. *Geschichte des dokumentarischen Films in Deutschland, Bd. I: Kaiserreich 1895–1918.* Stuttgart: Reclam.

Karstedt, O. 1914. *Deutsch-Ostafrika und seine Nachbargebiete. Ein Handbuch für Reisende*. Berlin: Dietrich Reimer (Ernst Vohsen).
Kauß, K. 1966. 'Die Deutsche Kolonialgesellschaft und die deutsche Kolonialpolitik von den Anfängen bis 1895', Ph.D. dissertation. Berlin (Ost): Humboldt Universität Berlin.
Keil, C., and S. Stamp (eds). 2004. *American Cinema's Transitional Era*. Berkeley: University of California Press.
Keitz von, U. and K. Hoffmann (eds). 2001. *Die Einübung des dokumentarischen Blicks*. Marburg: Schüren.
Klein-Arendt, R. 1996. *'Kamina ruft Nauen'. Die Funkstellen in den deutschen Kolonien 1904–1918*. Ostheim: Wilhelm Herbst Verlag.
Knoll, A.J., and L.H. Gann (eds). 1987. *Germans in the Tropics. Essays in German Colonial History*. New York, Westport, CT and London: Greenwood Press.
Köhler, J. 1907. *Schule und Kolonialinteressen*. Langensalza: Herman Beyer & Söhne.
Köhler, M., and G. Barche (eds). 1985. *Das Aktfoto. Ansichten vom Körper im fotografischen Zeitalter. Ästhetik, Geschichte, Ideologie, Ausstellungskatalog des Münchner Stadtmuseums*. Munich and Luzern: C.J. Bucher Verlag.
Königlich Preußisches Statistisches Landesamt. 1908. *Statistisches Jahrbuch für den Preußischen Staat 1907*. Berlin: Verlag des Königlich Statistischen Landesamtes.
Kolonialkriegerdank e.V..1926. *Koloniales Hand- und Adreßbuch 1926–27*. Berlin: Verlag Kolonialkriegerdank.
Kundrus, B. (ed.). 2003. *Phantasiereiche. Zur Kulturgeschichte des deutschen Kolonialismus*. Frankfurt: Campus Verlag.
Langbehn, V. (ed.). 2010. *German Colonialism, Visual Culture, and Modern Memory*. New York: Routledge.
Laukötter, A. 2007. *Von der 'Kultur' zur 'Rasse' – vom Objekt zum Körper? Völkerkundemuseen und ihre Wissenschaften zu Beginn des 20. Jahrhunderts*. Bielefeld: Transcript.
Liesegang, F.P. (ed.). 1920. *Wissenschaftliche Kinematographie. Einschliesslich der Reihenphotographie*. Düsseldorf: Ed. Liesegang.
Liliencron von, A. 1905. *Unsre Braven. Fünf Bilder aus dem Leben unsrer braven Truppen in Südwestafrika*. Mühlhausen:Verlag von G. Danner.
Lindner, U., et al. (eds). 2010. *Hybrid Cultures-Nervous States. Germany and Britain in a (Post)Colonial World*. Amsterdam and New York: Rodopi.
Lips, J. 1937. *The Savage Hits Back, Or The White Man Through Native Eyes*. New Haven, CT: Yale University Press.
Loiperdinger, M. 1999. *Film & Schokolade. Stollwercks Geschäfte mit lebenden Bildern*. Basel and Frankfurt: Stroemfeld/Roter Stern.
Loiperdinger, M. (ed.). 2011. *Early Cinema Today: The Art of Programming and Live Performance*. New Barnet and Herts: John Libbey Publishing.
MacKenzie, J.M. 1985. *Propaganda and Empire: The Manipulation of British Public Opinion 1880–1960*. Manchester: Manchester University Press.
Maß, S. 2006. *Weiße Helden. Schwarze Krieger. Zur Geschichte kolonialer Männlichkeit in Deutschland 1918–1964*. Cologne, Weimar and Vienna: Böhlau Verlag.
McClintock, A. 1995. *Imperial Leather: Race, Gender and Sexuality in the Colonial Contest*. New York: Routledge.

Medieu, G. 1916. *Le Cinéma Colonisateur*. Alger: Typographie Adolphe Jourdan, Imprimeur Libraire Editeur, Place du Gouvernement.
Messter, O. 1936. *Mein Weg mit dem Film*. Berlin: Max Hesse.
Michels, S. 2009. *Schwarze deutsche Kolonialsoldaten. Mehrdeutige Repräsentationsräume und früher Kosmopolitismus in Afrika*. Bielefeld: Transcript.
Mirzoeff, N. (ed.). 2002. *The Visual Culture Reader*, 2nd edn. London: Routledge.
Mitarbeiter des historischen Museums (eds). 1982. *Die Zukunft beginnt in der Vergangenheit. Museumsgeschichte und Geschichtsmuseum*. Frankfurt: Anabas Verlag.
Moltke von, J. 2005. *No Place Like Home. Locations of Heimat in German Cinema*. Berkeley: University of California Press.
Morlang, T. 2008. *Askari und Fitafita: 'Farbige' Söldner in den deutschen Kolonien*. Berlin: Ch. Links Verlag.
Müller, C. 1994. *Frühe deutsche Kinematographie. Formale, wirtschaftliche und kulturelle Entwicklung 1907–1912*. Stuttgart and Weimar: Metzler.
Müller, C., and H. Segeberg (eds). 1998. *Modellierung des Kinofilms. Zur Geschichte des Kinoprogramms zwischen Kurzfilm und Langfilm 1905/06–1918*. Munich: Wilhelm Fink Verlag.
Museum für Völkerkunde (Leipzig). 1928. *Jahrbuch des Städtischen Museums für Völkerkunde zu Leipzig* 9. Leipzig: R.Voigtländers Verlag.
Nagl, T. 2009. *Die Unheimliche Maschine: Rasse und Repräsentation im Weimarer Kino*. Munich: edition text + kritik.
Nead, L. 2007. *The Haunted Gallery*. New Haven, CT and London: Yale University Press.
Nipperdey, T. 1976. *Gesellschaft, Kultur, Theorie. Gesammelte Aufsätze zur neueren Geschichte*. Göttingen: Vandenhoeck & Ruprecht.
Noack, V. 1913. *Der Kino. Etwas über sein Wesen und seine Bedeutung*. Gautzsch b. Leipzig: Dietrich.
Noske, G. 1914. *Kolonialpolitik und Sozialdemokratie*. Stuttgart: Verlag von I.H.W. Dietz Nachf. GmbH.
Noyes, J. 1992. *Colonial Space. Spatiality in the Discourse of German South West Africa 1884–1915*. Chur: Harwood Academic Publishers.
Oksiloff, A. 2001. *Picturing the Primitive. Visual Culture, Ethnography, and Early German Cinema*. New York: Palgrave.
Parzer-Mühlbacher, A. 1910. *Photographisches Unterhaltungsbuch*. Berlin: Verlag Gustav Schmidt.
Paul, G. 2006. *Visual History Ein Studienbuch*. Göttingen: Vandenhoeck & Ruprecht.
Perraudin, M., and J. Zimmerer (eds). 2010. *German Colonialism and National Identity*. New York: Routledge.
Peterson, J.L. 1999. 'World Pictures: Travelogue films and the Lure of the Exotic 1890–1920', Ph.D. dissertation. Chicago: University of Chicago.
Peterson, J.L. 2013. *Education in the School of Dreams: Travelogues and Early Nonfiction Film*. Durham, NC: Duke University Press.
Pierard, R.V. 1964. 'The German Colonial Society, 1892–1914', Ph.D. dissertation. Iowa City: University of Iowa.
Prager, E. 1908. *Die deutsche Kolonialgesellschaft 1882–1907*. Berlin: Dietrich Reimer.

Ramirez, F., and Ch. Rolot. 1985. *Histoire du cinéma colonial au Zaïre, au Rwanda et au Burundi*. Brussels: Musée royal de l'Afrique centrale.
Reche, O. (ed.) 1929. *In Memoriam Karl Weule. Beiträge zur Völkerkunde und Vorgeschichte*. Leipzig: R. Voigtländers Verlag.
Reichhardt, H.J. (ed.). 1986. *Berlin in Geschichte und Gegenwart*. Jahrbuch des Landesarchivs Berlin. Berlin: Wolf Jobst Siedler Verlag.
Reichs-Kolonialamt. 1913. *Jagd und Wildschutz in den Deutschen Kolonien*. Jena: Verlag Gustav Fischer.
Rohrbach, P. 1911. *Das deutsche Kolonialwesen*. Leipzig: Verlag von G.A. Gloeckner.
Roters, E. 1995. *Jenseits von Arkadien- die romantische Landschaft*. Cologne: Du Mont.
Ryan, P. (ed.). 1972. *Encyclopedia of Papua and New Guinea*. Melbourne: Melbourne University Press.
Said, E. 1978. *Orientalism*. New York: Pantheon Books.
Schillings, C.G. 1905. *Mit Blitzlicht und Büchse. Beobachtungen und Erlebnisse in der Wildnis inmitten der Tierwelt von Äquatorial-Ostafrika*. Leipzig: R. Voigtländers Verlag.
———. 1906. *Flashlight in the Jungle: A Record of Hunting Adventures and of Studies in Wild Life in Equatorial East Africa*. New York: Doubleday & Page.
———. 1922. *Mit Blitzlicht und Büchse im Zauber des Elescho*. Leipzig: R. Voigtländers Verlag.
Schinzinger, F. 1984. *Die Kolonien und das Deutsche Reich. Die wirtschaftliche Bedeutung der deutschen Besitzungen in Übersee*. Wiesbaden: Franz Steiner Verlag.
Schnee, H. 1927. *Die koloniale Schuldlüge*, 3rd edn. Munich: Buchverlag der Süddeutschen Monatshefte.
Schöning, J. (ed.). 1997. *Triviale Tropen. Exotische Reise und Abenteuerfilme aus Deutschland 1919–1939*. Munich: edition text + kritik.
Schomburgk, H. 1922. *Bwakukama. Fahrten und Forschungen mit Büchse und Film im unbekannten Afrika*, 2nd edn. Berlin: Deutsch Literarisches Institut.
———. 1928. *Mein Afrika*. Leipzig: Verlag Deutsche Buchwerkstätten.
———. 1931. *Zelte in Afrika. Eine autobiographische Erzählung*. Berlin: R. Hobbing.
———. 1947. *Von Mensch und Tier und etwas von mir*. Berlin: H. Wijomkow-Verlagsanstalt.
———. 1959. *Zelte in Afrika. Fahrten-Forschungen-Abenteuer in sechs Jahrzehnten*. Berlin: Verlag der Nationen.
Schulz, C. 1922. *Jagd- und Filmabenteuer in Afrika*. Dresden: Verlag Deutsche Buchwerkstätten Dreden.
Schütze, C. 1994. 'Karl Weule und die Völkerkunde'. Master's thesis. Munich: Ludwig-Maximilians-Universität Munich.
Schweinitz, J. (ed.) 1992. *Prolog vor dem Film: Nachdenken über ein neues Medium 1909–1914*. Leipzig: Reclam Verlag.
Seemann, M. 2011. *Kolonialismus in der Heimat. Kolonialbewegung, Kolonialpolitik und Kolonialkultur in Bayern 1882–1943*. Berlin: Ch. Links Verlag.
Shohat, E., and R. Stam (eds). 1994. *Unthinking Eurocentrism. Multiculturalism and the Media*. New York: Routledge.
Smith, W.D. 1991. *Politics and the Sciences of Culture in Germany 1840–1920*. New York, Oxford: Oxford University Press.

Soénius, U. 1992. *Koloniale Begeisterung im Rheinland während des Kaiserreiches.* Cologne: Selbstverlag Rheinisch- Westfälisches Wirtschaftsarchiv zu Köln e.V.
Speitkamp, W. 2005. *Deutsche Kolonialgeschichte.* Stuttgart: Reclam.
Spittler, G. 2008. *Founders of the Anthropology of Work: German Social Scientists of the 19th and Early 20th Centuries and the First Ethnographers.* Münster and Hamburg: Lit Verlag.
Stam, R. 2000. *Film Theory an Introduction.* Malde, Oxford and Carlton: Blackwell Publishing.
Staehelin, B. 1993. *Völkerschauen im Zoologischen Garten Basel 1879–1939.* Basel: Basler Afrika Bibliographien.
Städtisches Museum für Völkerkunde (Leipzig). 1910. *Jahrbuch des Städtischen Museums für Völkerkunde zu Leipzig* 3. Leipzig: R.Voigtländers Verlag.
Stuemer von, W., und E. Duems. 1932. *Fünfzig Jahre Deutsche Kolonialgesellschaft 1882–1932.* Berlin: Deutsche Kolonialgesellschaft.
Stratz. C.H. 1901. *Die Rassenschönheit des Weibes.* Stuttgart: Verlag F. Enke.
Struck, W. 2010. *Die Eroberung der Phantasie. Kolonialismus, Literatur und Film zwischen Deutschem Kaiserreich und Weimarer Republik.* Göttingen: V&R unipress.
Suleri, S. 1992. *The Rhetoric of English India.* Chicago: University of Chicago Press.
Thilenius, G. (ed.). 1929. *Tagungsbericht der Deutschen Anthropologischen Gesellschaft. Bericht über die 50. Allgemeine Versammlung der Deutschen Anthropologischen Gesellschaft in Hamburg vom 1.-13. August 1928.* Hamburg: Friederichsen, de Gruyter & Co.
Thode-Arora, H. 1989. *Für fünfzig Pfennig um die Welt: Die Hagenbeckschen Völkerschauen.* Frankfurt and New York: Campus Verlag.
Tobing Rony, F. 1996. *The Third Eye: Race, Cinema, and Ethnographic Spectacle.* Durham, NC and London: Duke University Press.
Uricchio, W., and R.E. Pearson. 1993. *Reframing Culture: The Case of the Vitagraph Quality Films.* Princeton, NJ: Princeton University Press.
Van der Heyden, U., and J. Zeller (eds). 2002. *Kolonialmetropole Berlin. Eine Spurensuche.* Berlin: Berlin Edition.
Wagner, W. (ed.). 1992. *Rassendiskriminierung, Kolonialpolitik und ethnisch-nationale Identität,* Referate des 2. Internationalen Kolonialgeschichtlichen Symposiums. Münster and Hamburg: Lit Verlag.
Walgenbach, K. 2005. *'Die weiße Frau als Trägerin deutscher Kultur'. Koloniale Diskurse zu Geschlecht, 'Rasse' und Klasse im Kaiserreich.* Frankfurt and New York: Campus Verlag.
Warmbold, J. 1989. *Germania in Africa. Germany's Colonial Literature.* New York, Bern, Frankfurt and Paris: Peter Lang.
Warner, M. 2002. *Publics and Counterpublics.* New York: Zone.
Warnke, I. (ed.). 2009. *Deutsche Sprache und Kolonialismus: Aspekte der nationalen Kommunikation 1884–1919.* Berlin and New York: De Gruyter.
Weiss, M. 1910. *Die Völkerstämme im Norden Deutsch-Ostafrikas.* Berlin: Marschner.
Welch, D. 2000. *Germany, Propaganda and Total War, 1914–1918. The Sins of Omission.* London: The Athlon Press.
Weule, K. 1908. *Negerleben in Ostafrika. Ergebnisse einer ethnologischen Forschungsreise.* Leipzig: Brockhaus.

———. 1908. *Wissenschaftliche Ergebnisse meiner ethnographischen Forschungsreise in den Südosten Deutsch-Ostafrikas*. Ergänzungsheft der Mitteilungen aus den deutschen Schutzgebieten, vol. 1. Berlin: Ernst Siegfried Mittler und Sohn.

———. 1909. *Native Life in East Africa. The Results of an Ethnological Research Expedition*, trans. A. Werner. New York: D. Appleton and Company.

Wildenthal, L. 2001. *German Women for Empire, 1884–1945*. Durham, NC: Duke University Press.

Zeller, J. 2000. *Kolonialdenkmäler und Geschichtsbewußtsein: Eine Untersuchung der kolonialdeutschen Erinnerungskultur*. Frankfurt: IKO-Verlag für interkulturelle Kommunikation.

———. 2008. *Bilderschule der Herrenmenschen: koloniale Reklamesammelbilder*. Berlin: Ch. Links Verlag.

———. 2010. *Weiße Blicke. Schwarze Körper. Afrika(ner) im Spiegel westlicher Alltagskultur*. Erfurt: Sutton.

Zantop, S. 1997. *Colonial Fantasies, Conquest: Family, and Nation in Precolonial Germany, 1707–1870*. Durham, NC and London: Duke University Press.

Zimmerer, J., and J. Zeller (eds). 2008. *Genocide in German South-West Africa: The Colonial War of 1904–1908 and Its Aftermath*. London: The Merlin Press Ltd.

Zimmerman, A. 2001. *Anthropology and Antihumanism in Imperial Germany*. Chicago and London: University of Chicago Press.

Articles

Abel, R. 2006. 'Another "Forgotten" Part of the Program. Nonfiction', in *Americanizing the Movies and 'Movie-Mad' Audiences, 1910–1914*. Berkeley, Los Angeles and London: University of California Press, pp. 171–82.

Alexander, C. 1991. 'Annals of Exploration, "The White Godess of the Wangora"', *The New Yorker*, 8 April, pp. 43–76. Retrieved 20 March 2014 from http://www.newyorker.com/archive/1991/04/08/1991_04_08_043_TNY_CARDS_000359730.

Anon. 1901. 'Die Ausführung von Eingeborenen aus den Kolonien zu Schaustellungszwecken', *Koloniale Zeitschrift* 2(13): 183.

———. 1902. 'Der Deutsche Flottenverein als Schausteller', *Der Komet*, 27 December, 4.

———. 1905. 'Flottenverein und Kinematograph', *Der Komet*, 23 December, 5–6.

———. 1906. 'Bericht der "Kommission für die landeskundliche Erforschung der deutschen Schutzgebiete" an den Kolonialrat über ihre Tätigkeit im Rechnungsjahre 1905/06', *Mitteilungen von Forschungsreisenden und Gelehrten aus den deutschen Schutzgebieten* 19(4): 291–94.

———. 1906. 'Bericht über die landeskundlichen Expeditionen der Herren Prof. Dr. Karl Weule und Dr. Fritz Jäger in Deutsch-Ostafrika', *Mitteilungen von Forschungsreisenden und Gelehrten aus den deutschen Schutzgebieten* 19(4): 294–304.

———. 1907. 'Der Kinematograph', *Die Flotte* 10(1): 9.

———. 1907. 'Der Fortschritt', *Der Kinematograph*, 10 February.

———. 1909. 'Kinematographische Aufnahmen in Tanga', *Usambara-Post*, 4 September.
———. 1911. 'Kolonialer Verkehrsverein', *Deutsche Kolonialzeitung*, 20 May, 338.
———. 1912. 'Deutsche Jagdfilm-Gesellschaft', *Usambara-Post*, 2 November.
———. 1913. 'Die Gründung der "Kinematographischen Studiengesellschaft"', *Lichtbild-Bühne*, 8 February, 26–31.
———. 1913. 'Bund für Vogelschutz E.V.. Jahresbericht für die Zeit vom 1. Oktober 1911 bis 1. Oktober 1912', *Ornithologische Monatsschrift* 38(2): 129–39.
———. 1913. 'Koloniale Werbung und Aufklärung', *Deutsche Kolonialzeitung*, 10 July, 482–883.
———. 1913. 'Eine neue Filmfabrik', *Der Kinematograph*, 15 October.
———. 1913. 'Afrikanische Jagden im Film', *Lichtbild-Bühne*, 13 December, 24–28.
———. 1913.'Eine wissenschaftliche und belehrende Filmschau'. *Lichtbild-Bühne*, 27 December, 38.
———. 1914. 'Kinematographische Studiengesellschaft', *Lichtbild-Bühne*, 17 January: 30.
———. 1914. 'Wochen-Rundschau über neue Films', *Lichtbild-Bühne*, 31 January, 36.
———. 1914. 'Die "Kinematographische Studiengesellschaft"', *Lichtbild-Bühne*, 1 February, 16–21.
———. 1914. 'Kinematographische Studiengesellschaft', *Lichtbild-Bühne*, 14 February, 55.
———. 1914. 'Ein großer Erfolg der Deutschen Jagdfilm-Gesellschaft', *Lichtbild-Bühne*, 21 February, 48.
———. 1914. 'Streiflicher aus der deutschen Filmetropole', *Der Kinematograph*, 25 February.
———. 1914. 'Die Film-Schau der Woche', *Lichtbild-Bühne*, 28 February, 44.
———. 1914. 'Die Kinematographische Studiengesellschaft', *Der Kinematograph*, 1 April.
———. 1914. 'Die Tierdressur für Kino-Aufnahmen', *Lichtbild-Bühne*, 25 July, 63–64.
———. 1914. 'Die Kino-Expedition durch Deutsch Südwest-Afrika', *Lichtbild-Bühne*, 11 July, 40.
———. 1915. 'Bericht über die Tätigkeit vom 1. Oktober 1913 bis 1. Oktober 1914', *Jahresheft 1915 des Bundes für Vogelschutz*, 1–13.
———. 1916. 'Aus der afrikanischen Wildnis', *Lichtbild-Bühne*, 29 July, 55–56.
———. 1917. 'Fetischkönigin der Wangora', *Der Kinematograph*, 4 April.
Aubinger, J. 1914. 'Der Kinematograph in Kriegszeiten', *Der Kinematograph*, 12 August.
Ardener, E. 1970. 'Witchcraft Economics, and the Continuity of Belief', in Mary Douglas (ed.), *Witchcraft Confessions and Accusations*. London: Tavistock, pp. 141–60.
Benali, A. 2001. 'Le cinéma colonial: patrimoine emprunté', *Journal of Film Preservation* 63(10): 2–6.
Bhabha, H.K. 1994. 'The Other Question. Stereotype, Discrimination and the Discourse of Colonialism', in *The Location of Culture*. London: Routledge, pp. 66–84.

———. 1994. 'Of Mimicry and Man: The Ambivalence of Colonial Discourse', in *The Location of Culture*. London: Routledge, pp. 85–92.

Blesse, G. 1994. 'Karl Weule als Feldforscher (Zur wissenschaftlichen Expeditionstätigkeit Karl Weules in Südost-Tansania 1906)', Sonderdruck aus *Jahrbuch des Museums für Völkerkunde zu Leipzig* 40. Münster and Hamburg: LIT Verlag, pp. 155–67.

Bild- und Filmamt (1917). 1975. 'Bild- und Filmamt: Der Propagandafilm und seine Bedingungen, Ziele und Wege' in W. von Bredow and R. Zurek (eds), *Film und Gesellschaft in Deutschland. Dokumente und Materialien*. Hamburg, pp. 73–87.

Blankenship, J. 2006. 'Leuchte der Kultur: Imperialism, Imaginary Travel, and the Skladanowsky Welt-Theater', in *KINtop: Jahrbuch zur Erforschung des frühen Films* 14/15: 37–51.

Bleibtreu, K. 1917. 'Das Beiprogram und anderes', *Der Film*, 24 November.

Bottomore, S. 1985. 'Le théme du témoignage dans le cinéma primitif', in P. Guibbert (ed.), *Les premiers ans du cinéma français*. Perpignan: Institut Jean Vigo, pp. 155–61.

Bowersox, J. 2011. 'Boy's and Girl's Own Empires: Gender and the Uses of the Colonial World in Kaiserreich Youth Magazines', in M. Perraudin and J. Zimmerer (eds), *German Colonialism and National Identity*. New York: Routledge, pp. 57–68.

Bowser, E. 1979. 'The Brighton Project: An Introduction', *Quarterly Review of Film Studies* 4(4): 509–38.

Brauner, L. 1910. 'Der Kinematograph als Ausstellungsattraktion', *Der Kinematograph*, 13 July.

Brehl, M. 2008. '"The drama was played out on the dark stage of the sandveldt". The destruction of the Herero and Nama in German (popular) Literature', in J. Zimmerer and J. Zeller (eds), *Genocide in German South-West Africa: The Colonial War of 1904-1908 and Its Aftermath*. London: The Merlin Press Ltd, pp. 100–12.

Christadler, M. 1977. 'Zwischen Gartenlaube und Genozid', *Politik und Zeitgeschichte* 27(21): 18–36.

Christie, I. 2011. '"The Captains and the Kings Depart": Imperial Departure and Arrival in Early Cinema…', in L. Grieveson and C. MacCabe (eds), *Empire and Film*. London: Palgrave Macmillan, pp. 21–33.

Convents, G. 1988. 'Documentaries and Propaganda Before 1914. A View on Early Cinema and Colonial History', *Framework* 35: 104–13.

———. 1990. 'Film and German Colonial Propaganda for the Black African Territories to 1918', in P. Cherchi Usai and L. Codelli (eds), *Before Caligari: German Cinema, 1895–1920*. Venice: Edizioni Biblioteca dell'Immagine, pp. 58–77.

———. 2005. 'Africa: German Colonies', in R. Abel (ed.), *Encyclopedia of Early Cinema*. New York: Routledge, pp. 19–20.

Curtis, S. 1994. 'The Taste of a Nation: Training the Senses and Sensibility of Cinema Audiences in Imperial Germany', *Film History* 6(4): 445–69.

De Brigard, E. 1995. 'The History of Ethnographic Film', in P. Hockings (ed.), *Principles of Visual Anthropology*, 2nd edn. Berlin and New York: Mouton de Gruyter, pp. 13–43.

Eckart, A. 1992. 'Koloniale Stadtplanung und europäischer Rassismus: Die Enteignung der Dualla', in W. Wagner (ed.), *Rassendiskriminierung, Kolonialpolitik und ethnisch–nationale Identität* 2. Internationales Kolonialgeschichtliches Symposium 1991. Münster and Hamburg: LIT Verlag, pp. 206–16.

Eley, G. 1992. 'Nations, Publics, and Political Cultures: Placing Habermas in the Nineteenth Century', in C. Calhoun (ed.), *Habermas and the Public Sphere*. Cambridge, MA: MIT Press, pp. 289–339.

Elsaesser, T. 1986. 'The New Film History', *Sight and Sound* 35(4): 246–51.

Essner, C. 1986. 'Berlins Völkerkunde-Museum in der Kolonialära. Anmerkungen zum Verhältnis von Ethnologie und Kolonialismus in Deutschland', in H.J. Reichhardt (ed.), *Berlin in Geschichte und Gegenwart*. Jahrbuch des Landesarchivs Berlin. Berlin: Wolf Jobst Siedler Verlag, pp. 65–94.

Fraser, N. 1992. 'Rethinking the Public Sphere: A Contribution to the Critique of Actually Existing Democracy', in C. Calhoun (ed.), *Habermas and the Public Sphere*. Cambridge, MA: MIT Press, pp. 109–42.

Fricke, D. 1961. 'Der deutsche Imperialismus und die Reichstagswahlen von 1907', *Zeitschrift für Geschichtswissenschaft* 9(3): 538–76.

Fuhrmann, W. 1999. 'Lichtbilder und kinematographische Aufnahmen aus den Kolonien', *KINtop: Jahrbuch zur Erforschung des frühen Films* 8: 101–16.

———. 2002a. '"Nashornjagd in Deutsch-Ostafrika" – Die frühe Kolonialfilmindustrie', in U. van der Heyden and J. Zeller (eds), *Kolonialmetropole Berlin. Eine Spurensuche*. Berlin: Berlin Edition, pp. 184–87.

———. 2002b. 'Locating Early Film Audiences: Voluntary Associations and Colonial Film', *Historical Journal of Film, Radio and Television* 22(3): 291–304.

———. 2003.'Die Kinematographenkampagne der Deutschen Kolonialgesellschaft', in M.A. Denzel et al. (eds), *Jahrbuch für Europäische Überseegeschichte* 3. Wiesbaden: Harrassowitz Verlag, pp. 115–36.

———. 2005. 'Der Kinematograph in Afrika: Filme aus den deutschen Kolonien', in U. Jung and M. Loiperdinger (eds), *Geschichte des dokumentarischen Films in Deutschland, Bd. I: Kaiserreich 1895–1918*. Stuttgart: Reclam, pp. 149–60.

———. 2007a. 'Local Entertainment and National Patriotism: The Distribution of Colonial Films in Germany', in F. Kessler and N. Verhoeff (eds), *Networks of Entertainment: Early Film Distribution 1895–1915*. London: John Libbey Publishing, pp. 246–54.

———. 2007b. 'First Contact: The Beginning of Ethnographic Filmmaking in Germany, 1900–1930', *History of Anthropology Newsletter* 34(1): 3–9.

———. 2008a. 'Early Ethnographic Film and the Museum', in R. Abel, G. Bertellini and R. King (eds), *Early Cinema and the 'National'*. London: John Libbey Publishing, pp. 285–92.

———. 2008b.'Kolonie und/oder Heimat? Ein Stück ungeschriebener Filmgeschichte', in A. Barsch, H. Scheuer and G.M. Schulz (eds), *Literatur-Kunst-Medien. Festschrift für Peter Seibert zum 60. Geburtstag*. Munich: Martin Meidenbauer Verlag, pp. 321–34.

———. 2008c. 'Die Insel: Koloniale Unterhaltung in Altenburg', in U. van der Heyden and J. Zeller (eds), *Kolonialismus hierzulande. Eine Spurensuche*. Erfurt: Sutton-Verlag, pp. 337–42.

———. 2010a. 'The aesthetic of prison war camp film in early cinema', in R. Johler, C. Marchetti and M. Scheer (eds), *Doing Anthropology in Wartime and War Zones. World War I and the Cultural Sciences in Europe*. Bielefeld: Transcript, 2010, 337–51.

———. 2010b. 'Deutsche Kultur- und Spielfilme im Brasilien der 1930er Jahre: Eine transnationale Perspektive', in I. Schenk, M. Tröhler and Y. Zimmermann (eds), *Film – Kino – Zuschauer: Filmrezeption/Film – Cinema – Spectator: Film Reception*. Marburg: Schüren, pp. 399–418.

———. 2010c. 'Patriotism, Spectacle and Reverie: Colonialism in Early Cinema', in V. Langbehn (ed.), *German Colonialism, Visual Culture, and Modern Memory*. New York: Routledge, 148–61.

———. 2012. 'Trans-Inter-National Public Spheres', in M. Braun et al. (eds), *Beyond the Screen: Institutions, Networks and Publics of Early Cinema*. London: John Libbey Publishing, pp. 307–14.

———. 2013. 'Ethnographic Film Practices in Silent German Cinema', in J.A. Bell, A. K. Brown and R.J. Gordon (eds), *Expeditions, Anthropology and Popular Culture: Reinventing First Contact (1914–1939)*. Washington, DC: The Smithsonian Institution Scholarly Press, pp. 41–54.

Furkel, G. 1926. 'Film vor 30 Jahren', *Der Kinematograph*, 7 November: 15–16; 14 November: 11–12; 21 November: 11–12.

Garncarz, J. 2002.'The Origins of Film Exhibition in Germany', in T. Bergfelder, E. Carter and D. Göktürk (eds), *The German Cinema Book*. London: BFI, pp. 112–28.

———. 'Über die Entstehung der Kinos in Deutschland 1896–1914', in *KINtop: Jahrbuch zur Erforschung des Frühen Films* 11: 145–58.

Gewald, J.B. 2000. 'Colonization, Genocide and Resurgence: The Herero of Namibia 1890–1933', in M. Bollig and J.B. Gewald (eds), *People, Cattle and Land: Transformations of a Pastoral Society in Southwestern Africa*. Cologne: Rüdiger Köppe Verlag, pp. 187–226.

Gunning, T. 1990. 'The Cinema of Attractions. Early Film, its Spectator and the Avant-Garde', in T. Elsaesser (ed.), *Space-Frame-Narrative*. London: BFI, pp. 56–62.

———. 1995. '"The Whole World within Reach": Travel Images without Borders', in R. Cosandey and F. Albera (eds), *Cinéma sans frontières 1896–1918, Images across Borders*. Lausanne: Nuit Blanche Editeurs/Edition Payot, pp. 21–36.

———. 1997. 'Before Documentary: Early Nonfiction Films and the "View" Aesthetic', in D. Hertogs and N. de Klerk (eds), *Uncharted Territory. Essays on Early Nonfiction Film*. Amsterdam: Stichting Nederlands Filmmuseum, pp. 9–24.

Hagen. K. 1913. 'XLIV. Allgemeine Versammlung der Deutschen Anthropologischen Gesellschaft in Nürnberg', *Korrespondenz-Blatt der Deutschen Gesellschaft für Anthropologie, Ethnologie und Urgeschichte* 44(8/12): 61–134.

Harms, V. 1984. 'Das historische Verhältnis der deutschen Ethnologie zum Kolonialismus', *Zeitschrift für Kulturaustausch* 34(4): 401–16.

Hassert, K. 1908. 'Vorläufiger Bericht über einige Ergebnisse der Kamerun-Expedition 1907/08 des Reichs-Kolonialamtes', *Geographische Zeitschrift* 14(11): 625–28.

Herzog zu Mecklenburg, J.A. 1906. 'Die Auflösung des Reichstages und die Deutsche Kolonialgesellschaft', *Deutsche Kolonialzeitung*, 22 December (cover).
Honold, A. 2000. 'Flüsse, Berge, Eisenbahn: Szenarien geographischer Bemächtigung', in A. Honold and K.R. Scherpe (eds), *Das Fremde. Reiseerfahrungen, Schreibformen und kulturelles Wissen*. Beiheft 2 der Zeitschrift für Germanistik. N.F., pp. 149–74.
Hübner. 1904. 'Der Kinematograph in der Ausrüstung des Reisenden', *Deutsche Kolonialzeitung*, 24 March, 113–14.
Jäger, J. 2006. 'Bilder aus Afrika vor 1918. Zur visuellen Konstruktion Afrikas im europäischen Kolonialismus', in G. Paul (ed.), *Visual History. Ein Studienbuch*. Göttingen, pp. 134–48.
———. 2009. 'Colony as Heimat? The Formation of Colonial Identity in Germany around 1900', *German History* 27(4): 467–89.
Kennedy, K. 2002. 'African Heimat: German Colonies in Wilhelmine and Weimar Reading Books', *Internationale Schulbuchforschung* 24: 7–26.
Kessler, F. 2000. 'On Fairies and Technologies', in J. Fullerton and A. Soderbergh Widding (eds), *Moving Images: From Edison to Webcam*. Sydney: John Libbey Publishing, pp. 39–46.
———. 2002. 'Historische Pragmatik', *Montage/AV* 11(2): 104–11.
Kirschnick, S. 2002. '"Hereinspaziert!" Kolonialpolitik als Vergnügungskultur', in A. Honold and O. Simons (eds), *Kolonialismus als Kultur: Literatur, Medien, Wissenschaft in der deutschen Gründerzeit des Fremden*. Tübingen, Basel: Francke Verlag, pp. 221–41.
Krause, F. 1928. 'Dem Andenken Karl Weules', *Jahrbuch des Städtischen Museums für Völkerkunde zu Leipzig* 9. Leipzig: R.Voigtländers Verlag, 7–33.
Kreimeier, K. 1997. 'Mechanische Waffen und Haudegen überall. Expeditionsfilme: das bewaffnete Auge des Ethnografen', in J. Schöning (ed.), *Triviale Tropen: Exotische Reise- und Abenteuerfilme aus Deutschland 1919–1939*. Munich: edition text + kritik, pp. 47–61.
Lange, B. 2008. 'Die Welt im Ton – In deutschen Sonderlagern für Kolonialsoldaten entstanden ab 1915 einzigartige Aufnahmen', *iz3w. Informationszentrum 3. Welt* (307): 22–25. Retrieved 25 February 2014 from http://www.freiburg-postkolonial.de/Seiten/Lange-Welt-im-Ton.htm#_ftn2.
Lennox, S. 2010. 'From Postcolonial to Transnational Approachers in German Studies', in U. Lindner et al. (eds), *Hybrid Cultures-Nervous States. Germany and Britain in a (Post)Colonial World*. Amsterdam and New York: Rodopi, pp. xlvii–lxxiii.
Lewinsky, M. 2011. 'The Best Years of Film History: A Hundred Years Ago', in M. Loiperdinger (ed.), *Early Cinema Today: The Art of Programming and Live Performance*. New Barnet and Herts: John Libbey Publishing, pp. 25–35.
Levy, D. 1982. 'Re-constituted Newsreels, Re-enactments and the American Narrative Film', in Roger Holmann (ed.), *Cinema 1900/1906: An Analytical Study*. Brussels: Fédération Internationale des Archives du Film, pp. 243–60.
Loiperdinger, M. 1996. 'Lumières Ankunft des Zugs – Gründungsmythos eines neuen Mediums', *KINtop: Jahrbuch zur Erforschung des frühen Films* 5: 36–70.
———. 2002. 'The Beginnings of German Film Propaganda: The Navy League as Traveling Exhibitor 1901–1907', *Historical Journal of Film, Radio and Television* 22(3): 305–13.

McClintock, A. 2002. 'Soft-Soaping Empire. Commodity Racism and Imperial Advertising', in N. Mirzoeff (ed.), *The Visual Culture Reader*, 2nd edn. London: Routledge, pp. 506–18.

Maletzke, G. 1972. 'Propaganda: Eine begriffskritische Analyse,' in *Publizistik* 17(2): 153–64.

Märker, P., and M. Wagner. 1981. 'Bildungsreise und Reisebild: Einführende Bemerkungen zum Verhältnis von Reisen und Sehen', in P. Bopp, P. Märker and M. Wagner (eds), *Mit dem Auge des Touristen. Zur Geschichte des Reisebildes*. Tübingen: Eberhard-Karls-Universitaät, pp. 7–18.

Melber, H. 2000a. 'Rassismus und eurozentristisches Zivilisationsmodell: Zur Entwicklungsgeschichte des kolonialen Blicks', in N. Räthzel (ed.), *Theorien über Rassismus*. Hamburg: Argument Verlag, pp. 131–63.

———. 2000b. '"…dass die Kultur der Neger gehoben werde!" – Kolonialdebatten im deutschen Reichstag', in U. van der Heyden and J. Zeller (eds), *Kolonialmetropole Berlin. Eine Spurensuche*. Berlin: Berlin Edition, pp. 67–72.

Melcher, G. 1909. 'Von der lebenden Photographie und dem Kino-Drama', *Der Kinematograph*, 17 February.

Meyer, H. 1903. 'Die geographischen Grundlagen und Aufgaben in der wirtschaftlichen Erforschung unserer Schutzgebiete', in Deutscher Kolonialkongress, *Verhandlungen des Deutschen Kolonialkongresses 1902*. Berlin: Verlag Dietrich Reimer (Ernst Vohsen), pp. 73–82.

———. 1910a. 'Übersicht über die Ergebnisse der Expeditionen der Landeskundlichen Kommission des Reichskolonialamtes', in Deutscher Kolonialkongress, *Verhandlungen des Deutschen Kolonialkongresses 1910*. Berlin: Verlag Dietrich Reimer (Ernst Vohsen), pp. 5–10.

———. 1910b. 'Die Landeskundliche Kommission des Reichskolonialamtes', *Koloniale Rundschau. Monatsschrift für die Interessen unserer Schutzgebiete und ihren Bewohnern* 2(12): 722–34.

Miller, A. 1996. 'The Panorama, the Cinema and the Emergence of the Spectacular', *Wide Angle* 18(2): 35–69.

Moltke von, J. 2002. 'Evergreens: The Heimat Genre', in T. Bergfelder, E. Carter and D. Göktürk (eds), *The German Cinema Book*. London: BFI, pp. 18–28.

Montagne, L. 1907. 'Naturaufnahmen für Phono- und Kinematographen', *Der Kinematograph*, 14 April.

Mordhorst, C. 1913. 'Wie eine Löwenjagd gestellt wird', *Lichtbild-Bühne*, 25 October: 18.

Moyd, M. 2008. 'Askari and Askari Myth', in P. Poddar, R. Shridhar Patke and L. Jensen (eds), *A Historical Companion to Postcolonial Literatures: Continental Europe and Its Empires*. Edinburgh: Edinburgh University Press, pp. 208–09.

Mühl-Benninghaus, W. 1998. 'Exemplifikation des Militärischen zwischen 1914 und 1918. Die Darstellung des Ersten Weltkrieges im Nonfictionfilm', in C. Müller and H. Segeberg (eds), *Modellierung des Kinofilms. Zur Geschichte des Kinoprogramms zwischen Kurzfilm und Langfilm 1905/06–1918*. Munich: Wilhelm Fink Verlag, pp. 273–300.

———. 2001.'Der dokumentarische Film in Deutschland zwischen erzieherischen Anspruch und wirtschaftlicher Realität', in U. von Keitz and K. Hoffmann (eds), *Die Einübung des dokumentarischen Blicks*. Marburg: Schüren, pp. 81–102.

Müller, C. 1998. 'Variationen des Kinoprogramms. Filmform und Filmgeschichte', in C. Müller and H. Segeberg (eds), *Modellierung des Kinofilms. Zur Geschichte des Kinoprogramms zwischen Kurzfilm und Langfilm 1905/06–1918*. Munich: Wilhelm Fink Verlag, pp. 43–75.
Musser, C. 1990. 'The Travel Genre in 1903–1904: Moving Towards Fictional Narrative', in T. Elsaesser (ed.), *Early Cinema: Space, Frame Narrative*. London: BFI, pp. 123–32.
Neuhauss, R. 1906. 'Der Kinematograph auf wissenschaftlichen Reisen', *Photographische Rundschau und photographisches Centralblatt* 20: 290–91.
———. 1907a. 'Der Kinematograph', *Photographische Rundschau und photographisches Centralblatt* 21: 273–78.
———. 1907b. 'Neuere Photographische Hilfsmittel für den Forschungsreisenden', *Zeitschrift für Ethnologie* 39(4): 966–72.
———. 1911. 'Kinematographische und phonographische Aufnahmen aus Deutsch- NeuGuinea', *Zeitschrift für Ethnologie* 43(1): 136–38.
Neuser, D. 2008. 'Ein Platz an der Sonne – der neue Heimatfilm *Afrika, Mon Amour* und *Momella. Eine Farm in Afrika*' in A. Erll and S. Wodianka (eds), *Film und kulturelle Erinnerung. Plurimediale Konstellationen*. Berlin and New York: de Gruyter, pp. 107–37.
Nipperdey, T. 1976. 'Verein als soziale Struktur in Deutschland im späten 18. und frühen 19. Jahrhundert', in *Gesellschaft, Kultur, Theorie. Gesammelte Aufsätze zur neueren Geschichte*. Göttingen: Vandenhoeck & Ruprecht, pp. 174–205.
Normand, M. 1900/1997. 'Delia im Kinematographen und der Burenkrieg', *KINtop: Jahrbuch zur Erforschung des frühen Films* 6: 11–29.
Odin, R. 2000. 'For a Semio-Pragmatics of Film', in R. Stam and T. Miller (eds), *Film and Theory: An Anthology*. Malden, MA and Oxford: Blackwell Publishing, pp. 54–66.
Paasche, H. 1914. 'Der Jagdfilm', *Ethische Rundschau: Monatsschrift zur Läuterung und Vertiefung der ethischen Anschauungen und zur Förderung ethischer Bestrebungen* 3(5–6): 85–87.
Perlmann, E. 1908. 'Die Kinematographen-Theater und der Deutsche Flottenverein', *Der Kinematograph*, 19 February.
Peterson, J.L. 1997. '"Truth is Stranger than Fiction": Travelogues from the 1910s in the Nederlands Filmmuseum', in D. Hertogs and N. de Klerk (eds), *Uncharted Territory: Essays in Nonfiction Film*. Amsterdam: Stichting Nederlands Filmmuseum, pp. 75–90.
Peterson, J.L. 2004.'Travelogues and Early Nonfiction Film: Education in the School of Dreams', in C. Keil and S. Stamp (eds), *American Cinema's Transitional Era*. Berkeley: University of California Press, pp. 191–213.
Pöch, R. 1906. 'Dritter Bericht über meine Reise nach Neu-Guinea (Neu-Süd Wales, vom 21. Juni bis 6. September 1905, Britsch–Solomoninseln und Britsch Neuguinea bis zum 31 Jänner 1906)', *Sitzungsberichte der kaiserlichen Akademie der Wissenschaften* 65(6): 601–15.
———. 1907. 'Reisen in Neu-Guinea in den Jahren 1904–1906', *Zeitschrift für Ethnologie* 39: 382–400.
Polimanti, O. 1920. 'Die Anwendung der Kinematographie in den Naturwissenschaften der Medizin und im Unterricht', in F.P. Liesegang (ed.), *Wissen-*

schaftliche Kinematographie, einschließlich der Reihenphotographie. Düsseldorf: Ed. Liesegang, pp. 257–310.
Rath, W. 1992. 'Emporkömmling Kino', in J. Schweinitz (ed.), *Prolog vor dem Film. Nachdenken über ein neues Medium 1909–1914*. Leipzig: Reclam, pp. 75–89.
Reche, O. 1929. 'Karl Weule', in O. Reche (ed.), *In Memoriam Karl Weule. Beiträge zur Völkerkunde und Vorgeschichte*. Leipzig: R. Voigtländers Verlag, pp. 1–18.
Richelmann. 1911. 'Etwas über Vergnügungsreisen in Afrika', *Deutsche Kolonialzeitung* 28(13): 206 and 28(15): 249–51.
Richter, R. 1995. 'Die erste deutsche Kolonial-Ausstellung 1896. Der "Amtliche Bericht" in historischer Perspektive', in R. Debusmann and J. Riesz (eds), *Kolonialausstellungen-Begegnungen mit Afrika?*. Frankfurt: IKO-Verlag für Interkulturelle Kommunikation, pp. 25–41.
Rogowski, C. 2010. 'The "Colonial Idea" in Weimar Cinema', in V. Langbehn (ed.), *German Colonialism, Visual Culture, and Modern Memory*. New York: Routledge, pp. 220-38.
Roller, K. 2002. '"Wir sind Deutsche, wir sind Weiße und wollen Weiße bleiben"- Reichtagsdebatten über koloniale "Rassenmischung"', in U. von der Heyden and J. Zeller (eds), *Kolonialmetropole Berlin. Eine Spurensuche*. Berlin: Berlin Edition, pp. 73–79.
Rosenthal, A. 1913/14. 'Kinovorstellungen in Vereinen', *Bild und Film* 3(8): 198–200.
Rother, R. 1995. 'Bei unseren Helden an der Somme. Eine deutsche Antwort auf die Entente-Propaganda', *KINtop: Jahrbuch zur Erforschung des frühen Films* 4: 123–42.
Rowen-Steinbach, D. 2008. 'Defending the Heimat: The Germans in South-West Africa and East Africa during the First World War', in H. Jones, J. O'Brien and C. Schmidt-Supprian (eds), *Untold War. New Perspectives in First World War Studies*. Leiden, Boston: Brill, pp. 179–208.
Rübenstahl, M. 2002. '"Gedenket unserer Landsleute, die fern der Heimat krank liegen!" – Der Deutsche Frauenverein für Krankenpflege in den Kolonien', in U. von der Heyden and J. Zeller (eds), *Kolonialmetropole Berlin. Eine Spurensuche*. Berlin: Berlin Edition, pp. 56–63.
Ryan, M.P. 1992. 'Gender and Public Access: Women's Politics in Nineteenth Century', in C. Calhoun (ed.), *Habermas and the Public Sphere*. Cambridge, MS: MIT Press, pp. 259–88.
Sachers, H. 1921. 'Der Kolonialfilm', *Afrika Nachrichten*, 14 May, 94.
Schlüpmann, H. 1997. 'The Documentary Interest in Fiction', in D. Hertogs and N. de Klerk (eds), *Uncharted Territory: Essays in Nonfiction Film*. Amsterdam: Stichting Nederlands Filmmuseum, pp. 33–36.
Schneider, G. 1982. 'Das Deutsche Kolonialmuseum Berlin und seine Bedeutung im Rahmen der preußischen Schulreform um die Jahrhundertwende', in Mitarbeiter des Historischen Museums (eds), *Die Zukunft beginnt in der Vergangenheit. Museumsgeschichte und Geschichtsmuseum*. Frankfurt: Anabas Verlag, pp. 155–99.
Schomburgk, H. 1913.'Der Kinematograph im Dienste der kolonialen Propaganda', *Koloniale Zeitschrift*, 4 April, 219.
Schultz, H.D. 2006. 'Das "größere Deutschland" muss es sein!- Der koloniale Gedanke im Geographieunterricht des Kaiserreichs und darüber hinaus',

in R. Dithmar and H.-D. Schultz (eds), *Schule und Unterricht im Kaiserreich*. Ludwigsfelde: Ludwigsfelder Verlagshaus, pp. 183–234.
Singer Kovács, K. 1983. 'George Méliès and the Féerie', in J.L. Fell (ed.), *Film Before Griffith*. Berkeley, Los Angeles and London: University of California Press, pp. 244–57.
Sippel, H. 1995. 'Rassismus, Protektionismus oder Humanität? Die gesetzlichen Verbote der Anwerbung von "Eingeborenen" zu Schaustellungszwecken in den deutschen Kolonien', in R. Debusmann and J. Riesz (eds), *Kolonialausstellungen-Begegnungen mit Afrika?*. Frankfurt: IKO-Verlag für interkulturelle Kommunikation, pp. 43–64.
Smith, W.D. 1987. 'Anthropology and German Colonialism', in A.J. Knoll and L.H. Gann (eds), *Germans in the Tropics. Essays in German Colonial History*. New York, Westport, CT and London: Greenwood Press, pp. 39–57.
Sperling, W. 1989. 'Zur Darstellung der deutschen Kolonien im Erdkundeunterricht (1890–1914) mit besonderer Berücksichtigung der Lehrmittel', *Internationale Schulbuchforschung* 11: 387–410.
Stam, R. 2000. 'Semiotic Revisited', in *Film Theory: An Introduction*. Malden, MA and Oxford: Blackwell Publishing, pp. 248–56.
Ste, H. 1907. 'Der Kinematograph im Dienste der Völkerkunde', *Der Kinematograph*, 11 December.
Steiger, R., and M. Taureg. 1985. 'Körperphantasien auf Reisen. Anmerkungen zum ethnographischen Akt', in M. Köhler and G. Barche (eds), *Das Aktfoto. Ansichten vom Körper im fotografischen Zeitalter. Ästhetik, Geschichte, Ideologie*. Munich and Luzern: C.J. Bucher Verlag, pp. 116–36.
Steinke, M. 1917. 'Koloniale Propagandafilms', *Deutsche Kolonialzeitung*, 20 September, 137.
Strahl, G. 1907. 'Kinematographen', *Der Kinematograph*, 26 June.
Struck, W. 2003. 'Die Geburt des Abenteuers aus dem Geist des Kolonialismus. Exotistische Filme in Deutschland nach dem Ersten Weltkrieg', in B. Kundrus (ed.), *Phantasiereiche. Zur Kulturgeschichte des deutschen Kolonialismus*. Frankfurt and New York: Campus Verlag, pp. 263–81.
———. 2010a. 'The Persistence of (Colonial) Fantasies', in M. Perraudin and J. Zimmerer (eds), *German Colonialism and National Identity*. New York: Routledge, pp. 224–31.
———. 2010b. 'Reenacting Colonialism: Germany and Its Former Colonies in Recent TV Productions', in V. Langbehn (ed.), *German Colonialism, Visual Culture, and Modern Memory*. New York: Routledge, pp. 260–77.
Taureg, M. 1983. 'The Development of Standards for Scientific Films in German Ethnography', *Studies in Visual Communication* 9(1): 19–29.
Töteberg, M. 1999. 'Exotik und Tourismus. Die Reisefilme der Hapag', *Hamburger Flimmern* 5: 2–6.
Trebus, H. 2001. 'Carl Julius Friedrich Müller, genannt der "Insel Müller". Eine legendäre Persönlichkeit von Altenburg', *Familienforschung in Mitteldeutschland* 14(4): 160–64.
Wahl.T. 2010. 'Barbusig baden', *Berliner Zeitung*, 6 April. Retrived 28 February 2014 from http://www.berliner-zeitung.de/archiv/ein-zdf-dreiteiler-ueber-die-deutsche-kolonialgeschichte-setzt-vor-allem-auf-exotik-und-dramatik-barbusig-baden,10810590,10709114.html.

Weule, K. 1906. 'Der Stand der ethnographischen Forschung in unsern Kolonien', in Deutscher Kolonialkongress, *Verhandlungen des Deutschen Kolonialkongress 1905*. Berlin: Verlag Dietrich Reimer (Ernst Vohsen), pp. 17–30.

———. 1910a. 'Die nächsten Aufgaben und Ziele des Leipziger Völkerkundemuseums', in Städtisches Museum für Völkerkunde (Leipzig), *Jahrbuch des Städtischen Museums für Völkerkunde zu Leipzig* 3. Leipzig: R.Voigtländers Verlag, pp. 151–74.

———. 1910b. 'Die praktischen Aufgaben der Völkermuseen auf Grund Leipziger Erfahrungen', *Korrespondenzblatt der Deutschen Gesellschaft für Anthropologie, Ethnologie und Urgeschichte* 41(9–12): 74–78.

Waz, G. 1997. 'Auf der Suche nach dem letzten Paradies. Der Afrikaforscher und Regisseur Hans Schomburgk', in J. Schöning (ed.), *Triviale Tropen. Exotische Reise und Abenteuerfilme aus Deutschland 1919–1939*. Munich: edition text & kritik, pp. 95–109.

Weinstein, V. 2010. 'Archiving the Ephemeral: Dance in Ethnographic Films from the Hamburg South Seas Expedition 1908–1910', *Seminar: A Journal of Germanic Studies* 46(3): 223–39.

Zeller, J. 2001. '"Wie Vieh wurden hunderte zu Tode getrieben und wie Vieh begraben". Fotodokumente aus dem deutschen Konzentrationslager in Swakopmund/Namibia 1904–1908', *Zeitschrift für Geschichtswissenschaft* 49(3): 226–43.

———. 2002a. 'Berliner Maler und Bildhauer im Dienste der Kolonialidee', in U. van der Heyden and J. Zeller (eds), *Kolonialmetropole Berlin. Eine Spurensuche*. Berlin: Berlin Edition, pp. 159–67.

———. 2002b. 'Orlog in Deutsch-Südwestafrika. Fotografien aus dem Kolonialkrieg 1904–1907', *Fotogeschichte. Beiträge zur Geschichte und Ästhetik der Fotografie* 22 (85/86): 36.

———. 2010. 'Spurensuche light. ZDF-Historiker Guido Knopp scheitert an der deutschen Kolonialgeschichte', *iz3w. Informationszentrum 3. Welt* (319): 41.

CD-Rom

Filmmuseum, Amsterdam, the Netherlands (eds). 1998. 'The Eye of the Beholder', 3rd Amsterdam workshop.

Online Resources

'Colonial Film: Moving Images of the British Empire'. Retrieved 28 March 2014 from http://www.colonialfilm.org.uk/home.

Colonial Picture Archive. Deutsche Kolonialgesellschaft, or DKG (German Colonial Society). Retrieved 28 March 2014 from http://www.ub.bildarchiv-dkg.uni-frankfurt.de/Default.htm.

'Freiburg Postkolonial'. Retrieved 28 March 2014 from http://www.freiburg-postkolonial.de.

'Great Victoria Falls, Zambesis River'. Retrieved 28 March 2014 from http://colonialfilm.org.uk/node/503.
'Wider den Paradiesvogelmord. Lobby-Arbeit anno 1910: die ersten Naturschutzkampagnen'. Retrieved 28 March 2014 from http://www.nabu.de/nabu/portrait/geschichte/00346.html.

Journals and Periodicals

Afrika Nachrichten (Leipzig 1920–1943).
Afrika-Post, Organ für deutsche Interessen in Afrika Hamburg (Hamburg 1888–1914).
Die Flotte. Monatsblatt der Deutschen Flotten-Vereine im Auslande (Berlin 1889–1919).
Der Artist: Fachblatt für Unterhaltungsmusik und Artistik (Düsseldorf 1883–1936).
Der Film. Zeitschrift für die gesamten Interessen der Kinematographie (Berlin 1916–1943).
Der Kinematograph. Organ für die gesamte Projektionskunst (Düsseldorf 1907–1935).
Der Komet. Erste, Älteste und führende Fachzeitschrift des Schausteller-, -Kinematographenbesitzerstandes (Pirmasens 1894–1912).
Deutsche Kolonialzeitung. Organ der Deutschen Kolonialgesellschaft (Munich 1884–1943).
Koloniale Rundschau. Zeitschrift für koloniale Länder-, Völker- u. Staatenkunde. Zeitschr. für d. gesamte Eingeborenenwesen (Leipzig 1909–1943).
Kolonie und Heimat in Wort und Bild [from 1912 *Kolonie und Heimat: Unabhängige koloniale Wochenschrift. Organ d. Frauenbundes der Deutschen Kolonialgesellschaft*] (Berlin 1907/08–1918/19).
Lichtbild-Bühne. Älteste deutsche Fachzeitung des Films (Berlin 1908–1939).
Mitteilungen von Forschungsreisenden und Gelehrten aus den Deutschen Schutzgebieten: Mit Benutung amtlicher Quellen [from 1907 *Mitteilungen aus den Deutschen Schutzgebieten: Mit Benutzung amtlicher Quellen*] (Berlin 1888–1928/29).
Ornithologische Monatsschrift (Gera 1890–1937).
Phonographische Zeitschrift: Fachblatt für die gesamte Musik- u. Sprechmaschinen-Industrie (Berlin 1900–1933).
Zeitschrift für Ethnologie (Berlin 1869–).

Local Newspapers

Altenburger Zeitung für Stadt und Land, Altenburger Landeszeitung, Anhaltischer Staats-Anzeiger (Dessau), *Basler Nachrichten* (Switzerland), *Bergisch-Märkische Zeitung* (Hagen), *Berliner Tageblatt, Berliner Börsenzeitung, Berliner Lokal Anzeiger, Der Altmärker* (Stendal), *Chemnitzer Tagblatt und Anzeiger, Darmstädter Tageblatt, Deutsch-Ostafrikanische Zeitung* (Dar es Salaam), *Fränkischer Kurier. Nürnberg, Duisburger Generalanzeiger, General Anzeiger für Elberfeld-Barmen, General Anzeiger: Anzeiger für Essen und Umgebung, Gränzbote* (Tuttlingen), *Der Grenzbote. Heidenheimer Tages-Zeitung, Hamburger Fremdenblatt, Hagener Zeitung, Hohenzollerische Volkszeitung* (Sigmaringen), *Holsteinischer*

Courier (Neumünster), *Kieler Zeitung, Norddeutsche Allgemeine Zeitung, Kreis-Blatt für den Ober-Lahn-Kreis* (Weilburg), *Leipziger Neueste Nachrichten, Lübecker Generalanzeiger, Magdeburgische Zeitung, Pirnaer Anzeiger, Rhein- und Ruhr Zeitung* (Duisburg), *Rheydter Zeitung* (Berlin), *Schwäbische Chronik* (Stuttgart), *Stuttgarter Neues Tagblatt, Stadt-und Landbote* (Calbe an der Saale), *Taunusbote* (Homburg vor der Höhe), *Usambara-Post* (Tanga), *Velberter Zeitung, Vossische Zeitung, Weser-Zeitung* (Bremen), *Zeitzer Neuesten Nachrichten*.

Unpublished Sources

Noirot, M.L. 1966/67. 'Landmann Chronik'. Typescript.

Bundesarchiv, Berlin-Lichterfelde

BArch, R 1001/5637-2 Expeditionen. Wissenschaftliche Erforschung Ostafrikas.
BArch, R 1001/6620 Forschungreisende in Afrika.
BArch, R 1001/6621 Forschungreisende in Afrika, Empfehlungen Bd.: 4.
BArch, R 1001/6630 Kinomatographische Unternehmungen.
BArch, R 1001/6632 Reise des deutschen Kronprinzen in die deutschen Kolonien.
BArch, R 1001/6688 Deutsche Kolonialgesellschaft, Bd.: 4.
BArch, R 1001/6994 Sitzungen des Kolonialrats. - Vorlagen und Protokolle: 7. Sitzungsperiode, 1904/1907.
BArch, R 1001/7771 Jagd. Wildschutz. Fischerei.
BArch, R 1001/7779 Jagd und Wildschutz in Deutsch-Ostafrika, Bd.: 4.
BArch, R 8023/154 Deutscher Frauenbund und dessen Einrichtungen, Bd.: 2.
BArch, R 8023/232 Expeditionen und Studienreisen Allgemein, Bd.: 1.
BArch, R 8023/328 Deutsche Kolonial-Filmgesellschaft mbH.
BArch, R 8023/329 Überseefilm Aktiengesellschaft.
BArch, R 8023/510 Auflösung des Reichstages wegen Ablehnung einer kolonialpolitischen Forderung der Regierung am 13. Dez. 1906, Bd.: 2.
BArch, R 8023/646 Deutsches Kolonialmuseum zu Berlin, Bd.: 3.
BArch, R 8023/683 Ausschußsitzungen der Deutschen Kolonialgesellschaft. Berichte, Bd.: 1.
BArch, R 8023/1048a Kolonialkriegerspende, Opfertag.
BArch, R 8023/1089 Werbekommission der Deutschen Kolonialgesellschaft, Sitzungsberichte Bd.: 1.
BArch, R 8024/81 Deutsch-koloniale Kino- Gesellschaft mbH.

Bundesarchiv-Militärchiv, Freiburg

BArch MA, RM 9901 Film- und Lichtbild-Propaganda: Organisation während des Krieges.
BArch, MA, RM 3/9914 Anträge der Flottenvereine auf Verleihung von Auszeichnungen, Bd. 1.
BArch, MA, RM 3/9925 Hauptausschuß des Deutschen Flottenvereins für Berlin und die Mark Brandenburg, Bd. 1.

Landesarchiv Berlin

LAB, A Rep. 342-02, no. 2476.

Historisches Archiv der Stadt Köln

File 614, no. 364.

Stadtarchiv Leipzig

Kap. 31. Nr. 12, Akten des Museums für Völkerkunde, Bd. 5, 1907.
Kap. 31. Nr. 12, Akten des Museums für Völkerkunde, Bd. 8, 1913.

Archiv des Museums für Völkerkunde zu Leipzig

File: Aktenstück Expedition 1908/09 Prof. Weule.
File: C 17 AF.
File: Museumsgeschichte (MUGE) Diverses.

Archiv für Geographie, Leibniz-Institut für Länderkunde, Leipzig.

Box 434: Deutsche Kolonial-Gesellschaft.

INDEX

Aar Kinematographen-Werk (projector company), 186
Afrikahaus (Africa House), DKG, 33; Woermann, 58
Afrikanisches Idyll, Ein (An African Idyll) (1907), 217
Aktionsausschuss (DKG, Action Committee), 248–49, 254n19
Alexander, Georg, 7, 257
Alldeutscher Verband (Pan-German League), 40n23, 73
Altenloh, Emilie, 107
Amateur Aufnahme Kino (film camera), 165–167
Askari, 28, 179, 199, 204, 209
Audubon Society, 237
Aus dem Innern Afrikas (From Inner Africa) (1911), 202, 214, 277
Aus dem Leben der Kate auf Deutsch Neuguinea. Aufnahmen aus dem Jahre 1909 (From the Life of the Kate in German New Guinea. Pictures from 1909), 133, 276
Aus der Afrikanischen Wildnis (From the African Jungle) (1916), 227, 234, 241n18

Bagne en Afrique orientale allemande, Un (A Penitentiary in German East Africa) (1910), 221n27
Bastian, Adolf, 134, 137, 152, 159, 207
Bau der nördlichsten Station in Togo, Der (The Construction of the Northernmost Station in Togo) (1916), 250

Bau einer Eisenbahnlinie in Afrika (Construction of a Railway in Africa) (1908), 221
Bebel, August, 29
Befreien Sie Afrika (Free Africa) (1999), 274
Bethmann Hollweg von, Theobald, 228
Bild und Filmamt (BUFA, Photography and Film Office), 247–49, 253, 259, 261, 262, 264, 269n22, 269n25
Bilder aus Deutsch-Süd-West-Afrika (Scenes from German South-West Africa) (1912), 200
Boer War, 96
Boese, Carl, 7, 257, 267
Boxer Uprising (1900–1901), 31, 36
British Royal Society for the Protection of Birds (RSPB), 237
Brunner, Karl, 183
Bülow von, Bernhard, 3, 83, 87, 95
Bund für Vogelschutz (BFV, League for the Protection of Birds), 237, 239
Buschmann spricht in den Phonographen (Bushman speaks into the Phonograph) (1908), 212

Cameroon, 3, 6, 27; Carl Müller, 46–47, 48; film, 57, 58, 65, 78, 118, 120, 183, 246, 255n34
Censorship, 184, 185, 245, 266
Cinématograph des Colonies, Le (Production company), 272

Circus Busch, 30
Colonial education, 45, 107–12, 272; in Africa, 69, 184, 205–09. *See also* cultural mission
Colonial film audience, African, 43; female, 105–07, 113n31; German youth, 107–112; working class, 103–05; variety, 31
Colonial Ideology, 3, 260; and movement, 66–69; technology, 68, 69, 200–03, 213, 214; cultural mission, 203–13; travelogue aesthetic, 213–20
Colonial Office Visual Instruction Committee, 272
Conradt, Walther, 180

Dernburg, Bernhard, 68, 85, 103, 109, 181
Deutsch-Afrikanische Film-und Vortragsgesellschaft (German-African Film and Lecture Company), 251
Deutsch-Neuguinea (German New Guinea), 3, 66, 222n48, 223n77, 229. *See also Mit dem Norddeutschen Lloyd nach Neu Guinea*
Deutsch-Ostafrika (DOA, German East Africa), 3, 4; Carl Müller, 43–44; film, 6, 68, 74, 75, 210–213, 226, 273; Robert Schumann, 226
Deutsch-Südwestafrika (DSWA, German South-West Africa), 4, 45, 47; Carl Müller, 46–48, *Der Verräter*, 257–58; film, 44, 54, 55, 68, 76, 184, 197–98; Robert Schumann, 91–92, 95–96; tableaux vivants, 86–90
Deutsche Armee- Marine- und Kolonialausstellung (DAMUKA, German Army, Navy and Colonial Exhibition), 118, 184, 215
Deutsche Bioscop Gesellschaft mbH (film company), 7, 72, 73, 115–24, 129n1
Deutsche Erdkundliche Kinogenossenschaft (German Geographical Cinema Co-Operative), 182
Deutsche Jagd-Film-Gesellschaft (DJFG, German Hunting Film Company), 171, 224, 226–29
Deutsche Kolonial-Filmgesellschaft (DEUKO, German Colonial Film Company), 7, 247, 249, 252–53, 256–68, 269n25
Deutsche Koloniale Eisenbahn- und Betriebsgesellschaft (DKEB, German Colonial Railway- and Operating Company), 118
Deutsch-Ostafrika:eine grosse öffentliche Schule der Provinz Usambara (A Big Public School in the Usambara Province) (1912), 210–213, 276
Deutsche Ost-Afrika Linie (DOAL, German East Africa Shipping Line), 58, 62n52
Deutsche Kolonialgesellschaft (DKG, German Colonial Society), 5, 12–14, 23n59, 32–34; collaboration with associations, 72–73; DEUKO 256, 259–60, 263, 267; DFV, 13, 71–72; film shows, 64–69; Hottentot election, 83–91, 92, 94, 97–98; Kinematographenkampagne, 100–129; lantern slides and film, 34–39; film propaganda, 69–75; 247–49, 251–253, 254n17. *See also* Carl Müller, Robert Schumann, Hans Schomburgk
Deutsche Lichtbild-Gesellschaft (DEULIG, German Cinematographic Company), 247, 253, 259
Deutschen Kolonien, Die (The German Colonies) (TV documentary 2005), 274
Deutscher Flottenverein (DFV, German Navy League), 13, 40n23, 57, 60, 71–73, 78, 90, 109, 115–24, 127
Deutscher Frauenverein für Krankenpflege in den Kolonien

(DFKK, German Women's Association for Nursing in the German Colonies), 106
Deutscher Frauenverein vom Roten Kreuz für die Kolonien (German Women's Association of the Red Cross for the Colonies), 107
Deutsches Kolonialmuseum (German Colonial Museum), 1, 51, 54, 69, 108, 163n42
Deutschkoloniale Kino- Gesellschaft m.b.H. (German Colonial Cinema Company), 127
Diamantenfelder in Deutsch-Südwestafrika (Diamond Fields in German South-West Africa) (1914), 223n82
Dokumentaraufnahmen vom Bau der Telefunken-Großstation, Kamina/ Togo (Afrika) für die drahtlose Verbindung des ehemaligen deutschen Schutzgebiets Togo mit Berlin (Images of the Construction of the Telefunken-Großstation, Kamina/ Togo [Africa] for the Wireless Transmission of the Former Colony Togo with Berlin) (1913), 191n42, 276

Elefantenjagd am Viktoriasee in Afrika, Eine (An Elephant Hunt at Lake Victoria) (1913), 185
Eine öffentliche Schule in Ostafrika (A Public School in East Africa), 222n48
Eisenbahnbau bei Kindu (Railway Construction near Kindu) (1911), 221
Ende der Alma Bonar, Das (The End of the Alma Bonar) (1918), 257
Ernemann (film company), 140, 143–46, 159, 162n12, 166, 187. *See also* Amateur Aufnahme Kino
Eröffnung der Kolonialausstellung in Berlin am 2. Mai durch seine Kaiserliche Hoheit den Kronprinzen (Opening of the Colonial Exposition on 2 May in Berlin by his Imperial Majesty the Crown Prince) (1907), 184
Erste staatliche Fachschule in Tanga (First Vocational School in Tanga) (1911), 222n48. *See also Fortschritte der Zivilisation in Deutsch-Ostafrika, Die*
Ethnographische Aufnahmen aus Deutsch –Ostafrika (Ethnographic Images from German East Africa) (1906–1907), 141–142, 276. *See also* Karl Weule
Express-Films Co., G.m.b.H. (film company), 185, 188

Fahrt durch den Urwald (Trip Through the Jungle) (1910?), 216–17
Farmer Borchardt (1917), 7, 257, 258, 259, 260–63, 268–69
Féerie, 76, 79n43, 80n43, 297
FIAF conference (Brighton), 8, 20
Fière, Octave, 168, 170,187
Filming in the colonies (technology), 165–72
First World War (colonial propaganda), 243–68
Fortschritte der Zivilisation in Deutsch-Ostafrika, Die (The Progress of Civilization in German East Africa) (1911), 6, 178, 184, 205, 207–09, 222
Foy, Wilhelm, 156–57, 163
Frauenbund der Deutschen Kolonialgesellschaft (FDKG, Women's League of the German Colonial Society), 106, 128
Frauenleben in Westafrika (Women's Life in West Africa) (1916), 250, 254
Frenssen, Gustav, 93–94, 200
Frobenius, Leo, 152–54, 160–162
Furkel, Georg, 118, 129, 168, 197, 215

Gefangene von Dahomey, Der (The Prisoner from Dahomey) (1918), 257–59, 264–66

Gehrts, Emma Augusta (Meg), 250–51, 267
German, Paul, 161
Gestörte Liebesidyll im afrikanischen Laubenurwald, Das oder: Ein Freibad im Urwald (The Disturbed Love Idyll in the African Jungle or: A Public Bath in the Jungle) (1914), 226–27
Gnu- und die Onix-Jagd, Die (The Gnu and Oryx Hunting) (1914), 229
Goldfieber (Gold Fever) (1920), 267
Goldindustrie in Afrika (Gold Industry in Africa) (1911), 223n82
Graetz, Paul, 14, 187–89
Gusmann von, Wilhelm, 183

Haddon, Alfred Cort, 134, 150, 151
Haase, Lene, 258–59, 270
Häfker, Hermann, 181–82
Hagenbeck, Carl, 10, 24
Hagenbeck Stellinger Zoo, 226, 241n18
Hamburger Kolonialwoche (Hamburg Colonial Week), 267
Heimat, 16, 19, 20, 50, 93, 117, 128, 180, 182, 194–95, 213, 220, 260–64
Heldin von Paratau, Die (The Heroine of Paratau) (1918), 254, 257, 268
Herero (people), 4, 19, 28–29. See also Herero War
Herero War (1904–1907), 4, 14, 27, 262; *Farmer Bochardt*, 258,262; film, 65, 76, 90–91, 197–98; Hottentot election, 83, 85; literature, 93–95; lantern slides, 36; popular media, 28–32; prison camp, 49–51; tableaux vivants, 86–90; *Two Worlds*, 261–62
Hinterland von Tanga, Das (The Tanga Hinterland) (1914), 229
Historical pragmatics, 11
Hodgson, Jimmy S. (operator), 188, 250
Hottentot election, 83–99

In Deutsch-Ostafrika während des Ersten Weltkriegs. Aufnahmen aus den Jahren 1914–1916 (In German East Africa during the First World War. Images from the Years 1914–1916), 276
Im Deutschen Sudan (In the German Sudan) (1917), 250, 251–53, 255, 276
Im Reich der Diamanten (In the Land of the Diamonds) (1907), 184
In Afrika, der schwarze Kontinent (In Africa, the Black Continent) (1915), 185
Iris (film company), 185–86, 189

Jagd auf den Silberreiher in Afrika (Shooting Egrets in Africa) (1911), 236–37, 239, 277
Jagd auf Riesenschlangen (Hunting Boa Constrictors) (1913), 229

Kampf um Diamantenfelder, Im (In the Battle over Diamond Fields) (1921), 267
Karalus, Karl, 256, 257
Kiautschau im Film (1914), 246
Kilimandscharo zum Nil durchs verbotene Afrika, Vom (From the Kilimanjaro to the River Nile Through Forbidden Africa) (1925), 267
Kine Messter (Camera), 167, 168
Kinematographenkampagne (cinematograph campaign), 100–129, 178, 268
Kinematographic map, 152–153. See also Frobenius, Leo
Kinematographische Studiengesellschaft (Cinematographic Study Society), 228–29
Kinetographie, 181, 190n15
Kinoreformbewegung (cinema reform movement), 135–36; and colonial discourse 179–82
Königliches Museum für Völkerkunde, Berlin (Royal Museum for Ethnology), 108, 134, 158–59

Kolonialabteilung des Auswärtigen Amtes (KA, Colonial Department of the Foreign Office), 14, 33, 37, 39, 43, 45, 62n50, 85
Koloniale Schuldlüge (colonial guilt lie), 255n37, 265
Kolonialer Verkehrsverein (Colonial Tourist Office), 194
Kolonialkriegerdank, 251, 255n32
Kolonialland Afrika, Das (The Colonial Land Africa) (1924), 267
Kolonialrat (KA, Colonial Council), 58, 138
Kolonialschau (colonial exposition), 9, 10, 52, 108, 217. See also DAMUKA
Kolonie und Heimat (Colonial journal), 50, 128
Kommission für die landeskundliche Erforschung der deutschen Schutzgebiete (Commission for the Geographic Exploration of the German Protectorates), 138
Kongo, Der (The Kongo) (1913), 6, 202, 221n26, 221n39
Krause, Friedrich (Fritz), 137, 161
Kulturkreislehre (Diffusionism), 135–36
Kulturmission (Cultural Mission), 3, 203–8, 223n81

Land und Leute in Deutsch-Südwest-Afrika (Land and People in German South-West Africa) (1907), 178
Landeskundliche Kommission des Reichskolonialamtes (Geographic Commission of the Imperial Colonial Office), 147n26
Lange, Konrad, 181
Leben und Treiben in Tanga (Deutsch-Ost-Afrika) (Hustle and Bustle in Tanga [German East Africa]) (1909), 178–79, 184, 199, 200–04, 209–10, 213, 215, 246
Lebende Bilder (living pictures), 86. See also tableaux vivants

Letzte Augenblick, Der (The Last Moment) (1918), 257, 268
Leute in Südwest Afrika (1907), 221
Liliencron von, Adda, 86, 88–89
Lips, Julius, 210
Löwenjagd in Afrika (Lion Hunt in Africa) (Fragment before 1914), 235, 276

Machin, Alfred, 128
Maji-Maji rebellion, 4, 28, 32, 36, 40n3, 204
Mecklenburg zu, Adolf Friedrich, 117, 155–56, 167, 188
Mecklenburg zu, Johann Albrecht, 33, 84, 86, 248–249, 254n21
Mensch und Tier im Urwald (Man and Animal in the Jungle), (1924), 267
Meyer, Hans, 138, 140, 147n23, 148n37, 158, 191n35
Minerva (film company), 121
Mit dem Norddeutschen Lloyd nach Neu-Guinea (With the Norddeutschem Lloyd to New Guinea) (1907), 66, 117, 129n6, 133, 217–218, 223n81
Moderne Landwirtschaft (Modern Agriculture) (1912), 203, 277
Museum für Völkerkunde zu Leipzig (Leipzig Museum for Ethnography), 14, 134, 137, 142, 152, 158–60
Müller, Julius Friedrich Carl, 8,14, 18, 37–38, 149; Altenburg, 53–57; DKG film shows, 64–73, 83, 86, 90–91, 101–02, 106, 108–10, 116, 118–20, 209; film lecturer, 75–78; in the colonies, 42–52, 61n15, 62n50, 67; Woermann, 57–61

Nama (people), 4, 28, 32, 49, 51, 76, 83, 138, 204, 262; *Südwest-Afrika*, 197–98. See also Herero War
Nashornjagd in Deutsch-Ost-Afrika (Rhinoceros Hunting in Africa) (1913), 229–34, 235, 276

Neu-Guinea 1904–1906 – In memoriam Professor Dr. Rudolf Pöch (New Guinea 1904–1906 - In memoriam Professor Dr. Rudolf Pöch), 277
Nilpferdjagd in Deutsch-Südwest-Afrika (Hippo Hunt in German Southwest Africa) (1907), 214
Neuhauss, Richard, 133, 161, 166–68, 170, 173n14, 234
Norddeutscher Lloyd (shipping line), 117, 119

Oberländer, Hans, 248, 257, 268n6
Oberste Heeresleitung (High Command), 247, 264
Öffentliche Schule in Ostafrika, Eine (A Public School in East Africa) (1912), 222n48. See also Deutsch-Ostafrika. Eine grosse öffentliche Schule der Provinz Usambara
Opfertag für die Kolonial-Kriegsspende (Sacrifice Day for the Colonial War Donation) (1918), 257
Ost-Afrika /Östliches Afrika (East Africa), 277

Phantom Ride, 45, 118, 215, 216
Peter Moors Fahrt nach Südwest. Ein Feldzugbericht (Peter Moor's journey to Southwest Africa. A narrative of the German campaign), 93, 94, 95, 170, 200
Phonograph, 139, 140, 144, 145, 154–56, 160, 210–13, 222n61, 276
Pöch, Rudolf, 66–67, 134, 142, 148n53, 149, 150, 151, 161, 167, 212, 276
Propaganda-Gesellschaft für die deutschen Kolonien (Propaganda Society for the German Colonies), 126, 127, 269

Raub in den Sudu-Bergen, Der (The Outlaw of the Sudu Mountains) (1916), 251
Railway (colonial), 45, 46, 57, 68, 69, 78, 118, 181, 183, 185, 188, 197, 201, 204, 208, 209, 213, 215, 216, 221n37, 240, 252
Rautenstrauch-Joest-Museum (Cologne), 156, 163
Regnault, Felix, 134, 135, 136, 151
Reichskolonialamt (RKA, Imperial Colonial Office), 14, 85, 138, 139, 150, 157, 159, 224, 235; film companies, 185–87, 189, 191n26, 240; wildlife protection, 234, 242n41; Schomburgk, 251; DEUKO, 256, 257, 259, 264, 268n3, 268n12; Ufa 269n25
Reisen und große Jagden im Innern Afrikas/Voyage et grandes chasses en Afrique (1913), 128
Reisebild, 178. See also travelogue
Roebel-Kulturfilm (film company), 267, 270

Sachers, Heinz, 183
Schillings, Carl Georg, 18, 167, 233, 235, 237, 242n41
Schomburgk, Hans, 14, 167, 169, 170, 172n4, 173n20, 183, 188–89, 191n42, 225–26, 247, 248, 249–53, 254n26, 255n31, 255n34, 267, 268n9, 276
Schule in Neu-Guinea, Eine (A School in New Guinea) (1909), 222
Schulz, Christoph, 226, 241n9, 241n18
Schumann, Robert, 8, 14, 17, 91–8, 98n27, 170–71, 179, 200, 224–35, 239, 240, 240n4, 241n9, 241n18, 242n33, 249–53, 255n38, 276
Schutztruppe (Colonial Troops), 39, 97, 181, 258, 268n3. See also Unsere Schutztruppe in Deutsch-Süd-West-Afrika (1911), Unsere Schutztruppe im Krieg (1916)
Schwarze Hölle, Die (The Black Hell) (1904), 31–32
Schwarze Truppen in Dar-es-salam (Black Troops in Dar-Es-Salaam) (1914), 229
Sigifälle in Kamerun (Sigi Falls in Cameroon) (1914), 7, 246. See also

Sigifälle in Deutsch-Ostafrika (The Sigi Falls in German East Africa) (1910), 223n73

Sittenverbesserung eines Negers, Die (The Moral Improvement of a Negro) (1911), 222n52

Solf, Wilhelm (state secretary), 188–189, 198, 191n26, 191n42, 205, 228, 237, 264

Staatssekretär Dr. Solf in den Kolonien. (Togo im Film) (State Secretary Dr Solf in the Colonies [Togo on Film]) (1914), 188–189. See also *Staatssekretär Dr. Solf besucht im Oktober 1913 Togo*

Staatssekretär Dr. Solf besucht im Oktober 1913 Togo (State Secretary Dr. Solf visits Togo in October 1913) (1913), 189, 205, 277

Stachow, Leo, 186, 188–89. See also Aar Kinematographen-Werk.

Steinke, Martin, 256, 263

Südwest-Afrika (South-West Africa) (1907), 196–98, 203, 204, 214, 218, 272, 274

Süd-West-Afrika (South-West-Africa) 1914), 246

Tableaux Vivants, 86–90, 97

Thilenius, Georg, 149

Togo (colony), 3, 27; on film 46, 57, 118, 188, 189, 191n42, 204, 205, 250–51, 267, 277. See also *Im deutschen Sudan*

Travelogue, 15–17, 75, 252, colonial travelogue, 16–17, 19, 192–220, 224, 230, 232, 240, 259–60, 272, 274

Travelling exhibitor, 122–25, 178

Tropengift (Tropical Poison) (1919), 267

Übersee–Film A.G. (film company), 267

Unsere Polizeitruppe in Togo (Our Police Troops in Togo) (1916), 250

Unsere Schutztruppe im Krieg (Our Colonial Troops in Wartime) (1916), 250

Unsere Schutztruppe in Deutsch-Süd-West-Afrika (Our Colonial Troops in German South-West Africa) (1911), 184

Unsre Braven (Our Brave Ones), 86–90. See also tableaux vivants

Variety (theatre), 10, 11, 18, 19, 27, 30–32, 61, 75, 91, 177

Verlorenes Land (Lost Country) (1925), 267

Verräter, Der (The Traitor) (1917), 7, 257, 259, 260, 268, 269

Viktoriafälle, Die (The Victoria Falls) (1907), 6, 215, 223, 277

View ('view' aesthetic), 1, 15, 31, 36, 46, 75, 76, 79n40, 89, 119, 127, 192–93, 196–98, 200–04, 213, 216, 217, 218, 224, 232, 252; and programming, 214

Völkerkunde (ethnography), 5, 19, 129; filmmaking, 131–147

Völkerkundliche Aufnahmen aus der Südsee aus den Jahren 1908–1910 (Ethnological Film Documents from the Pacific from the Years 1908–1910), 133, 277

Völkerschau (Human zoo), 4, 9, 10, 22, 143

Voluntary association, 12–13, 19. See also Deutsche Kolonialgesellschaft

Weisse Göttin der Wangora, Die (The White Goddess of the Wangora) (1916), 251, 267

Weisse unter Kannibalen (Fetisch), Eine (A White among Cannibals [Fetish]) (1921), 267

Weltreich der Deutschen, Das (The German's World Empire) (TV documentary 2010), 274

Werbekommission (DKG, Publicity Committee), 35, 41n34, 78, 100, 115
Weule, Karl 14, 18, 19,117, 134, 137–146, 149–161, 162n12, 164n55, 165–68, 170–172, 186, 212, 266, 267
Wie ein Brief von den grossen Seen Zentral-Afrikas zu uns gelangt (How a Letter travels from the Great Lakes of Central Africa) (1911), 7, 218–19, 277
Wie Fritzchen sich die Reichtags-Kämpfe und Neu-Wahlen denkt (How Fritzchen Imagined the Reichstag's Quarrels and the New Elections) (1907), 7

Wilden beim Eisenbahnbau, Die (The Savages Constructing a Railway) (1907), 19, 185, 201, 208, 209, 221n37
Woermann, Adolph, 58
Woermann Carl, 57
Woermann Linie (Woermann shipping line), 46, 51, 57–61, 70
Wolfram, Wilhelm, 44, 55, 56

Zentrale für wissenschaftliche und Schulkinematographie (Centre for Scientific and School Cinematography), 183
Zimmermann, Emil, 248, 254n17
Zwei Welten (Two Worlds) (1911), 261

Film Europa: German Cinema in an International Context
Series Editors: **Hans-Michael Bock** (CineGraph Hamburg); **Tim Bergfelder** (University of Southampton); **Sabine Hake** (University of Texas at Austin)

The Concise Cinegraph: An Encyclopedia of German Cinema
General Editor: Hans-Michael Bock
Associate Editor: Tim Bergfelder

International Adventures: German Popular Cinema and European Co-Productions in the 1960s
Tim Bergfelder

Between Two Worlds: The Jewish Presence in German and Austrian Film, 1910–1933
S. S. Prawer

Framing the Fifties: Cinema in a Divided Germany
Edited by John Davidson and Sabine Hake

A Foreign Affair: Billy Wilder's American Films
Gerd Gemünden

Destination London: German-speaking Emigrés and British Cinema, 1925–1950
Edited by Tim Bergfelder and Christian Cargnelli

Michael Haneke's Cinema: The Ethic of the Image
Catherine Wheatley

Willing Seduction: *The Blue Angel*, Marlene Dietrich, and Mass Culture
Barbara Kosta

Dismantling the Dream Factory: Gender, German Cinema, and the Postwar Quest for a New Film Language
Hester Baer

Belá Balázs: Early Film Theory. *Visible Man* and *The Spirit of Film*
Bela Balazs, edited by Erica Carter, translated by Rodney Livingstone

Screening the East: Heimat, Memory and Nostalgia in German Film since 1989
Nick Hodgin

Peter Lorre: Face Maker. Constructing Stardom and Performance in Hollywood and Europe
Sarah Thomas

Turkish German Cinema in the New Millennium: Sites, Sounds, and Screens
Edited by Sabine Hake and Barbara Mennel

Postwall German Cinema: History, Film History and Cinephilia
Mattias Frey

Homemade Men in Postwar Austrian Cinema: Nationhood, Genre and Masculinity
Maria Fritsche

The Emergence of Film Culture: Knowledge Production, Institution Building, and the Fate of the Avant-Garde in Europe, 1919–1945
Edited by Malte Hagener

Imperial Projections: Screening the German Colonies
Wolfgang Fuhrmann

Cinema in Service of the State: Perspectives on Film Culture in the GDR and Czechoslovakia, 1945-1960
Edited by Lars Karl and Pavel Skopal

German Television: Historical and Theoretical Perspectives
Edited by Larson Powell and Robert R. Shandley

www.ingramcontent.com/pod-product-compliance
Lightning Source LLC
Chambersburg PA
CBHW072144100526
44589CB00015B/2089